Germany an

Germany and Its Gypsies

A POST-AUSCHWITZ ORDEAL

Gilad Margalit

The University of Wisconsin Press

The University of Wisconsin Press
1930 Monroe Street
Madison, Wisconsin 53711

www.wisc.edu/wisconsinpress/

3 Henrietta Street
London WC2E 8LU, England

2   4   5   3   1

Printed in the United States of America

Library of Congress Cataloging-in-Publication Data

Margalit, Gilad.
[Germanyah ha-aheret veha-Tso'anim. English]
Germany and its gypsies: a post-Auschwitz ordeal / Gilad Margalit.
p. cm.
Includes bibliographical references and index.
ISBN 0-299-17670-3 (alk. paper)—
ISBN 0-299-17674-6 (pbk.: alk. paper)
1. Romanies—Germany—History—20th century.   2. Germany—Ethnic relations.
3. Race discrimination—Germany.   I. Gross, Tom.   II. Title.
DX229 .M3713 2002
943'00491498—dc21

2001006535

I dedicate this book to my wife, Vardit Gvuli,
and to my children, Ili, Roni, Gaia, Gili, and Ruti.

Contents

Illustrations

Illustrations

Preface and Acknowledgments

On 9 January 1957, less than twelve years after the end of the Nazi persecution of the Gypsies, the Administration and Construction Committee of the local parliament (Landtag) of the German state of Baden-Württemberg debated a bill for the regulation of vagrancy. The bill, proposed by Joseph Vogt, a member of the Christian Democratic Party (CDU), was inspired by the Bavarian Law concerning Vagrancy *(Landfahrerordnung)* of 1953 and was designed to limit the free movement of Gypsies in the state, supposedly to defend the inhabitants from the Gypsies' alleged criminal activity. In the middle of Vogt's speech, a member of parliament from the opposition liberal party, the Free Democrats (FDP), Emmi Diemer-Nicolaus, rose to her feet to express her objections. The bill contravened the Basic Law (Grundgesetz) of the Federal Republic and was an example of unacceptable overlegislation, she said. Vogt, no doubt irritated by his colleague's interruption, responded by saying that he wished a wagonload of Gypsies were placed in front of her home so that the housewife in her would triumph over the lawyer.[1] In other words, as soon as the sensible humanist was confronted with the concrete expressions of Gypsy existence, she would abandon her abstract and unrealistic ideas and would support a drastic solution for the "problem." Vogt's argument did not persuade Diemer-Nicolaus and her colleagues to support his legislation in the Landtag at Stuttgart, however, and his attempt failed.

The conflicting viewpoints of Vogt and Diemer-Nicolaus reflect two German approaches to Gypsies in the aftermath of Auschwitz. The question is which of them more truly represents the "German attitude" toward this Nazi persecuted and despised minority—the conservative bigot or the enlightened liberal?

The study of German preoccupation with various aspects of Nazi persecution of Gypsies and its implications for German society, culture, and institutions can afford us perhaps not answers but at least a perspective on two central and interlocked questions that have intensely engaged the minds of both Germans and non-Germans since the collapse of the Nazi regime on 8 May 1945: How did Germans confront and come to terms with their own Nazi past? Was there in the "New Germany" any continuity of institutions or patterns of government activity that had existed before the collapse of Nazism?

In the late 1980s, the collapse of the German Democratic Republic (GDR) elicited a lively public debate in the former East and West Germany about confronting and coming to terms with Communist dictatorship. In the 1990s, this led to revival of public and academic discourse on how Germans coped with the Nazi past, especially in the early years of the Federal Republic of Germany (FRG) and of the GDR.[2]

Historians and other participants in this debate reached varied and different conclusions. The predominant view in liberal and leftist circles was that German society and its various institutions found it very difficult to cope frankly and courageously with their Nazi past. In a book entitled *Die zweite Schuld oder von der Last Deutscher zu sein* (The second guilt, or the burden of being German), published as early as 1987, the German Jewish author Ralph Giordano asserted that, in addition to their guilt from murdering Jews, the Germans had a "second guilt" because "Hitler was defeated only militarily but not ideologically."[3] On the other side, German historians of the new right, such as the young historian Manfred Kittel, contradicted this assertion. In *Die legende von der "Zweite Schuld": Vergangenheitsbewältigung in der Ära Adenauer* (The legend of the "second guilt": Coming to terms with the Nazi past in the Adenauer era), Kittel referred directly to Giordano's accusation. Although Kittel did not deal explicitly with the case of the Gypsies, he claimed that, in comparison with other post-Nazi states such as the GDR and Austria, the FRG as a state and German society in general had coped properly with the moral, political, and judicial aspects of its Nazi past. He denounced the claims of the kind Giordano made as a political myth created by the German left during the 1960s.[4]

The debate on the *Vergangenheitsbewältigung* (coming to terms with the past) is part of an academic and public discourse on the political and social meaning of the aftereffects of Nazism, which has been ongoing in Germany since 1945. Most experts regard 1945 as a profound turning point in German history.[5] In contrast, a few leftist and Marxist historians have argued that 1945 symbolizes the restoration of the economic, social, and political patterns of the Weimar Republic.[6] Jürgen Kocka stated that the very presentation of these different analyses as contradictory alternatives is false. While there was a basic continuity in the economic system and in the civil service, in other fields many innovations had taken place, so he concluded that 1945 was no less a significant turning point than were 1918–1919 and 1933.[7]

The relationship between German society and its Gypsy minority in the postwar era was formally placed on the public agenda for the first time in Germany only in 1979, when a campaign for equal civil rights for Sinti and Roma was launched in the FRG. This campaign was initiated by the German civil rights organization, the Society for the Threatened Peoples (Die Gesellschaft für bedrohte Völker). Several books were published, and documentary films were made. Although most of these books and films concentrated on the Gypsy fate during the Third Reich, some also referred to German policies and attitudes toward the treatment of Gypsies after the war.[8] Commonly embedded (explicitly or, more usually, implicitly) in these publications and films were the claims that postwar German society and its institutions had failed to cope—morally, politically, and judicially—with the implications of the Nazi persecution. Naturally, the authors and filmmakers focused on aspects that they regarded as manifestations of continuity of Nazi racism toward Gypsies, most notably racist perceptions among specialists on the Gypsy issue in various police departments in the FRG during the 1950s and 1960s. The narration of these films and books emphasized the continuity of Nazi patterns in policies and attitudes toward the Gypsies in the democratic era after the war. They used terms borrowed from the vocabulary of the Final Solution, such as *Untermenschen* (subhuman) and *Sonderbehandlung* ("special treatment," a euphemism in Nazi Germany for killing) to illustrate post-1945 German attitudes and policies toward Gypsies, and they chose to define the policies of the various authorities of the FRG toward Gypsies as persecution *(Verfolgung)* rather than as discrimination *(Diskriminierung)*.[9]

The principal spokesperson for the German Gypsies, Romani Rose, who chairs the Central Council of German Sinti and Roma (Zentralrat deutscher Sinti und Roma), even went so far as to claim that the democratic FRG had continued the extermination policy of the Third Reich, albeit using milder methods.[10] Was there really such a continuous line from Nazi dictatorship to the democratic Federal Republic?

This book covers the entire postwar period: the era of the Allied military governments in Germany (1945–1949); the years after 1949, when two German states, the FRG and the GDR, existed side by side; and the first years after the collapse of the Berlin Wall in 1989 and the beginning of German reunification. As German law does not allow access to official documents until thirty years after they have been written, the discussion in this volume of official German policies terminates at the beginning of the 1960s. The chapters on the period since then center on the public debate on the Nazi persecution of the Gypsies in the German political culture.

Two main Gypsy groups live in Germany today: the Sinti (the largest group) and the Roma (a smaller group). Until the 1970s, these two self-appellations in the Gypsy language, Romany, were unknown to the German public. In 1960, when Walter Strauss and Wilhelm Weiss, two German Roma from Frankfurt, founded the first Roma organization in the Federal Republic, they had no qualms about calling it the Zentral Komitee der Zigeuner (Central Committee of the Gypsies).[11] From the late 1970s on, however, the political organizations of the Sinti and the Roma, influenced by the International Romany Union and the German minority rights organization, the Society for the Threatened Peoples, began to regard the German term *Zigeuner,* meaning Gypsy, as bearing derogatory connotations. They therefore replaced it with the artificial phrase "Sinti and Roma." Since the early 1980s, the German media and official bodies have followed their lead, although in public, the term *Zigeuner* remains in widespread usage. Nevertheless, the new German term "Sinti and Roma" barely captures the denotation of Zigeuner. Sinti and Roma pertains only to the unique composition of the Gypsy population in Germany, where the Sinti form the majority; it is not applicable to other groups in the eastern and southern European countries, where Gypsies are mostly Roma with very few Sinti. In western Europe, the French Sinti prefer to call themselves *Manush* and the Spanish Gitanos call themselves *Cale.* Although the German Sinti also used both these terms for themselves until the late eighteenth century, apparently "Sinti" gradually replaced them in the nineteenth century.

Therefore, it is clear that changing the general reference from "Gypsies" to "Sinti and Roma" cannot be done outside the concrete context of the German Gypsy population. One simply cannot replace terms such as *Zigeunermusik, Zigeunerbild* (Gypsy image), *Zigeunerromantik* (Gypsy romance), and, naturally, *Zigeunerschnitzel* (Gypsy roast).

This volume concerns German attitudes toward and policies about Zigeuner in the earlier era, when the German authorities, media, and public did not know the term Sinti and Roma. In fact, for generations Germans have used Zigeuner as an appellation for both groups, and sometimes they have even used the term to denote another itinerant minority of mixed German-Sinti descent known as *Jenisch.* Before the late 1970s and early 1980s, the only Germans who knew the Romany terms "Sinti" and "Roma," and could distinguish them, were linguists (the two groups speak different dialects of Romany) and racial scientists and personnel who had participated in the Nazi persecution of the Gypsies. For these reasons and to prevent any anachronism, I have decided to use the term "Gypsy" in this book as the English equivalent of *Zigeuner* in the German sources. It is a general ethnic definition for the Gypsy groups in Germany and has no derogatory connotations. I use the terms "Sinti" and "Roma" only in cases where a specific group is under discussion.

The attitude expressed by post-1945 German society about Gypsies reflects various patterns of continuity and change. Generally, the patterns of continuity originated before the Third Reich, but they were crystallized during the Nazi era. Newer patterns emerged in postwar Germany, primarily within the political culture and under the guidance of the Western Allies' declared policy of denazification in political and cultural spheres. The denazification process made use of punishment, as well as education: sanctions were taken against anyone who dared to violate its rules and break its taboos, while reeducation during the first postwar years exposed the German public to the crimes and atrocities committed under the Third Reich and implied the existence of collective guilt of all Germans for these crimes. In the German population, this policy created a reluctance to utter anything publicly that might be interpreted as identifying with Nazism and its atrocities. Consequently, for many years the postwar German population largely refrained from talking openly about subjects not regarded as legitimate under the new political culture.

This phenomenon encouraged the civil service, the political system, and the social elite in Germany to acquire and use a unique discourse that was designed to circumvent the communicative taboos and to enable people to state opinions that deviated from the new rules set under the auspices of the Allies. The use of this discourse compelled me to adopt a somewhat complex method of analysis for this book, so that I could uncover the meaning that often lay behind the refined form of discourse. This analysis distinguishes official public expressions (such as speeches in parliament and articles in the press) from conversations held in more intimate social circles (such as meetings of governmental bureaucracy and closed sessions of committees in German local parliaments). The former may be defined as public discourse *(öffentliche Diskurs)* and the latter as semipublic discourse *(halböffentliche Diskurs)*. Public discourse tends to be articulated in formalistic codes that reflect the official and legitimate positions that were shaped within the political culture of postwar Germany. This is also the case, but to a lesser degree, in semipublic discourse. The lack of any professional research by others in the field of what I would term German antigypsy discourse has obliged me to adopt psycho- and sociolinguistic methods developed by Ruth Wodak in her research on the antisemitic discourse in postwar Austria.[12]

By the 1980s, literature on German Gypsies tended to define each antigypsy expression as racist, even in cases where, in fact, there was no racist element present. Hatred of Gypsies, based on a whole range of reasons, has existed ever since their arrival on German soil in the fifteenth century. Most common was the stereotypical image of the Gypsy as thief, fraud, and parasite living at the expense of his "host peoples" *(Wirts-völker)*. Aversion on specifically racist grounds in the modern sense constitutes only the top layer in antigypsyism, as in antisemitism. This was added at the end of the nineteenth century (appearing initially on the fringe of the anthropological racism at that time) onto centuries of underlying layers of preexisting discrimination.

The racial descent of Gypsies then became emphasized, and their supposed traits and instincts (such as "wanderlust"), which in the past had been attributed to "the Gypsy mentality," were now determined as being innate. Furthermore, the racist attitudes toward Gypsies were not solely negative but had a "positive" romantic side, which is discussed in chapter 1 of this book. Other forms of racist antigypsyism—such as application of racial hygiene terminology and conceptions, reference to the level of racial purity of the Gypsies, and so on—were developed in the first decades of the twentieth century and later characterized much, but not all, of the Nazi preoccupation with Gypsies. The racial-hygienicists regarded the personal traits of each individual Gypsy as hereditary. Gypsies whom they defined as "racially pure" *(Reinrassige)* were given the romantic stereotype of an ancient and noble Aryan tribe. Other Gypsies, in contrast, were stigmatized as *Mischlinge* (half-castes; hybrids or mongrels) and stereotyped as a dubious rabble.

As mentioned, a recurrent pattern in the postwar German discourse is the substitution of terms contaminated by Nazism; for example, the term "race" *(Rasse)* was replaced by the more neutral euphemism "people" *(Volk)*. But the audience's knowledge and experience enabled them to construe the hidden meaning within such terms. Another method of circumventing the taboo was to use arguments known from German antisemitic discourse. A number of such strategies have frequently been used in the German antigypsy discourse, mainly with the aim of mitigating the severity of Nazi crimes. Some speakers cited their own alleged experience with Gypsies as a supposedly rational basis for their prejudices. The most familiar strategy was to turn Gypsy victims into criminals—the *Opfer-Täter Umkehr*—thereby presenting the Gypsies as persecutors and the Germans as true victims; implicit in this was the notion that the Gypsies themselves were somehow responsible for their fate under the Nazis.[13] Generally, the communicative limitation that the Allies set on racist expressions with regard to the Jews was not imposed as severely in respect to the Gypsies. For that reason, the German discourse connected with the Nazi persecution of the Gypsies acquaints us with hidden layers in the German consciousness, which then either support or mitigate the most horrible aspects of Nazism, which usually are not expressed in the German discourse on the Jewish Holocaust.

This book is based primarily on the official records and sources in the following: the Office of the Military Government of the United States (OMGUS); the British military government; the public security departments of the Ministry of the Interior in various German states; the criminal police and compensation offices of some states *(Länder)* of the Federal Republic of Germany; the welfare and assistance authorities for the victims of fascism in the Soviet occupation zone and, later, in the German Democratic Republic; the minutes of the sessions of the Landtag committees in Bavaria, Baden-Württemberg, and Hesse; the minutes and documents of investigations in the cases of Nazi perpetrators; and court rulings in the FRG with regard to compensation matters.

Many documents and records cited in the book are collected in the main Federal Archives (Bundesarchiv) of the FRG in Koblenz and Berlin and in both main and local archives of several German states. Not all the relevant records were available in the various German archives; a number of ministries and government offices in several states have not yet made public their archives covering German policy toward the Gypsies during the second half of the 1940s and the 1950s. In particular, the Bavarian Ministry of the Interior refused me access to study its files on several aspects (including compensation and public safety) of its policy toward Gypsies from 1945 to 1961. The reason given was that the relevant files include personal data, which if exposed could harm the privacy of the individuals involved. At the Bavarian compensation office, a senior official claimed that some files of 1945–1953 had been partly destroyed by fire and other files had been damaged by the great humidity in which they were kept. I was unable to establish any independent confirmation of these claims.

In contrast to the lack of assistance extended to me by the Bavarian Ministry of the Interior, the following did grant me access to certain files on the subject, and to them I am deeply grateful: the Ministries of Justice in Bavaria, Baden-Württemberg, and Hesse; the Ministries of the Interior in Hesse and Lower-Saxony; and the Senator for Interior Matters and Sport in Bremen.

I would also like to thank the following for making documents available: the National Archives in Washington, D.C.; the Yad Vashem Archive in Jerusalem; the archive of the Organization of the Victims of the Nazi Regime (VVN) in Stuttgart; and the Archive of the Otto Pankok-Gesellschaft in Hünxe-Drevenack.

In conducting my research I drew on articles and readers' letters published in the German press and upon literature, folk songs, speeches, public opinion polls, and documentary and feature films. Many of these articles are from collections in the following archives: the *Frankfurter Rundschau* newspaper in Frankfurt aM., the Sender Frei Berlin (SFB) radio station in Berlin, the *Neues Deutschland* newspaper in Berlin, the Landtag archive of Baden-Württemberg in Stuttgart, the private collection of the late priest Georg Althaus (which are partly kept in the archive of the Lutheran church in Braunschweig and partly by his family), and the Wiener Library in Tel Aviv and in London. Most of the interviews with Germans and Gypsies (generally Sinti) for the purpose of researching this book were conducted between 1991 and 1993.

This book was originally written as a dissertation under the supervision of Prof. Moshe Zimmermann and Prof. Dan Diner, and I thank them for their support and encouragement. In 1995 the dissertation was submitted to the Senate of the Hebrew University in Jerusalem.

I am grateful to the following organizations for their support through scholarships, which enabled me to conduct research in Germany: the Richard Koebner Center for German History in the Hebrew University in 1991–1994, the German Academic Exchange Service (DAAD) in 1991–1993, and the Friedrich Ebert Foundation in 1993–1994.

The conceptual crystallization of this book owes much of its inspiration to many conversations and discussions I held with the following teachers, colleagues, and friends on various issues and problems I confronted during the research and the writing: Prof. Frank Stern, director of the Center for German Studies, Ben-Gurion University of the Negev, Beer Sheva, Israel; Dr. Constantin Goschler, Humboldt University, Berlin, Germany; Dr. Yaron Matras, University of Manchester, United Kingdom; and Dr. Georgia Rakelmann and Prof. Reimer Gronemeyer, both at Justus Liebig University, Giessen, Germany.

I owe special gratitude to my mentor, Prof. Dan Diner, of the Hebrew University in Jerusalem, Israel, and director of the Simon Dubnow Institute at the University of Leipzig, Germany. Professor Diner officially guided me in the framework of the DAAD scholarship between 1991 and 1993, and he has voluntarily continued to accompany my writing process through its conclusion.

Germany and Its Gypsies

1

Images and Impressions of Gypsies in the German Collective Memory

GYPSIES AS A UNIQUE ETHNIC GROUP IN GERMANY

T HE SINTI (also written and pronounced Sinte and Cinti) arrived in the German domain of Europe in the fifteenth century. To this day, they are the largest group of Gypsies in Germany. They call themselves "Gadschkene Sinti," which means German Sinti. After 1870, other Gypsy groups emigrated to Germany from eastern Europe. Collectively known as East European Roma, these groups have a dialect and customs that are distinct from those of the Sinti. Nevertheless, the Sinti and the East European Roma are actually different branches of one ethnic group—the Roma (or Romany) people, who are believed to have originated in North India and are now dispersed all over Europe; in more recent times, the Roma settled elsewhere in the world. In Romany, the language of European Gypsies, the name *Roma* (the singular of which is *Rom*) probably derives from *Dom*. Dom is the name given up to the present day to a mixture of tribes in India, who are of an inferior social status. Accounts from the sixth century A.D. characterize the Dom as wandering musicians. Indeed, the meaning of the term in Sanskrit is a low-class person who makes a living through music and song.[1]

The consolidation of Gypsies as a unique ethnic group probably occurred only after they left India. The circumstances of their leaving are not clear, since there is no Gypsy tradition to shed light on this chapter of their history; moreover, Indian, Arabic, and Persian sources do not

3

provide any definitive answers, either. Persian and Arabic texts do refer to Indian elements serving in the Arab armies that were settled throughout the Muslim empire, but this was mostly before the eleventh century, the time at which most linguists believe the Dom/Roma first left India.

In contrast to the Jewish people, who have a well-developed historical consciousness and who preserved both orally and in scripture their history and the memory of their homeland, Gypsies did not until recently have a historical consciousness, so that the Gypsy culture and language have not traditionally been written or passed down orally. Popular Gypsy tradition makes no reference to India or the Gypsies' past, which seems to have been forgotten.

The study of Romany by non-Gypsy linguistic experts has been the main source of the early history of Gypsies. By the end of the eighteenth century, some linguists, mostly German, discovered that Gypsies spoke an Indo-Aryan language.[2] Romany (also spelled Romani) is related to the new languages of India (Hindi, Punjabi, Bengali) and preserves not only the Indian vocabulary but also the Indian morphology. From the research in linguistics, it seems that Gypsies originated in the south of Punjab, perhaps in the area known as Sind (some argue that this is the origin of the name the German Gypsies call themselves, Sinti). For a period there was a mistaken but popular belief in the West that Gypsies were of Egyptian origin, and the terms used in English, French, and Spanish—*gypsy, gitan,* and *gitano*—are derived from "Egyptian."

The cultures through which Gypsies passed on their long journey to Europe left their imprint on Romany. For example, the vocabulary is strewn with Persian and Greek words and is evidence of the period when they lived in the domain of the Byzantine Empire. The absence of Arabic words in Romany strongly suggests that they lived under Arab domain for only a relatively short time.

Although Gypsies had no historical consciousness, and notwithstanding the division and antagonism that existed and still exists between and within different Gypsy groups,[3] Gypsies as a whole always had a unique consciousness and identity in Europe, and they perceived themselves separate from their non-Gypsy surroundings.

Romany makes a clear distinction between a Gypsy (Sinto or Rom) and a non-Gypsy, known as a *Gadjo* (the plural of which is *Gadje*); in certain Romany dialects Gadjo is roughly akin to "peasant," "farmer," or "settled."

As was the case with traditional Jewish society, traditional Gypsy society separated itself from its surrounding environment and did not internalize either its values or the negative image that the majority population attributed toward them. Gypsies regarded Gadje with a certain disrespect and even believed themselves to be somewhat superior, which more than

4

once served to cover up a sense of inferiority. To the Gypsy, the Gadjo corresponded with the figure of the gentile in the folklore of the Jewish Diaspora. Gypsies sometimes regarded Gadje as foolish, awkward, and immoral and impure.[4]

Notwithstanding the diversity between different groups of Gypsies, some common characteristics of a Gypsy ethnic identity can be found. For instance, the Sinti and the Roma speak different dialects of the same Romany language. Moreover, both cultures are based on customs, lifestyle, and a social structure that is unique to the Gypsies of Europe.

Some of these customs are of a non-Christian religious nature, apparently brought by the Gypsies from their essentially Hindi homeland or from along their route to Europe. From the earliest days of their arrival on German-speaking territory, six centuries ago, Gypsies presented themselves as Christians, but the expressions of their Christianity were fairly superficial. It is interesting that the Romany term for the cross is *Trushul* (trident); in Hinduism the trident is the symbol of the god Shiva. The Sinti adopted certain components of Christian ritual—including the belief in the Virgin Mary and the pilgrimage to sacred Christian locations, such as the Bergkapelle (mountain chapel) at Illingen in the Saarland—which, as a matter of fact, by that time probably had been integrated with previous pagan rituals. But Gypsies also continued to cling to their pre-Christian beliefs and to maintain customs that derived from these beliefs. These customs include a system of impurity and purity; various prohibitions on eating and sexual relations; and customs and rituals concerning birth, marriage, death, and illness. An individual who disregards these rules is perceived as impure *(Baledschido)* and might be temporarily or permanently excommunicated.[5] However, not all Roma groups strictly adhere to these rules.

Even today, many German Gypsies live according to traditional social frameworks (although these have been weakened in the last century as modernization has taken hold in society in general). The basic social unit of traditional Gypsy society is the extended family. Grouping several families together creates various clans, and each clan has a quasi autonomy. A group of clans constitutes a tribe. Each extended family is headed by its patriarch, who enjoys among his kin authority as a judge and arbitrator and in this role exerts sanctions against those who violate traditional laws. This leader, known by Sinti as a *Tschatschopaskero,* holds certain functions with a religious significance, too. For example, he can determine if an artifact or a person is impure and thus cannot be touched.

In the past, most Gypsies in Germany maintained a vagrant way of life. During the spring and summer months they wandered along fixed routes; in the winter they settled down in permanent locations. Over generations they developed an affinity with the areas in which they wandered;

they mastered the local German dialects and became part of German country life. Their nomadic lifestyle was accompanied by traditional occupations—producing metal handicrafts, dealing in haberdashery and used articles, trading in horses and domesticated animals, providing entertainment and musical performances—and by the traditional trades through which they are perhaps best known: palm reading, fortune telling, healing, and blessing, all of which were much sought after by the rural populations.[6] These occupations rarely brought in much by way of income; instead, they provided Gypsies with mere subsistence as they survived under tough conditions of material distress. The reports of missionaries who encountered Gypsies at the beginning of the nineteenth century described the way in which they lived in extreme poverty, were clad in rags, and owned almost no other possessions. This hardship of existence frequently led them to beg for money, and even to steal and to cheat.[7] These deeds were regarded by the settled population, however, not primarily as an expression of the Gypsies' distress but as a sign of their inherent evil.

The process of industrial modernization, which had started in German lands in the second half of the nineteenth century, adversely affected the Sinti's traditional occupations and undermined the shaky economic basis that had facilitated the maintenance of their traditional lifestyle. This process and the new possibility of enjoying the country's welfare support, which was conditioned on permanent settlement, led the German Gypsy groups to move away from their nomadic existence at the beginning of the twentieth century. Previously vagrant groups now lived in poverty-stricken neighborhoods on the peripheries of major German cities.[8] No longer a foreign itinerant or vagrant group with a different lifestyle, the Sinti now became an integral part of the under and lower classes of German society. although, certainly, the surrounding population did not regard them as such.

The movement of the Sinti into the poor areas of large cities was accompanied by social phenomena similar to what other German laborers and peasants experienced after modernization; but the "otherness" of Gypsies, and the public prejudice against them, made it much more difficult for Sinti than for other Germans in a similar socioeconomic situation to extricate themselves from a vicious circle of distress and backwardness.

The rejection by German society, which makes it difficult even today for young Sinti to secure places as apprentices (which is a necessary precondition for the advancement of tradespeople in the German labor market), leads many Gypsies to choose independent occupations in the area of small commerce. Many deal in textiles, carpets, or scraps. As in the past, only a small minority make a living exclusively through music. The material distress and the lack of education and occupational training that

Sinti children with a dog at the Heinefeld site in Düsseldorf, 1933. (Otto Pankok Museum Haus Esselt, Hünxe-Drevenack. Photo by Otto Pankok.)

might have enabled them to be integrated into the labor market also led some Sinti to turn to crime. This problem was recognized by a friend and sympathizer with the Sinti in Düsseldorf, the painter Otto Pankok, during the late 1940s and the 1950s.[9]

Many Gypsies now depend on state support. The Federal Family Ministry claimed in the early 1980s that many of the 12,000 Gypsies known to the ministry were recipients of welfare stipends. According to different and contradictory assessments from the late 1970s and early 1980s, the number of the Sinti and Roma population in the FRG (Federal Republic of Germany, or West Germany) was between 12,000 and 50,000, while in the GDR (German Democratic Republic, or East Germany) there were only a few hundred Sinti left. During the early 1990s the Zentralrat deutscher Sinti und Roma assessed this population at 70,000 people.[10]

THE GYPSY IMAGE IN THE GERMAN LANDS

Despite knowing very little about what actually constituted Gypsy culture, German society nevertheless regarded Gypsies as a foreign element.

The descriptions of Gypsies in the earliest German chronicles of the fifteenth century illustrate that the images and stereotypes of Gypsies known to our generation were already consolidated at that time. The passing on of these images and stereotypes through generations derives in part from their substantiation over time, but also from their processing in the collective German consciousness and their formation in symbols that became engraved on the collective memory and in culture. The prevalence of the Gypsy's image as a nomadic vagrant in our generation—an image that no longer reflects the Gypsy lifestyle in Germany today—is only one example of the way the present attitude toward Gypsies wrongly reflects the influence of the collective memory. It will be argued in this book that the German collective memory toward Gypsies, built up over many centuries, had a great influence not only on the formation of attitudes toward them after 1945 but also on the interpretation of their persecution by the Nazis.

Jan Assmann has established the existence of two layers in the German collective memory, which applied here to the Gypsies: (1) a historic layer, expressing the processing of the encounter with Gypsies across generations (it is this layer that has been canonized in German culture); and (2) a later and less consolidated layer, stored in the memory of the last few generations, which preserved daily experiences of their encounters with Gypsies. Although Assmann has argued that these two layers are distinct, my research indicates what Zuckerman had already theoretically asserted—that, in fact, there is constant interaction between the contents stored in these two layers.[11]

Gypsies in the Historic Layer of German Collective Memory

The historic layer of German collective memory of Gypsies is torn between two diametrically opposing images: a stronger negative image that is in marked contrast to a romantic, enchanted image, which took root in Germany during the seventeenth century. In fifteenth- and sixteenth-century chronicles, Gypsies are variously described as a vagrant people, black in appearance, dirty and clad in rags, and wandering without purpose or aim throughout the country.[12] The chronicles report that Gypsies lived by pickpocketing, thievery, robbery, palm reading, witchcraft, and magic.[13] In some of these chronicles and also in later sources, Gypsies are frequently referred to as Tartars *(Tataren, Tartaren)* or pagans *(Heiden)*.[14] Their identification with the Tartars, who invaded Europe in the Middle Ages, leaving a trail of destruction and anxiety in their wake, indicates the fear that Gypsies awoke in the European population. This identification may also be connected with fear of a Turkish invasion of the Holy Roman Empire in the sixteenth century. As the Turks advanced toward central Europe, Gypsies were accused of disloyalty, treason, and espionage. Such accusations are reflected in the decision of the Reichstag of the Holy Roman Empire as early as the year 1497, which ruled that Gypsies would not be permitted to pass through or be tolerated within the empire's boundaries. The Reichstag decision of 1530 repeats the former one and explicitly accuses Gypsies of spying for the Turks and therefore of being enemies of the Christian world. The weight of this component of the Gypsy's image was reduced after the Turks withdrew from Europe in the seventeenth century.[15]

The use of the term *pagan* as a synonym for Gypsy showed that German Christian society did not recognize the Gypsies' claim to Christianity. Sebastian Münster argued in his book *Cosmographia Universalis* (1550) that there was no faith at all among Gypsies.[16] Their preoccupation with black magic contributed to this view, and they were perceived as having links with Satanic forces. The Gypsies' dark complexion was defined in Europe as black, which was regarded by European folklore as the color of the devil and the kingdom of evil.[17] Nevertheless, in spite of Martin Luther's denunciation of Gypsy fortune tellers as liars, there was at the same time a strong demand among the Christian population for the Gypsies' supposed supernatural powers to bless, to tell fortunes, and to heal. Even the alchemist and physician Paracelsus noted that one could learn black magic from old Gypsy women, and he held their art of chiromancy in some esteem.[18] The position of the church—and even of the Spanish Inquisition—to the Gypsy practice of black magic was mild, and Gypsies were never the target of religiously motivated persecution in Christendom because of it.[19] In contrast to antisemitism, hostility toward Gypsies lacked a religious temper and its demonizing characteristics. For example, Gypsies were accused of kidnapping Christian children, but not of slaughtering them for religious purposes.

The image of Gypsies as an immoral and lawless people did not derive solely from the accusations that they were cheats, thieves, and robbers. Luther claimed that Gypsies baptized their children more than once, in order to receive additional gifts from Christian godfathers. In a sermon the religious reformer made in 1543, in which he compared Jews to Gypsies, Luther transferred the false stereotypes that were already attributed to the Jewish "other" to the Gypsy "other." He asserted that "the Gypsies make it difficult for people by charging high prices, giving away information and being traitors, poisoning the water, burning, kidnapping children, and cheating in all kinds of ways in order to cause damage."[20]

Even at this early stage, the way Gypsies were described and the accusations leveled against them indicate that such perceptions played a role in the way Germans established their own national identity. The attributes of the identity given to the Gypsy were in many respects the exact opposite of the characteristics that German society attributed to itself. Settled Christian society regarded itself as white not only in complexion but also metaphorically, as an expression of moral purity. The negative stereotype of the Gypsy "other" crystallized into a cultural memory over the generations and helped Germans form their own sense of belonging. This is at least partly true even today.

The emphasis on Gypsy paganism and the Gypsies' alleged collaboration with Christianity's enemies, as a central component of the image of the Gypsy, has been largely diminished since the seventeenth century, while the weight of the social component of the image has increased. Gypsies were defined as a useless mob *(Gesindel)* of thieves and whores, and differences between them and the German underworld *(Gaunertum)* were blurred. By the nineteenth century, this identification in the German consciousness was so strong that the criminologist Friedrich Avé Lallement actually suggested that, etymologically, the term *Gauner*, used to describe the German criminal underworld, was an abbreviation of the term *Zigauner* or *Zigeuner* (Gypsies, in German).[21] That is, the very definition of Gypsies in the German consciousness was tied to belonging to the lowest level of society. The demonization and the characteristics attributed to Gypsies in these descriptions express the hatred that German society, through all its generations, like other European societies, felt for Gypsies. This hatred was nourished by irrational feelings of fear and aversion, but it was also substantiated after encounters with Gypsies.

In the period after the Thirty Years War, a different attitude, seen as positive by many, penetrated German culture through the influence of Spanish culture. Two motifs of presenting Gypsies passed from Spanish to German literature and gained a considerable degree of popularity. The first of these motifs was the stereotype of the exotic young Gypsy woman, a pretty and seductive figure. This became a common character not only in literature but also in opera and folklorist art, and it was in stark contrast to the traditional image of the ugly old Gypsy woman who engaged in witchcraft, a stereotype that continued to exist alongside the new romantic motif.[22]

The romantic motif of the Gypsy woman originated in the figure of Perziosa, the protagonist in Cervantes' *The Gypsy of Madrid* (1613). It became really popular when Goethe adopted this motif about a hundred years later in the figure of Mignon in *Wilhelm Meister's Wanderjahre* (The wander years of Wilhelm Meister). In the early 1600s, Cervantes' novel also was performed as a musical drama on the German stage. That this new romantic motif proved so popular is no doubt connected to the attraction many German men felt toward the new image of young Gypsy women, who were a kind of forbidden fruit. It may also have represented a subconscious attempt in the German psyche to overcome the fear of

Gypsies through the conquest of the Gypsy girl. That during the course of some popular stories the Gypsy girl, in fact, turned out to be a non-Gypsy who had been kidnapped in childhood by Gypsies only added to the attraction of this stereotype—the girl's "superior descent" now being explained by proto-racist reasoning. Her moral virtues and the nobility of her figure were now explained by her non-Gypsy origins, allowing the traditional antigypsy image to be resubstantiated.

The other new stereotype that originated from the influence of Spanish literature portrayed Gypsies as a free people, relative to the other subjects of the Holy Roman Empire (although this, too, was combined with the traditional antigypsy image). It appeared for the first time in the German picaresque literature *(Schelmenroman)*. Two well-known examples of this depiction are in Johann (Hans) Jakob Christoffel von Grimmelshausen's works, *Courasche* and *Springinsfeld* (1670). In both these stories, Gypsies have a key role in the plot. They are presented as living a free, easy, and cheerful life, in complete contradiction to the lifestyle of the settled society all around. This literary motif gained so much popularity because it reflected an authentic component of German society's attitude toward Gypsies and their way of life; this element was envy, as Gypsies were viewed as having attained a state of freedom that the German society did not have.[23]

This image is also found in several popular folk songs, which as a collective creation reflect the image of Gypsies in the German collective consciousness. Here is one of them:

> Lustig ist das Zigeunerleben . . . Faria, Faria, Ho
> Er braucht dem Kaiser
> Kein Zins zu geben;
> Lustig war es im grünen Wald,
> Wo der Zigeuner Aufenthalt.[24]

> [Jolly is the Gypsy's life . . . Faria, Faria, Ho
> He needs to pay
> The Kaiser no tribute;
> Jolly it is in the green forest
> Where the Gypsy lives.]

In projecting the achievement of this freedom, a sterilizing element of social control is hidden, which actually presents the inferior and low status of Gypsies as the price of that freedom.

Goethe was the great popularizer of romantic motifs in depicting Gypsies in German literature. Through the figure of Mignon in his novel *Wilhelm Meister's Wanderjahre* and in his play *Götz von Berlichingen of the Iron Hand,* Goethe bequeathed to German culture what has come to be called Gypsy romanticism *(Zigeunerromantik).*[25] The sentimental depiction of Gypsies in his plays expresses the enthusiasm of the Storm and Stress (Sturm und Drang) movement, of which Goethe was a principal figure, with regard to the people perceived as "nature people" *(Naturvölker)*. According to the Storm and Stress perception, these people— who, in their view, remained close to nature, in contrast to people in the civilized nations—preserved a degree of primeval authenticity and purity. The Gypsy is depicted as a loyal person with values, ready to sacrifice his life for freedom and justice.[26] This positive presentation of the Gypsy was characteristic of many works of the Romantics in the early nineteenth century, such as Achim von Arnim's *Isabel of Egypt* (1811).

Despite its popularity, the romantic motif in literature nonetheless reflected an image of the Gypsy that was prevalent only among a relatively limited circle. Popular folk songs—such as "Wir arbeiten nicht und verdienen doch" (We don't work and still we earn) and "Zick Zack Zigeunerpack" (Zig zag, pack of Gypsies)[27]—show that in wide classes the components of freedom and nature were combined with traditional negative images and were often based on actual encounters between Germans and Gypsies, which for the most part were negative. Thus, contradictory memories about Gypsies became crystallized in German culture: on the one hand, Gypsies were viewed as repulsive and intimidating; on the other hand, they were seen as attractive and enchanting. This multiple image and the formation of the Gypsy as a symbol in the German consciousness indicate that, during the generations that Gypsies lived in Germany, like Jews, they turned from being unknown strangers into a familiar other and thus became an integral part of the German homeland *(Heimat)*.[28]

Encounters with Gypsies during Recent Generations

While the weight of the Gypsy romanticism in the historic layers of the German collective memory was significant, in the memory of the most recent generations it occupied only a marginal place, compared with extremely hostile feelings toward Gypsies. What positive images remained relied on Gypsy images stored in the German culture, images not of the concrete Gypsy but of a synthetic "Gypsiness" such as the Gypsy girl motif that originated in Cervantes' work. An article in the *Frankfurter Rundschau* pointed out the paradoxical nature of this attitude: "We love Gypsy melodies, Gypsy cellar [the cellar of a cafe in which Gypsies play the so-called Gypsy music], Gypsy romance, Gypsy schnitzel [a cutlet in pepper sauce—the influence of the Hungarian kitchen. Hungary was regarded as the homeland of the Gypsies. The traditional "Gypsy" music that was played by Sinti in Germany was Hungarian (Czardash)], but apparently we do not respect and appreciate those who gave their name to these things."[29]

The superiority of the antigypsy contents over the romantic contents in the memory of recent generations derived from, among other elements, the fact that the German encounter with Gypsies during this period, as in previous times, tended to substantiate the antigypsy prejudices and stereotypes rather than to undermine and refute them. The reasons for this are rooted in the nature of the human coping with the "other." Research by social psychologists shows that encounters between two ethnic groups have often served to enhance preexisting stereotypes rather than to refute them. In fact, almost no deep relations developed between the majority and the minority (Germans and Gypsies), and the relations were expressed mostly by external and superficial interaction, so that the knowledge about the minority also tended to be one-dimensional. Even when an encounter with the other occurs and undermines the stereotypical expectations, it is difficult for the majority to abandon its prejudices. The frequent coping pattern of the majority with the behavior of a single minority member (who contradicts the attributed stereotype) results in classification of this individual as an exception confirming the rule, rather than repudiation of the stereotype.[30] A study done in Hungary in 1980 presented this general phenomenon about Gypsies. It was found that while ethnic Hungarians are usually very tolerant to the Gypsies they work with, they are prejudiced in principal to the idea of sharing living quarters with Gypsies, to integrating Gypsy children into schools, and to marrying Gypsies.[31]

The German majority (like most other national groups) tends to identify itself as better than the other and to attribute unique behavior patterns to minority groups. Since in the German collective consciousness Gypsies functioned as a kind of negative founding element for its own identity, to abandon stereotypes of Gypsies might have implications for the German identity, too. Furthermore, the power of negative deeds performed by minority members to enhance the negative image is much greater than the power of positive deeds of the minority to undermine the negative stereotypes associated with their image. Thus the German public was more inclined to recall negative experiences from encounters with Gypsies than positive ones, and the continuous friction between the two populations again substantiated the antigypsy stereotypes stored in cultural memory and passed from generation to generation.

In the nineteenth century, protests by individual Germans against the perceived inability of the authorities to deal with Gypsies appeared in citizens' complaints and in readers' letters to the local press. These show that, in particular, the rural population felt exposed to and unprotected against what they regarded as threats by Gypsies. It was no longer a case of Germans feeling threatened by the supposed black magic properties attributed to Gypsies but by the fact that the population started to attribute to Gypsies intentions of murder and property abuse against the German population.[32] These feelings evolved further in the twentieth century and applied to both urban and rural populations. For example, hundreds of citizens of Frankfurt registered written complaints with the municipal authorities in the 1930s, both before and after the Nazis came to power. These complaints, protesting the permission given by the municipality to Gypsy groups to live in or near the town, show these concerns about personal and property safety after the movement of Gypsies to the city's outskirts. This anxiety was in part authentic in periods of instability and economic, political, and social crises in Germany, but for the most part it was inflated beyond any plausible proportion.

Even during the early years of the Third Reich, citizens in Frankfurt felt that the municipal authorities had "abandoned" them to the Gypsies and failed to provide adequate protection. Many citizens called for Gypsies to be forcibly driven out of the city. Some expressed their anger because they believed that Gypsies did not work and instead lived at the expense of the public, either by receiving welfare from the authorities or by begging and committing crimes.[33] The desire to get rid of Gypsies is also documented in the report of the SD *(Sicherheitsdienst;* security service of the SS) of October 1939, concerning the Austrian population's attitude: "An urgent suggestion for the solution of the Gypsy problem is their incarceration in closed camps. . . . The population awaits the elimination of this asocial element."[34] Nevertheless, even during the Nazi regime, as we shall see later, both antigypsy and romantic stereotypes were integrated into the racist beliefs about Gypsies.

In the early 1960s, the German sociologist Lukrezia Jochimsen conducted a survey among Germans about their feelings toward Gypsies, in which she asked the respondents to define "Gypsy." The answers, mainly negative, reflect the factors and concepts that shaped the German collective memory concerning Gypsies in the generations that experienced the Third Reich. Jochimsen concluded that Germans perceived Gypsies as "vagrants of a strange race, who wandered into our country from foreign countries (Hungary, the Balkans, Asia), having particular negative characteristics (they were asocial, savage, parasites, work shy, and criminals)."[35] While some of these definitions are traditional, others, it seems, are associated with racism and with the theory of *Asozialität* (asociality) that developed during the Third Reich.

Images of Gypsies among Children

Negative stereotypes about Gypsies were often formulated in childhood. The first "encounter" young children in Germany had with Gypsies occurred in many cases not as a real meeting but in stories told to them

Two Gypsies kidnapping Frieda, illustration from *Onkel Knolle,* 1918.

by adults. As a significant other in almost any possible domain (lifestyle, religion, appearance, origin), the image of the Gypsy in Germany, as in other European countries, served for generations as an aid in the educational process of young children. The frightening stereotype of the child-kidnapping Gypsy was embedded at a very early stage in the minds of children, as Jochimsen noted.[36] These stories and warnings, usually communicated orally, were also written down and integrated into educational literature for children. In 1910 the first edition of the children's book *Onkel Knolle* appeared in Germany. One of its rhymes relates the story of "Frieda the Gypsy" (Zigeunerfrieda). Frieda, the impudent, bad, and dirty girl, who would not listen to Uncle Knolle, eventually met her punishment:

> Zwei Zigeuner, schwarz und greulich,
> Packten jetzt die Frieda eilig;
> Warfen sie, trotz ihrem Schrei'n
> In den Wagen, schwupps, hinein![37]

> [Two Gypsies, black and frightening,
> Now grasp Frieda, quick as lightning;
> They threw her in spite of her crying
> Into the wagon, whoops, inside!]

The story, accompanied by attractive illustrations, ends with the Gypsies making Frieda work very hard; she walks a rope and juggles for whole days in markets and fairs. Only then does she repent her bad behavior, but it is too late. The book proved very popular in Germany throughout most of the twentieth century. By 1960, twelve separate editions had been published. In the same year another "educational" story, Alexander Roda's "Zigeuner sind ehrlich" (Gypsies are honest), was published. This attributed negative characteristics to the figure of the Gypsy using other methods. The story takes place in a German village in Siebenburgen. The Gypsy character is no longer an overtly frightening figure, but, instead, he is seemingly friendly and acquires the trust of the naive little German girl—then steals money and other items from her.[38]

Such negative messages about Gypsies have continued to be embedded in children's stories up to the present time. They were also expressed in essays by German children about Gypsies, the writing of which was initiated by Joachim Hohmann. In 1979, Hohmann conducted a poll of 130 pupils, aged ten to fourteen, from a variety of social backgrounds. A little more than 69 percent of the children responded positively to the statement "Gypsies live on money-begging and stealing," and 61.5 percent responded positively to the statement "Gypsies are sometimes crooks."[39]

INFLUENCE OF RACISM

Toward the last quarter of the nineteenth century, ideas that originated in racism began to spread throughout German culture. These concepts became very popular. The racist interpretation assumed that the Gypsy lifestyle was not a result of mentality or external circumstances, as had been the understanding during the Enlightenment, but rather was composed of unchangeable properties and instincts. Racism did not create new images but gave new interpretations and rationalization to the antigypsy and romantic myths and images already present in the German collective consciousness. Racism did contribute to the enhancement of the importance of anthropological and physiognomic data about Gypsies, however, and, according to the principles of racism, these data provided concrete scientific proof for the Gypsy essence *(Zigeunerwesen)*.

Beginning in the late 1880s, racist perception regarding Gypsies appeared in the realm of German speaking and culture. A stereotypic observation of Gypsies and Jews caused racists to ignore the great difference between these two peoples and their unique cultures and to attribute to them superficial similarity qualities, such as "black," vagrants, and peddlers. This fictional similarity caused the racists, like the generations who preceded them, to bind the origin of Gypsies with that of Jews.[40] At the margins of his book, *The Law of Nomadism and the Present Jewish Domination* (1887), written in the spirit of the racist antisemitism, the Orientalist Adolf Wahrmund referred to Gypsies as an example of an Asian vagrant people, who, like Jews, were not capable of working and therefore made a living by easy ways, such as kidnapping children and carrying on inferior trades.[41] Yet despite this binding, and contrary to the antisemitism, the antigypsy trend within the realm of German culture did not bear a political nature.

A conventional motif in popular literature since the end of the nineteenth century is the rejection of the romantic argument that the Aryan roots of the Gypsy language were an indication of their Aryan origin. In an entry about Gypsies in an encyclopedia published in 1911, the author, Reinhold Urban (who was a missionary who had ministered to Gypsies), followed Wahrmund's approach, according to which Gypsies were closer to Jews than to Aryans: "The language does not necessarily indicate national belonging *[Volkszugehörigkeit]*. . . . Anyway, this is not far from the notion that the Gypsy fate, similar to that of the Jews, also has a similar meaning."[42]

At the fringes of this antigypsy racism, a more romantic form of racism also prevailed, together with a belief that Gypsies were Aryans. This romantic view might have originated within the circles of the Gypsy Lore Society, a body established in England in 1888. Certain members of the society believed Gypsies were the most ancient of the Aryan race and sought to protect them from mixing with non-Gypsy elements and from modernization, which threatened to eliminate them.[43] This view was probably brought to Germany by Houston Stewart Chamberlain, since he believed the genial musical gift of Gypsies to be a typical expression of an Aryan essence.[44]

The racial preoccupation with Gypsies in the press, popular literature, and encyclopedias increased during the early twentieth century and reached its peak during the Nazi regime, although it did not stop with the collapse of the Third Reich. Through these sources, racist concepts penetrated the public consciousness and became a part of common knowledge about Gypsies in Germany.

The centuries-old images and stereotypes gained a new rationalization. In the first decades of the twentieth century, contrary to the study of Gypsies in England, German *Ziganologie* (Gypsy studies) centered more on anthropology and criminal biology than on the study of Gypsy language and culture. In Germany, the physical and social expressions attributed to race gained more importance than the Aryan origin of the Gypsy language. Indeed, many German ethnologists did not believe Gypsies to be Aryans, and this belief filtered down to the general public. They emphasized that although Gypsies spoke an Indo-Aryan language, ethnologically they were a national mixture *(Mischvolk)* and should not be perceived as Aryans.[45]

Even Felix von Luschan, an anthropologist and ethnologist who did not accept the idea of inequality between races and held that there were no pure races, treated both Gypsies and Jews as foreign elements in western Asia. In his book of 1922, Luschan declared that most Gypsies look like the people of the Mediterranean and only a small minority of them appear to be of Indian origin.[46]

Nazi anthropologist Hans F. K. Günther did not accept Chamberlain's Aryan concept and established explicitly that among Gypsies, as among Jews, the imprint of the Oriental race and the West Asian *(Vorderasien)* race is expressed. Günther defined Gypsies as an Oriental–West Asian mixture of races *(Rassengemisch)*, which also included Indian, central Asian, and European elements.[47] A similar attitude was adopted by the principal German encyclopedias published in the 1930s.[48] From at least 1935 onward, the notion that Gypsies were a foreign race in Germany became official Nazi policy and led to the penetration of racist ideas about Gypsies into the educational system and the media. The press and popular magazines of the 1930s expressed different prevailing racial attitudes about Gypsies, but common to all of them was the notion that Gypsies were a foreign race in Germany.

In the first years after the Nazis assumed power, there still appeared in the German press articles that reflected the romantic racist approach toward Gypsies. A report of the NRG information agency in August 1935 emphasized that many of the vagrants in Germany were not in fact "pure race" *(Rassenechte)* Gypsies but, rather, *Jenische* (non-Gypsy nomads), the descendants of mercenaries of the Thirty Years War. The report said that pure race Gypsies would not like to be confused with the latter. It was mentioned that although pure race Gypsies did not greatly respect the rights of the Gadje to their property, they did maintain strict morals within the tribe. In addition, it was emphasized that although petty property offenses committed by vagrants were a routine matter, the serious crimes attributed by the public to Gypsies were not really committed by Gypsies but, rather, by the representatives of the rabble *(Gesindel)*, because these crimes did not suit the Gypsies according to their race.[49] Such romantic racism could not perceive that a member of a noble Aryan race was capable of committing a crime. This attitude was not far from the position expressed by anthropologist Martin Block in an interview he gave in 1936 to the *Mittag* newspaper, in which he stated, "Gypsies are members of a pure Aryan race."[50]

Later on, articles in the spirit of antigypsy racism became much more dominant in the German press. For example, Georg Nawrocki wrote a series of pieces about the Sinti in Hamburg in the Nazi newspaper *Ham-*

burger Tagblatt in August 1937, expressing strong racist views. Naw-rocki documented that from the first days of their arrival in Germany, chronicles reported the involvement of Gypsies in cheating, thefts, robbery, and murder. The author asserted that, in spite of the strict actions of the authorities, which were intended to eliminate the nuisance they created, and in spite of the Draconian penalties, "the Cinti adhere to each other in a gang and multiply like rats." Furthermore, through "compassionate" authorities, the Gypsies of foreign race *(fremdrassige)* even manage to acquire German citizenship to serve as a cover for the commitment of new crimes. Later in the series, Nawrocki emphasized that Gypsies did not work but were parasites of a foreign race *(fremdrassige Schmarotzer)* living on German toil—"people who hate labor as if it were a sin and who despise laborers as if they were slaves."[51]

Nawrocki mixed the traditional antigypsy image with racial terminology and used new biological metaphors. Nevertheless, he outlined the same threat to Germans from Gypsies about which traditional antigypsyism had warned—the danger to property and life—rather than the "dilution" of the racial purity of the German people, in the spirit of racial hygiene *(Rassenhygiene)* (known in English as eugenics). At the time, this racial hygiene approach was confined to the relatively small readership of racist magazines[52] and was only widely disseminated in the national press in 1941, when in February and March of that year, the principle results of the racial hygiene survey, conducted by Robert Ritter on behalf of the Reich's Ministry of Health about German Gypsies, were proliferated through the news agencies in the German press. The press reported that Ritter found that "most of those called Gypsies are not in fact nomads of a pure Indian origin *[Indischer Herkunft stammechte Nomaden]* but rather mongrels *[Mischlinge]* of Gypsies who mixed in recent generations, especially with asocial and hereditarily inferior elements."[53]

But the racial terminology prevalent in the press and popular magazines in early twentieth-century Germany, and the theories about social deviation (asociality) that were prevalent since the 1920s, paved the way for the acceptance of the wider German public (and not only those in explicitly racist circles) to absorb the theories from the field of racial hygiene concerning Gypsies, as disseminated by the Nazis.

INFLUENCES OF THE THEORY OF ASOCIALITY

The concept of asociality first appeared in the German encyclopedia *Der Grosse Brockhaus* in 1928. Under the entry "Asocial," two terms, having a close meaning, appeared: *Asocial* and *Antisocial*. Asocial was defined as the behavior of a person who is indifferent to the society around him; antisocial was defined as behavior that is aimed against society. From about that time, asocial began to be used to mean antisocial, and Germans have attributed this inaccurate meaning to the term up until the present day.[54] The 1928 encyclopedia entry for "Asociality" was based on criminologist Cesare Lombroso's ideas about the connection between degeneration and crime, which gained much popularity in Germany in the early twentieth century.[55] The asocials were defined as beggars, vagrants, "work shys" *(Arbeitsscheue)*, eccentrics, whores, drunks, and delinquents.[56] The seeming absence of the social instinct in asocials was portrayed as a form of degeneration, since most people were said to possess a well-developed social instinct. It was also argued that the inclination of the asocials was to act in a criminal way. These ideas, which originally were not necessarily formulated by racists, became more and more integrated into racism. In the 1920s, the causes of asociality were explained as being primarily developmental and environmental. By contrast, research from the 1930s onward pointed to hereditary factors as causes.

Like racism, the theory of asociality is pseudoscientific, imparting scholarly rationalization to prejudices that were already prevailing in wide layers of society. Backwardness and social distress were denounced as expressions of behavioral deviation that derived from a mental and moral defect. In racist circles, all causes were attributed to hereditary defects. This approach reflected a pessimistic attitude toward the self-assurance of the Enlightened approach that the "social problems" *(Soziale Frage)* of poverty and backwardness—which assumed very large proportions in Germany after the industrialization and modernization processes at the end of the nineteenth century—could be solved through education and welfare. Thus it was not only the Gypsies' traditional image that led them to be included in the category of asocials but also the collapse of their traditional lifestyle, leading to their migration to the cities, which rendered them a part of the city's poor and the "social problem" in Germany.

Articles written about the Sinti in the 1930s emphasized that the men did not work and passed their days in total idleness, while their women carried the burden of sustaining the large families.[57] Even Gypsies who settled down and found stable work, and who in their lifestyle did not break the conventional morals of the "decent" public, were perceived, because of their different customs, to be asocial. Under the influence of Physiocratic perceptions (which surfaced in the eighteenth century but continued to shape attitudes toward Gypsies during the twentieth century), the Gypsies' occupations frequently involved peddling and begging, which were perceived as nonproductive and therefore also morally faulty.[58] Lack of self-discipline and perseverance were regarded as characteristics common to Gypsies and asocials. The adherence of Gypsies to these ways of life, which sometimes did not derive from choice but from lack of other alternatives, was interpreted as a challenge and threat to "conventional" lifestyles.

INFLUENCE OF ROMANTICIZATION

The decline in the intensity of the romantic view of Gypsies in recent generations derives not only from the friction between Gypsies and Germans but also from cultural changes that occurred in Germany at the beginning of the nineteenth century. Even so, the romantic image of Gypsies in Germany never fully died but continued to exist among the public and even among a minority of the Nazi leadership during the Third Reich.

With the decline of the romantic view, the romantic motif about Gypsies disappeared from German literature after 1830 and in its stead the traditional negative image reappeared. Toward the end of the nineteenth century, literature identified with and expressed the values of the bourgeoisie, which regarded the Gypsy lifestyle as an antithesis to the bourgeois healthy and moral lifestyle. This trend was especially salient in the Gypsy images in children's literature of that period.[59]

By the nineteenth century, legal experts and criminologists began to study Gypsy culture and language, not out of purely scientific or romantic motives, however, but to acquire tools to fight these people, who were regarded in Germany as an integral part of the underworld.[60] This view also influenced the information about Gypsies that was distributed to the public.

The figure of the Gypsy in German operettas written at the end of the nineteenth century proved an exception to this trend. Perhaps for artistic reasons alone, operettas preserved characteristics of the romantic approach.[61] From the turn of the century and during the first half of the twentieth century, the romantic trend reappeared among those who wrote critiques of bourgeois society and progress, but this had little influence on wider attitudes toward Gypsies by either society or the state.

At the end of the nineteenth century and the beginning of the twentieth, the very rejection of Gypsies by society caused some of the critics of modernization and progress to perceive the characteristics attributed to them as expressions of authenticity and vitality. This was especially so in art and literature. Those who wished to escape materialism regarded the vagrant life of Gypsies in nature as more free than the confined bourgeois way of life, and they made the Gypsy lifestyle an object of their desires. One of the prominent representatives of this trend was the novelist and poet Hermann Hesse. The Gypsy figures in his work symbolized the instinctive and vital elements of life: freedom and nature. The figure of Goldmund in the novel *Narcis und Goldmund* presents this stereotype, although he is not a Gypsy. Goldmund is a wandering artist swept by his impulses to a life of adventure. The event that changed Goldmund's life was an encounter with a Gypsy woman, with whom he had his first sexual experience. "I met life itself," he told his friend Narcis.[62] Also, in his poem, "Glorious World," from his collection *Wandering* (1974), Hesse contrasts the modern, artificial, and terrible world with the world of "dreams and blessed folly," of which Gypsyhood is one of the symbols:

> Schwüler Nachtwind im Baum, dunkle Zigeunerin;
> Welt voll törrichter Sehnsucht und Dichterduft;
> Herrliche Welt, der ich ewig verfallen bin,
> Wo dein Wetterleuchten mir zuckt, wo deine Stimme mir ruft![63]

> [Sultry wind in the tree at night, dark gypsy woman,
> World full of foolish yearning and the poet's breath
> Glorious World I always come back to,
> Where your heat lightning beckons me, where your voice calls!]

Gypsyhood is perceived by Hesse as a kind of personification of the spirit of freedom, impulsiveness, and vitality. The outstanding expression of this trend in art was the painter Otto Müller. The Gypsy figures in his work are naturally integrated into nature, so much so that some even thought Müller himself must have been of Gypsy origin.[64]

Even during the Third Reich, the romanticization of Gypsies did not disappear completely, although it no longer always derived from the same motives that had evoked it among the modernization critiques. During this period the romanticization was sometimes bourgeois, reminiscent of the Gypsy operettas of the turn of the century, such as Franz Lehar's *Zigeunerliebe* (Gypsy love) and it afforded an artistic release to the subconscious desires to escape the modern, sophisticated, and rational world into a simpler and emotion-intensive life. These desires were projected onto Gypsies. The romanticization was expressed by articles in the press; by the Gypsy operettas that continued to be performed on German stages even after 1933; and, perhaps most surprisingly, by films made during Nazi times. These films presented romantic and indubitably Gypsy figures, such as the nameless Gypsy violinist, who played beautifully in *Die Czardasch Fürstin* (The Czardash princess [1934]),[65] or figures having Gypsy characteristics, such as the dancer and beggar from Spain, Martha, played by none other than Leni Riefensthal, the Führer's darling herself, in her film *Tiefland,* the production of which was completed only at the end of the war. According to the director, Fritz Hippler, who was in charge of films under Goebbels, the financing of the film was achieved through the head of the Hitler chancellery, Martin Bormann.[66]

In Nazi circles and in the Third Reich's press, the romanticization of Gypsies gained a racist rationalization, which emphasized the Aryan origin of Gypsies and the strictness of the pure race Gypsies' moral laws,

Postcard, "Gypsy life *[Zigeunerleben]*; A quiet place in the forest is a sufficient resting place for him," circa 1910.

especially sexual modesty. As explicit evidence of the consistency of this romanticization among the German public under Hitler, we can see the frequent need to denounce this attitude in the press, by representatives of various circles of the Nazi Party.[67] In his series of articles, Nawrocki denounced the romanticization of Gypsies as an approach that characterized the petits bourgeois *(Spiesser)*.[68]

The German collective memory of Gypsies continued to be characterized in recent generations by this duality, although the antigypsy contents always predominated over the romantic contents. These rooted patterns continued to influence and shape the attitude of Germans toward Gypsies even after Auschwitz, although mainly in a cultural rather than in a political context.

2

Policy toward Gypsies until the Collapse of the Third Reich

THE SO-CALLED GOLDEN AGE AND ERA OF DEPORTATION AND PERSECUTION

GROUPS of Gypsies first arrived in the German-speaking domain of Europe at the beginning of the fifteenth century. Contemporary chronicles report that these groups were headed by leaders bearing aristocratic titles, who carried patronage letters *(Schutzbriefe)* from Christian rulers. The patronage letters seemed to confirm the Gypsies' claim that they were undertaking a seven-year repentance voyage that had been imposed on them for abandoning Christianity. The letters requested that they receive assistance wherever they went, and these groups roamed throughout western Europe. Gypsies' pretension to be pilgrims and the patronage letters protected and helped them for a few decades, a period later referred to as the Gypsies' golden age in Europe. For example, in 1418 the "needy people of little Egypt" received sums of money from the town of Frankfurt to buy bread. By the middle of the century, however, attitudes toward them changed for the worse throughout the continent. Contemporary reports indicate that by 1449 they were being expelled from Frankfurt, and by 1463 the people of Bamberg were willing to give an amount of money to a group of Gypsies to prevent them from entering the town.[1]

These events set in motion a pattern of behavior that was to become the official policy of the Holy Roman Empire over the next 300 years.

25

Between 1497 and 1774, 146 decrees were enacted against Gypsies, most of which ordered their deportation from the domain of the German nation. The first such decree was published in the principality of Brandenburg in 1482, following an abuse of the emperor's patronage letter. A few years later, in 1497, the Reichstag of the Holy Roman Empire followed suit, ruling that Gypsies would not be permitted to pass through or be tolerated within the boundaries of the empire since they were suspected of spying for the Turks. This declaration was repeated in the Reichstag's decree of 1500 and again in a further decree of the Reichstag published in Augsburg in 1530, about a year after the Turks had been turned back at the gates of Vienna. The decree stated explicitly that Gypsies were spies for the Turks and thus enemies of Christianity. The decrees gave Gypsies a specified period of time to leave the boundaries of the German nation, after which it was stated that they would no longer be protected by the law and would be included in the category of *Vogelfrei*—"free as a bird." This means that the empire's subjects would be allowed to hurt them, even to kill them, whether or not they were thought to have committed a specific crime.

These decrees were published in the framework of decisions concerning other fringe groups in society, like beggars and vagrants. The Reichstag decision of 1551 targeting Gypsies was similar to the attitude prevailing toward Jews. However, the need to publish six different decrees between 1497 and 1551, repeating the instructions of the previous ones, indicates the inefficiency of these decrees. In 1571, a German who stabbed a Gypsy with a knife was acquitted in Frankfurt, on the grounds of a Reichstag decree, and a similar such acquittal followed an incident in Breslau in 1584.[2]

In the course of the sixteenth century the German principalities followed the Reichstag's decrees and ordered the expulsion of Gypsies from their domain; these decrees also contained threats toward any Gypsy who dared reenter the boundaries of the principality. The reason the Reichstag had cited in its decisions for the deportation of Gypsies— that they were collaborators with the Turks—did not appear in the principalities' enactments, however. (In many principalities, the enactment was directed not only toward Gypsies but also toward vagrants and beggars, and, in the principality of Wittgenstein, also toward Jews.) Similar to the Reichstag's course of action, some principalities also published further decrees about Gypsies during the course of the sixteenth century, repeating the language of the previous ones, and this, too, is probably an indication that the previous decrees were not being effectively enforced.[3]

The substantial changes that took place in central Europe over the course of the Thirty Years War diverted the attention of the authorities away from dealing with Gypsies and vagrants. During this war many Gypsies served in the warring armies in special units under Gypsy command, while others made their living from the various armies by serving as peddlers, spies, entertainers, and musicians. At the end of the war, many soldiers remained unemployed, and the number of beggars and vagrants greatly increased throughout the German lands. This phenomenon, which caused a certain degree of distress to the general population, led the authorities to renew their battle against groups of vagrants, including Gypsies. Again, the main objective of the policy was the deportation of vagrants and Gypsies.[4]

The consolidation of the absolutist regime in Prussia at the beginning of the eighteenth century and its influence on German principalities caused the aggravation of accusations against Gypsies and other vagrants and led to even harsher punishments. The reasons given for the persecution were connected to the vagrant way of life rather than to their foreign origin. The authorities accused the vagrants of robbery, arson, and murder, not just with cheating and petty theft as they had done in the past. The rationalization of the severe punishments that characterized absolute regimes meant the substitution of deportation with forced labor and with lashing. A mark was branded with hot fire on the bodies of Gypsies who were caught, and repetition of the offense meant death through brutal torture, without any preliminary legal procedure.[5] This punishment awaited both men and women.

The aggravation of punishment was accompanied by an attempt, in the spirit of the utilitarian approach of absolutism, to correct the "delinquents'" offspring. A decree published in Hesse in 1722 ordered children over the age of ten to work in the fields or to learn a trade with a craftsman. Children under ten were placed in orphanages and monasteries to provide them with a Christian education, so that when they grew older they would choose an occupation and abandon their parents' "wicked" ways. For this purpose, penitentiaries and educational institutions were erected. Concurrently, a state mechanism was consolidated; it was intended to fight the vagrants and to make living on the roads difficult for them.[6]

Despite the heavy penalties, it seems that the early absolutist regimes had no apparatus for enforcing these decrees on a continuous basis. The forces against Gypsies were not operational units that continually controlled the vagrants but ad hoc forces. The political division of Germany, which was then separated into about 300 political entities, enabled Gypsies to sneak into a neighboring territory, where the authorities were less strict. The great German kingdoms took significant measures against Gypsies, while many of the smaller ones tolerated them. Although the full legal possibilities were not fully implemented, the punishments were nevertheless often harsh and brutal,[7] and as the absolutist state apparatus was enhanced, Gypsies found it harder to avoid them.

Influences of the Enlightenment and the Beginning of the Modern Policy

In the course of the first half of the eighteenth century, Gypsies were mobilized for military service in some of the German principalities. An attempt was even made to settle them permanently in the earlhood of Wittgenstein; similar attempts followed elsewhere during the second half of the eighteenth century. Experience showed that it was not always easy to deport Gypsies, and the influence of the Enlightenment led to the gradual abandonment of the idea of brutal punishment.

Instead, some attempt by the state was made to integrate the Gypsies with the rest of its inhabitants. The policy of the Hapsburg (Austro-Hungarian) Empire toward Gypsies in its domain is an example of this. In 1762 a decree of the Court in Vienna was published, stating that Gypsies were honest citizens and had to serve in the militia.[8] In 1768 some decrees were published in nearby Hungary, which obliged Gypsies to settle permanently and abandon their traditional occupations. The aim behind the decrees was to assimilate the Gypsies in the Hungarian population and to eradicate their unique ethnic character. These Hapsburg initiatives did not have much influence on the German principalities in the eighteenth century, although there were exceptions. For example, by 1771 a first Gypsy settlement was established in Germany, in Berleburg.

The concepts of the Enlightenment started to affect the Gypsy policy in Germany later than in the Hapsburg Empire. In 1787 the second edition of the book *Dissertation on the Gypsies* by linguist Heinrich Moritz Grellmann was published; in the spirit of the Enlightenment, Grellman advocated their "civic correction" (*Bürgerliche Besserung,* not *Bürgerliche Verbesserung,* or "civic improvement," which was the Enlightenment term for the goal for Jews) and integration into the state. This book was read by state officials, and the influence of the book's Enlightenment ideas are evident in their writings.[9]

In 1807, for the first time in the realm of the German states, Gypsies in the kingdom of Württemberg were able to attain citizenship. The authorities' approach was first to tie the vagrant population to a particular place by the enticement of welfare assistance and then to make them economically productive. The goal was keeping Gypsies under close control rather than inflicting harsh penalties, and this control was augmented over time. In Württemberg, for example, during the course of the nineteenth century, the police forces that walked the roads and controlled the vagrant population were greatly increased. Even before, in the late eighteenth century, certain Gypsies who were prepared to collaborate with the authorities (sometimes against their own kinfolk) were integrated into the police as rangers *(Hatschier)*.

In the spirit of the Enlightenment, a great emphasis was placed on education as a means to achieve the "civic correction" and assimilation of Gypsies. Although the state began to demonstrate a willingness to let Gypsies become legal citizens, officials were nevertheless reluctant to allow the number living there to increase. Thus a distinction was made (first in the kingdom of Württemberg in 1828 and later elsewhere) between local Gypsies *(inländische)* and foreign ones *(ausländische),* and the latter continued to be deported. Local Gypsies were defined as Gypsies who had lived within the domain of the kingdom for a long period.[10] This distinction has continued to characterize the German policy toward Gypsies up to the present day. Such Gypsies were separated in the legislation from the other vagrants with which they had been associated in the past and were presented as a special group in need of state assistance.

This new policy contained an inner contradiction. On the one hand, the authorities acknowledged that the era in which Gypsies existed outside the law should come to an end and that Gypsies should be given the right to settle within the state and become "useful" citizens. On the other hand, the authorities did not, and perhaps could not, cease to regard Gypsies as criminals and to discriminate against them relative to other subjects. To gain the right to exist legally, Gypsies had to give up wandering, join a German community, and settle within it. Close control over their everyday lives and education were the two main devices for integrating Gypsies into society, so, in fact, in the spirit of the Enlightenment, they were expected to cease being Gypsies. Gaining future citizenship was conditioned upon proving a faultless past.

The principal difficulty in realizing the plan to integrate Gypsies and award them citizenship derived from the objection by German communities themselves, who were reluctant to receive Gypsies into their midst. Opposition to accepting Gypsies derived both from the inhabitants' prejudices and from their fear that integrating them would commit the community to support them economically, proving a great financial burden. The kingdom's officials wanted to settle the Gypsies but showed no willingness to invest resources by establishing special settlements for them.[11] They sought to restrict the Gypsies' activities as tradesmen and peddlers by limiting the issuing of licenses, but they did not give them alternative possibilities of making a living legally. Thus Gypsies were pushed into the same kind of illegal existence that they had before the nineteenth century. Gypsies who were caught dealing without a license were susceptible to imprisonment or deportation out of the Reich's domain. The provisions of the different decrees published by the German states concerning

Gypsies and other vagrants, especially after the foundation of the German Reich (Kaiserreich) in 1871, provided the authorities with almost unlimited rule over Gypsies and aggravated the struggle of the state against them.[12]

Another important act that was intended to force Gypsies to settle down permanently was the separation of young children from their families to facilitate their regular schooling. When they finished school, however, because of popular prejudice against them, Gypsy children found it hard to secure a place of apprenticeship with craftsmen in order to acquire occupations that society regarded as productive; in fact, they had little choice but to make a living following their ancestors' traditional occupations, such as peddling.

Increased Control during the Kaiserreich and the Weimar Republic

The failure of the new policy aimed at solving the problem of vagrancy and at settling Gypsies caused the decline of the optimistic attitudes many officials held at the beginning of the nineteenth century and led to the adoption of a skeptical and sometimes even racist approach. Although the central government had enhanced its control over Gypsies and prohibited the issuing of licenses to peddlers, it did not succeed in enforcing this policy on many local officials, who issued Gypsies with licenses to get rid of their presence in their area.[13]

At the same time, in the middle of the nineteenth century there was a general increase in the number of non-Gypsy vagrants. This was especially so from the 1870s onward, as an outcome of industrialization. Complaints by the agricultural population against vagrants increased significantly, leading the authorities to try and increase control over Gypsies as part of the general vagrant population. The number of offenses with which it was possible to indict Gypsies and other vagrants was increased in some states in the 1880s, so that the authorities had in their disposition a variety of legal means to either deprive Gypsies of peddler licenses or deport them.[14] In most cases the police were the authority charged with determining whether a Gypsy should receive a license, and thus in effect the police became an instrument of the state for repressing Gypsies.

The first chancellor of the German Reich, Otto von Bismarck, dealt with the question of Gypsy policy. In an 1886 letter, he repeated the principles of distinguishing between local and foreign Gypsies; he called for deportation of the foreign ones, prevention of new Gypsies from entering the Reich, dismantling the gangs of local Gypsies, and dealing with Gypsies in general through a combination of punishment and education. In 1889, Bismarck expressed interest in whether his policy in regard to local Gypsies had been successful, especially the removal of children from their parents and placing them in educational institutions.[15]

This increased control over Gypsies was accompanied from the beginning of the twentieth century by the stigmatization of Gypsies as criminals. This phenomenon was contradictory to the general trend of legislation in the Kaiserreich. Despite partial successes in certain areas, the "problem" was not solved. The prevalent attitude was that a "total solution" was conditional upon legislation that covered the whole Reich. In the framework of making the battle against Gypsies more efficient, an information agency was established in 1899 in the police headquarters of Munich in Bavaria *(Zigeunernachrichtendienst)*.

This agency collected general information about Gypsies. It attempted to compile up-to-date information from local police stations concerning all appearances of Gypsies in Bavaria, personal data about the groups' members, and general information about the property and the travel direction of the Gypsy caravans. In 1909, a central collection of fingerprints of Gypsies was opened. Beginning in 1913, the agency also received information from the public prosecutor about indictments of Gypsies and current reports from the population registration offices *(Standesämter)* about the births, marriages, and deaths of Gypsies. All this information was cataloged on cards and in files. The reputation of the information agency spread, and states outside Bavaria soon asked for its assistance. But plans to establish similar agencies in other states did not materialize, and in effect the Munich information agency became a center for Gypsy issues for the whole Reich. In 1931, the German states began to participate, proportionally to the size of their population, in financing the Munich agency's activities.[16] Bavaria, the motivating power behind these decrees, was then joined by other states that, because of their geographic location along the Reich's border, had a special interest in fighting Gypsies—states such as Württemberg, Baden, Saxony, and Alsace.

In 1911, the Bavarian authorities initiated a convention in Munich, in which police experts on the Gypsy issue from all over Germany participated; the goal was to consolidate a cooperative action against Gypsies. During World War I Gypsies were regarded as potential spies, but their freedom of movement was not restricted. After a Gypsy from Cologne was caught in possession of a large number of certificates and seals, which he had been issuing to foreign Gypsies, to prevent such abuse in the future, a prohibition was issued throughout Germany forbidding the issuing to Gypsies of any certificate or other formal document.[17]

During the economic crisis that followed World War I, the number of beggars and vagrants on the streets increased, and this led to new decrees against Gypsies and vagrants.

In Bavaria a law for "combating Gypsies, vagrants, and 'work shys' "

(Gesetz zur Bekämpfung von Zigeunern, Landfahrern und Arbeitscheuen-unwesens) was enacted in 1926. The character of this law was more preventive than punitive, and it indicated a trend that would increase during the Third Reich—lumping Gypsies together with other stigmatized fringe groups in society. The law's provisions indicate that it referred to vagrant Gypsies alone, hence its aim was to fight the vagrant way of life rather then Gypsies per se. Nevertheless, Article 9 imposed the obligation of permanent work on every Gypsy over the age of sixteen. This law authorized Gypsies, vagrants, and work shys to be imprisoned in workhouses (a kind of correction institution), according to an executive decision of local authorities *(Landräte)* or heads of municipalities *(Oberbürgermeister),* without any prior legal procedure.[18] Combining Gypsies and work shys within one law suggests that the legislators regarded Gypsies, like the work shys, to be asocial, and their distress was perceived to be the result of idleness, lack of self-discipline, and lack of perseverance. The workhouses were supposed to be the appropriate institution for correcting these weaknesses, and the imprisoned were to be educated through hard work. Other articles imposed heavy limitations on the vagrant lifestyle.

The desire to control the Gypsy "problem" led in the last years of the Weimar Republic to much more efficient methods for registering and controlling Gypsies. In 1927, the Prussian Ministry of the Interior published a decree ordering the fingerprinting of all Gypsies and all non-Gypsy vagrants to be taken. Fingerprints of all Gypsies over the age of six were taken. In 1929, Hesse passed a similar law to the one that Bavaria had enacted in 1926. This time it concentrated on Gypsies alone.[19] By the middle of the 1930s the Munich agency had opened files on about 19,000 Gypsies (which constituted the large majority of all Gypsies present in Germany), material that was soon to serve the Nazis in their persecution of Gypsies.

The hardening of the Gypsy policy during the Weimar period might be interpreted as a first stage for the persecution of the Gypsies during the Third Reich. The horrible and unprecedented character of the Nazi policy toward the Gypsies, however, points to a gap rather than to a continuous aggravation of the Gypsy policy from Weimar to the Nazi period.

"GYPSY QUESTION" DURING THE THIRD REICH

Beginning in 1933, Gypsies who lived in the German Reich were exposed to unprecedented discrimination and harassment, mostly by local and other authorities, although these measures were not uniformly or universally enforced.[20] Thus in some parts of Germany there was no substantial change in the first years of Nazi rule in the policy toward Gypsies from that which had prevailed during the Weimar Republic. For example, the municipality of Frankfurt am Main changed its Gypsy policy only in 1936. In July 1933, because they regarded the policy of the authorities as wholly inadequate, residents of Ginnheim, a suburb on the outskirts of the city, made a request to the Nazi Gauleiter (the leader of a district of the Nazi Party) in Hesse-Nassau that he assist in driving away Gypsies who had parked in the area and were a nuisance to citizens. In reply to an approach by a party representative, the mayor of Frankfurt wrote that the municipality had no measures to force Gypsies to leave the neighborhood and that it was not possible to prevent citizens from leasing unbuilt land to Gypsies to park on.[21]

Bavaria had conducted relatively harsher measures against Gypsies for many years. In the period 1933–1935, however, compared to 1930–1932, the number of Gypsies incarcerated in workhouses on the grounds of the 1926 law increased. The number of Gypsies indicted in 1935 under this law, however, was identical to the number indicted in 1927.[22]

The year 1936 marked the turning point in the Gypsy policy of the Third Reich. In this year, as part of the reorganization process known as the *Gleichschaltung* (coordination or synchronization of the institutions of the German Reich with those of the Nazi Party), an institutional infrastructure to deal with Gypsies was established within the office of the Reich's criminal police (RKPA [Reichskriminalpolizeiamt]). The Munich Gypsy police department was integrated into the Prussian state criminal police office *(Landeskriminalpolizeiamt)* in Berlin and became the Reich's Center for Combating the Gypsy Nuisance (Reichzentrale zur Bekämpfung des Zigeunerwesens). Creation of this central Reich body made control and domination of Gypsies inside the Old Reich (Alt Reich) more efficient. From this period on, measures unprecedented in modern German history began to be taken against Gypsies by the authorities.

In June 1936, a circular entitled "Combating the Gypsy Plague" was issued by the Minister of the Interior of the German Reich and Prussia. This circular, intended to regulate the treatment of Gypsies on the national level, continued the traditional distinction by German officials between local and foreign Gypsies, but it also included some innovations. The decree ordered, for the first time, that Gypsies be settled in one place.[23] Even in the year before, 1935, there were plans in several cities, including Cologne and Düsseldorf, to concentrate all Gypsies who parked or settled in their jurisdiction in one location and place them under guard. In Cologne a camp was erected, surrounded by a barbed-wire fence, in which about 400 Gypsies were housed. The camp was supervised by a member of the SS *(Schutzstaffel)*, who lived on site with his family. In Düsseldorf, the municipality erected at its own expense a special site,

33

Höherweg, into which all Gypsies living in the town or on the outskirts were collected in 1937. Buildings were specially constructed to house Gypsies, and the camp was supervised by a policeman, who lived on site. In Berlin, too, Gypsies were concentrated in a camp near Marzahn, on the outskirts of the city, under police supervision. In this camp some Gypsies lived in their wagons and some in shacks that were erected on the site. In contrast to other cities, in which police and welfare authorities undertook the task of concentrating Gypsies in one location, in Berlin bodies of the Nazi party, such as the the local district Nazi party leader (Gauleiter) and the race issues office (Rassenpolitischesamt), were also involved.

In the second half of the 1930s, similar camps were also established in Frankfurt, Gelsenkirchen, and some other cities.[24] In these camps Gypsies were prohibited from working in their traditional occupations, and they were employed in compulsory work in construction and in factories. They were also denied welfare and children's pensions, as Gypsies were stigmatized as asocials who were not eligible for welfare.

Although historian Sybil Milton regards this process as the first stage in realization of the intention to exterminate Germany's Gypsies, no one at the ceremony that laid the cornerstone of the Gypsy camp in Düsseldorf could have foreseen Auschwitz. In fact, the representative of the German Labor Front (DAF) in the city expressed his joy at the vision that Gypsies would be settled in the future like everybody else and be integrated into the National Socialist order.[25]

Measures against Gypsies also began to take on a more overtly racist tone, as in the circular "Combating the Gypsy Plague" Gypsies were there defined as "the Gypsy people who are foreign to the German people." The racial laws published in 1935 had referred only to Jews. But in 1936, when the commentary to the racial laws of 1935 was published, it was mentioned therein that Gypsies, too, were "of foreign blood" *(artfremdes Blut)* and they also were forbidden to marry Germans.[26]

In 1936 a psychiatrist in Tübingen, Dr. Robert Ritter, became the head of the Research Unit for Racial Hygiene and Population Biology (Rassenhygienischen und Bevölkerungsbiologischen Forschungesstelle), which operated in the Reich's Ministry of Health. Ritter's reports indicate that the Ministry of the Interior authorized his institute to hastily promote the "clarification" of the asocial problem, which included Gypsies, "in order to investigate whether through preventing offspring infected with hereditary diseases, the restriction of the increase lately occurring in the asocials and criminals might be achieved." A memorandum written by a senior official of the Ministry of the Interior on the issue of future legislation concerning Gypsies confirms that they intended to expand the sterilization law of July 1933 (Law for Prevention of Offspring from People

Suffering with Hereditary Illnesses, or Gesetz für Verhütung erbkranken Nachwuchses) to include the Gypsy *Mischlinge* (*Mischlinge* is a typically racist term that denotes mongrels or hybrids; it is taken from breeding dogs and horses), who were defined as asocials.[27]

In 1937, teams from Ritter's institute started to collect data on Gypsies all over Germany. They were aided by the Reich's criminal police and by the newly created Center for Combating the Gypsy Nuisance. The purpose of the study was to collect material about Gypsies and asocials that would enable the Gypsy population to be classified according to its social value and thus assist policymaking. There were plans to pass a special law to regulate the treatment of Gypsies by the German state, but in the end no such law was enacted.[28]

However, the Nazi policy on Gypsies had always contained the social element; in a December 1939 letter to the DFG recommending Ritter's research, Paul Werner, Arthur Nebe's deputy in the criminal police (RKPA), defined the nature of the problem: "The Gypsy problem is now the most urgent part of the entire social problem to be handled. This is indeed mainly a racial problem, but in its practical effect it is mostly a problem of asocials."[29] Within the Reich's boundaries, the German bureaucracy regarded the "Gypsy question" as an integral part of what it defined as a "social problem" for the *Volksgemeinschaft* (the German national community), however, not as a political or existential problem. In her dissertation, Ritter's assistant Eva Justin established that the Gypsy problem so far should not be compared with the "Jewish problem," as the "Gypsy breed" *(Zigeunerart),* in contrast to the Jewish intellectuals *(jüdischen Intelligenz),* could not undermine or endanger the German people. Most German Gypsies were traditionally stigmatized as "asocial elements" who allegedly lived like parasites off German toil (by committing crimes or receiving welfare handouts).[30]

Some had already begun to regard the Gypsy problem as one of race. On 8 December 1938, Heinrich Himmler, then commander of the German police, and under the influence of Ritter's activity, issued a second circular entitled "Combating the Gypsy Plague." Himmler stated that, in light of the information accumulated thanks to the racial biology studies, regulation of the Gypsy question "will attack the essence of this race."[31]

Ritter provided the Nazi regime with a theory about Gypsies that combined racism with the theory of asociality. He argued that almost none of the Gypsies were pure nomads of Indian origin, but rather they were Mischlinge of different origins and combinations. The asocial properties that he claimed were prevalent among those who conducted a Gypsy way of life were, he said, a consequence of mixing Gypsy blood with that of disreputable elements in German society. Ritter argued that most of those named "Gypsies" were in fact Asoziale Mischlinge (asocial mongrels) and that there were no longer any actual pure race Gypsies left in Europe.[32] As he believed that the asocials were a hopeless case and could not be integrated into respectable and productive society, he had recommended as early as 1935, in a lecture given to an international congress of population science in Berlin, that it should be examined whether the solution of the asocial problem was to prevent their reproduction, "just as the state has already begun to successfully treat retarded people." Presumably, his wish to consider expanding the use of sterilization as a preventive social treatment beyond populations to which the 1933 law had been designed was shared by other bureaucrats in the Ministry of the Interior, and about a year later this fact facilitated his appointment as head of the racial hygiene research unit in the Ministry of Health.[33] The practical effect behind his suggestion to sterilize the asocial among the German Gypsies would be to eliminate most German Gypsies in one generation.

The historian Gisela Bock has written that even before the Nazi regime officially adopted a policy of sterilization as a means of solving the Gypsy problem, dozens of Gypsies had already been sterilized under the 1933 law to eliminate offspring of people suffering from hereditary diseases. They were, she says, victims of both what she terms hygienic racism *(hygienischer Rassismus)* directed against asocials and the anthropological racism directed against ethnic minorities. Bock estimated that the rate of sterilization among Gypsies was higher than the general rate of sterilization in German society.[34]

Ritter held that the "pure race Gypsies" should be allowed to continue their traditional lifestyle and customs, as these constituted no danger to the German people.[35] Ritter thus upheld the traditional distinction accepted among German officials since the early nineteenth century—that is, between local Gypsies, who had to be controlled, and foreign Gypsies, who had to be deported. Ritter determined that a small core of the Sinti were "pure race" *(Reinrassige)*; alternatively, he used the term "Gypsies of genuine Gypsy tribes" *(Stammechte Zigeuner)*. In various places in his writings Ritter determined that the term "pure race," which he used with regard to the Sinti, is a practical term, not referring to the notion of racial purity in its most accurate meaning, for, according to him, no pure race Gypsies were left in Europe. Therefore, in fact, Ritter did not contradict the German anthropologists, who had never believed Gypsies to be members of an Aryan race, as they were perceived by racial romanticists. Nazi anthropologists regarded all Gypsies as "an Oriental–West Asian mixture of races," like Jews.[36]

Ritter's chief assistant, Eva Justin, wrote that although they had mixed with German blood, the Sintis still showed evidence of characteristics of their Indian origin. She also asserted that the physical characteristics of the Roma were Oriental and West Asian, and that they did not look at all like Gypsies but rather resembled East Europeans. Some of them even looked Jewish, she said.[37]

It may be that Ritter's wish to keep for himself a small group of Gypsies for research purposes lay behind his making a quasi-scientific distinction between the "positive" and "negative" elements in Gypsyhood. Not incidentally, Ritter attributed the pure element in Gypsies to a small group of the Sinti, not to the Roma, and he bestowed a privileged status on those Sinti (in relation to other Gypsy groups), as if they were Aryans. A study of Ritter's writings and of questionnaires prepared by his assistants for the purpose of collecting the information through which the extent of the racial purity of Gypsies was to be ascertained showed that the criteria for classifying Gypsies were taken not only from the field of racial hygiene but also from the domain of the old anthropological racism. The classification of Gypsies was not based, as assumed by the historian Detlef Peukert, on family genealogies alone (the history of which, he said, Ritter believed to indicate the existence of a hereditary inclination toward crime or honest living). It was also based on physical characteristics (such as skeleton, physical structure, and hair and eye color) and cultural characteristics (such as the mastering of the Romany language, the extent of strictness about upholding traditional customs, and the extent of "wandering lust" *[Wandertrieb]*).[38]

Gypsies who did not fit, either racially or culturally, the ideal type of the pure Gypsy were immediately stigmatized as Mischlinge and asocials. In 1935, before he had even started to conduct his studies, Ritter determined that only about 10 percent of Gypsies were real Gypsies. This brings to mind the German anthropologist Felix von Luschan's statement that only between 5 and 10 percent of Gypsies look like they are of Indian origin.[39] Ritter's research findings from 1937 on apparently substantiated his hypothesis. In 1941 Ritter completed his primary survey, and he then aimed to finish his analysis of all Gypsies in the Reich, but he was not able to complete this task in full.[40]

Ritter's recommendations to sterilize and incarcerate most German Gypsies and to allow only a small number to remain free met the expectations of the bureaucracy in the Ministry of the Interior, which authorized him to perform the research. They hoped that the use of sterilization could also be expanded to solve the asocial problem. These expectations reflected the wish prevalent among the Nazi leadership to see a complete and radical solution for the Gypsy problem in the Reich's domain, as a part of a larger utopian vision of purifying the German nation of "elements with little value."[41]

There is no explicit evidence that before 1942 the Nazis had intended to exterminate Gypsies. During the criminal investigation process conducted against them after the war, Ritter and Justin both argued that as early as 1935 the intention prevailed within the SS's office for race issues *(Rassenpolitischesamt)* to exterminate all German Gypsies by loading them on a ship and sinking it out at sea. Ritter claimed that during the war, he himself had frustrated similar plans for total extermination of Gypsies. During the investigation (which began in 1947), Ritter used these arguments as an alibi to justify his own recommendation for sterilization and incarceration of Gypsies during the Third Reich. He presented them as an attempt to protect Gypsies against the intention by others to totally exterminate them. The reliability of these details, like others he submitted during the testimony, is rather dubious.[42] However, expressions indicating intentions of annihilation (as opposed to the concrete extermination plans concerning European Jewry of late 1941 and early 1942) were circulating within the Nazi Party in the 1930s,[43] so that it is possible that some functionaries in 1935 may have expressed themselves in a similar manner with regard to the "solution of the Gypsy problem."

The Radicalization of the Gypsy Policy during World War II

The attitude of the Nazi leadership with regard to the solution of the Gypsy problem was apparently influenced by global events. While in 1938 the SS discussed sterilization and incarceration as a "solution," by 1940 Himmler and Reinhard Heydrich wanted to deport all Gypsies—without any distinction between Mischlinge and pure race—to the Government-General in occupied Poland.[44] After the first 2,330 Gypsies were deported from the Reich to Poland in May 1940, this initiative was stopped due to the opposition of Hans Frank, the governor-general. Frank said the deportation of Gypsies was to be postponed until the "Jewish problem had been resolved."[45] Both Ritter and Leonardo Conti, the state's secretary for health issues and head of the Reich's physicians' organization, opposed this step. They advocated sterilization as the only means to deal with "the problem" effectively.[46] In 1941 the sterilization law of July 1933 was invoked and expanded to include sterilizing those who were labeled as asocials, including many Gypsies over the age of twelve. Although even the Nazis were aware that the legal foundation for sterilizing Gypsies who were not infected with hereditary diseases was shaky, this policy continued to the end of the war. Almost 2,000 German Gypsies, who had not been deported to Auschwitz, were sterilized between 1943 and 1944.[47]

The war and the extermination of Jews contributed to the radicalization of opinion among the Nazi upper ranks about how best to "solve" the Gypsy problem. In a conversation with the Minister of Justice, Otto Thierack, in September 1942, Joseph Goebbels stated that the "asocial life of Jews and Gypsies simply has to be exterminated."[48] As has already been mentioned, Ritter used this label "asocial" to refer to most of the Gypsies in Germany. And apparently Goebbels and Thierack found no meaning in the racist distinction between Mischlinge and "pure race Gypsies." In 1941 Heydrich suggested including the asocials in the euthanasia program. It is likely that he also supported a similar treatment for Gypsies, who were regarded by the criminal police and the bureaucracy as an integral part of the asocials.[49]

Even when the Gypsy problem began to be regarded as a distinct racial question after 1938, the treatment of Gypsies was different from that of Jews, whose legal status as German citizens had been denied since the Nuremberg Laws were enacted in September 1935. Only on 26 November 1935 did the Ministry of the Interior extend the ban against Jews marrying Aryans to Gypsies and blacks *(Neger)*.[50] Although both Gypsies and Jews were regarded as carriers of foreign blood, and despite the explicit provision that formally likened the status of both groups, officially Gypsies continued to hold their citizenship status as Reichsbürger until the twelfth directive in the Reich's citizenship law of April 1943.[51] However, many of them were deprived of certain civil rights, such as the right to vote for members of the Reichstag, to receive welfare grants, and to move freely.

Directives issued in November 1937 by the Reich's Ministry of the Interior and the War Ministry explicitly stated that Gypsies may not serve in the military, but these were disregarded when the war broke out in 1939. As German citizens, several hundred young German Sinti were conscripted to the Wehrmacht during the first years of the War. An ex-Wehrmacht soldier, Walter Winter, recalled that at least 500 of the inmates in the Gypsy camp at Auschwitz-Birkenau were former Wehrmacht soldiers.[52]

In May 1940 Hitler was informed of the service of Gypsies as soldiers in the Wehrmacht by his assistant for Wehrmacht issues. This information upset him, and he stated that because Gypsies were a foreign element *(artfremd)* they should be treated according to the special law *(Ausnahmegesetz)* that applied to Jews, who were no longer permitted to be enlisted for military service. Hitler claimed that Himmler had been given clear instructions about how to handle Gypsies.[53] But Hitler's bidding was not carried out in full until the beginning of 1943. Most Gypsies continued to serve in the Wehrmacht until 1942–1943, when they were discharged, in many cases only several months after the decrees ordering them to be discharged had been issued.[54]

In most cases the Wehrmacht authorities were aware that these soldiers were Gypsies. For example, as late as March 1942 the Sinto Walter Winter could remain with his naval unit, but as a Gypsy he was not entitled to rank or promotion.[55] He preferred to leave the navy. Since Ritter claimed that almost 90 percent of the German Gypsies were Mischlinge, probably most of the Gypsy Wehrmacht soldiers were defined as such. Considerably many more Jewish Mischlinge served in the Wehrmacht during World War II. When World War II broke out, Jewish Mischlinge of both first and second degree were called up to military service. Then in summer 1940 the Wehrmacht authorities excluded "half-Jews" and those married to Jews and "half-Jews," but they allowed "quarter-Jews" to remain in the Wehrmacht. Hitler and the Wehrmacht's leadership were reluctant to release soldiers from service as the situation in the front became more and more disastrous. In the course of World War II, however, the Nazi regime and consequently the Wehrmacht had hardened his ideological position, and finally Gypsy soldiers were discharged in 1943.[56]

The number of Gypsies—around 20,000 in Germany before their destruction by the Third Reich, as against approximately 500,000 Jews—was of course much smaller, as was their prominence in German cultural, economic, social, and political life. Unlike the case of Jews and Judaism, which greatly engaged Nazi thinkers and politicians, references to Gypsies in writings, speeches, and discussions of the leading Nazi figures and in Nazi propaganda were extremely sparse. The Nazi preoccupation with Gypsies lacked the political aspect that characterized the Nazi position on Jews. Neither German Sinti nor Eastern European Roma were ever regarded by the Nazis as the political enemies of Germany as Jews were.

Hitler himself showed very little interest in Gypsies, and he did not initiate the antigypsy policy. He referred only twice to Gypsies in his table talks, and he never once talked about them in public. Hitler's remarks about Gypsies reflected antigypsyism, which was not always scientifically racist. While in May 1940, Hitler indeed established that Gypsies were foreigners and had to be treated like Jews, by contrast in a conversation with Heydrich in 1941, Hitler described Gypsies in the spirit of their traditional image, as thieves and frauds who were a nuisance to the rural population. "Gypsies are romantic," Hitler ruled, "only in the bars of Budapest."[57] The Gypsy topic was so marginal to the Nazi agenda that no uniformly negative attitudes or opposition to Gypsy culture emerged, even among the SS officers, who formed the ideological spearhead of Nazism. Almost every week for over two years (March 1938–May 1940), the SS bulletin, *Das Schwarze Korps,* carried an advertisement for the Gypsy Cellar (Zigeunerkeller), which operated in Cafe Vienna in Berlin. The advertisement was decorated by a figure of a Gypsy violinist dressed in Hungarian costume. The cafe offered daily concerts of "Gypsy" music, in the afternoons and evenings. The contents of the advertisement did not clarify whether the musicians were genuine Gypsies; however, it is

Advertisement for the "Gypsy Cellar," from the SS newspaper *Die Schearze Korps,* 1938–1940.

hard to imagine the official SS journal carrying a similar advertisement for a Jewish cellar *(Judenkeller)* in which Klezmer music was played.

Moreover, it should be noted that even the pseudoscientific reason that Ritter gave for sterilizing Gypsies and denying their freedom had not been their Gypsy essence but, rather, their asociality. These properties they had inherited from their German asocial ancestors. In 1941, when

Ritter completed his survey of Gypsies in Germany and Austria, his conclusions were published in the German press; he claimed to have found that most Gypsies in Germany were not really Gypsies but rather descendants of German asocials and hereditary inferior elements of German society.[58]

Many senior Nazis adopted the antigypsy policy, which became increasingly extreme after the outbreak of World War II. But a different, more complicated approach toward the German Gypsies did not undergo a process of Nazi radicalization. This approach was typical of the Deutsches Ahnenerbe (German Ancestors' Heritage), an institution established by Himmler within the SS for the purpose of investigating the ancient Germanic past. This approach incorporated the romantic attitude toward Gypsies. As has been noted earlier, from the end of the nineteenth century, the romantic stream was the least dominant one within German racist thinking about Gypsies. This racist perception was similar to that held by Houston Stewart Chamberlain, who regarded them as Aryans and probably had considered less the physical appearance of Gypsies than their culture. In his writings about the ancient Germanic past, Walther Wüst, who headed the Ahnenerbe, also referred to Gypsies and their culture. In a lecture delivered in 1939, Wüst said that "a thorough examination of the Gypsy legends, which were originally told in a Indo-Aryan dialect, never fail to reveal a treasure of Aryan thinking and perception that has not been corrupted." The Ahnenerbe had plans to conduct research on Romany and Gypsy customs.[59]

Himmler's access to the foundation's ideologists meant that the Ahnenerbe's romantic concepts about the German Gypsies had some influence on Nazi policy toward Gypsies during 1942–1943. (Himmler, the founder of the institution, was the leading player in charge of conducting the Gypsy policy of the Third Reich.) In that period, Himmler's Gypsy policy combined Ritter's eleminationist concepts with the romantic notions of the Ahnenerbe. Ritter's research was used by Himmler as a pseudoscientific foundation for his policy, although Ritter himself opposed the racial romanticization of Gypsies. While in 1938 research Ritter had established that, despite its mixed nature, the Gypsy language belonged to the Indo-Germanic languages and that the Gypsies' origin lay among the nomad pariah of northern India, in articles and later publications he denied this finding so that he might protest the Ahnenerbe's romanticization of Gypsies as Aryans. In an article published in February 1941, summarizing his three years of research about the Gypsy population in Germany, Ritter wrote, "although in the commentaries [about the racial laws] Gypsies are mentioned, together with blacks, as carrying foreign blood. Nevertheless, the wrong approach that Gypsies wandered from India, their language contains Sanskrit elements, and they are in fact 'Aryans' finds itself not seldom represented."[60] This change in Ritter's attitude was apparently a response to the Ahnenerbe's romantic perception of Gypsies during that period.

Like Ritter, most of the Nazi functionaries who referred in some way or other to Gypsies attributed no significance to the Aryan myth. Hitler and Alfred Rosenberg, for example, did not regard the Indians as Aryans and therefore opposed their struggle for independence.[61] The romantic perception was not acceptable among the SS. The SS newspaper wrote about this issue after an interview that ethnologist Martin Block gave to the *Mittag* newspaper in 1936. Block, who had published a book about the Balkan Gypsies, among whom he had lived for several years, stated, probably with the intention of protecting Gypsies, that they were an original Aryan human race ("echt arische Menschenrasse"). Block was subjected to much contempt and reproof by *Das Schwarze Korps*. "Block and the *Mittag* might try to present Jews as a pure Aryan race yet!" the journal wrote. "It should be established that Gypsies, like Jews, are 'bastard peoples' [Bastardvölker]."[62] Beyond the strong language, the journal reflected the attitude of German anthropology, according to which Gypsies were not Aryans. After this article, the issue was not raised again in *Das Schwarze Korps*, perhaps because it was controversial.

A similar attitude against the Ahnenerbe's position was expressed by various publications of the National Socialist Party. For example, an article in the publication of the Reich's Ministry of Law (Reichsrechtsamt) implicitly protested against any romantic attitude toward Gypsies: "Whoever wants to fight them [the Gypsies] successfully should first free himself of all the romantic and sentimental attitudes toward Gypsies, their origin, race, customs, and lifestyle."[63]

Whereas Himmler officially headed the bodies that dealt with the German Gypsies (the criminal police and the concentration camps' administration), the influence of the Ahnenerbe's romantic perceptions had apparently influenced actual Nazi policy concerning them. Himmler used only certain elements of Ritter's theory and combined these with some romantic elements.

Nazi Policy on the East European Roma

Most of the Gypsies murdered by the Germans during the war were from eastern Europe. The fate of the Roma, the eastern European Gypsies in the German occupied territories, differed from the fate of the Sinti, the German Gypsies. In most of the occupied territories in the east, the Roma were not persecuted systematically, as were the Sinti inside the Reich's borders. The beginning of the killing was connected to the war against the Soviet Union that broke out on 22 June 1941. In late summer that year, in occupied Serbia, a few hundred Gypsy men were taken hostage, together with Jewish men, and were executed in reprisal for partisan attacks on German soldiers.[64]

Reports of the Einsatzgruppen (operating groups of the Security Service [SD] of the SS), which operated behind the advancing Wehrmacht units in the German-occupied territories of the Soviet Union, indicate that their firing squads began to execute Gypsies in late August 1941.[65] On 22 August 1941 the commander of the Einsatzkommando A/3, Karl Jäger dryly reported for the first time on the killing of Gypsies in Dünaburg: "3 Gypsy men, 1 Gypsy woman, 1 Gypsy boy."[66] We do not know of any specific order to exterminate Gypsies, but it seems that certain commanders of the Einsatzgruppen interpreted Hitler's Commissars Order of June 1941 (an order to kill political commissars of the Red Army, as well any other elements who might endanger the security in the occupied territories of the Soviet Union)[67] and other guidelines issued in early summer 1941 to the SS and police leaders in the Soviet-occupied territories as pertaining also to the extermination of Gypsies, mentally ill persons, and others considered to be asocials. Michael Zimmerman presumes that the killing of Gypsies was connected with Himmler's order to the Einsatzgruppen at that time to begin with total annihilation of the Jewish population (including women and children), anticipating the collapse of the Soviet Union.[68] Until the end of July 1941, the Einsatzgruppen had mostly executed Jewish men older than fifteen.[69]

Einsatzgruppen A, B, and C did not search out Gypsies systematically, but nevertheless 3,500 Gypsies were murdered in the Baltic states. Einsatzgruppe D, which was active in the Crimean Peninsula, murdered between 2,000 and 2,400 Gypsies in 1941–1942.[70] During the Einsatzgruppen trial at Nuremberg in 1948, Otto Ohlendorf, the commander of Einsatzgruppe D, claimed that the assignment of these troops was to keep the occupied Soviet territories free from subversive elements by killing Jews, Gypsies, Communist functionaries, and anyone who might threaten security. He asserted that past experience had taught that, like Jews, Gypsies had always been active as spies.[71] Another SS general, Erich von dem Bach-Zelewski, stated at the Nuremberg trials that killing Gypsies was part of the assignment of the Einsatzgruppen.[72]

Ohlendorf's line of defense was that he and the other commanders of the Einsatzgruppen had received a general order to murder Jews and Gypsies even before the beginning of the war against the Soviet Union. This apologetic claim originated from his desperate attempt to escape the death penalty for his crimes. He thought he might get a milder sentence if he could only prove that the mass killings he had ordered were the implementation of a superior's order and not his own initiative. (Ohlen-

Treatment of Eastern
Roma

German soldier with Gypsies, probably somewhere in the occupied territories of the Soviet Union.

45

Treatment g Laron Rom

dorf did not succeed and was hanged in Nuremberg.) Ohlendorf's claim could not be substantiated by historical research.[73]

Not only the Einsatzgruppen but also the representatives of German civil administration in the occupied territories in the East supported the killing of Gypsies in their jurisdiction. On 4 December 1941 the Reichs-kommisar of the Reichskommissariat Ostland, Hinrich Lohse, expressed his consent with the directive of the commander of the Order Police *(Ord-nungspolizei)* to execute the Gypsies of Libau. On the following day the entire Gypsy population of Libau was killed. Lohse ordered that vagrant Gypsies should be treated as Jews. However, in spite of his consent, the local order police and the security police *(Sicherheitspolizei)* disagreed about the definition of "Gypsy" and the question whether only the va-grant Gypsies or also the settled Gypsies were to be killed. In January 1942 the commander of the security police and the Sicherheitsdienst in Latvia had interpreted Lohse's position as pertaining only to vagrant Gypsies and that Gypsies who had a permanent place of residence and stable work should have been spared. But the commander of the order police held the opposite opinion, that all Gypsies had to be executed. Thus, both vagrant and settled Gypsies were killed in Latvia in the first months of 1942. In certain communities such as, for example, in Talsi, the lives of settled Gypsies were spared. Since the directives about the measures to be taken against Gypsies had seemed to be obscure, the com-mander of the Order Police sent several inquiries to the commanding of-fice of the gendarmes, the SS, and the police in late March and early April 1942 in which he demanded clear orders. The commander of the police constabulary *(Schutzpolizei)* in Latvia ordered the Security Service of the SS to take measures against Gypsy vagabonds only.[74]

The first murder of Gypsies by gas took place at Chelmno in January 1942. The victims were Gypsies from the Austrian Burgenland, who had been deported to the Lodz ghetto and had survived the epidemics and the hunger there.[75]

On 20 April 1942, Himmler noted in his diary: "No extermination of the Gypsies" ("Keine Vernichtung d. Zigeuner") following a telephone conversation with Heydrich, the head of the Reich's main security office *(Reichssicherheithauptamt)*.[76] I interpret this as an expression of his ob-jection to the murder of Gypsies by the Einsatzgruppen from the start of the war against the Soviet Union. I do not agree with the assumption by historian Michael Zimmermann that this note referred to the release of 292 Roma women and children from the camp in Semlin near Belgrade in Yugoslavia, where they had been incarcerated together with Jewish women and children.[77] The Roma women and children had already been released at the beginning of March 1942, when a special wagon was sent from Berlin to gas all the Jewish inmates in that camp.[78] I see no reason why Himmler should have discussed this particular decision with Heydrich a month and a half after it had been implemented.

In my view Himmler's note reflects a universal perception he held at that time. I do find a direct connection between this note and the directive Himmler issued to the Security Police and the Order Police in occupied Poland some months later, in August 1942. Himmler stated that those units should not take steps against Gypsies merely because they were "Gypsies": measures should be taken only against Gypsies who participated in criminal activities or who collaborated with the partisans.[79]

Contrary to the "common-sense" approach of Ohlendorf and Bach-Zelewski and the civil administration in Latvia, which condemned thousands of Roma to death, Himmler probably believed they should be spared from the total extermination he designed for the whole of European Jewry. Parallel to his racist-romantic perceptions regarding the German Sinti, Himmler seemingly also took a more moderate approach than his Nazi colleagues to the Roma in eastern Europe.

According to the July 1942 draft of a decree for dealing with the East European Gypsies, Alfred Rosenberg's Ministry for the Occupied Territories in the East (Ostministerium), Gypsies were to be treated as Jews, and no distinction should have been made between permanently settled and vagrant Gypsies. In the final version of May 1943, the intention was then to concentrate Gypsies in camps and special settlements rather than to exterminate them. In June 1943, the ministry sent the draft to various authorities to consult them before issuing the decree. It was rejected by Himmler and by its subordinate authorities (the criminal police, the Order Police, and the SS). They supported their conception of 1942 that permanently settled Gypsies and Gypsy Mischlinge were to be distinguished from vagrants, and thus should be treated in the same way as the rest of the German population, while Gypsies and Mischlinge who were not permanently settled were to be treated like Jews (namely, murdered). It is not at all clear to what extent those executing the policy in the occupied territories in the East actually followed Himmler's instructions.[80] In occupied Poland, about 8,000 Polish Gypsies out of 20,000 were murdered.[81] The contrast with the almost total annihilation of 3 million Polish Jews might point out that at least there Himmler's instruction were indeed followed.

In fact, Himmler's orders for the east European Roma reflected a view that was the reverse of that toward German Gypsies. In the east it was the vagrant Gypsies who were perceived as an element to be exterminated, rather than the permanently settled Gypsies. In Germany, as noted above, Ritter held the opposite position. The murder of the Roma by Wehrmacht units, Einsatzgruppen, and collaborators among local populations all over Europe was not preceded by any racial hygiene

47

Treatment of Eastern Roma

classification and evaluation, as was done with regard to a large part of the Gypsies in Germany.

The crucial reasons for murdering Gypsies, as submitted to the executives by the operation orders, were not always purely racist. In some cases, traditional antigypsy arguments and prejudices, dating back to the sixteenth century, were cited. These included spying for the enemy, spreading diseases and plagues, and the argument that Gypsies played no useful role in society. For example, in October 1941, the command in Serbia decreed that Gypsies were an element not to be trusted and thus constituted a danger to public order: "The Gypsies, due to their internal and external constitution cannot be useful members of the community of nations [*Völkergemeinschaft*]." [82] As these victims, like the East European Jews, had no contact with the German population, it seems unlikely that the extermination of the Roma constituted part of the German attempt to protect the racial purity of the German population, as implied by Peukert's model. [83]

Nazi Policy on the German Sinti

In October 1942, without consulting Hitler, Himmler issued a decree ordering that "the pure race Sinte" [*reinrassigen Sinte-Zigeuner*] will be awarded freedom of movement, which will enable them to wander in a certain area, to live according to their customs and habits, and to continue with their unique occupations." Himmler established in this decree that only Gypsies of unblemished behavior (*einwandfrei*) would be accepted. In this decree, contrary to Ritter's belief (Ritter opposed mixing Gypsy Mischlinge with pure race Gypsies), Himmler ordered that "Gypsy Mischlinge who are good with regard to their Gypsyhood" be joined with the clans (*Sippe*) of the "pure" Sinti, so that they would be integrated into the Sinti clan, provided the Sinti would not oppose their joining. The Gypsy men were intended to serve in a special unit of the Wehrmacht. [84]

Himmler's opinion of Gypsies was racial-mystical, while Ritter's was derived from the field of racial hygiene; Himmler was therefore less strict than Ritter in defining Mischlinge and pure race. According to the data of the criminal police, in November 1942, out of about 18,000 Gypsies in Germany, the pure race numbered 1,079, while the "Gypsy Mischlinge, who were more Gypsy than German," accounted for 6,992 persons. Because the issue was not the merging of the two categories but rather integrating the Mischlinge into the pure tribes, apparently only a few out of this pool of Mischlinge could have joined the pure tribes. After the war, Ritter estimated that the number of pure Gypsies did not exceed 4,000. [85] The task of joining Mischlinge with the pure race tribes was imposed by Himmler not on the scientific expert, Ritter, but on nine

Gypsy leaders *(Rechtsprecher)*, who were described in the German documents as tribe heads *(Hauptlinge)*. The transfer of the allegedly scientific task to the Gypsies themselves apparently derived from the interest either Himmler or the Ahnenerbe's experts had in consolidating organic rather than synthetic clans. The classification according to Ritter's harsh criteria destroyed the organic texture of Gypsy families and could have harmed their ability to maintain community life.[86] Rudolf Höß, the commandant of Auschwitz, reported in his diary that the two pure race Gypsy tribes were intended for settlement in the Neussiedler lake area, namely Sopron in the district of Ödenburg in Hungary, and would enjoy certain freedom of movement. Zimmermann claims that they were to stay in a reservation in the Government-General in Poland.[87]

This plan was opposed by Reichsleiter Martin Bormann, who headed Hitler's chancellery. Bormann protested in a letter to Himmler in early December 1942, after he had accidentally heard about it from Arthur Nebe, the head of the criminal police. "Special treatment of those who were called pure race Gypsies will constitute a significant deviation from the measures taken for combating the Gypsy nuisance, and it will in no way be accepted with understanding among the population or in the party's corridors," wrote Bormann. He added: "The Führer also will not allow the old liberties to be returned to part of the Gypsies."[88]

In December 1942 Hitler, Himmler, and Bormann met to discuss the issue. A remark by the Minister of Justice, Thierack, in his notebook makes clear that Himmler succeeded in convincing Hitler and Bormann to accept his policy by explaining that there were valuable racial elements among Gypsies.[89] What might have accounted for Hitler's acceptance of Himmler's argument was the distinction Himmler made between the Mischlinge and the racially pure Gypsies, and this suggested the exclusion of the romantic layer of the Gypsy image from the hated aspects of Gypsyhood. The romantic perception of the Gypsy (as discussed in chapter 1 of this volume) was embedded in the collective German consciousness. This romanticism might even have been attractive to Hitler, especially as Himmler's plan was intended only to preserve a small and limited number of German Gypsies. Ritter's distinction between Mischlinge and "pure race Gypsies" apparently corresponded to a hidden desire to isolate from Gypsyism the elements that charmed the Germans, as it did other Europeans—elements expressed in the German classics by the images of the dancing Gypsy girl and the Gypsy violinist.

In January 1943 Himmler issued a circular ordering the deportation of the Reich's Gypsies to a special family camp at Auschwitz-Birkenau. The circular included some categories that were to be exempted from deportation—the pure race among the Sinti and the small Lalleri tribe (which, in fact, was culturally closer to the East European Roma tribes than to the Sinti) in accordance with Ritter's approach. The circular also exempted categories contradictory to Ritter's, thus increasing the number of Gypsies who were allowed to remain free, beyond the range Ritter had recommended. Among the exemption categories were "high-quality Gypsy Mischlinge," Gypsies married to Germans, and those who were socially integrated (the decree determined that the criminal police would establish the extent of their integration, not Ritter); another exempted category were Gypsy soldiers who had not yet been dismissed and those who had been released after participating in the war and who had been injured or awarded medals. But the decree established that all those who were exempt from deportation would be obliged to sign their willingness to be voluntarily sterilized.[90] In 1940 Himmler replied to Gunther d'Alquen, of the Sicherheitsdienst, and the editor of *Das Schwarze Korps,* that "the fact that someone proved his racial value by his courage at war would definitely be recognized, even if he was not of Nordic pure race."[91]

Himmler's racist perception of Gypsies was therefore not as harsh as other Nazi leaders and functionaries. In Himmler's eyes, the willingness of Gypsy soldiers to sacrifice themselves for Germany and the Führer, as well as their social integration, carried more weight than their racial classification as determined by Ritter. Himmler's policy was a very radical version of a combination between two opposing trends in German society: antigypyism and the romantic attitude toward Gypsies. The antigypsy views were common among the police apparatus and the state bureaucracy in Germany. The romantic elements in his policy probably originated in the Ahnenerbe and can be regarded as a continuation of the traditional romantic approach toward Gypsies. The racist nature of the Third Reich had to provide both trends with a racist rationalization. As both German and Nazi anthropology had never regarded Gypsies as an Aryan race, even though they spoke a language of Aryan origin, the Ahnenerbe's researchers provided reasons prevalent in the romantic racial stream as grounds for their romantic attitude.

However, the way in which the circular's instructions were actually carried out and the way Gypsies were treated in Auschwitz are consistent with the functionalistic theories about the processes that led to the extermination of Jews, since they indicate that some kind of anarchy prevailed between the various power centers of the Nazi system and that Himmler's orders were not followed by his subordinate ranks.[92] The criminal police stations throughout the Reich, which were responsible for carrying out the deportation, whether because they wished to get rid of the Gypsies under their jurisdiction or because they lacked racial hygiene opinions of Gypsies, were not strict about following the circular's instructions for exemptions from deportation to Auschwitz. In the vast majority of cases, they did not discriminate between pure race and Gypsy *Mischlinge,* and only a few Gypsies were allowed to stay in Germany, most of them under police control. Many of these were sterilized, and they were not allowed to move freely or engage in their traditional occupations. Höß and Pery Broad, who served in the political department at Auschwitz, bear witness that in the "transports" after the decree that ordered deportation of Gypsies to Auschwitz, many arrived who were not intended to arrive at all; among them were members of the National Socialist Party or various Nazi organs, and soldiers who were dismissed from the Wehrmacht, including several who had received war decorations. However, the Center for Combating the Gypsy Nuisance in the criminal police in Berlin firmly refused to grant the requests from the camp's staff and from relatives and friends to release these people from Auschwitz.[93]

There is no evidence that in 1943 the SS planned to exterminate the Gypsies who were deported from Germany and some other countries to Auschwitz, as was the clear intention in the case of the "final solution" for the Jews who were deported there. Theoretically, Roma and Sinti Mischlinge were included among the deported, and, according to Ritter's theory, they were asocial and had to be sterilized, while according to Goebbels's and Thierack's perceptions, they probably had to be exterminated. Höß argued that the purpose of their incarceration in Auschwitz was to hold them there until the end of the war. Broad received explicit instructions from Berlin that Gypsies were not to be treated like Jews when they arrived (namely, they were not to be exterminated), and until 1944, when a decision was taken to eliminate the Gypsy camp, the Gypsy prisoners there were not exterminated by gas. (The only exception was a transport of 1,000 Gypsies that arrived at Auschwitz in 1943 from Bialystok and were gassed on the spot, allegedly because they were infected with typhus.)[94]

A special camp was erected for Gypsies in Auschwitz-Birkenau, and there they enjoyed certain privileges and conditions that were not afforded to Jews or any other group of prisoners. These privileges caused enmity toward them by other prisoners and friction. Some prisoners gave testimony to this effect after the war. For example, John Heinrich, a German political prisoner who served in the camp as a paramedic, claimed that Gypsies held a status of "civil internees" in the camp and not a status of prisoners (as Jews were). Wieslaw Kielar, a Polish political prisoner in Birkenau, stated that the Gypsy camp was not a concentration camp but a "family camp," and until a certain time, even such luxuries as milk were provided for the Gypsy children.[95] Although personal numbers were indeed tattooed on the prisoners' forearms and on the babies' feet, and the letter Z (which stood for Zigeuner—Gypsy) was stitched on their clothes, they were exempted from wearing prisoners' uniforms and work duty was not imposed on them, at least at the beginning. Money, valuables, and personal possessions were not taken away from the Gypsy prisoners, and they were able to purchase food staples and products in a so-called canteen erected in the camp.[96]

Hundreds of Gypsies who were dismissed from the Wehrmacht were also brought to the camp. Most of them served in the army until 1942–1943. During the first months they and their families lived in a special block at the camp; only later were they dispersed among other blocks. The presence in the camp of these Wehrmacht Gypsies, according to one of the survivors, was probably what caused the authorities in Berlin to frustrate the intentions of the camp's administration to close the Gypsy camp and send all its prisoners to the gas chambers.[97]

During 1943, Himmler lost almost all interest in the fate of Gypsies. The extent of Himmler's will on what happened in the camps became limited, in spite of the fact that the system was directly subordinate to him, especially regarding the appalling conditions that prevailed in the camps from 1943 on. Different needs and interests of local level functionaries may well have caused the leadership's intentions to be frustrated. Conditions for Gypsies worsened considerably, and soon the crowded accommodations, the poor hygiene conditions, the miserable nutrition, and Dr. Mengele's sadistic torture dressed up as "medical experiments" led to the outbreak of plagues, and many of the incarcerated Gypsies died as a result.

At the beginning of August 1944, a decision was taken to close the Gypsy camp. According to Höß, the terrible conditions into which the camp had deteriorated were the reason for its closure; Höß's claim is supported by testimonies of Polish and German doctors.[98] Between May and July 1944, the healthy Gypsy prisoners and ex-Wehrmacht soldiers and their families were transferred, the men to Buchenwald and the women to Ravensbrück. It might have been that Himmler himself was responsible for that selection, which saved the ex-Wehrmacht soldiers and their families from immediate extermination in the gas chambers. Their deportation to Buchenwald and Ravensbrück did not spare them from hard labor and in many instances to sterilization, however, and in the case of some, to ghastly medical experiments; many died as a result of these and other crimes.

The 2,897 Gypsies who were left in Auschwitz—the sick, the old, children, and those who had no relatives who served in the Wehrmacht—were murdered in the gas chambers. The Gypsy camp was later intended for the incarceration of Hungarian Jews, who were now arriving at Auschwitz by the hundreds of thousands, and it seems that the need for extra camp space to help speed up the extermination of Hungarian Jewry overrode the romantic wish of Himmler to preserve the last of the German Gypsies.[99] The Gypsy family camp in Birkenau had existed almost seventeen months.

There are certain similarities between this camp and the family camp of the mostly Czech Jews who had been deported to Auschwitz from Theresienstadt that existed between September 1943 and July 1944. The lives of those Jews also were spared for some months; they were not gassed immediately on arrival at Auschwitz, and Jewish families could remain together there. Correspondence between the International Red Cross and the office of Adolf Eichmann illuminates the motives for erecting this unique camp in Auschwitz-Birkenau. In view of a forthcoming visit of Red Cross officials to Auschwitz, the Nazi authorities wished to refute rumors that had spread in Europe and in the world that systematic extermination of the European Jews was taking place in this camp. Thus, each of the two groups of Theresienstadt Jews survived in Auschwitz exactly six months, and then they were murdered in the gas chambers.[100] There is no evidence for similar motives for erecting the Gypsy family camp at Auschwitz-Birkenau.

In the last two months of the war, a few hundred German Gypsies who had been incarcerated in the concentration camps were then coercively enlisted into the Dirlewanger unit, which was enlisted from of the ranks of German prisoners (mainly criminals and asocials, but also some German political prisoners), and were sent to the Russian front on the River Oder.[101] This might show that, despite everything, Gypsies, in contrast to Jews, were perceived by Himmler, who gave his consent to Dirlewager's initiative, to be part of the German fatherland and not its foe.

In the end, Ritter and his institute only succeeded in performing a bureaucratic procedure of classification according to the racial hygiene method with regard to about 23,000 out of the 32,000 Gypsies who resided in the Reich, including Austria.[102] As did the preceding policy on Gypsies since the nineteenth century, the Nazi policy distinguished between German Gypsies and foreign Gypsies, but the Nazis assigned a racist meaning to these categories, which, in contrast to the preceding policy, determined whether they were to live or die. Unlike the case of the German states in the nineteenth century, which simply were not able to control and thus deport all their Gypsies and therefore decided to let them exist on their land legally, the decision by the Nazis to allow a small number of German Gypsies to survive was taken deliberately, and it derived from the racist romantic attitude.

Estimations of the Number of Gypsy Victims under the Nazi Regime

There are various estimates regarding the total number of Gypsies murdered by the Nazis and their collaborators in eastern European countries, or who died as a consequence of their deportation and confinement. The number of victims cannot be definitively established, since there is a lack of accurate data on the dimensions of the killing in the former Soviet Union, Poland, Hungary, Serbia, Croatia, and Romania. In contrast, well-kept German documents enable us to ascertain the number of Gypsy victims in Germany, Austria, Holland, northern France, the Baltic states, and Crimea.

In 1972, Donald Kenrick and Grattan Puxon assessed the number of Gypsy victims of the Nazis and their collaborators (both inside and outside the Reich) at 219,600 men, women, and children. When the Society for the Threatened Peoples opened its public campaign in 1979 for equal civil rights for the German Gypsies, they published an unfounded and greatly exaggerated assessment that the number of Gypsy victims exceeded half a million,[103] an estimate that had appeared in the German press in the early 1960s (as far as I know) and has been accepted unquestionably, but wrongly, by many journalists and others ever since.[104] In 1989, Hermann Arnold, Ritter's successor in the racial hygiene field in the FRG, challenged these assessments. He confronted Kenrick and Puxon's assessments with the German documents (e.g., the Einsatzgruppen reports on the scale of their killing) and argued that the number of Gypsy victims throughout Europe was at most 100,000.[105]

Michael Zimmermann recently supplied the most up-to-date and possibly most accurate and best-researched assessment. He stated that the number of Gypsy victims of Nazi Germany amounted to 50,000 persons, 15,000 of whom were German Gypsies. To this one should add the number of Gypsy victims of the fascist regimes in Croatia and Romania, which might exceed 35,000. These figures add up to 90,000. Zimmermann indicated that the total number of victims might exceed these figures.[106]

Although, since the end of the fifteenth century, Gypsies on German soil had suffered many cruel persecutions, the objective of which was to drive them away from the Reich's domain, their persecution by the Nazi regime, especially during the war, was entirely different in nature from the persecutions they had endured in the past and constituted a unique phenomenon in the history of the state's attitude in Germany. This was the first time that a government would attempt to get rid of German Gypsies, primarily through a plan of physical extermination. Whereas in the 1930s the common opinion held by the regime's technocrats was that the Gypsy entity could be eliminated within one generation by mass sterilization, during the war some radicalization occurred among the Nazi leadership. Apparently inspired by the extermination of Jews, they began to think of substituting sterilization with mass murder. Ironically, Reichsführer Heinrich Himmler, who supported and enthusiastically participated in the extermination of Jews, adopted some romantic attitude elements of the Ahnenerbe perception of Gypsies and protected German Gypsies from immediate murder in the gas chambers. This was the first and only time since the first Gypsies landed on German soil in the fifteenth century that the phenomenon of romanticization of this hated minority had any influence on the formation of policy concerning them in Germany.

But the benefits of Himmler's protection were very dubious because he entrusted their fate to a system that had been erected specifically for the extermination of human beings. Furthermore, the romantic attitude toward Gypsies was in the exceptional minority within the Nazi leadership and was totally contradictory to the general concept of the German national community *(Volksgemeinschaft)* that was shared by Hitler and other prominent Nazi leaders and by wide circles of the Nazi bureaucracy; Himmler's view therefore had little chance of success within the Nazi system. The Messianic radicalism in Nazi ideology led to the radicalization process that ended with the genocide of tens of thousands of Europe's Gypsies. In the Reich, it was a part of a criminal eugenic vision of eliminating crime and backwardness from the Volksgemeinschaft by means of murder. In the German-occupied territories, it was an integral part of the annihilation war waged against Judeo-Bolshevism as Gypsies were there often regarded by the Germans as agents of the Jews.[107]

3

Policy toward Gypsies in the Shadow of Auschwitz

THE GYPSY policy of the Nazi regime collapsed along with the Third Reich in May 1945. The collective incarceration, enforced sterilization, and mass murder came to an end, and the bodies in the Reich's criminal police office (RKPA), which had centralized the persecution, were dismantled. The formulation of a "Gypsy policy" after 1945 posed for the state's authorities a moral and political challenge that was unprecedented in the history of German–Gypsy relations. This chapter concentrates on that challenge, in particular the way in which the German authorities dealt with Gypsy issues during the period of the Allies' military government (1945–1949) mostly in the American occupied zone and in the Federal Republic of Germany during the 1950s.

GYPSIES IN WEST GERMANY AT THE END OF THE WAR

Although there are no official statistical assessments on the number of Gypsies who resided in Germany in 1945 or thereafter, it is clear that the murder and mass sterilization of Gypsies during the Third Reich greatly reduced their number. In May 1940, an estimated 18,330 Gypsies had lived within the borders of the German Reich; in 1945, according to an unknown expert, Karl-Heinz Sippel, fewer than 5,000 remained. Of these, 2,000 were survivors of concentration camps and the rest had escaped incarceration. However, this assessment may well have underestimated the true number of Gypsies.[1]

After being released from concentration camps, the survivors began returning to the cities and villages from which they had been deported, in search of their families and kin. As most of the wagons in which many Sinti had lived up until the end of the 1930s had been confiscated by the police and burnt or sold, they had to find other accommodations. Some of them acquired new wagons and returned to a traditional vagrant way of life, but most either joined their few surviving relatives who had remained in the holding camps the Nazis had erected in various German cities or otherwise went to live in temporary housing. Thus, small concentrations of Gypsies were created anew throughout Germany.[2]

Nazi persecution had severely aggravated the Gypsies' socioeconomic situation, which had already been marked by poverty and distress even before Hitler seized power. The Nazi regime robbed them of what valuables they had (mostly gold and jewelry), and after the war the Gypsies found it difficult to prove their ownership and recover their property, an issue which (as in the case of the Jews) largely remains unresolved until this day. The concentration camp survivors were physically and mentally broken. Some could hardly function, let alone make enough living to support their families.

Although modernization had impaired the profitability of the Gypsies' traditional ways of earning a living even before the Hitler era, the possibilities of their finding new occupations now were extremely limited, since most of them were illiterate. Thus many continued with their traditional occupations after the war, such as horse trading, peddling, and dealing in carpets, textiles, and haberdashery. Even though Gypsy women participated in these small businesses, Gypsy men rarely made enough to supply the needs of their often large families, and many found themselves in need of welfare support. In some cases the distress was so acute that they were driven to break the law. Otto Pankok, the Düsseldorf painter, and a well-known friend of the Sinti, wrote in 1950: "It is as clear as daylight that among people in distress, criminal offenses, begging money, stealing food, etc., are more frequent than among officials who earn good salaries or citizens who are well-established."[3]

The Gypsies did not reappear simultaneously all over Germany. In one or two places, such as Hamburg, they returned as early as May 1945. They reappeared in other states, such as Hesse, Bremen, and Württemberg-Baden, over the next twelve months. Throughout Germany, their return was met by a negative response, both by the local population and by the authorities. For example, police reports compiled in rural areas near Hamburg in June 1945 state that the local German population accused Gypsies of illegally taking fodder from the fields for their horses and of demanding, under threats, especially of women, that they be given vegetables and fruit. Similar reports were made throughout Germany, at least up until the establishment of the FRG in 1949. These complaints were

Site of the Gypsy camp *(Zigeunerlager)* at Höherweg in Düsseldorf, 1947. (Otto Pankok Museum Haus Esselt, Huenxe-Drevenack. Photo by Otto Pankok.)

referred to the Ministries of the Interior of the various states. In Bremen, for instance, citizens who lived in a neighborhood close to an area where Gypsies had parked their wagons complained that the Gypsies defecated and threw trash all over the place and that their presence had become a sanitary nuisance.[4]

Although the Gypsies' bitter fate during the Third Reich became known after the defeat, only a few Germans expressed any sympathy or empathy toward them. Pankok described the attitude of German society: "Hitler has sunk, but the racial hatred has remained unchanged; to those who do not believe this, I recommend a walk, accompanied by a Gypsy, in the streets of a city."[5]

In the early 1950s, citizens submitted complaints to the town (municipal) council *(Magistrat)* of Frankfurt am Main, demanding that the city authorities remove Gypsies, who were described as a plague, from the area of the city. It is hard to believe that those who submitted such demands in the 1950s held a negative attitude toward the way in which the Nazi regime had responded positively to similar petitions by the citizens of Frankfurt in the early 1930s, although apparently they were reserved about the eventually murderous nature of the Nazi "solution" to the "Gypsy problem."[6] The removal of Gypsies from cities and villages during the Third Reich (on the basis of circulars issued by Heinrich Himmler, on 8 December 1938 and later) apparently had raised expectations among the population that even after the defeat of Nazism the authorities would agree to the demands by citizens that Gypsies be deported. Indeed, after 1945, in at least one German town, Marburg in Hesse, the Gypsies were deported, with the approval of the military government of the United States.[7]

STRUGGLE AGAINST THE "GYPSY NUISANCE" DURING THE ALLIES' MILITARY GOVERNMENT

While those citizens who demanded that the authorities take strict measures toward Gypsies were resolute in their calls for action, the attitude of many minor officials in the police, local authorities, and various interior ministries, who were asked to deal with these complaints, was far from decisive. The fact that Gypsies, like Jews, were defined as victims of Nazi racial persecution led many officials to fear the legality of acting against them. They were also concerned that the occupying Allies might attribute a political significance if the authorities took steps against Gypsies, and the Allies might even impose sanctions.

For the first time in German history, the authorities were hesitant about carrying out measures to deport Gypsies from their jurisdiction. A letter of November 1946 written by the head of a local government *(Regierungspräsident)* in Kassel to the Ministry of the Interior in Hesse complained that "the authorities and police officers treat Gypsies carefully today, because Gypsies were persecuted for racial motives in the Nazi state, and almost all of them hold certificates of persecuted people." (Likely, he meant membership cards of the VVN, the association of those persecuted by the Nazis.) In 1947, in a letter to the Ministry of the Interior of Stuttgart, the head of the local government in Baden grumbled that these certificates served some of the Gypsies as "protection letters for their dubious activity" and that because of this dealing with them was difficult. The police department of the local government in Darmstadt reported to the public security department of the Hessian Ministry of the Interior that at the end of 1945 Gypsy horse traders had arrived in the region of Bergstrasse and exchanged horses with the local citizens. In some of these exchanges the Gypsies had allegedly cheated the local citizens, giving them in exchange for a young and healthy horse an old horse that had been tampered with in order to hide its age and condition. The authorities in Heppenheim launched an investigation, aware that many Gypsies held certificates confirming that they were former inmates of Nazi concentration camps, and this led them to avoid initiating legal proceedings.[8]

Yet, the field ranks of the various German authorities who were in contact with Gypsies sought to remove not only vagrant Gypsies, who proved to be a nuisance to the population, but also those Gypsies who after the war were making an attempt to settle down and abandon their vagrant lifestyle. In January 1946, the mayor of Laufen am Kocher tried to deport the Reinhardt family, some of whose members had survived the concentration camp in Belsen and who now wished to settle down in the Laufen jurisdiction. The mayor refused to give this Gypsy family their food coupons. In a letter to the authorities he claimed that because the Gypsies had made such a fuss in response, he had had to change his mind and give them the coupons.[9]

The case of the Reinhardt family indicates that not only had the attitude of German officials toward Gypsies changed after the Nazis were defeated, but so had the behavior of Gypsies toward the German population and authorities. They no longer feared confronting officials and insisting upon their legal rights as equal citizens. In late June 1945, an officer at police station no. 101, on the southern outskirts of Hamburg, reported to the police headquarters of the city-state that, as people released from concentration camps, the Gypsies had demanded an improved attitude and had requested that they be registered at the police station, which was usually only done in the case of permanent inhabitants.[10] Gypsies now wished to be registered, as registration was a condition Nazi victims needed to fulfill in order to receive immediate assistance. The office wrote that before 1933 the police "endured" the Gypsies for only a short time before deporting them to neighboring areas. His words imply that he understood that after the Nazi defeat it was no longer possible to treat Gypsies this way, and therefore he requested instructions from headquarters, asking "whether anything could be done to prevent the continued stay of Gypsies in their parking lot."

The records of the authorities in Hesse and Lower Saxony indicate that Gypsies not only claimed that they were victims of Nazi persecution but also that they belonged to the "united nations," or to the "friendly nations," that is, to the Allies who fought Nazism.[11] According to the Allies' policy, the citizens of the united nations were not subjected to the authority of the German police and judicial system but, instead, to the police and legal authority of the military government, which was the aim of the Gypsies.[12] The authorities in Lower Saxony submitted the matter to be ruled on by the British military government at Lüneburg, which in early November 1945 refused the Gypsies' request, thereby authorizing the German police to continue to act against them.[13]

Similar claims were made by some Gypsies in 1946 to the gendarmery command in Hesse. Not wanting to act against the instructions of the military government, the command appealed to the head of police to make a quick decision regarding the Gypsies' status. The appeal reached the public security department at the Hessian Ministry of the Interior and from there was passed to the U.S. Office of Military Government for Germany (OMGUS) in Hesse. The American military government delayed making a decision, and a reminder was sent from the public security department in November. A draft answer was prepared by the legal department of the military government, but apparently it was never sent. It said that Gypsies were not recognized internationally as an independent nation, therefore their nationality would be determined according to the rules referring to the establishment of citizenship.[14]

According to the circular issued in mid-November 1945 by Maj. Gen. Clarence Adcock, head of the OMGUS, it was established that a displaced person's nationality should be determined according to the citizenship they held. According to this interpretation, Ernst Anspach, of the German administrative legal branch of the American military government in Hesse, wrote to Mr. Ellenbogen of the legislative branch in mid-March 1947, saying that he believed that Gypsies were subject to the jurisdiction of the German courts if they belonged nationally (i.e., with regard to their citizenship) to the nationals of enemy nations, namely, Germans, Austrians, and so on, and were not subjected to this authority if they belonged to the Allies' united nations or if they held no citizenship. Only in March 1947 did the American military government specifically reply to the public security department of the Ministry of the Interior in Hesse. The Hessian military government had requested that Gypsies who violated the law, or who were suspected of doing so, should be treated according to German rules and instructions; however, the Americans said that if the relevant Gypsy presented a certificate confirming that he had been politically or racially persecuted, he should immediately be transferred to the nearest office of the American military government or to a military police station. This reply was sent through a circular of the public security department to the head of the local administration *(Regierungs-präsidenten)* in Hesse and to the different branches of the police. No reference to the establishment of the nationality of Gypsies was made in the circular, a matter which Anspach discussed and also brought up in his conversation with the representative of the Ministry of Justice in Hesse.[15]

Although the postwar Allied military governments acknowledged that Gypsies had been victims of racial persecution,[16] this was not acceptable to the representatives of the German criminal police and to many bureaucrats in the German local authorities, the welfare system, and the compensation system for victims of Nazism. In fact, the Allied military governments demonstrated virtually no interest in policy issues concerning Gypsies. While it is true that they were fewer in number than Jews and other groups, it is nevertheless surprising that during this whole period

(1945–1949) no attempt was made by the Allies to deal with the Gypsies' unique problems or to formulate an overall plan for their rehabilitation and integration into German society. The abolishment of the antigypsy legislation of the Nazis, the main part of which was contained in the circulars issued by Himmler, had been implied by the second article of the first law the Allies enacted concerning the repeal of the Nazi laws, an article that annulled any law, decree, or regulation based on racial principles.[17]

But the Allies made no explicit statement to the German public and authorities to unambiguously clarify their attitude about the abolishment of this legislation. Apparently, it was not obvious to all police officers in Germany that Himmler's circulars on combating the Gypsy plague were based on racial principles. In October 1945, the head of the Order Police (Ordnungspolizei) in the province of Hannover approached the province's president and asked him to issue general instructions for "combating the Gypsy nuisance" (Zigeunerunwesen) in the province. As a legal basis for antigypsy actions he proposed relying on the Ministry of the Interior's circular of 8 December 1938, which had been issued by Himmler. He requested that the main points of the circular should be maintained, but not the racist components and distinctions: "The distinction between Gypsies and Gypsy Mischlinge [Zigeunermischlingen] has little significance; whoever lives according to the Gypsy style and demonstrates the asocial properties of Gypsies has to be treated as a Gypsy, without reference to his racial belonging. It is no longer possible to treat someone differently because of his racial belonging." The head of the Hannover Order Police stated that it was necessary to maintain a central agency for combating the Gypsy plague and noted that the criminal police had already submitted its proposals for this issue to the military government.

In another letter sent by the criminal headquarters of the Hannover police to the provincial president, it was emphasized that the grounds for the steps to be taken against Gypsies were not racial, "but that according to experience, the rate of crime among this people is especially high." They called for the establishment of an information service in the criminal police to manage a surveillance card index of Gypsies and issue certificates to them. They urged that no additional Gypsies be admitted to the region of Hannover; that local Gypsies be deported to their former place of residence; that vagrant Gypsies be reported to the police information service, where they should be registered; and that all requests made by Gypsies for certificates and approvals would have to pass through the police information service.[18] Hannover's attitude toward the use of the Third Reich's regulations against Gypsies was exceptional; in general, other authorities ruled that the measures taken against Gypsies could no longer legally lean on Himmler's instructions.

Caravans of Sinti at the campsite at Höherweg in Düsseldorf, 1949. (HSTA Dusseldorf RWB 1775. Photo by Karl Heinz Stachelscheid.)

As many police and interior authority officials really did believe that Gypsies constituted a plague for the German population, they sought a valid legal basis, free from the stain of Nazi racism, for the measures to be taken against them. An attempt was made to consolidate a Gypsy policy by relying on legislation that preceded the Nazi period, partly from the Kaiserreich and partly from the Weimar Republic.

The general supervisor for Gypsy matters in the criminal police department of Hamburg, Commissar Jehring, wrote in July 1945 that, with the annulment of the racial laws, the legal basis for the measures the criminal police had taken against Gypsies were no longer valid. But, he added, antigypsy steps could be based on the decrees issued by the Prussian Ministry of the Interior on 17 February 1907 and on 6 June 1936. The aim of the new Gypsy policy, as indicated by a memorandum issued by Jehring at the end of September 1945, was the "driving away of the Gypsy plague" and the "guiding of the Gypsies into a settled lifestyle." This latter aim expressed the Enlightenment idea of "civic correction *[bürgerliche Besserung]* of Gypsies." Such a declaration by a representative of the very authority that had deported the Hamburg Gypsies to Auschwitz during the Third Reich reflects the profound change that had taken place after 1945 among even those officials from the Nazi period who retained their posts in the German police. A similar solution was also discussed in Württemberg-Baden. It was suggested that an investigation be held there to establish whether the decree about Gypsies that had been issued by Württemberg's Ministry of the Interior in 1921 could still be used.[19]

In a 1946 letter to the Ministry of the Interior in Hesse, Inspector Berger, an official of the police command, doubted whether the decree issued by the Prussian Ministry of the Interior on 17 February 1906 could serve as a legal basis for measures now to be taken against Gypsies. According to him, no legal basis for police action against Gypsies remained after the validity of the racial laws was annulled on orders of the occupying military government. Therefore he challenged the Ministry of the Interior in Hesse to re-regulate the Gypsy question.[20] However, in Hesse, as in Bavaria, no new legislation was needed to regulate the Gypsy question, for in the domain of these two states, contrary to the other German states, the laws from the Weimar Republic were still valid and had not been abolished by the Allies. In Hesse, some Gypsies were indeed deported from at least one community, relying on this law and carried out with the approval of the American military government (OMGUS).[21]

The Bavarian authorities continued to use the antigypsy law of the Weimar Republic until the OMGUS repealed it in 1947. A routine inspection of the workhouse at Rebdorf, performed that year by the prisons branch at the OMGUS in Bavaria and aimed at ensuring that prisoners had not been incarcerated without due legal procedure, found that eleven prisoners, eight of them Gypsies, had been incarcerated there as instructed by city mayors and municipal councils. The prisoners, both men and women, had been jailed for periods between nine months and two years, on the grounds of the law for combating Gypsies, vagrants, and work shys of 1926, which permitted the imprisonment in workhouses of individuals who, due to a moral fault, were deemed to be a burden to the public welfare or to another person. The head of the prisons branch believed this law should be annulled and reported this to the legislation department of the OMGUS.[22]

Contrary to the impression created with time among Bavarian political circles, this law was abolished not because of its discriminatory nature against Gypsies but rather for violating the democratic principle of division of power, which enabled an executive body to perform a judicial procedure against Gypsies, vagrants, and work shys. These categories also were applied to Germans (especially work shys), not only to Gypsies. In a letter to the Bavarian prime minister, in which the military governor of Bavaria, Murray Van Wagoner, instructed him to immediately annul the law and release the incarcerated prisoners, it was emphasized that the provisions of this law, allowing judgment and punishment of people by executive rather than judicial decision, intruded on the judiciary and constituted a violation of both the military government's policy and the principle of division of powers between the executive and the judiciary. Van Wagoner explained in his letter that this law lacked the minimal requirements demanded of a law, and it violated the rights and immunity guaranteed by the third declaration of the control council.[23] In fact, the annulled law included nineteen articles, and only one of them (article 9) included an instruction for judging offenders by executive power. All the other articles imposed different restrictions on Gypsies' and vagrants' freedom of movement in Bavaria. In 1946 the OMGUS closed all the workhouses within its jurisdiction and revoked the legal basis for their existence,[24] although in the other Allied occupation zones the workhouses remained open.

OMGUS held that merely purging German law books of Nazi legislation was insufficient; instead, every law that contradicted the principles of American democracy should be struck off. As the incarceration in workhouses of people labeled as "asocial" was an important element of German welfare policy, officials of the military government believed that a reform in and the democratization of this system should be carried out and that laws regarded by them as injuring basic human liberties should be annulled, even if they were not typical Nazi laws. The political establishment of Bavaria accepted the OMGUS orders without appeal. The Bavarian prime minister, Dr. Hans Ehard, announced that the law concerning Gypsies, vagrants, and work shys would be removed from the Bavarian law book and informed the military government that all prisoners would be released.[25]

Beyond the abolishment of this law, the OMGUS did not interfere with or seek to change in any way the "Gypsy policy." In the framework of the reorganization of the Bavarian police force, the OMGUS approved the continuing existence of a unit dealing with and gathering information on Gypsies. Gypsies were mentioned as a police target along with the asocials, or beggars and vagrants, in a document submitted to the OMGUS on 14 October 1947, dealing with the structure of the criminal investigations department in Munich.[26] When the Bavarian office of criminal identification, which was subordinated to the Bavarian Ministry of the Interior, was established in May 1946, an information agency concerning Gypsies (Nachrichtenstelle über Zigeuner) was included therein. This body had already operated within Munich police headquarters since 1899. In the days of the Weimar Republic it served as a de facto national center for police surveillance on Gypsies, and all the German states *(Länder)* used its services and helped finance it. In 1936, in the framework of the *Gleichschaltung* (coordination, synchronization) policy (which aimed at integrating the National Socialist Party's bodies, such as the SS, in the Reich's authorities), the roles of the unit were transferred to the national center for Gypsy issues of the criminal police (RKPA), which was established in Berlin. This unit continued to exist in the Munich police after 1945 and was only officially dismantled in 1965.[27]

The OMGUS legitimized the structural foundation on which the discriminating Gypsy policy that preceded the Nazi period was based. This policy included keeping close control over Gypsies and collecting and accumulating information on them. The name of the department, known by the officials as the "Gypsy police" *(Zigeunerpolizei),* was changed sometime between 1947 and 1951 and officially was called the Chamber for Gathering Information and Collecting Material about Vagrants *(Landfahrer).* Notwithstanding the change in name, the unit continued to be interested in Gypsies who no longer led a nomadic lifestyle, which apparently went beyond the department's mandate.[28] In the late 1940s and early 1950s, the head of the department was Joseph Eichberger, who during the Third Reich had been in charge of deporting German Gypsies to concentration camps.[29] Some of the "experts on Gypsy issues," who acquired their knowledge on this matter during the Third Reich, continued their career in the criminal police after 1945. Even those persons in charge of the Gypsy issue who had not been active Nazis, it seems, were to a large extent imbued with racist theories about Gypsies and perceived all Gypsies to be delinquents, to judge by articles on Gypsies they published in German magazines on police issues during the 1950s.[30] They kept and made use of files on Gypsies from the Nazi period and followed up and accumulated new information about them, irrespective of whether they had a criminal record. In spite of the biographical continuity of the personnel involved and the harassment they inflicted on Gypsies, they certainly could not continue implementing Nazi "Gypsy policy."

The department's personnel seemed unaware of the reason for the annulment of the 1926 law by the OMGUS and were convinced the repeal was associated with the Gypsy persecution in the Third Reich. Articles published in police magazines explained the necessity of the legislation, thus providing the general public with false information that also was absorbed in political circles and by government officials.[31] After the annulment of the legislation in Bavaria, the American military government then failed to properly examine whether similar laws existed in other states in Germany and consequently ignored the state of Hesse's law for combating the Gypsy nuisance of 1929. This law, which duplicated the articles concerning Gypsies that had been contained in the Bavarian law of 1926, was thus saved from annulment.

In May 1947 the public security department of the Hessian Ministry of the Interior requested the ministry's legal department to investigate whether the 1929 law was still valid and, if it was not, to prepare a fresh bill identical to the former law of 1929 "for the current state of Hesse" (the borders of post-1945 Hesse were not identical to those Hesse held in 1929, which had also included part of the Rhine-Palatinate). But the legal department's reply of October 1947 added a new dimension to Germany's Gypsy policy, which had not existed before 1945: "As today the state is committed to the correction of the wrong done [this is the literal meaning of the term *Wiedergutmachung*, but, practically, it meant compensation for the victims of Nazi persecution] to Gypsies, as a group persecuted as a result of racist motives, I contacted the department for compensation in the Ministry for Political Liberation and asked for instructions as to how we can appropriately reconcile the viewpoint of Wiedergutmachung with the interests of public security."[32]

The legislation against the "Gypsy plague," an issue which in the past had always been dealt with by German bureaucrats and politicians in light of exclusive considerations for German public security, was now to be limited and balanced by concerns representing the Gypsies' interests. In the years when Germany was ruled by the Allies, the officials who actually represented these considerations were those who worked in the divisions established by order of the military governments, such as the Ministry for Political Liberation in Hesse. These officials were in many cases not the kind traditionally found in German bureaucracy. They included a high number of anti-Nazi personnel, among them several Jews, including Dr. Curt Epstein, who served as director of the compensation department of the Ministry for Political Liberation in Hesse. These individuals felt a strong commitment to ensure that justice was awarded to the victims of Nazism, including Gypsies.

From the moment the Ministry for Political Liberation interfered, it played a role that could not be ignored. Dr. Epstein wrote a harsh letter to the Ministry of the Interior, placing the blame for the public's complaints that Gypsies had become a nuisance mainly on the municipal authorities. Epstein accused the authorities of categorically avoiding helping Gypsies in their request to find suitable accommodation. By this neglect, Epstein argued, Gypsies had little choice but to search for their livelihood on the streets. Epstein declared that he was aware that it was impossible to settle all the Gypsies as "vagrancy is in the blood of this race," but at the same time, he indicated that experience showed that a large part of them did seek—especially in light of their past sufferings—to find a regular occupation and a place to live. If adequate assistance was provided to allow them to settle down, Epstein argued, only a small minority would remain nomads, and these could be guided in a friendly way into following wise routes without any need for special laws.

Epstein also expressed his opinion about the law from the Weimar Republic. He determined that using this or a similar law would amount to renewing the notorious racist legislation, and he said that Gypsies should never again be subjected to such special laws.[33] Epstein's position doomed the attempt made by the department of public security and other authorities in Hesse to renew the validity of the 1929 law. A review prepared by the department of public security in March 1956 concerning the possibility of reenacting the 1929 law stated explicitly that the Ministry for Political Liberation opposed the legislation and recommended that the housing ministry take all necessary measures to give Gypsies proper accommodations.[34]

However, both Dr. Epstein and the Ministry for Political Liberation believed that distress was a prime cause of crime; their position was not acceptable to the officials of the Ministry of the Interior or to the police who were handling Gypsy questions all over West Germany; they regarded the Gypsy question as an exclusive public security issue and completely ignored its social aspects. The intervention of the Ministry for Political Liberation failed to lead to a comprehensive plan to settle Gypsies and provide education and vocational training for the young generation. But the intention to renew Weimar-era legislation was not carried out, in spite of the interest it evoked in the public security department and in the police.[35] Politicians and officials in Hesse and Bavaria agreed to confine the Gypsy policy within the restriction dictated by the OMGUS and the Ministry for Political Liberation.

However, they did not wish to annul the Weimar Republic's antigypsy legislation for good, and so they decided to wait for an opportunity to restore it. The establishment of the Federal Republic of Germany in September 1949 was taken as a sign by the officials of the public security department of the Hessian Ministry of the Interior to resume their attempts to reenact the Weimar law. The department adopted a legal interpretation made by the Hesse police school in Bad Homburg that the 1929 law for combating the Gypsy nuisance was still valid. It was argued that the provisions of this law were not directed against Gypsies as a race, but rather against all vagrants, and it did not therefore contradict the Hessian constitution. The Ministry of the Interior decided the question should be examined by the Hessian Ministry of Justice, which disagreed with the opinion adopted by the Ministry of the Interior. The Ministry of Justice ruled that the law contravened the principle of legal equality, for it referred only to Gypsies on the grounds of their origin and therefore contradicted the Basic Law *(Grundgesetz)* of the FRG.[36]

For several years this ruling prevented attempts in Hesse to renew the 1929 law. Despite the avoidance of legislation, representatives of the committee for state law and the administration of the states' council in the American occupation zone sought in December 1948 to restore one important component of the Gypsy policy that preceded Nazi racial policy: a special police unit to control the Gypsy population, which would also rely on information found in the population registry offices *(Standes-ämter)*. The committee unanimously determined that while it was obvious that special instructions against a certain group for racist reasons could not endure, it was nevertheless desirable that people who might constitute a threat to public security due to their antisocial behavior should be subject to special supervision. The committee therefore confirmed the validity of section 157 of the service instructions of the population registry clerks. This section required that the offices report every case of a birth, marriage, or death of a vagrant. They were to do this as close as possible to the time of registry and to inform the local police station of their report. Furthermore, the committee drew the attention of the states' representatives to the fact that an information-collecting agency concerning people without permanent living quarters was already active at police headquarters in Munich, and they encouraged the states to recommend that their local criminal police stations submit information about such persons to this information agency.[37] This call to the states to use the agency's services can be seen as part of an attempt made by German officials to restore the patterns of the Weimar Republic's Gypsy policy. In July 1949, during discussions on whether to issue identification certificates to Gypsies, the committee empowered the coordination office to investigate with the Bavarian Ministry of Interior whether a central agency for vagrants was operating there, and if so what tasks it fulfilled and which zone it concerned.[38]

Now the police and the public security departments in the Ministry of the Interior again attempted to reinstate the Gypsy policy of the Weimar Republic, intentions that had been curbed during the period of the military government. A letter dealing with the issue of personal certificates to people living in wagons, sent at the end of June by the planning and population authorities of Hamburg to the head of the local administration in Hamburg, stated that according to the report of the criminal police office for the British occupation zone, it was not possible to maintain a central registration of "vagrant people" *(fahrende Volk)*, as had been done in the past, because the military government would not now have agreed to it.[39] With the foundation of the FRG in September 1949 this limitation was apparently removed. That month a convention discussed the establishment of a "federal center for fighting the criminal vagrant nuisance" and of an information and registration service that would pass every document concerning vagrants to the center. It was also agreed that legal steps for "combating the vagrant plague" should be considered.[40] The ministers of the interior of the regional states held a work group in October 1949 and expressed their wish to maintain a list of vagrants and, if possible, to compile a central index card list for the whole FRG, but this question remained open. They also discussed the possibility of concentrating the issuing of personal certificates in the hands of one central body.[41] Yet, despite the committee's attempts, it did not succeeded in restoring to the Munich agency the status it had held during the Weimar Republic and the beginning of the Third Reich. Notwithstanding the cooperation of all the criminal offices of the FRG, the Munich agency never again actually constituted a federal center in the way that it had done during the Weimar Republic, and over the years similar information centers were established in the criminal police offices of other German states, including Hamburg and North Rhine–Westphalia.[42]

In contrast to the OMGUS and the other military governments in Germany, who did not intervene in the Gypsy policy beyond taking a few steps following the general policy of denazification of German legislation, in neighboring France, by 1949 the Interior authorities had begun to consolidate a general social policy toward Gypsies. This was characterized by an understanding approach; it was acknowledged that the "public security" aspects of the problem, including criminal activity among Gypsies, were not the result of any inherent evil but, rather, were the symptom of social distress. The French authorities apparently believed that to solve the problem, it was necessary to concentrate on the problem's roots rather than on its symptoms.[43] After the foundation of the FRG, however, treatment of the Gypsy question in Germany was still characterized by a hostile attitude. The "Gypsy question" was perceived exclusively as a problem of public security and was discussed without any reference to its social aspects, let alone to the human and moral duty to correct the wrong done under Hitler. In this reality, the exceptional attitude of the Ministry for Political Liberation in Hesse, which had tried to rehabilitate Gypsies, did not yield any practical results.

GYPSY POLICY IN THE FRG: BETWEEN TRADITION AND CHANGE

In the wake of the Nazi crimes and the reeducation program established by the Allies in occupied Germany, the legitimacy of central components of the traditional Gypsy policy, which included restrictions on basic freedoms, was undermined, and a democratic trend, nonexistent in Germany in the past, developed within the political establishment and even among government officials. However, although they realized that it might no longer be possible to continue with traditional discriminatory Gypsy policies, most of the advocates of this democratic trend in the German political establishment nonetheless continued to view Gypsies as a nuisance and regarded themselves as committed to protecting the public and its property from Gypsies. Much of the German population continued to regard vagrant Gypsies as a plague, as well as those Gypsies who had settled in poverty-stricken dwellings on the outskirts of cities, and complaints by both ordinary citizens and local officials weighed heavy on the political establishment, who were under pressure to find a solution.

In January 1949, the Committee for Basic Questions of the Parliamentary Council (Parlamentarische Rat) debated what policy the state should adopt. Willhelm Heile, of the DP (Deutsche Partei), and Frederike Nadig, of the SPD (Social Democratic Party), had suggested limiting by law the Gypsies' freedom of movement, but Dr. Herman von Mangoldt of the CDU (Christian Democratic Union), and the committee chairman, opposed this. Mangoldt stated that the equality principle determined that nobody should be discriminated against on grounds of his race or because he possessed a "wandering drive." Restricting freedom of movement and vesting too much authority in the legislature, as he put it, would constitute a return to Nazi ways. He held that certain courses of action could be taken without legislation, and he argued that, according to the existing laws under which the police operated, there already were measures by which theft could be prevented if it turned into a plague. He believed that freedom of movement could be maintained, while at the same time Gypsies could be obliged to find themselves a permanent address.

The majority of members of the local parliaments in the FRG, fearing an overinvolvement by the legislature on this question, sided with Mangoldt. The only exception was the Bavarian Landtag, which enacted a law concerning Gypsies and which expressly supported the restoration of the traditional discriminating Gypsy policy. However, the legislators felt they had to semantically disguise the discriminatory nature of the law so that it would not appear to be based on origin and race but, rather, aimed at the treatment of exceptional social behavior, namely, vagrancy.[44]

CONSTITUTIONAL SOLUTION: THE BAVARIAN VAGRANT REGULATION

The Bavarian attempt to reenact discriminatory legislation against Gypsies, an attempt that was eventually successful, was one component of the struggle waged by a coalition of major parties—the leftist SPD and the rightist CSU (Christian Social Union)—in Bavaria, to try and revoke the American revision of the local punitive law. The Anglo-Saxon perception of democracy was rejected by Bavarian politicians, who sought to maintain in state hands a great deal of control over elements society labeled as asocial, without restricting this power by legal principles that protected the individual's liberties. The basic democratic duty to ensure individual freedoms for all citizens was outweighed by the value of protecting public security, which was perceived as being far more important.

In 1951, three of the Landtag's CSU members promoted a bill in the law and constitution committee of the Landtag aimed at regulating those "so-called wandering people" *(so genannten fahrenden Volk)* who have no permanent address. By avoiding the explicit term *Gypsies (Zigeuner)* the committee indicated the desire to present a law that would not appear to actually discriminate against an ethnic group. In Bavaria, the Gypsies had already been defined in terms of race during the Weimar Republic, and since according to the Basic Law *(Grundgesetz)* of the FRG discrimination on the grounds of race, origin, or ancestry was prohibited, the promoters of the bill referred to the Gypsies by this well-known synonym *(fahrenden Volk)* in Germany, enabling them to argue that the law related not just to Gypsies but to all vagrants, including those of German origin.

The bill was brought before the Landtag's plenary session in June 1951. The vote was to urge the Bavarian government to take measures to expedite the bill into law so that the welfare duties of the state and the local communities, in particular, would be limited.[45] The Landtag members sought to legalize the denial of welfare support to the needy among Gypsies. The Chancellery of the Bavarian government passed the Landtag's decision to the Ministry of the Interior, which brought together this decision with a previous decision the Landtag had made in September 1950 about the renewed drive to confine criminal elements in workhouses,[46] and they began preparing a draft of a bill concerning vagrants and work shys based on the Bavarian law of 1926 for combating Gypsies, vagrants, and work shys.

The most prominent change in the new draft law was the elimination of any explicit reference to Gypsies. Justification for the law, as prepared by the Ministry of the Interior, stated that because the constitution provided that no person should be discriminated against because of his origin or race, the special terminology of "racial Gypsy" *(Rassezigeuner)* was to be abandoned and substituted by the racially neutral term, "a vagrant, who in private cases might also be a Gypsy."[47] Although the term *racial Gypsy* did not appear at all in the 1926 law, the instructions for activating the law given by the Bavarian Ministry of the Interior stated that "the race theory provides information concerning whoever should be regarded as a Gypsy."[48]

The definition of the term *vagrant (Landfahrer)* subsequently provided by the Ministry of Interior's clarifications also repeated that Gypsyhood constituted a racial rather than an ethnic state. Because this closely resembled Nazi thinking, in 1950, Ministry of Interior officials felt the need to substitute the terminology perceived as racist to legitimize the law. But beyond this semantic change, the officials did not believe there was a need to make substantial changes to the law or its spirit. The joining together in one law of Gypsies (now called vagrants) and work shys derived not only from both groups being frequently labeled asocial but also from the nature of the political culture that came into being in Germany after 1945, which denounced racist discrimination as illegitimate for political reasons but did not reflect any profound change of values.

The chairman of the Landtag committee for social issues, Heinrich Stöhr, told the committee that in a conversation with the Bavarian Minister of the Interior, Dr. Willhelm Hoegner, who was a member of the SPD, he discovered that the government had avoided preparing legislation that dealt only with vagrants, fearing that it would create the impression that the law was intended to target a particular race. Typically, the actual discrimination against Gypsies did not trouble Hoegner; rather, he disliked the idea that it might be viewed as racial (and hence Nazi-like) discrimination. Hoegner believed that lumping the two categories together would blur the impression that this law constituted a plot against Gypsies. All the Landtag members were thus made aware of the discriminatory nature of the law, yet most of them did not consider this to be the substantial problem. The desire of the Landtag to limit the assistance the welfare authorities gave to Gypsies was not expressed in the bill, because this would contradict the principles of the Basic Law.[49]

The first version of the bill was criticized by the Bavarian Ministry of Justice. Dr. Koch, a senior official at the Ministry of Justice, submitted an opinion to the Ministry of the Interior in which he wrote that the bill relied too much on the 1926 Bavarian law for combating Gypsies, vagrants, and work shys and that in its substantial provisions it did not relate at all to the change in legal attitudes since 1945 about the preconditions through which the state is entitled to intervene in the domain of the individual. Koch asserted that preventive confinement in workhouses contradicted the principle of the right to freedom from any enforced labor anchored in the Basic Law. However, he never once referred to the fact that although the explicit reference to Gypsies that was included in the 1926 law had been omitted, the new law continued to be directed mainly against a certain ethnic group and therefore violated the principle of equality before the law.[50]

Among the leading members of the Bavarian judiciary, who were asked by the Ministry of Justice to submit their opinion of the bill, only Dr. Konrad, the president of the Bavarian supreme court, related in his opinion to the question of Gypsies being discriminated against by this law. He emphasized that if the personal characteristics creating the term *vagrant* were associated with a certain race (Gypsies), the bill was in contradiction with the Basic Law. He further stated that the 1926 law defined vagrant as "a person wandering according to the Gypsy custom." "If the terminology of 'Gypsy custom' was introduced into the bill so that it included the established custom of wandering and the imbedded custom of resisting settlement, it seems that the racial labeling of Gypsies was only substituted by the description of their properties," he said.[51] The Bavarian Ministry of Justice informed the Federal Ministry of Justice of this, and Bonn joined this position and criticized the Ministry of the Interior's interpretation of the legislation.[52] However, the Ministry of the Interior, headed by Hoegner, stuck to its opinion and claimed that the confinement of vagrants and work shys, who lived at the expense of others and evaded work, like the removal of mental patients from the public, constituted a clear act of protecting public security and that this subject fell within Bavaria's authority. The ministry rejected the claim that this was not an act of punishment deriving from punitive law and that it should be under the exclusive authority of the federal bodies. A few semantic adjustments were made to please the Ministry of Justice, such as substitution of the term "workhouse" *(Arbeitshaus)* by the term "confinement house" *(Verwahranstalt),* and this enabled the bill to be handed over for consideration to the Landtag in July 1952.[53]

The bill prepared by the Ministry of the Interior was submitted to the Landtag Committee for Social Issues in September 1952. The committee's members criticized the Bavarian government for uniting vagrants and work shys in one law, in contradiction to what the Landtag had demanded. The Landtag's sole interest had been a law concerning Gypsies, and the committee rejected the bill because it regarded the "joining together of vagrants and Gypsies in one law an injury to the reputation of the respectable vagrants" and demanded that the government prepare two separate bills, one dealing with vagrants and the other with work shys.[54]

Following the rejection of the bill, the Ministry of the Interior prepared a new draft, leaving in only the sections referring to vagrants. The new law was termed the "vagrant regulation" *(Landfahrerordnung)*. (The substitution of the so-called racial label *Gypsies [Zigeuner]* by the apparently unloaded term *vagrants [Landfahrer],* was thought to ensure that no one could accuse the law of racism.) In May 1953 the law was submitted to the Landtag, and in October 1953 it was accepted by majority vote in the Landtag plenary session.[55] The vagrant law explicitly and consciously concentrated on imposing restrictions on vagrants, in order to make it difficult for them to maintain their lifestyle. It limited various basic rights to which the Gypsy vagrants were as much entitled to as other Bavarian citizens. The social aspects of the vagrancy problem were barely mentioned in the law, although government officials did not deny they existed.

Advocates of the legislation differed sharply over its purposes. Karl Weishäupl, a Social Democrat member of the Landtag, represented the Enlightened approach and stood for "civic correction" of Gypsies. He regarded the legislation as a means to eventually settle Gypsies in the way they had been settled in the Austro-Hungarian Empire in the reign of

Maria Theresa and her son, Joseph II, and he thought that this would solve the problems their vagrant lifestyle caused to the settled society. But other members of the Landtag, from all parties, adopted the traditional line that Gypsies were a danger to public security in Bavaria, not a social problem.[56]

NAZI PAST AS A CAUSE FOR REJECTING A LEGISLATIVE SOLUTION

Even before the vagrant law was enacted in Bavaria, control over Gypsies was being tightened in accordance with the instructions from the Ministry of the Interior. The central agency for combating the vagrants, which operated within the national Bavarian criminal police office in Munich, observed that, as a result, the "vagrants" moved to the neighboring states of Hesse and Baden-Württemberg.[57] "In the face of the undesirable possibility, from a police and security point of view, that the entering of undesirable elements into Hesse would be enhanced, when the law came into effect," in May 1953 the public security department of the Hessian Ministry of the Interior issued circulars on the issue to the local government. They asked that they be kept informed about the movements of vagrants throughout Hesse, as well as their numbers, citizenship, occupations, involvement in crime, and attempts to settle them permanently, along with the education of their children.[58]

In October 1953, Hesse's criminal police office drew the attention of the federal criminal police office to the situation, and in early March 1954, the latter informed all the states' criminal police offices about the enactment of the new Bavarian vagrant law. The need for coordination between states was emphasized, as well as the need to prepare for the possibility that the vagrants would move from Bavaria to other states where no such legislation was in effect.[59] This approach raised the question of the need to adopt similar legislation, not only in nearby Hesse and Baden-Württemberg, which were the likely places any Gypsies leaving Bavaria would head, but also in far away Hamburg. The Hamburg police, like the criminal police offices of most states of the FRG, supported the adoption of the Bavarian legislation. They said that "our experience showed that a substantial part of this public makes a living by criminal activity, especially cheating and theft."[60]

The Hessian Ministry of the Interior approached the Ministers and Senators of the Interior in charge of interior issues in all states to find out whether other states planned to adopt the Bavarian vagrant law. That they felt the need to do this suggests they feared taking any independent action because, as in Bavaria, the legitimacy of such action would be undermined if it were associated with the Nazi past. The ministries and senators of the interior were less enthusiastic than the offices of the criminal police: Berlin, Bremen, and North Rhine–Westphalia came to the conclusion that the law was unnecessary, while Hesse, Lower Saxony, Baden-Württemberg, Shleswig Holstein, and the Rhine-Palatinate reported that the adoption of similar legislation in their domains would be considered.[61] During the course of 1954 the issue was discussed in several federal frameworks. In April 1954 the issue was raised at a meeting of the heads of the criminal police offices of the German states. The representative of the federal criminal office, Dr. Ochs, established that the problem of the vagrants could only be solved at a federal level, and he therefore recommended that the heads of the criminal police act within the ministries of their states so that the various legislation procedures would be unified throughout the FRG.[62]

The German Conference of Mayors (Deutscher Städtetag) adopted the position of the police concerning the Gypsy question, albeit for different reasons. The issue of the Gypsy nuisance was raised at the beginning of 1954 during the German mayors' conference, as part of their discussions concerning a new law for regulating housing. This law was intended to help refugees who had lost their homes during the war to move from temporary accommodations into permanent dwellings. The mayors noted the difficulty of finding housing for Gypsies, due to the unwillingness of the population to rent them apartments and allow them to live in their neighborhood. The alternative—to house Gypsies in shacks or in old railway wagons—was a heavy economic burden on the cities, especially cities that in any case suffered from severe housing shortages, having taken in many German refugees who had been expelled from or were fleeing from eastern European countries *(Heimatvertriebene)*. The meeting emphasized the need, on the federal level, to find housing solutions for Gypsies by settling them or by specifically establishing Gypsy settlements in which they would be trained to become farmers according to the model of Friedrich the Great.

The chair of the mayors' conference decided to transfer the matter to the social issues committee of the conference and to ask them to determine whether this was a social problem or a problem of law and order. In February the social issues committee ruled that this was a law-and-order problem, a decision that was apparently motivated primarily by their unwillingness to assume the financial burden necessary for finding housing and occupational solutions for Gypsies. A conscious decision was therefore taken to neglect Gypsies and turn their already poverty-stricken dwellings on the city outskirts into even more extreme places of social distress. It was clear from this decision that the interests of the newly arrived ethnic German expellees from the east took preference over those of the states' long-time resident Gypsy citizens.

After this decision, handling of Gypsies was transferred in June 1954 from the welfare department to the law and order department of the German Mayors' Conference, which maintained contact with the federal criminal police office. The following month, the criminal police recommended to the city associations (Landesverbände des Deutschen Städtentag) in the FRG that they examine whether an arrangement in the spirit of the Bavarian precedent should also be established in their states.[63]

In July of the same year, the federal criminal police office issued instructions for combating the Gypsy nuisance, ordering an increased level of control on the movement of vagrants, especially that of Gypsies.[64] Hesse and Baden-Württemberg, which were the prime targets to be affected by the Bavarian legislation, did not hurry to adopt the Bavarian vagrants' law. Mr. Keil, a senior jurist at the Hessian Ministry of the Interior, argued that the Bavarian law contradicted the principle of freedom of movement that was ensured by the Basic Law, and he proposed submitting the issue for examination to a legal committee of the work group of the Interior Ministries in the FRG. When the committee convened in September 1955, they failed to reach a conclusion. Dr. Pioch, the representative of the federal criminal police office, clarified that the federal authorities (namely, the federal Ministry of the Interior) was not especially interested in enacting new legislation in this field.[65]

Notwithstanding the support of the police and the German Mayors' Conference in adopting the Bavarian precedent, Bavaria remained the only state in the FRG in which a constitutional solution to the Gypsy problem was maintained. The Bavarian precedent was not adopted on the federal level or by any other state of the FRG. Bavaria itself finally repealed its antigypsy law in 1970, after the authorities realized that since 1966 no certificates had been issued by the Bavarian state to vagrants as defined by the law's provisions, because all the Gypsies in Bavaria by then had permanent addresses and therefore ceased to be subject to its instructions.[66]

But among the states that considered adopting the Bavarian legislation, only in Hesse did the government's representative explicitly state that the decision not to adopt was a result of the political illegitimacy of legislating against a group persecuted by the Nazis, as well as being in contradiction to the Basic Law, which ensured freedom of movement to all, including Gypsies. In 1956, in the plenary session of the Hesse Landtag, the Hessian Minister of the Interior, Heinrich Schneider, replied on behalf of the government to a bill promoted by a Christian Democrat member of the Landtag, Dr. Ernst Holtzmann. Schneider emphasized that the bill touched on a sensitive issue, which had to be dealt with very delicately to avoid the impression that the law to be enacted included any racial discrimination, and he criticized the bill for relying too heavily on

77

the 1929 law, despite the modernization of the vagrants' lifestyle since that time. He suggested that the bill be submitted for examination and consultation on a federal level and that it only be adopted in Hesse if other states also adopted it.[67]

In the final discussion of the bill in the Landtag plenary session, the Gypsies' persecution in the Third Reich was again cited as a reason for rejecting the draft. Gustav Krämer, a Landtag member from the Social Democrats, was the first to express his party's opposition to the bill on this basis, and he said that for this reason the Landtag should take extra care. Minister of Interior Schneider added that the bill was to be rejected not only because of the constitutional problems it raised but also because of the psychological and political factors Krämer had pointed to. "By no means do I want the state of Hesse to enact a law resembling any racial laws of the Third Reich," he declared to calls of support and approval from the benches of his own party, the SPD. "The law refers exactly to the circle of people who were hurt by the discriminating laws of the Third Reich. Even if there is no substantial similarity between the bill and Nazi laws, the enactment of such a law evokes bad memories and does not prevent undesirable interpretation," he said. Schneider concluded by determining that these reasons were sufficient for rejecting the bill and that the bill raised additional constitutional problems.[68]

Although Schneider himself had rejected the bill, a senior official in the Hessian Ministry of the Interior, Mr. Keil, clarified in a letter to the heads of the Hesse local government that "even if the enactment of the vagrant law was not passed for constitutional and political reasons in Hesse and most other states in the German federation, the police will not absolve themselves from their responsibility to take as much care as needed that this circle of people behave according to the law."[69] For this purpose, in June 1957 the Hessian criminal police office distributed among police field ranks a document concerning the "combating of the vagrant nuisance," in which all the existing legal means with which the police could deal with vagrants were specified. This was itself based on a document issued in 1956 in Lower Saxony.[70] This avoidance of overt legislative discrimination, while at the same time practicing discrimination in secret, was characteristic of policies toward Gypsies throughout Germany in the 1950s and 1960s, by both of the states' Ministries of the Interior and by their criminal police offices.

One of the most dramatic means taken by the Ministries of the Interior against both Roma and Sinti from North Rhine–Westphalia, and in particular from Cologne, was to deny them German citizenship. The denial of citizenship relied on a provision of the passport law, which enabled the state to take away a passport if its holder could not present, to the authorities' satisfaction, a certificate confirming he was German according to subsection 1 of section 116 of the Basic Law. This section determined that a German was a person already holding proof of German citizenship, or was himself an ethnic German refugee or expellee, or a spouse or child of such a person, who was living in the domain of the German Reich in December 1937. Usually, it was difficult for Gypsies to provide such proof.[71]

In January 1954, Dr. Mittelstädt, acting on behalf of the North Rhine–Westphalian Ministry of the Interior, gave written instructions to the municipal authorities (the Regierungpräsidenten and the Verwaltungen der Landkreise) to investigate the question of the Gypsies' citizenship. Mittelstädt stated that the few cases that had been investigated raised doubts about the Gypsies' citizenship, and he reviewed the possibilities and conditions demanded since 1842 for attaining citizenship of Prussia and later the Reich through bequeathance or naturalization. He claimed that it could not be presumed that Gypsies met the conditions demanded for the attainment of citizenship in Prussia until 1871, the main condition being that the applicant had been permanently settled in one place for ten years, and he gave instructions that evidence attesting to past German citizenship be examined carefully. He ruled that even when a Gypsy held a German passport, this should not be regarded as a proof of his German citizenship, because it was known that after World War II citizenship matters were not thoroughly investigated and procedures for awarding citizenship were generous, especially to people released from concentration camps. He also stated that proof of naturalization or another decision concerning citizenship should be accepted only if there was a detailed listing of the date of the act and the number of the file in the column of the citizens' registry.[72]

The West German authorities relied on the findings of Ritter and his fellow Nazis in the early 1940s to deny the citizenship of German Roma families. According to Ritter's research, Roma who immigrated to Germany from Hungary between 1880 and 1887 adopted German names, such as Strauss and Weiss, and gained Prussian citizenship unlawfully. They were therefore stripped of their citizenship by the Third Reich and declared to be stateless. After the war, their German citizenship was restored, but at the beginning of the 1950s it was denied again in light of the information from the Nazi period provided by the criminal police.[73]

Paul Jochum, a lawyer from Cologne, claimed that he succeeded in returning German citizenship to between ten and fifteen Sinti families. He did this by bringing proof, as required by the passport law, from the genealogical tables prepared by Ritter and his team for the German Gypsies. In the 1950s and 1960s, these tables were kept under the supervision of the Gypsy researcher, Dr. Hermann Arnold of Landau in the Palatinate, who dealt with questions of racial hygiene.[74] Through these tables it was possible to trace the history of certain Sinti families back to the eighteenth century. Jochum asserted that the Gypsies had not appealed the denial of their citizenship by the authorities in time to the court for administrative questions *(Verwaltungsgericht)*. Had they done so, they would also have been able to further appeal against the authorities before the court of constitutional questions *(Bundesverfassungsgericht)*. The Gypsies' lack of understanding and awareness of the legal possibilities open to them, and the fact that no legal measures were taken on their behalf, resulted in their German citizenship being lost.

Their wish to have their citizenship restored obliged the Gypsies to submit a request for naturalization in the FRG, as if they were newly arrived immigrants.[75] In order to be naturalized in Germany, one had to meet several conditions: one had to demonstrate mastery of the German language, both orally and in writing; prove that they had never broken any laws; and prove economic independence, namely, not to need welfare.[76] But many Gypsies—lacking a regular education, not holding any occupation, and sometimes possessing a criminal record—could not meet these demands. The inability to be naturalized according to the jus soli in the FRG (until recently) denied German citizenship not only to the holders of the passports themselves but also to all their offspring born in the FRG.

The conditions for citizenship, in addition to other forms of discrimination, gave the Gypsies in the FRG the not unfounded notion of being singled out for attack by the German state. One of these sources of discrimination was at the hands of the criminal police, who targeted Gypsies over other Germans. A number of these policemen had already "dealt" with Gypsies during the Third Reich and continued to hold racist perceptions. Although they did not directly influence the formulation of postwar Gypsy policy, they undoubtedly provided the policy with a dimension of continuity with the Nazi past, a dimension that was significant enough to prevent the wounds of the Nazi persecution of the Sinti and Roma from healing. Such a discriminatory policy has continued up to the present time. Just as in the late 1940s the authorities had substituted the term *Gypsy* with the social term *vagrant,* so in the early 1980s the police also used a semantic disguise, this time referring to Gypsies by a new term, HWAO *(häufig wechselnder Aufenthaltsort),* which meant "frequently changing his place of living."[77]

The police also continued to hold and use files opened on Gypsies during the Third Reich and to collect material about them on a family basis, not on the basis of concrete suspicions held against an individual for allegedly committing an offense. Discrimination was caused less by limiting Gypsies' freedom of movement than by the actions of the police, which had the backing of the government in what they did.

The fear of Gypsy crime prevalent among officials and the political establishment was not reduced until the early 1960s, when for the first time since 1945 reliable statistical data was compiled that showed a relatively low rate of crime by vagrants, relative to overall crime. It was revealed that out of the total number of crimes committed in the FRG in 1959, only 1,197 (constituting 0.09 percent of the total) were committed by vagrants.[78] (In one state, Baden-Württemberg, the Minister of the Interior had already realized that there was a low rate of crimes committed by vagrants in his state, in 1957.) These new statistics no doubt contributed to ceasing the attempts to enact special laws against the Gypsies in the FRG.

Opinions about the Gypsy question in the political system of the FRG in the 1950s were mixed. CSU members in Bavaria and CDU members in Hesse supported discriminatory legislation, while the CDU representative in the parliamentary council, Mangoldt, objected. The disagreements within the SPD over this issue ran even deeper. The SPD representative in the parliamentary council, Frederike Nadig, as well as the SPD faction in Bavaria, under the leadership of Dr. Wilhelm Hoegner, supported the discriminatory legislation, but the SPD members in the Hessian Landtag opposed it.

Most government officials of the FRG, as well as representatives of the police and public security departments in the Ministries of the Interior in most of the German states, tended to support the regulation of state-Gypsy relations through legislation that restricted the Gypsies' basic rights. In contrast, officials in the federal and state Ministries of Justice opposed this, believing that the basic rights of the Gypsy citizens of the FRG should not be harmed. Therefore, it seems that, on the one hand, the traditional approach common among officials before the Nazi policy was established in 1936 was still prevalent, while, on the other hand, a reformist trend established by the Allies in occupied Germany and by the officials appointed by them was also supported by many representatives of the German political establishment after 1945. But even the traditional approach contained two main contradictory positions: the enlightened stance, which sought to "improve" Gypsies by settling them and turning them into a "productive" element of society, and the hostile one, which sought to deport them or otherwise limit as much as possible the freedom of movement of vagrant Gypsies.

Those with a reformist bent were also not of one mindset. Not all the liberals who were reserved about excess legislation in the face of the Nazi past necessarily perceived the "Gypsy problem" as a result of social

Germany and Its Gypsies

distress requiring a comprehensive positive plan of action rather than police repression. Some "liberals" in Hesse were not even opposed to practicing discrimination against Gypsies.

The actions of these contradictory and complex trends resulted in a policy that usually respected the principle of equality before the law in theory, but in practice discriminated against Sinti and Roma because of their origin.

4

Compensation Policy toward Gypsy Victims of Nazism

FTER winning the war, the Allies forced Germany to offer assistance and compensation to the victims of Nazism who had been persecuted for political, religious, or racial reasons.[1] A specific demand to compensate Gypsy victims was never presented by the Allies, as was done with regard to Jewish victims, but the German obligation to compensate this group derived from the general demands of the Allies. The policy of recognizing Gypsies as victims of Nazi persecution, a policy that was designed and consolidated by the welfare and compensation government authorities in Germany through involvement of the Allies, was a compromise. It combined the need to respond in principle to the Allies' demands and the need to consider the opposition to compensating Gypsies that was prevalent among both the German officials and many former political prisoners.

While no one in the German welfare and compensation divisions questioned that the persecution of Jews derived from racist motives, as early as 1945 many officials and former political prisoners argued that Gypsies were persecuted by the Nazis not for racist motives, which would have entitled the victims to be officially regarded as "victims of Nazism," but for being asocial. The German government authorities and society at large regarded asociality as a crime, against which every proper government ought to act, and did not perceive the persecution of Gypsies as a typically Nazi one.

The Nazi persecution of Jews was implemented after decades in which Jews had been regarded as ordinary citizens and were fully integrated members of society; that of Gypsies continued a policy from the late

83

fifteenth century when Gypsies were regarded as a "delinquent group"—and this attitude remained acceptable from that time on, even during the democratic Weimar Republic. The barbaric and murderous nature of the Nazis' treatment was not a sufficient reason to convince most officials and even many former political prisoners that there was a substantial difference between the persecution of Gypsies in the past and that which had occurred under the Nazis. This undermined the racial motive for Gypsy persecution and denied many Gypsies their recognition by the authorities as victims of Nazism, and thus they were excluded from eligibility for special welfare and compensation for their persecution and suffering. The history of this recognition policy toward Gypsies from 1945 to 1965 is one of discrimination and denial.

This chapter concentrates on the years 1945–1953, during which the policies of the welfare and compensation authorities in the two postwar German states—the FRG and the GDR—were designed and consolidated. It ends when the dispute among the compensation authorities in the FRG on the question of eligibility of Gypsies to be recognized as victims of Nazism was decided in favor of the harsh approach, which then denied them their due recognition and compensation.

In the early 1950s, the debate over the Gypsies' recognition shifted from the compensation authorities to the legal system, which heard appeals by Gypsies against the authorities that had not recognized them as victims of Nazism. The compensation authorities of the FRG did not recognize Gypsies as victims of Nazism until they were forced to do so by the supreme court rulings of 1956 and 1963.[2] The way in which the FRG's legal system dealt with this question will be discussed in chapter 5. At the end of the 1960s, the authorities in the GDR also showed a willingness to correct the injustice inflicted on Gypsies from the earliest years of Soviet occupation by the discriminatory recognition policy that had been established with regard to them.[3]

WELFARE AND COMPENSATION AUTHORITIES
FOR THE VICTIMS OF NAZISM

Many victims of Nazism had not previously been clients of the German welfare authorities, but they became such when they were released from concentration camps. Many of them had nowhere else to go, and they needed basic help in securing food, clothing, housing, medical care, and in finding employment, as well as general financial help. Many of the former prisoners now crowded the community welfare offices, which were overwhelmed with the number of applicants: released prisoners, Wehrmacht soldiers, and German refugees from the East.[4] In the face of the heavy distress of the victims of Nazism, and wanting to distinguish between them and others who needed welfare, special departments were established. Thus, responsibility for granting service to victims of Nazism was imposed on the local authorities: the councils *(Landräte)* in rural areas *(Landesbezirke)* and the mayors *(Oberbürgermeister)* in cities.[5]

In a letter of late October 1945, the head of the American military government (OMGUS) in Bavaria, Gen. Walter Muller, wrote to the Bavarian minister president, Dr. Wilhelm Hoegner, that an important policy objective of the military government was to provide assistance to Germans who suffered as a result of discriminatory Nazi rules or because of their militant resistance to Hitler. Muller demanded that Hoegner provide the victims with housing, furniture, appropriate clothing, fuel supply, full medical care, and enlarged food rations and that everything should be done to enable them to become economically independent.[6]

The other occupying military governments also instructed the German administrations in their domains to finance help for the victims of Nazism. The Russian military government did so in September 1945, and the British military government followed suit in December of that year. The operation of these special departments on the local level was coordinated by a central authority in each state *(Land)*.

In Bavaria, a special body was established in early December 1945 within the Ministry of the Interior to deal exclusively with persecuted Jews: the Staatskommissariat für Betreuung der Juden in Bayern. A few months later, in late March 1946, a special body for people who had been politically persecuted was established: the Staatskommissariat für die politisch Verfolgten. In September 1946, the two commissariats were unified for the first time under the name "State Commissariat for Victims of Fascism." The name of this authority was identical to the name of the same body in the Russian occupation zone, and it was changed after the outbreak of the Cold War. By instruction of the American military government, it became known as the State Commissariat for Victims Persecuted for Racial, Religious, and Political Motives. In November 1949, after the Bavarian Compensation Law was enacted, the name was changed to the Bavarian Compensation Office (Bayerisches Landesentschädigungsamt).[7]

In 1947, the Bavarian model was adopted in Hesse. But the authorities in Baden-Württemberg rejected the Bavarian model; the compensation department was originally established within the Baden-Württemberg Ministry of the Interior but later was transferred to the Ministry of Justice. By 1946 offices were established within one of these ministries in all the other states in the American-occupied zone; most were known as the Office for Correcting the Wrong Done (Amt für Wiedergutmachung) and were charged with handling the different problems of all the victims of Nazism.

In the British occupation zone, as in Württemberg-Baden, these kinds of special offices were not established, and the persecuted were cared for by various departments in one of the ministries: in North Rhine–Westphalia departments in the Ministry of the Interior and in the Ministry of Social Issues were established in 1946 for this purpose, while in Lower Saxony the department was in the Ministry of the Interior.[8]

Thus, in the part of Germany that was controlled by the Americans and British, each state managed the local assistance and compensation policy toward Nazi victims according to the regulations and decrees established there by, or with the approval of, the respective military governments. Although the Allies issued instructions for and decrees about the assistance and compensation policy, carrying out the policy was a priori imposed on the German assistance authorities, which included at the outset a substantial representation of the different organizations of the victims. These executive bodies did not just carry out the policy of the Allies; rather, they designed the policy on how to recognize victims, although formally this policy was approved by the military governments until they came to end in 1949.

The greatest unity in coordinating the assistance policy, and in the structure of the authorities handling it, prevailed in the Soviet-occupied zone. In June 1945, the Department for the Victims of Fascism (Opfer des Faschismus, or OdF) was already established within the division of labor and social welfare in the German administration of the Soviet occupation zone. This body governed the whole system of aid to victims of Nazism in that zone. The department was headed by Ottomar Geschke, a veteran Communist who had been incarcerated in concentration camps through the entire duration of the Third Reich. Geschke also managed the department for social issues in the municipal council (Magistrat) of Berlin and held a position in the Organization of the Victims of Nazism (Vereinigung der Verfolgten des Naziregimes [VVN]) in the Soviet occupation zone. In each of the five states in that zone—Thuringia, Brandenburg, Saxony, Saxony-Anhalt, and Mecklenburg Pomerania—a division within the welfare department of the local Ministry of Labor and Welfare managed all the issues related to caring for the victims of Nazism in its domain.[9]

With the initiative of the military governments, the preparatory work for the enactment of compensation laws in the states *(Länder)* had begun. In 1946, Thuringia was the first state to issue a law for helping victims of fascism. In 1947, compensation laws were enacted in North Rhine–Westphalia and in Baden-Württemberg. In 1949, the authorities in most states enacted compensation laws. While the laws in the American occupation zone were overall compensation laws, those enacted in the British occupation zone concentrated only on compensation for the denial of freedom *(Haftentschädigung)*.[10]

In the Soviet occupation zone and afterward in the GDR, the policy of compensation to victims of Nazism assumed an entirely different nature than in the West. In the East there were two categories of Nazi victims: victims of fascism and fighters of fascism. The latter was regarded as a more prestigious category by the Communists. Upon retirement—or immediately, if they had been handicapped by the persecution—those recognized as persecuted were granted an honorary pension *(Ehrenrente)*; pensions for fighters were approximately 10 percent higher than pensions for victims. In contrast to the capitalist West, the amount of pension in the socialist regime was fixed and quite low, and financial compensation was not awarded according to the length of time spent in a concentration camp or according to the severity of the physical or mental injury suffered.

As Jews and Gypsies were persecuted on racial grounds, they were considered to be passive victims, and in the early summer of 1945 the OdF was reluctant to recognize them as victims at all. Probst (Prior) Heinrich Grüber and the Jewish representatives Julius Meyer and Heinz Galinski had to fight for a few months until the OdF finally announced in September that "Jews are also victims of fascism." The announcement also recognized all those who "were persecuted on grounds of race," a clause that pertained to Gypsies as well. In spite of the announcement, however, the reluctance to recognize the so-called passive victims and the traditional negative image of Gypsies had a tremendous influence on recognizing Gypsies as victims of fascism in East Germany. The tiny uneducated and unorganized Sinti minority could not successfully cope with its discrimination by the recognition procedure in the GDR.[11]

The compensation laws defined those who would benefit as people who had been persecuted by Nazism for racist, political, or religious reasons and included no reference to the ethnic identity of the victims or to the nature of their political or religious beliefs. The Ministries of Justice in the states in the American occupation zone coordinated the enactment of the compensation laws, thereby ensuring that the legislation in these states was unified. By 1950 compensation laws had been established in every state in the FRG. By 1946 the compensation offices in the American, British, and French occupation zones were maintaining contact and coordinating with each other about compensation issues. Through the VVN (which will be elaborated on later) and other means, contacts were maintained between the representatives of the various welfare authorities in all four occupation zones in Germany. It was through these representatives that information about the welfare and compensation policy toward victims of Nazism was spread.

After the outbreak of the Cold War, an interministerial working group was established in West Germany in early September 1948. It dealt with issues of compensation to victims of Nazism in the occupation zones of the Western Allies and coordinated the compensation policy of the authorities in the states of West Germany. This working group discussed all the problems that arose in the course of carrying out the compensation policy, with the purpose of managing a unified compensation policy in the whole area in which the three great Western powers intended to found the Federal Republic. The group's coordinating office was situated in Munich and headed by Philipp Auerbach, the president of the Bavarian Office of Compensation. After the FRG was established, this framework continued to operate and consolidated the compensation policy of the FRG.

When the GDR was founded in October 1949, a Ministry for Labor and Health was established, and the office for dealing with victims of Nazism continued to function under its auspices. (Formerly this office had operated in the Department of Labor and Welfare in the German administration of the Soviet occupation zone.) In early 1950, detailed instructions for recognizing the various victims of Nazism were published in the GDR's book of laws, and thus the consolidating stage of the recognition of Nazism victims in the GDR was in fact completed.

In the FRG a federal compensation law *(Bundesentshädigungsgesetz)* was enacted only in 1953. In contrast to the GDR, however, no detailed instructions were published with it concerning people who were entitled to be recognized as victims. The procedure and the policy of recognizing victims was consolidated in the FRG by senior officials in the various compensation authorities, some of whom were also the authors of commentaries to the compensation laws.[12]

The backgrounds of the officials in the compensation offices at that time were quite varied. Many of the officials, including some of the senior ones, were themselves victims of Nazism. In three of the most important states in West Germany, Jews headed the compensation authorities: in Bavaria, Philipp Auerbach, a chemist, merchant, and outstandingly active person in the Jewish community in Germany; in North Rhine–Westphalia, Dr. Marcel Frenkel, a lawyer and a member of the German Communist Party (KPD); and in Hesse, Dr. Curt Epstein. These ex-victims did not constitute a homogeneous group with a unified conception. In Munich, for example, tensions arose in the compensation office between Jewish officials and non-Jewish German officials who had been politically persecuted; they had contradictory opinions on several issues. Even among the Jews themselves there were tensions and disputes between German Jews and Jews of east European origin *(Ostjuden)*.

In the Soviet occupation zone, the inclusion of Jews in the system was much lower than in the West. The head of the department for victims of the Nuremberg laws, which operated within the main committee for the victims of fascism in Berlin, was Julius Meyer, a Jewish survivor of Auschwitz; however, his authority did not go beyond the treatment of Jews.

Many of the various victims' representatives were not professional officials by training. Otto Aster, the state commissar for political victims in Bavaria, was originally a butcher. These persons assumed their roles through the special circumstances that brought about the establishment of compensation authorities in Germany. The lack of appropriate training was shown by some officials (Auerbach, for example) in courses of action that were not common among the German bureaucracy. But the main expression of this in the West was the way in which the ex-victims regarded their role: they perceived themselves as representing the victims' interests and, quite often, representing the victim group to which they themselves belonged more than representing the financial interests of the German state in which they operated.

Not all the senior and junior officials in the compensation offices were victims of Nazism. There were many officials in the compensation authorities in West Germany whose backgrounds and activities did not differ from those of the professional officials in other government offices at that time. In the years after the Federal Republic was established, the number of such officials in the compensation systems increased and their influence on overall policy was enhanced. More than those who were themselves victims of Nazism, these officials tended to deal with questions of compensation first and foremost as representatives of the financial interests of the German state and taxpayers, and they considered it their role to reduce the burden of compensation on the public financial purse as much as possible.

Treatment of Gypsies by Assistance Organizations for Victims of Nazism

Immediately after the liberation, former concentration camp prisoners throughout Germany established aid organizations for their various communities. The political prisoners and Jews, who constituted the majority of prisoners in the camps, were the most organized among the various groups of victims and established aid agencies *(Hilfsstellen)* for their members. As the Jewish bodies mostly assisted those who were persecuted for their Jewish origin, many of the Gypsy victims turned for help to the Organization of Victims of the Nazi Regime, the VVN. Representatives of the former political prisoners established this organization, and by 1946 branches of the VVN had been established in all of Germany's main cities.

At first, there were members of all political parties among the victims in the organization. After the Cold War broke out in 1946, Communist Party (KPD) influence on the organization increased. In June 1948, when the representatives of the KPD and the Socialist Unity Party, the SED (which joined the Social Democratic Party [SPD] and the Communist Party in the Soviet occupation zone in 1946) became a majority on the organization's council, the SPD representatives left, anticipating the division of Germany and protesting that the VVN had been turned into a Communist organization.[13] Indeed, the temporary establishment regulations of the VVN in Stuttgart in late June 1945 declared that only those who were incarcerated or persecuted in the Third Reich for their political struggle against Nazism should be accepted as members of the organization.[14]

In spite of this, the VVN did help Gypsies who were incarcerated for their origin rather than for any political opposition to the Nazis. Between May and November 1947, about 400 Gypsies were recognized as victims of Nazism by the VVN agencies *(Betreuungsstelle)* in Württemberg-Baden. The organization helped in a variety of matters, including claims for returning property, claims for financial help, and help in financing medical treatment and convalescence. At the end of 1945, when the military governments issued instructions to ensure that immediate aid was given to victims of Nazism, the VNN agencies gained a semiofficial status, and they were first (although not the exclusive) agency integrated into the government compensation system.[15] From time to time, VVN representatives from all the occupation zones in Germany convened to discuss the various issues they dealt with, so that the conditions for recognition, which originated in the Soviet occupation zone, were adopted by the Western organization's representatives and were integrated into the procedures and regulations of the compensation offices in West Germany. The VVN agencies were subject to regulations and criteria for recognition of victims established by the government compensation authorities and, in this respect, they constituted an integral part of the compensation system. The demands that the VVN made for Gypsies to be recognized as victims usually derived from the policy of the compensation offices (for example, not acknowledging the Höherweg camp in Düsseldorf, in which local Gypsies were incarcerated from 1936 on, as a concentration camp).[16] In certain periods, Gypsies who requested that the VVN agencies in certain states recognize them as victims were then asked to fulfill special criteria as a condition for being recognized as such.

The VVN was not a homogeneous organization, and different Gypsies received different treatment, depending on which office they dealt with. For example, a random study of files about Gypsies that are held in the VVN archive in Stuttgart suggests that, in some cases, being accepted into the organization (and thus also being recognized as a victim of Nazism) depended (or at least some Gypsies received the impression it depended) on proving an identification with the Communist Party (KPD). For instance, some Gypsies noted in the application form that they had voted for the KPD in the elections of 1932 and 1933. Another Gypsy, whose application to be accepted as a member of the organization was rejected, wrote: "Neither Moscow nor you will determine whether I was persecuted for racist motives, but the American military government!!"[17]

Another large aid organization that helped Gypsy victims of the Nazis was the Bavarian Help Organization for Those Injured by the Nuremberg Laws (Bayerisches Hilfswerk für die von der Nürnberger Gesetzen Betroffenen). This organization, established in early January 1946, operated exclusively in Bavaria and helped all those who were persecuted for racial reasons: Jews, Germans of Jewish descent, and Gypsies. In 1947, 16,000 people were registered as victims there. It is not clear what number among these clients were Gypsies.[18]

Allies' Attitudes about Recognizing Gypsies as Victims of Nazism

The Allies defined nationality according to one's political, rather than ethnic, entity. As Gypsies were not recognized as a nation, they were assigned to different national groups according to the citizenship they held. Those who had no citizenship were placed in a special category of members of various nations who held no citizenship.[19] For this reason, there are no specific data about Gypsies in the statistics of the military governments and the International Refugees Organization. But the estimated number of Gypsies who remained in Germany at that period was about 5,000, of whom fewer than 2,000 were survivors of concentration camps.[20] Even if these estimates are, in fact, too low, and Gypsies numbered about 10,000, what is clear is that, compared to Jews and to the political victims of Nazism, Gypsies were a small group; they were not homogeneous and not internally cohesive, and they lacked both status and public influence on German society and on the Allies' military governments.

These data and the marginal, almost insignificant, place Gypsies occupied in Nazi ideology meant that Gypsies, in contrast to Jews, were not explicitly mentioned in documents of the Allies and of the International Refugees Organization as a special category of victims of Nazism. In a letter of late October 1945 from Gen. Walter Muller, the head of OMGUS in Bavaria, to the Bavarian minister president Dr. Wilhelm Hoegner, there is no explicit reference to Gypsies. Jews, by contrast, appear at the top of the list of the victims of Nazism and as a category separate from the general category of victims persecuted by the Nazis for political, racial, and religious motives.[21] Despite the lack of any explicit reference, documents of the American military government in Hesse and testimonies of German Gypsies concerning their treatment indicate that the military governments did regard the Nazi persecution of Gypsies as racist persecution, similar to the Nazi persecution of Jews.

The Allies maintained that the German authorities should help anyone persecuted by the Nazi regime for political, racial, or religious reasons and should compensate them for both health and material damage.[22] Political instruction *(Zonenpolitische Anweisung)* no. 20, issued by the British military government, emphasized that this help also had political and educational goals: to show the Germans clearly that anyone who had suffered as a result of their resisting Nazism would be appropriately rewarded.[23] The focus on three categories of persecution was intentional. The Allies aimed to distinguish between, on the one hand, persecution that stemmed from racial, political, or religious motives and, on the other hand, persecution and even incarceration in concentration camps of criminal elements, which was not perceived as a typical Nazi persecution but as part of the legitimate fight against crime. In the spirit of the Allies' instructions, the commands issued by the German authorities a few months after the defeat, outlining whom to recognize and aid as a victim of Nazism, excluded those who had been convicted and imprisoned for committing a crime that was recognized as a crime according to the principles of international law.[24]

Limited Recognition by Aid and Compensation Authorities of Gypsies as Victims of Nazism

The officials of the compensation authorities and from among the associations of former political prisoners denied the eligibility to be recognized as victims of Nazism not only to criminals but also to those who were persecuted by the Nazis for asociality.[25] They shared the widespread consensus in German society to incriminate and deny rights to those labeled by the Nazis as asocial. Attitudes had changed little. For example, in January 1948, the federation of trade unions in Bavaria proposed solving the food shortage problem by incarcerating all the asocials in a labor camp.[26]

The former political prisoners were troubled by the German population's attitude toward them. This hostile stance was not founded only on prejudice or on bad experiences during their shared incarceration. Those recognized as victims enjoyed privileges in obtaining rationed products, and the German population, which suffered various shortages in the first years after the war, was hostile and jealous. It was a common view that the victims enjoyed economic privileges that enabled them to obtain most commodities available in the market, while the general public had to make do with scraps.

The former political prisoners also felt that public hostility toward victims of Nazism was fueled by Nazi remnants, who continued to degrade them "as the Gestapo used to do, and to present them in public as criminals and asocials who were lawfully incarcerated by the Nazis." The very incarceration of asocials in concentration camps was perceived by the former political prisoners as a plot the Nazis had devised to harm their public reputation. In the face of the public's attitude toward them, the "politicals" felt the need to emphasize the difference between them and the "asocials." The compensation of those labeled asocials was presented by the politicals as a degradation for the true opponents of fascism and its victims and a slight to their name.[27] At a meeting of the work committee of the aid agencies for victims of Nazism in the state of Hesse, which took place in Wiesbaden in January 1947, Dr. Curt Epstein was elected state commissar for treatment of the victims of Nazism in Hesse; he stated: "It is necessary to draw public attention to the necessity of fighting the Nazi defamation, that the prisoners of the concentration camps were criminals, asocials, murderers, and thieves."

Words to this effect were also written by Philipp Auerbach, the Bavarian state commissar for the victims of Nazism, to the welfare department at the local office of OMGUS in early May 1947. Like Epstein and other colleagues throughout Germany, who expressed themselves in a similar way, he held that the "chaff" (criminals and asocials) should be separated from the "grains" (the true victims) and that efforts should be made to deny recognition and aid to unworthy prisoners.[28] Gypsies were perceived by a wide stratum of German society as an integral part of the asocials and thus as people who were justifiably persecuted and incarcerated in concentration camps by the Nazi regime.

The writer of a letter in mid-August 1945 from the mayor's office in Cologne to the welfare department in Düsseldorf emphasized that not every case of persecution by the Gestapo or the Nazi courts should be regarded as a political persecution since "only persecution for obvious anti-Nazi political activity constitutes political persecution." Continuing, he suggested that it be established in an unequivocal manner that Gypsies did not belong to the circle of those persecuted for racist motives.[29] An opinion written in 1946 by a VVN official (concerning a Gypsy who had requested that he be recognized as a victim) demonstrates that the image of the Gypsy among the circles of former political prisoners was no different from that prevailing among the German public at large: "He is of an asocial and delinquent nature and, like most Gypsies, lives only on trading in stolen goods and dubious business in order to achieve in a dishonest way an unemployment pension. His story about acquiring the horse is a typical Gypsy trick, the only purpose of which is to steal money from other people."[30]

To this traditional prejudice were sometimes added sentiments of hostility toward Gypsies that derived from the experiences of living with them in concentration camps. For example, a protest letter from the former political prisoners in Detmold, written in response to the claim that Gypsies officially should be recognized as victims, states: "When a Gypsy was incarcerated [in a concentration camp] in the years 1933–1940, the grounds for the imprisonment was generally the suspicion that he had committed a criminal offense. . . . In most cases the prisoners were Gypsies who avoided the duty of compulsory labor. In the concentration camps Gypsies behaved in an uncollegial manner, especially the Gypsy children, who were sent to the blocks during roll calls. They would climb through the back windows of the blocks and steal what simple possessions the poor prisoners still had, possessions like a comb, a spoon, etc. The prisoners could recover their stolen possessions only if they gave the children a part of their miserly food ration. This was reported to me from Ravensbrück and Uckermark. It was also reported that Gypsies acted in the camps as informers for the Gestapo, but I cannot provide evidence concerning specific cases."[31] Negative experiences of encounters with Gypsies in concentration camps only supported and reinforced the prejudices that were already predominant among the public in pre-Nazi days. The very incarceration of Gypsies in concentration camps did not generally generate among the political prisoners a feeling of solidarity and empathy toward them.

Doubts about the Gypsies' eligibility to be recognized as victims of Nazism were also raised in October 1946 among the welfare and compensation authorities for the victims of Nazism in the British zone. Dr. Marcel Frenkel, who headed the compensation department in North Rhine–Westphalia, noted in his report of a meeting held in Hamburg that Gypsies were assigned to a category of victims whose eligibility to be recognized was not clear *(Sonderbetreuung);* also belonging to this group were homosexuals (who were punished according to paragraph 175 of the German Punitive Law) and the victims of the Nazi sterilization policy. Frenkel went on to say that in North Rhine–Westphalia Gypsies were still regarded as having been incarcerated in concentration camps for racial reasons, but he also added a note in the document's margin that recognition by the district committees for special aid of those who submitted claims for being persecuted should be made only after a very careful examination had confirmed a faultless past of the claimant.[32] This conditioning was valid with regard to all victims and did not discriminate against Gypsies in particular.

Frenkel's attitude was common among his fellow ex-political prisoners and VVN members. They also believed that those who had a criminal past should not be helped at all, notwithstanding their origin, even if their conviction had occurred after the defeat of Nazism. The activation of this

Personal identification card *(Personalausweis)* of Norwegian Gypsy Zolo Karoly, a prisoner at Buchenwald concentration camp. (Bilderdienst Süddeutscher Verlag.)

principle with regard to Gypsies was problematic for two reasons. First, certain acts of the Nazi regime against Gypsies had automatically been defined in police documents as a fight against crime rather than as racist persecution. Second, the police and judicial authorities' had continued to discriminate against vagrant Gypsies even after 1945, and the likelihood that a Gypsy had been targeted by the police and convicted of an offense was much greater than for a member of any other group of victims of Nazism. The authorities' policy did not derive simply from a wish to prevent damaging the reputation of the former political prisoners, even at the expense of other victims, but from the perception that criminal conviction for even a small offense was a convincing evidence of asociality.

Notwithstanding his uncompromising demand that recognizing someone as being a victim of Nazism should be conditioned on a faultless past, Frenkel regarded Gypsies and the Gypsy Mischlinge as victims of racial persecution. In 1948, he wrote the following reply to a request made by a provincial office of a compensation authority: "The conditions for recognizing Gypsies as victims of Nazism are identical to those concerning Jews and half-Jews, and I ask that all applications for recognition are dealt with in this spirit." In January of that year, after publication of an article in the Communist newspaper *Freiheit* about the difficulties that officials in the compensation authorities piled on Gypsies who approached them, Frenkel asked the VVN to help Gypsies, many of whom were illiterate, to complete the forms for claiming recognition and show good will with regard to Gypsy applicants.[33]

During the discussions that the committee of representatives of the Ministries of Justice of Bavaria, Württemberg-Baden, and Hesse had held in 1947 to coordinate the preparation of compensation laws in the states in the American occupation zone, a different opinion was heard. In contrast to Frenkel's demand for a faultless past, most of the participants in the discussions stated that the compensation law should be applied also to victims who were not considered typical victims of Nazism—namely, mental patients, victims of Nazi sterilization policy, criminals, and asocials. They argued that these people should be compensated, provided they could be regarded as "innocent victims," because "this matter was publicly sensitive." Contrary to the perception guiding the instruction of the British military government of December 1945, and guiding the circles of former political prisoners in the years after that, German officials held that "the goal of the compensation law is not to award a prize to resistance fighters but to compensate victims." The officials believed that there was no room for enacting separate laws on the same issue, just because certain interested circles (the former political prisoners) raised special demands for reasons of prestige.[34]

The attitude of the officials in the Ministries of Justice in the American occupation zone did not derive from a feeling of commitment to the asocials; rather, it expressed considerations of efficiency and rationalization of legislation. If compensation were to be awarded for the very fact of persecution rather than for the reason behind the persecution, it would be possible to enact one single compensation law that would apply to all victims, including the "nontypical" victims, and thus remove the need for additional legislation for compensating groups of victims who were not included in the law. The compensation laws enacted in the American occupation zone included a paragraph enabling the compensation authorities to apply the compensation law to everyone who was harmed by Nazi persecution, whether or not they were included in the circle of victims of Nazism as defined by the existing law;[35] however, in the compensation laws of the British occupation zone, and also in the Federal Republic compensation laws of 1953 and 1956, the opinions of the former political prisoners prevailed, and a similar paragraph was not included. Only in 1957 was the General Law for the Results of the War (Allgemeine Kriegsfolgengesetz) enacted in the FRG; it was intended to comprehensively compensate all those harmed by the Nazis, such as minor offenders and asocials who were imprisoned in the concentration camps, who were not entitled to be recognized as victims of Nazism according to the federal compensation law.[36]

As early as 1945, in order to prevent criminals and asocials from receiving financial help or compensation, the aid authorities in Hamburg were assisted by representatives of the criminal police, who verified the claimants' appeals and checked that they had a clean past. In Württemberg-Baden, the state agency for political victims was assisted in this way since 1946.

By 1947 the state commissar for victims of Nazism in Bavaria, Auerbach saw to it that the Gestapo files and punishment reports from the police were received, and in addition he employed an official of the criminal police to examine the problematic cases. In the Soviet occupation zone and thereafter in the GDR the formal recognition of the status of victim of fascism was also conditioned on a faultless past, and the names of those claiming recognition were checked in the police records.[37] The cooperation of the compensation authorities with the criminal police acquainted the authorities with "experts for Gypsy matters," who operated within the criminal police; some of them had been responsible for enforcing sterilization and deporting Gypsies to concentration camps during the Third Reich.[38] Absurdly, these people had changed from Nazi criminals into allegedly neutral experts, submitting their "impartial" opinions to the compensation authorities about the motives for deporting Gypsies to concentration camps. As the motives rather than the fact of persecution determined the victim's eligibility, the ex-persecutors usually exploited their status to frustrate granting official recognition and, hence, compensation to their former victims. These experts indicated that the persecution of Gypsies did not derive from racist motives but from the asocial nature of the victims; they placed so many obstacles that only a small number of the Gypsy victims of Nazism were officially recognized as such. In Düsseldorf, for example, by 1949, only 19 out of the 138 Gypsies who had applied to be recognized as victims had been so recognized by the District Special Help Committee. The reasons for the authorities' refusal were varied: lack of evidence, camps in which Gypsies were kept under control in Germany were not recognized as concentration camps, and law-breaking for offenses such as stealing since 1946.[39]

HOW INSTRUCTIONS FOR RECOGNITION OF VICTIMS OF NAZISM DISCRIMINATED AGAINST GYPSIES

The first versions of the instructions *(Richtlinien)* for recognition of victims of Nazism, issued by the aid authorities and the voluntary organizations for victims of Nazism in 1945, did not generally make any specific reference to Gypsies. The definition of those persecuted for racial reasons usually mentioned only Jews or Germans of Jewish origin, according to the categories of the Nuremberg Laws.[40] When I was doing the research for this book, the earliest document that could be found in which an explicit reference to Gypsies appeared is a document of March 1946 with instructions for the treatment of political victims of the Nazi regime from Baden-Württemberg. In this document, Gypsies are listed alongside Jews as having been persecuted for racial motives, as defined in the Nuremberg Laws.[41] About two months later, Gypsies are also mentioned with Jews and the Mischlinge in the instructions for "issuing certificates to victims of fascism" that was issued by the chief committee for the victims of fascism (Hauptausschuss OdF), which operated in the office for social affairs in the magistrate's office of the city of Berlin.

But in these documents, restrictions for such recognition of Gypsies as victims of Nazism were already being set. This recognition was made conditional on their proving that they lived in a permanent dwelling and were employed in a steady job.[42] Setting such conditions was reminiscent of the conditions attached to the granting of state's services to Gypsies only if they met certain demands, relative to the German population, which had been first set in the early nineteenth century. At that time, the German principalities awarded citizenship and a license to practice an itinerant trade *(Wandergewerbeschein)* to local Gypsies only if they ceased to live a nomadic or seminomadic way of life. Of course, the inclusion of special conditioning after 1945 did not derive from the same reasons, although it shows that the formulators of the instructions were familiar with traditional measures the German bureaucracy had used against Gypsies. At the end of 1946 Hesse also set conditions that Gypsies must prove they had permanent living accommodations and a steady job before they could be recognized as victims of Nazism.[43]

A suggestion for a new formula of instructions for recognizing victims of fascism was issued by the section for the victims of fascism in the labor and social welfare department in the German administration of the Soviet occupation zone in early December 1946. This document made it a little easier for Gypsies since it required for recognition meeting only one of the two conditions that had appeared in the version of the chief committee for victims of fascism in Berlin of May 1946: either living accommodations or work. This document reflects not only the officials' prejudice but also their ignorance: they perceived Gypsyhood as a trait rather than as a matter of ethnic descent. The draft was passed for supervision to the labor and welfare issues department in the central secretariat of the Socialist Unity Party (SED), later the ruling party in the GDR. The party's clerk, who checked the draft, was sensitive enough to substitute the Nazi racist term *Mischlinge* on the draft with a less loaded term, *half-Jewish (Halbjude)*, but he did not at that time feel the need to correct the terminology in regard to Gypsies. This wording was later substituted by the following version: "Gypsies who were persecuted for their descent" *(Abstammung)*.[44] The instructions issued by the VVN throughout Germany for the recognition of victims of Nazism made such recognition conditional on their having a permanent address and steady work.[45] By 1947 the welfare and compensation authorities all over Germany had already granted the recognition of Gypsies as victims on the condition of their having a permanent settlement.

In the Bavarian compensation office's instructions for issuing certificates of identity for people who had been released from concentration camps *(KZ-Ausweise)*, the category of "Gypsies permanently settled" *(ansässige Zigeuner)* appeared under the title "victims persecuted due to racial background." The same formula appeared in similar documents in the British occupation zone.[46] These documents gave no explanation for the conditions for the recognition, which was not repeated with regard to any other group of victims. The absence from the instruction of a corresponding category of "permanently settled Jews" apparently created the impression that this was a discriminating restriction, as part of the tendency to deny recognition as victims of Nazism to those people who were stigmatized as asocials.

In reality, this matter may have been much more complicated. One of the VVN veterans argued that this condition did not derive from the desire to discriminate against Gypsies but, rather, from administrative causes. According to him, aid was afforded only to victims who were permanently settled in the domain of the aid authorities they approached, and this condition also appeared in versions of the compensation laws. He believed that stressing the demand for a permanent dwelling only concerned Gypsies, because many of them still led a nomadic way of life at that time, and this problem did not arise with other victims.[47]

The authorities for aiding the victims of Nazism operated on a communal basis and with communal financing, based on the operating patterns of the German welfare system since the nineteenth century. The city mayors and the councils in the rural areas bore the burden of aid to people who applied for assistance and who lived permanently in their jurisdiction.[48] A document issued by the compensation office in Stuttgart in January 1946 stated explicitly that the committees would take care of the victims of Nazism who lived in their jurisdiction *(Verfolgten . . . die jetzt in Württemberg ansässig sind)*.[49] Apparently, these bodies had no interest in helping victims who did not live in their jurisdiction. In 1946, the problem of providing financial help to needy people requesting assistance from welfare bodies in places where they did not normally reside was raised. In a circular issued by the public welfare department in the OMGUS in August of the same year, the British representative on the Allies' welfare committee reported that the welfare offices in the American zone were demanding reimbursement for people who were not permanently settled *(nicht-ansässige Personen)* from offices in the British zone, in accordance with German law. The British suggested that the costs be borne by the local welfare association in which the needy person was living and that all the German laws according to which one welfare office was reimbursed by another would be annulled.[50]

Although this explanation might support the claim that making recognition conditional on a permanent place of residence did not derive from discrimination but from the traditional and rigid patterns of the German welfare authorities, it cannot obscure the discriminatory nature of the other conditions Gypsies had to meet so they would be recognized as victims of Nazism. A letter that the local senior administrative official *(Regierungspräsident)* in Detmold sent to the Ministry for Social Affairs in Düsseldorf in May 1947, in response to making welfare help conditional on a permanent residence, shows that there were some officials who regarded such action as an instrument for preventing "nondecent elements" from being recognized as victims. The writer, a Mr. von Lüpke, complained to the compensation authority in North Rhine–Westphalia that conditioning recognition on having a permanent place of residence alone seems to him very dangerous because it would enable "indecent elements" to penetrate the victims' circles.[51] He suggested making the conditions for recognizing Gypsies as victims much more severe.

The Gypsies and their few supporters among the German public regarded these demands as discriminatory, that tended to make it difficult for Gypsies to attain recognition. When they complained about this to the VVN, the organization's leadership in North Rhine–Westphalia sought to refute the claims about discrimination of Gypsies in the VVN's journal of February 1948: their statement said that a confirmed license to practice an itinerant trade was regarded as proof of having permanent work.[52] This clarification sought to refute the claims that the VVN wanted to use this condition as a way of tricking the Gypsies, most of whom were self-employed and did not work in any formal, organized workplace.

In practice, Gypsies had difficulties actually receiving licenses from the relevant authorities, and many failed to get them. This demand discriminated against Gypsies in relation to other victims, who were not required to meet such a condition, and it encapsulated the hidden assumption that every Gypsy is an asocial until he proved otherwise. The condition for recognizing Gypsies as victims, as consolidated in the GDR, provides proof that setting conditions for recognizing Gypsies as victims of Nazism was a discriminating means deliberately intended to deny them such recognition and that the use of it derived from the fact that Gypsies were without exception regarded as asocial.

Shortly after it was established, the Ministry of Labor and Health Affairs in the GDR wanted to introduce instructions for recognizing victims of Nazism into the GDR's statute books. The original version, which had been prepared in May 1946 by the chief committee for victims of fascism in Berlin, was used as a basis for the revised draft, but to the old conditions was added a new one, of an ideological nature: Gypsies were asked to prove that they had democratic antifascist beliefs. No victims other than Gypsies were ever asked to meet such a criterion. It is clear that these conditions derive from the perception that Gypsies were asocial and from the desire to keep them separated from the privileged circle of the victims of fascism. The way in which Gypsies' beliefs were examined also indicated the wish to foil them, as could be seen from the evidence brought by Reimar Gilsenbach: "One could establish that the illiterate [Gypsy] is not revealing a democratic antifascist attitude by his inability to correctly answer the simple opening question, 'Now, comrade, what do you know about General Stalin? "[53]

Thus, recognizing Gypsies as victims depended on eliminating the components of Gypsy identity that were identified by society as expressions of asociality: wandering and the lack of a steady job. While most Gypsies could have coped with the demand to establish a permanent residence, as they had done this already in the nineteenth century (when this demand appeared for the first time) by renting a fictive apartment and showing up at the local registration office,[54] the demand for a steady job from people who had just been released from concentration camps was patently unfair, taking into account the employment opportunities in Germany in the first years after the war.

In 1947, Karl Hauff, head of the VVN branch in Württemberg-Baden, argued that many victims were unemployed. In the Soviet occupation zone there was also a high rate of unemployment among the "victims of fascism" that year. The state of employment among the victims did not improve even by 1950. In Munich, the VVN representative in Bavaria claimed that 60 percent of the victims were unemployed.[55] Considering the prevailing prejudice against Gypsies in German society, their chances of finding work in a period characterized by high general unemployment were not good. Furthermore, Gypsies released from concentration camps had special problems deriving from their persecution, which made it more difficult for them than other ex-prisoners to be integrated into the labor market. Before the war most German Gypsies had made their living by traditional occupations: small commerce, peddling, and various simple trades and crafts. The modernization processes that occurred in the German economy even before Hitler came to power reduced the profitability of these occupations and did not enable those who engaged in them to sustain their families. The denial of recognition as victims to Gypsies who did not meet this condition was a blatant infringement of the concept for which victims' organizations, such as the VVN and the compensation authorities, had been established.

GYPSIES' ELIGIBILITY FOR COMPENSATION
FOR DENIAL OF FREEDOM

By the end of 1949, compensation laws had been introduced in all states in the FRG, enabling the victims of Nazism to receive compensation for the period in which their freedom was denied. One group claiming compensation for denial of freedom were those Gypsies, mainly from the western parts of the FRG, who had been deported to Poland in May 1940. The question first came up in the compensation offices of Hamburg and Bremen.

In early January 1950, Mr. Wanschura of the compensation office in Bremen took evidence from Gypsies who survived the 1940 deportation to clarify the conditions in which the deported then lived in Poland until the end of the war. Luise Lafontain from Düsseldorf gave evidence that she had been interned for four years in the concentration camp at Belczeck, together with many of her "race-fellows" *(Rassengenosse)* from Bremen. This and other testimonies of Gypsy citizens of Bremen indicated to Wanschura that the deported were not settled in Polish villages and did not enjoy freedom but, rather, were imprisoned in concentration camps and ghettos throughout Poland.[56] However, while on business in Hamburg, Hans Travitz of Bremen, who also had been persecuted by the Nazis and was given assistance by the compensation office, "met the Gypsy Mischling Rudolf Weiss." Weiss explained that the Gypsies deported to Poland in May 1940 were kept only for a short time in the concentration camps at Belczeck and Krichow and thereafter were settled in the surrounding villages. Weiss argued that they enjoyed freedom of movement and some even engaged in commerce. Travitz hurried to report what Weiss said to the compensation office. After receiving this unexpected information, Weiss was summoned to the Hamburg compensation office, where testimony was taken from him. The following day, he went to Bremen and repeated his story. In light of this evidence, the Bremen compensation office immediately decided to stop the payment of compensation for denial of freedom *(Haftentschädingung)* to Gypsies who had been deported to Poland from Hamburg and the Rhineland in May 1940, until the matter had been investigated further and clarified.

About a week and a half later, using Weiss's evidence, the Finance authorities in Hamburg (to which the compensation office was subordinated) rejected a compensation claim made by a Gypsy who had been deported in May 1940. In appealing the claimant's argument that between May 1940 and his release in February 1944 he was imprisoned in Belczeck concentration camp, the authorities cited Weiss's argument that Gypsies were settled *(worden umgesiedelt)* in the Government-General that their freedom in general was not limited, and that they enjoyed freedom of movement.[57] In response, the VVN in Hamburg distributed a long memorandum among the compensation authorities, in which it laid out its criticism of the attitude of the Hamburg authorities. The VVN complained that the authorities accepted the Nazi terminology at face value: "All the deportation operations against Gypsies and Jews were performed under the term 'resettling' *[umsiedeln]*. All these 'resettlements' ended, with regard to the involved persons, without exception—and this has to be especially stressed—in ghettos and concentration camps. . . . The aim of the steps taken against Gypsies under the cover of 'resettlement' was extermination." Referring to the Gypsies who were released from concentration camps before May 1945 and remained in Poland, the writer of the memorandum emphasized that from the day of their deportation from Germany until the fall of the Nazi regime, Gypsies, like Jews, were outlawed *(Freiwild)*. Therefore he believed that even if they had been released before the defeat, the end of denial of freedom should be regarded as only having occurred on 8 May 1945 (the official termination of World War II).

On the same day that the Hamburg authorities rejected the claim of the Gypsy who had been deported to Poland, the Bremen compensation office published an interim report about the treatment *(Betreuung)* and recognition of Gypsies (from 18 January 1950). In contrast to the attitude of the Hamburg authorities, the Bremen compensation office rejected Weiss's testimony and instead accepted the evidence of the Bremen Gypsies. The office's memorandum stated: "In this case it is simply not possible to speak about resettlement (in the ordinary meaning of the term), especially when speaking about whole extended families remaining together."[58] Furthermore, the Bremen office went so far as to include Gypsies themselves in the procedure for examining whether Gypsies were eligible to be recognized as victims of Nazism. It determined, with regard to the Gypsy families in Bremen, that the evidence of reliable clan patriarchs *(Stammesoberhäupter)* could be used to help them verify the eligibility of compensation claimants. The memorandum noted that in Bremen three Gypsy family heads *(Stammesväter)* served as claims confirmators.

Hamburg did not take long to respond. In a letter addressed to Auerbach (head of the interoffice coordination office for matters of compensation in Munich), Frenkel (of Düsseldorf), and Wanschura (of Bremen), Dr. Franz of the local compensation office *(Wiedergutmachungsstelle)* in Hamburg protested against the policy of recognizing Gypsies in Bremen. Franz repeated the opinion of the Hamburg compensation authority about the May 1940 deportation and also expressed his opposition to the procedure consolidated in Bremen for the verification of the eligibility of Gypsy applicants: "Investigations showed that interested Gypsies methodically coordinate their evidence with each other and threaten to murder people whose reliable evidence is not compatible with their interests. In such circumstances one should oppose that the [eligibility for compensation] is determined according to Gypsies' evidence, even according to the evidence of the so-called Gypsy clan patriarchs *[Stammesväter]*."[59]

By discounting the reliability of the evidence of deported Gypsies themselves, Franz effectively left to the authorities only the evidence emerging from Nazi documents. Many senior officials interpreted the term *resettlement (Umsiedlung)* that the Nazis had used in their document literally—the resettlement of Gypsies in villages—while, in fact, most of the Gypsies deported to Poland in May 1940 had been incarcerated in camps. However, the compensation office in Bremen was not the only compensation authority in Germany to recognize that the deported Gypsies were entitled to compensation for denial of freedom. The compensation department of North Rhine–Westphalia, headed by Dr. Frenkel, followed Bremen's line of thinking. A memorandum was formulated in Frenkel's department on that issue, which closely resembles the position of the VVN in Hamburg. It was published a short time later: "The base assumption in determining the Gypsies' eligibility for compensation is that they were persecuted for racial motives like Jews and were all targeted for extermination. The first actions against Gypsies began in 1938 with the general measures taken against the asocials. Then, as with others, many Gypsies who broke the rules as such were caught, but they were not convicted (by any judicial process) but instead were arrested by the Gestapo and thrown into concentration camps."[60]

Following the opinion of the Hamburg VVN's memorandum, the compensation department in North Rhine–Westphalia also held that the period in which freedom was denied should not be regarded as having ended until the date of the armistice. In accordance with the predominant opinion, however, the memorandum stated that people with a criminal past were not entitled to compensation at all and issued instructions for the careful examination of whether a Gypsy applicant had a criminal history. In 1949–1950, in North Rhine–Westphalia, 373 Gypsies received compensation for denial of their freedom in the framework of the 1949 law.[61]

Since there was no unified compensation policy concerning Gypsies in the Federal Republic as a whole, the fate of compensation claims of survivors of the May 1940 deportation was determined according to the perception of each local compensation office head. Claimants in Bremen and North Rhine–Westphalia received compensation, while those in Hamburg were rejected. Such a situation did not comply with the aims of the coordinating committee, which sought to unify the compensation policy in all of the FRG's states. However, in early 1950 the prevailing contradictory attitudes of the different senior officials had not yet been bridged, and perhaps it would prove impossible to bridge them.

The question of the motives and nature of the Nazi persecution of Gypsies had not been removed from the compensation authorities' agenda. In October 1949, the administrative court *(Verwaltungsgericht)* in Stuttgart decided in favor of a Gypsy who had appealed a ruling of the regional compensation agency *(Landsesbezirksstelle)* that his confinement had not been due to racial persecution because he had been jailed for dealing in stolen goods before being incarcerated in a concentration camp.

The Württemberg-Baden Ministry of Justice then appealed this verdict at the supreme administrative court *(Verwaltungsgerichthof),* and the compensation office criticized the ruling of the lower instance. It determined that in no way should the persecution of Gypsies be compared to that of Jews, as there was a significant difference between the two persecutions. While the Jew was persecuted for his racial background without any reference to his personal traits, the Gypsy was usually a target of the Nazi regime only if he was regarded as a criminal or asocial. Race did not constitute a cause for persecution, but was only perceived as a cause for the Gypsy's asocial behavior. The agency also argued that the meaning of the race question was expressed within the framework of the actions the Nazi state took against Gypsies only in that it attributed a bad hereditary constitution to dangerous habitual criminals. The compensation agency's official stated that "the aim of the persecution was not the extermination *(Auslöschung)* of the race, but rather the elimination *(Beseitigung)* of elements perceived as asocial."[62]

This attempt to blur the collective nature of Gypsy persecution by the Nazi regime, and to present it as a legitimate measure to eliminate crime, characterized the attitude of "Gypsy experts" of the criminal police. They no doubt played a role in formulating the attitude of the compensation authority in Württemberg-Baden. The authority did not decide to completely deny compensation to Gypsies but was satisfied with putting them on an equal footing with the persecuted asocials and criminals (in accordance with article 50 of the Württemberg-Baden compensation law), rather then with those persecuted on racial grounds (according to section 1 of the same compensation law).

In mid-January 1950, while clarifying the May 1940 deportation issue, the public prosecutor in Stuttgart, who represented the state in the matter of a Gypsy's compensation claims, requested that the vagrant police station in Karlsruhe provide an opinion concerning the circumstances of this Gypsy's incarceration in a concentration camp. (The latter had sued the state for failing to recognize him as a victim for the purpose of compensation.)[63] The police body continued to hold files opened for

Gypsies even before the Nazis had come to power and which contained much information about them. In the Nazi period the racial opinions of Robert Ritter's institute concerning the extent of the file's owner's purity of race had been added to these files. These opinions determined the fate of Gypsies in the Third Reich—whether they were to be sterilized or sent to concentration camps. Mr. Hoffmann, an official of the vagrant police station in Karlsruhe, replied to the public prosecution that among the 5,000 vagrants registered in the station from before the war, as well as in the fingerprint collection in the station, there was no person with personal details similar to those given by the public prosecutor, and he concluded that a person by this name did not reside in Baden when Gypsies had been registered. Hoffmann was not satisfied with this reply but took advantage of the appeal to the vagrant police to warn of the danger of cheating on the part of Gypsies: "There is a fear that the vagrants will try to exploit the compensation system, in order to obtain a pension, using a fictitious identity or that of a dead person." "In fact, up to now no concrete cases are known," wrote Hoffmann, "however I am taking the liberty in this situation to draw attention to the fact that vagrants were known in the past to use fictitious names."[64]

In the departments for Gypsy affairs, which continued to exist after 1945 within the criminal police divisions in most states of the FRG, Gypsies continued to be regarded, as they had been during the Weimar Republic and the Third Reich, as a basically criminal element, even when no concrete proof had been found to support this; to this end, they went on collecting information about Gypsies on the basis of their ethnic background.

In a letter of November 1951, Mr. Meinert, the head of the central office of criminal identification and police statistics in Bavaria, detailed the tasks of his office. He wrote the following about the "Gypsy" unit, which had in the meantime adopted a more neutral name, Agency of Information and Fact-Collecting about Vagrants (Nachrichtensammel- und Auskunftsstelle über Landfahrer): "This agency deals with verifying claims for help and compensation submitted by Gypsies to the Bavarian compensation office and the Bavarian organization for helping victims of the Nuremberg Laws. As a result, it was found on the basis of the agency's information reservoir that in many cases the claims were not justified, and the state of Bavaria could have avoided significant financial damages." According to this letter, the exclusive role of this unit was the investigation of Gypsies' compensation claims, and it had no other police role. A total of 10,995 personal files and subject files were found in this unit in 1962, including files of Gypsies from the time of the Third Reich, which contained racist opinions from Ritter's institute.[65]

The Munich compensation office had already begun to cooperate with the criminal police in 1947, and thus, when investigating Gypsies' claims, the criminal police drew the attention of the compensation office to the existence of the so-called Gypsy police. At some point between 1947 and 1949, cooperation began between the compensation authorities for the victims and their former persecutors. After another reform in April 1952 in the criminal departments in the police headquarters *(Polizeipräsidium)* in Munich, the term referring to Gypsies *(Zigeuner)* was substituted with a less loaded term—*vagrants (Landfahrer)*.[66]

As a method for preventing any cheating in compensation issues, Hoffmann, of the Karlsruhe vagrant police station, suggested that suspected claimants consent to their fingerprints being taken and compared to the fingerprints in the police collections in Karlsruhe and Munich. The suggested procedure constituted and still constitutes part of police treatment of criminals; however, its introduction with regard to civilians without a criminal past was an assault on their basic rights. Regarding Gypsies as potential criminals was not limited to the "Gypsy experts" in the criminal police departments.

Among the officials at the compensation department of the Ministry of Justice in Stuttgart, to which the public prosecution sent a copy of the letter, was a senior official who treated the apprehension Hoffmann raised as a real danger and was quick to adopt the suggested procedure. The senior official in question, Hans Wilden, was a jurist and later one of the authors of the commentary on the federal compensation law (BEG), as well as a judge of the supreme court in Karlsruhe. About two months earlier, the compensation office of Bremen, which was disturbed by the possibility that Gypsies might submit several compensation claims concurrently in several states, had asked Wilden to provide it with a list of Gypsies who submitted compensation claims in Württemberg-Baden. Wilden replied to the office in Bremen that he had no statistical data about this community and suggested that Bremen clarify with the Stuttgart compensation office every case where a Gypsy had made a claim for compensation to find out whether a corresponding claim had been submitted elsewhere. Wilden attached a copy of Hoffmann's letter. In addition, he prepared a draft for a memo on the issue of Gypsies' claims. Wilden quoted the principles of Hoffmann's statement in the draft.[67]

The fear that Gypsy claimants would fraudulently receive compensation money, which apparently was connected in Wilden's mind with the traditional image of Gypsies, was for him enough to justify the establishment of a discriminating and degrading attitude toward the group. Wilden, contrary to Wanschura, the head of the Bremen compensation office, decided to acquaint himself with the subject of Gypsy persecution in the Third Reich from the point of view of the criminal police, which participated in the Gypsies' persecution, rather than from the victims' own testimonies. For this purpose in February 1950 he summoned a working meeting on the issue of "the treatment *[Behandlung]* of Gypsies in the Third Reich," with representatives of three police bodies in Stuttgart: the office of criminal identification and police statistics in Württemberg-Baden, the police headquarters *(Polizeidirektion)* in Stuttgart, and the criminal police of the city.[68]

The very use Wilden made of the term *treatment (Behandlung)* to define the Gypsies' persecution and murder, rather then the term *persecution (Verfolgung)*, might indicate that Wilden was not convinced that Gypsies were indeed genuine victims of Nazism. The new version of the circular's draft prepared by Wilden about two days after meeting with the police expressed without reservation the criminal police's attitude toward Gypsy persecution, an attitude that denied the racist nature of this persecution during the Third Reich. The wording of the circular is as follows: "The investigation of Gypsies and Gypsy Mischlinge eligibility to compensation, according to the compensation law, concluded that in many cases, this group was not persecuted and incarcerated for racial reasons, but for its asocial and criminal behavior."[69] Therefore it was established in the document that compensation claims of Gypsies and Gypsy Mischlinge would be passed for investigation to the criminal identification office in Stuttgart, and that the compensation office would carry out its investigations in cooperation also with the central office for criminal identification and police statistics of Munich in Bavaria and with the vagrant police station in Karlsruhe.

Wilden determined that this decree could be applied not only to new compensation claims but also to claims already being dealt with. The decree, therefore, gave authority to "experts on Gypsy affairs," who had actively participated in Gypsy persecution during the Third Reich, and to others who based their actions on the persecutors' opinion, to decide the fate of the victims' compensation claims in the state of Württemberg-Baden. The circular also gave authority to return the countrywide status the body for Gypsy affairs in Munich had enjoyed in the Weimar Republic, when it was called the Center for Combating the Gypsy Nuisance. The following paragraph was added to the final version of circular E-19:

> As Gypsies and Gypsy Mischlinge do not usually have a permanent place of residence, but wander all over the country, it should be taken into consideration that double claims [for compensation] would be submitted [in several states]. Furthermore, it should be mentioned that this circle of people frequently use incorrect names, or at least nicknames, according to which their owners cannot be located in the registry offices *[Standesämter]*.[70]

This final version was signed by Otto Küster, who headed the compensation department; Küster himself made only slight changes in the text, and it no doubt generally expressed his opinion, too. Küster's attitude toward Gypsies emphasizes how deeply rooted was the Gypsies' image as asocial at this time, even among persons who supported the unpopular compensation policy and who sought to atone for the wrongs of the Third Reich. In contrast to most German officials who did not come from among the ranks of the persecuted and whose attitude was guided by considerations of how to minimize the public expenditure on compensation, Küster was perceived, and expressed himself more than once, as one who regarded compensation not only as a legal act but also as a means of reinstituting justice and as a moral duty.[71] Since the negative image of Gypsies was deeply rooted in the collective consciousness in Germany, and since in the post-1945 political culture in Germany a discriminatory attitude toward Gypsies did not entail sanctions, Küster and many of his contemporaries failed to develop sensitivity to and criticism of discrimination against Gypsies, in the way many of them would have done regarding discrimination against Jews.

The attitude of the compensation authorities toward the so-called professional opinion of the criminal police was crucially influenced by the personal attitude of the senior officials. Officials who believed that the compensation policy should first aim to serve the state's interests, tended, like Wilden and Küster, to adopt without question any opinion that might have reduced the cost of compensation to the state finance, especially regarding a group of victims who had a highly negative public image. Officials who were concerned with the victims' interests, such as Wanschura, showed a critical attitude in the face of such opinions, even when they came from among the criminal police officials.

Copies of circular E-19 were distributed by the Württemberg-Baden compensation authority and sent to all the compensation authorities in Germany. The attitude of Stuttgart evoked the rage of Auerbach, head of both the Bavarian compensation office and the compensation offices' coordinating committee.

In March 1950 the Bavarian compensation office distributed a long circular, signed by Oskar Zelger, the head of Auerbach's chamber, who expressed the Munich office's opposition to the Stuttgart argument that the Gypsy persecution did not derive from racial motives but from the fight against antisocial behavior and crime. The circular reviewed the Gypsy persecution from 14 December 1937 on, when the decree for combating crime of the Reich's Ministry of the Interior was published. Zelger determined that the interpretation given to the term *asocial* in this decree was arbitrary, as was the application of this term to a certain population. The circular emphasized that all actions taken against Gypsies in the

Third Reich stemmed from racial motives, although the actions before 1942 also derived from motives of combating asociality: "It is not possible to regard Gypsies incarcerated in concentration camps as asocials and criminals, simply because Himmler's circular and the decrees of the racial hygiene institute in Berlin presented them as such."[72]

Zelger concluded by retreating from the conviction of the racial nature of Nazi persecution of Gypsies. He maintained that verification of whether a Gypsy had been imprisoned for racial reasons or mainly for asociality could be established only by cooperating with the center for criminal identification in Munich and the corresponding police departments in the other regional states. Although Zelger accepted the police registrations of the Nazi period as acceptable for the purpose of making such decisions, he thought one should recognize that before 1942 the incarceration of Gypsies in concentration camps was a result of their "asociality" more than was the incarceration of those after 16 December 1942 (the date the "Auschwitz decree" [Auschwitz Erlass] was issued).

Several days later, the coordinating committee for compensation issues of the eleven states of the FRG convened in Munich, under the leadership of Auerbach. The eleventh issue on the meeting's agenda was the question of compensation to Gypsies. In the meeting the deep controversies among the senior officials on the issue of compensation policy surfaced and, in fact, cut to the heart of the very role of the compensation system. Auerbach opened the discussion with strong reservations about the E-19 circular, saying that he regarded its publication as itself a form of racial discrimination against Gypsies. With regard to the claim of Stuttgart that Gypsies were persecuted in the Third Reich primarily because of their alleged tendency to commit crime, Auerbach determined that Gypsies were convicted only for very slight offenses, and that serious crimes such as murder and robbery were very rare among Gypsies. Auerbach declared that he regarded any Gypsy who was convicted of minor crimes fewer than ten times to be a decent person. Auerbach showed understanding and awareness of the unique circumstances of Gypsies, and, contrary to the predominant opinions of the compensation authorities and Frenkel, he stated that special criteria should be considered for any criminal past a Gypsy might have had. Auerbach held that it was not right that the compensation authorities investigated the criminal record of Gypsy claimants with the same measure of strictness by which the criminal record of the other claimants was investigated, because the lifestyle of Gypsies and the draconian legislation that sought to eliminate it had led to constant friction between Gypsies on the one hand and the police and the legal authorities on the other. Auerbach argued that it was the extent of the severity of their criminal convictions that should be taken into account when examining the eligibility of a Gypsy to be recognized as a victim of Nazism, rather than simply the existence of those convictions. At this stage, Auerbach introduced a personal tone into his words: "When I was incarcerated for two years in Alexanderplatz [in Berlin], I saw with my own eyes the transports of Gypsies passing through the jail, Gypsies and Jews in the same hall. I saw people whose only "crime" was to be a Gypsy or Gypsy Mischlinge, deported with their children. In Auschwitz I experienced personally one night how Gypsies were burned alive. These were crimes against the race that cannot be justified." Auerbach further clarified why he had so vehemently attacked the circular issued by the Stuttgart compensation department. "It might be," he said, "that in a few years it would be explained that Jews were also persecuted not for racial reasons [but because] they were mostly criminal and degenerated people *[entartete Menschen]*. That is why I defend by all means against the possibility that in our circle and in our authorities the fact of racist discrimination might even be established."

The division between those who supported and those who opposed the Stuttgart position in the meeting was clear. The non-Jewish speakers, Dr. Heiland of the Ministry of Finance in Freiburg and the jurist Hans Ehrig of the Hessian Ministry of the Interior, who had not personally suffered at the hands of the Nazis, supported the Stuttgart position. Hans Wilden, who prepared the circular that led to the dispute, chose to remain silent, although he was present at the discussion. The Jewish speakers, Auerbach and Hirsch both of the Munich compensation office (Auerbach and Hirsch themselves survivors of the Nazi concentration camps) and Marcel Frankel from Düsseldorf opposed it passionately.

Heiland presented two arguments against Auerbach's statement, one practical and the other based on principle. He claimed that, in principle, it was a complete mistake to regard the Nazi persecution of Gypsies only from a racial point of view: "Exactly the fact that Hitler had regarded Gypsies as pure Aryans enables me to claim that the fight against them had begun not in 1933 but at the beginning of the twentieth century or before, because they were then already regarded as an antisocial element." Heiland questioned the centrality that racism played in the Nazi persecution of Gypsies: "This was only a device of Hitler and the Nazis, that Jews and Gypsies were suddenly mentioned together. It was not Gypsies they wanted to defame by this, but rather Jews. In the people's voice, a Gypsy is a person who has a bad reputation as asocial." Heiland mentioned that in each case of a Gypsy's claim for compensation, there was a need to investigate what the motive for his persecution was. On the practical level he warned that if the compensation claim of every Gypsy was approved without investigation, the result would be, as had already happened in Bremen, that one Gypsy family received 80,000 marks and spent it in a very short time. Such phenomena, argued Heiland, hurt the

Philipp Auerbach, first president of the Bavarian compensation office until his impeachment in 1951. (Bilderdienst Süddeutscher Verlag.)

compensation policy *(Wiedergutmachung),* because people said, "you see where you get to with your compensation."[73]

Heiland took out of context a few words that had appeared in a report of the Bremen compensation office of January 1950. The report said that one should avoid paying Gypsies large sums on a one-time basis, but instead pay them in installments over a long period to prevent Gypsies, some of whom were young and illiterate and in any case inexperienced in managing large sums of money, becoming the victims of crooks who would exploit their inexperience and deprive them of their money. For the same reason, the Bremen office recommended purchasing for the Gypsies any new wagons to replace those that were taken from them when they were deported to the East.[74] Heiland raised this issue to justify the denial of compensation to Gypsies. His last argument resembled the attitude of the former political prisoners with regard to aid and compensation to victims labeled as asocials in 1946–1947: he examined the question of Gypsies' eligibility to compensation not with regard to applying the law, in light of the fact that their freedom was denied, but in light of the possible reaction of the public to compensating these victims.

After Heiland spoke, Frenkel took the platform and disagreed with him, saying that if the acts against Gypsies "took different forms," eventually the crucial cause for their persecution on the one hand and the pardon to those among them who were declared as pure race on the other hand were racial motives. Frenkel emphasized that in a set of actions performed against Gypsies they were treated by the police or the Gestapo "en bloc," without any investigation of whether the relevant individuals had actually committed any offense. Frenkel believed that serious criminals should not be awarded compensation for denial of freedom but that the burden of proof about the criminal past of the claimant was on the compensation authority: "If we cannot provide such proof, then we must let him benefit from the doubt and assume that he was persecuted for racial motives, exactly like the thousands of Gypsies who were burned alive. We owe it to these people and to ourselves. Nobody ever asked how it was with Jews: they were also taken en bloc."[75]

In contrast to Frenkel, and in the spirit of the position accepted by the different government authorities in Germany concerning Gypsies, the Hesse representatives established that the burden of proof should be on Gypsies: "According to the general principles, the onus of proving eligibility is basically on the claimant. Accordingly, the Gypsy too has to prove that he was persecuted [by the Nazis] for racist motives."

At this point Auerbach intervened in the discussion and repeated Zelger's statement in the circular that it was possible to decide whether Gypsies had been incarcerated for reasons of asociality or race only in cooperation with the central office of criminal identification in Munich, where a department for Gypsy affairs existed, or with corresponding departments in the other regional states. Ironically, the same Auerbach who supported awarding compensation to Gypsies also established the need to cooperate with experts for Gypsy affairs in the criminal police to investigate compensation claims submitted by Gypsies. Auerbach described the services provided by the central office for criminal identification in Munich to the compensation office as "exceptionally good." He added that "we have to supervise the criminal police offices and they have to supervise us," and he showed no reservations about cooperating with the office's personnel, who partly participated in the Nazi persecution during the Third Reich. It is probable that in Auerbach's time the opinions of the experts on Gypsy affairs were much more moderate than the opinions they prepared after he was dismissed from his office and after the vagrant regulation *(Landfahrerordnung)* was enacted in Bavaria in 1953. But Auerbach was caught up in the prevailing conception of his generation concerning asocials, and side by side with his decisive and courageous statements about any previous convictions of Gypsies, he also expressed himself apologetically, repeating the principles conditioning the Gypsies' eligibility to be recognized as victims on a permanent place of residence and stable work: "I wish to suggest considering in the framework of the question under discussion whether it could not be assumed that Gypsies without criminal convictions, or those with petty convictions, who lived before their incarceration in permanent accommodations or worked in a stable workplace, were indeed persecuted for racial motives." Auerbach's statement reveals the discriminating concept: in addition to vagrant Gypsies who did not have a permanent dwelling and stable work, this category included Gypsies who sustained their families and did not depend on welfare pensions, but nevertheless did not possess an official license to practice an itinerant trade. These latter were also considered asocial and therefore undeserving of compensation.

The only speaker at the meeting who showed exceptional sensitivity (in comparison to the other speakers) to the way in which Gypsy victims were suspected of being asocial was Hirsch of the Munich compensation office: "The term *Gypsy* is a term defining descent, and this is a term defining also race. If we explain that a Gypsy as such is already suspected of being asocial, this is a racist discrimination, whether he was justifiably persecuted or not. In any case this is an accusation of asociality of a whole group of people. We who had been persecuted should not do it, even if, and I sincerely admit that in many cases it seems that they were asocials. They were persecuted, and we should not prevent them from being entitled to compensation due to asociality." Hirsch's statement caused Auerbach to express himself decisively and emotionally: "We have here full reports from Ravensbrück of how eight- and nine-year-old girls were made guinea pigs and were killed; to explain here that they were criminal elements contradicts any principle of the Wiedergutmachung [literally, 'correcting the wrong', practically, compensation]. How could the children who were exterminated here—children aged eight and nine—be criminals?"

At this stage, Ehrig made a remark to Auerbach, which was censored from the minutes, apparently due to its excessive bluntness. With it a part of Auerbach's response was also censored. From the text of the representative from Lower Saxony, Dr. Fenyes, who wished to reconcile the positions of Ehrig and Auerbach, one can reconstruct Ehrig's main argument against Auerbach: "As the representative of the Hessian Ministry of the Interior, I have to observe the exclusive interests of the state rather than the one-sided interests of the victims."

Fenyes, who had been active in the committee of ex-prisoners of concentration camps in Hanover in 1945, and was, therefore, in a position to mediate between the two parties, sought to blunt the personal dimension of Ehrig's assault on Auerbach by arguing that Ehrig did not express his personal view but, rather, wanted to illuminate the question for which the committee had been convened. However, he agreed with Ehrig's argument that Auerbach's attitude represented a particular interest of the victims rather than the state's interest, which, according to him, was represented by Ehrig and himself. His words also implied that he viewed as negative the seniority awarded to the victims' representatives (the Jews) in the coordination committee. Auerbach, although using a conciliatory tone, did not seek to hide his different perception of his role: "I feel personally that I was called to the duty of the Bavarian compensation office's president, both in order to harmonize the interests of political and racial victims with the existing legislation and to carry out what can be done according to law. I would like to take this opportunity to say that after the publication of the compensation laws my hands are tied more than in the past. Today I am tied by the law, but I am trying to interpret it in favor of the victims as much as it can be made consistent with the oath I took to be faithful to the constitution." In conclusion, he replied personally to Ehrig and the other supporters of the Stuttgart opinion: "We do not have the right to hurt any group because of its racial or another belonging. . . . I interpreted Ehrig's expression as a question. He himself did not have the experience a part of us, unfortunately, acquired in the concentration camps; he only tried to clarify the issue. . . . we who have been in Auschwitz know what happened to the Gypsies."[76]

This discussion of the issue of the Gypsies' eligibility to compensation certainly reflected the vast disagreements over policy among the senior officials of the compensation authorities. The gap it exposed between the attitudes of the representatives of the Jewish collective and those of the

German collective toward the persecution of Gypsies reflected the chasm Auschwitz had torn between the consciousness of the two collectives to which the officials belonged. The opinion of the Jewish officials represented only a minority of the German public in 1950, but it expressed the Jewish collective consciousness, which regarded the persecution of Gypsies as an evil and racist persecution, like the persecution of Jews. The opinion expressed by the German officials represented the attitude of the German political establishment and the opinion of the majority of the German population in the early 1950s. They accepted the Nazi side: that the persecution of Gypsies had been a legitimate persecution of criminals and asocials, and not a typical Nazi criminal persecution. While Auerbach and his colleagues perceived the Gypsy persecution through the mirror of the Jewish collective memory and their personal memories from the Holocaust, the German officials perceived the same event through the mirror of the German collective memory, which focused on maintaining law and order in Germany's streets during the Third Reich, by incarcerating the asocial elements, to which, according to the Nazi concept, Gypsies also belonged. Some Jewish officials feared that depriving the rights of Gypsies might set a precedent in the future for depriving the rights of Jews to receive compensation for their persecution. In contrast, the German officials understood their role, according to the traditional principle of state bureaucracy, as a commitment to protect the financial interests of the state, and they acted to reduce the scope of the state's expenses for compensation. They perceived their Jewish colleagues' attitude as contradictory and as representing particular interests.

The differences in opinion were also expressed by the language used. While the German officials expressed themselves in an unemotional manner, using bureaucratic terminology and principles, the Jewish speakers spoke emotionally about the moral debt to the murdered and to the surviving victims.

COMPENSATION POLICY FOR GYPSIES IN THE FEDERAL REPUBLIC, 1950–1953

Although it seemed from the discussions of the coordination committee on compensation issues in Munich that Auerbach and Frenkel's position prevailed, Küster and Wilden did not alter their position, and their circular E-19 remained valid in the domain of Baden-Württemberg.

Notwithstanding Auerbach's opinion, in November 1950, a significant change took place in the practices of the Bavarian compensation office. The office rejected a claim for compensation of a Gypsy woman, Elisabeth Gutenberger. She had been denied her freedom for twenty-five months, during which time she was imprisoned in Birkenau, Ravensbrück, and other locations. The office explained the reasons for rejecting her claim by saying that the question of racial motive for Gypsy persecution had not been sufficiently clarified.[77] This position was even more extreme than that of Stuttgart, and since the state of Bavaria even today does not allow researchers to study the material of the compensation office from that period, it is difficult to explain exactly why change occurred in the Munich office's position.

In 1950, the Minister of the Interior in Lower Saxony also issued temporary instructions that Gypsies' claims for compensation for denial of freedom should not be handled.[78] At Auerbach's suggestion, the question of the Gypsies' eligibility for compensation was brought up as one of the issues on the agenda of the coordination committee for compensation issues' meeting, which convened in Bonn in the presence of the federal Minister of Finance, Fritz Schäffer, in November 1950. But the minutes of the meeting contain only a short and ambiguous sentence, which does not assist us in understanding the change in the compensation policy toward Gypsies. It stated that the Gypsies' eligibility to compensation in North Rhine–Westphalia and Hamburg, namely, in the British occupation zone, was equal to the eligibility of all the victims in the states of the American occupation zone.[79]

In the early 1950s, some of the senior officials who headed the compensation authorities in the period preceding the establishment of the Federal Republic retired from their posts. Their retirement was crucial for the recognition policy of the compensation authorities all over Germany toward Gypsy victims of Nazism. Most of these officials were Jewish victims of Nazism. These positions were then usually filled by German bureaucrats, many of whom did not come from among the ranks of the victims and who usually showed rigid attitudes toward the victims. This development was not entirely accidental, but was engineered by some German politicians, who resented the status of the former officials and the generous compensation policy that they had established and even acted intensively for their dismissal.

Dr. Curt Epstein, who had headed the compensation department in the Hessian Ministry of the Interior, had to resign from his office in March 1950. The Hessian minister of the interior, Heinrich Zinnkann (SPD), claimed that Epstein did not satisfactorily fulfill his duties.[80] Dr. Marcel Frenkel, who had headed the North Rhine–Westphalia compensation department since late 1946, was sent on an enforced vacation due to his membership in the Communist Party and other pro-Soviet organizations at the end of 1950.[81] The attack on Frenkel was begun in 1949 by a Christian Democrat in the Landtag, Müller. At the Landtag's meeting in July 1949, Müller attacked the Social Democrat minister of the interior, Menzel, who had appointed Frenkel. Müller said that the way in which the minister made his appointments was not understood by the public and that the CDU, as the strongest party in the state, would not stand for it anymore. In October he accused Frenkel of plotting to transfer to the State of Israel the Jewish property that had been left in Germany without heirs.[82] After this unfounded attack, Frenkel did not resume his position. He was succeeded by one of his Jewish assistants in the department, Dr. Goldfarb. Initially this change in personnel did not result in a change in the favorable policy toward Gypsies.

But the retirement of Philipp Auerbach from the presidency of the Bavarian compensation office and from the influential status he had in the field of compensation policy in the Federal Republic had a much greater effect. Auerbach had made many opponents, and they had begun to gather material against him. As a result of this, in July 1950 an investigation was conducted against him. At the end of January 1951 the Bavarian police raided the Munich compensation office in order to investigate suspicions about alleged financial disorders and fraud. Legal procedures were taken against Auerbach; he was suspended, and then he committed suicide after he was convicted.[83]

This affair led to increased police supervision with regard to claims for compensation throughout Germany. The opinions of Auerbach and other Jewish colleagues were derived from their general perception of the compensation policy in the Federal Republic of Germany, and it expressed the deep commitment they felt toward the victims of Nazism. In 1945, their views had the support of the Western Allies, who held that it was important to show the Germans that whoever suffered at the hands of the Nazis was appropriately compensated.

The outbreak of the Cold War, and the intention of the Western Allies to integrate West Germany as an important member of the democratic Western defense against Communism, led many senior officials in military governments to feel that they had to be reconciled with the Germans. One of the expressions of this reconciliation was the change of the Allies' policy toward the victims of Nazism. By mid-1947 OMGUS officials were opposing any possibility that victims of Nazism become a privileged class in comparison with the rest of the German population.[84] As soon as the German bureaucratic and political establishment understood that with the establishment of the Federal Republic the Western Allies would no longer show any great interest in questions of compensation policy, and that this was now to be merely an internal German issue, some German politicians were quick to try and create "normalization" of the compensation policy and to replace any officials who showed too much commitment to the victims' interests.[85] Among the officials who were in effect forced to retire was Otto Küster, who had headed the compensation department in Stuttgart, and who was perceived to be too generous.[86] However, Küster's retirement in 1954 brought no change in the discriminatory policy he established toward Gypsies, whereas Auerbach's death and Wanschura's retirement abandoned Gypsies to the arbitrariness and prejudice of their successors, who limited the recognition policy of their predecessors and denied Gypsies their eligibility to compensation.

In 1951, following a verdict of the Karlsruhe court in the matter of Birkenfelder versus the state of Württemberg-Baden,[87] Wilden and Küster issued another circular, E-41, which was intended for the district agency *(Landesbezirksstelle)* for compensation in Stuttgart and Karlsruhe. That circular instructed that claims for compensation for the incarceration of Gypsies who had stayed in the Government-General in Poland since their deportation in May 1940 be rejected, on the basis that their stay in Poland was not recognized as a political arrest.[88] The E-41 circular was also addressed to the office of criminal identification in Stuttgart, which investigated the reasons for the Gypsies' incarceration.

Taking his lead from previous instructions established in Germany since 1946 concerning the recognition of the Gypsy victims of Nazism, Küster established in the document that when investigating the eligibility of a Gypsy to compensation, not only previous indictments would be taken into account but also the question of whether the Gypsy was employed in a stable workplace at the time of his arrest. Küster and Wilden's attitude toward Gypsies was a mixture of prejudice and rigid formalism. In 1951 they personally handled the claims of Sinti from Freiburg, who were victims of enforced sterilization during the Third Reich. The way they dealt with these victims showed no expression of the attitude presented in the E-19 circular and again in the E-41 circular. Küster and Wilden recognized the claims of these Sinti, and they were compensated according to the compensation law. These authors of the E-19 circular did not try to dismiss the claims by arguing that the sterilization of these Sinti did not derive from racist motives but from eugenic motives. The compensation law regarded an enforced sterilization committed during the Third Reich as legal whenever the act was derived from eugenic motives according to the Law for Prevention of Offspring from People Suffering with Hereditary Illnesses (Gesetz für Verhütung erbkranken Nachwuchses), a Nazi law legislated on 14 July 1933.[89] In this case it was recognized that Gypsies whose racial persecution was not in doubt, and who further met the criteria demanded by the authorities, were indeed recognized as racial victims of the Nazis.

Not later than 1953, the compensation offices in Bremen and North Rhine–Westphalia also stopped recognizing survivors of the May 1940 deportation to Poland as being entitled to compensation for the denial of their freedom. The contents and style of two letters issued by the Bremen compensation office in June 1953 describe and explain these changes in policy. In early June 1953, Mr. Hennings, an official of the Bremen compensation office, replied to questions that the criminal police of the city had raised about the office's experience in compensating Gypsies. He claimed that even before publication of the compensation law in August 1949, payment to Gypsies had already begun, based on procedures for paying compensation for denial of freedom in Bremen, which had been published in March 1949. Hennings wrote that there was initially opposition to paying compensation to Gypsies who "stayed in the 'resettlement' areas in Poland." But the Organization of Former Victims of the Nazis had then yielded to the pressure by the American military government and paid compensation to Gypsies only on the grounds that they provided an affidavit. To undermine the legality of the Bremen compensation office's decision to compensate those who were deported in May 1940, Hennings told the criminal police that the decisions to compensate Gypsy victims was a decision of the ex-victims' organization that had been made under pressure of the military government and was not truly an official decision of the office at Bremen. Hennings said that any return of compensation money paid illegally to the state depended on the political situation.

What Hennings wrote was far from the truth. The question of the eligibility of those who were deported in May 1940 came up in Bremen only in January 1950, months after the annulment of the American military government there. In a letter Hennings sent to the compensation department of the Ministry of the Interior of North Rhine–Westphalia only three weeks after his letter to the criminal police, he did not repeat the above-described explanation of the policy concerning deported Gypsies. Apparently, the fact that the head of the addressed compensation department, Dr. Goldfarb, was Jewish meant Hennings was careful not to repeat the false claims he had made in his letter to the criminal police. This time Hennings argued that the Gypsies' compensation claims were accepted because the authorities, due to reasons prevalent at that time, had failed to investigate the Gypsies' living conditions in the camps in Poland, and the reasons for settling Gypsies (Umsiedlung), according to Hennings, were purely military.[90]

The problem that many Gypsies faced was that they could not meet the criteria necessary for recognition, and even recognition did not itself necessarily ensure appropriate compensation. The Gypsies' lack of financial resources meant they were often not able to hire proper legal representation, and in many cases they had to bargain with officials in the compensation offices about the size of the sums of money and the way in which they would be paid (a small monthly pension or a relatively large bulk sum). Karlo Hessdörfer, the former president of the Bavarian compensation office, argued that Gypsies often preferred to receive a bulk sum of a few thousand marks instead of a small monthly pension for the rest of their lives, the accumulated value of which would be much higher than the bulk sum offered. The late Paul Jochum, an attorney from Cologne who represented Gypsies in various matters, argued that the officials often encouraged them to make this choice.[91]

Cooperation between the different compensation offices and the "experts for Gypsy matters" was intensified in the early 1950s; written opinions by these experts were prepared at the request of compensation offices and courts that dealt with Gypsy claims. The compensation authorities looked for the most prominent Gypsy persecutors in the Third Reich in order to receive their opinion on the motives for the Nazi persecution of Gypsies.

In July 1956, the Bavarian compensation office approached Eva Justin, who was then working as a youth psychologist in the Frankfurt municipal health service. During the Third Reich, Justin had served as Ritter's devoted assistant and partner in preparing the racial hygiene opinions, on which basis Gypsies were to be sterilized and sent to concentration camps.[92] The Bavarian compensation office probably sought her opinion to clarify what the motives for sterilizing Gypsies were. The issue of the reasons behind the Third Reich sterilization policy was critical. Eugenic motives were perceived as legitimate by the compensation authorities, and the victims of such sterilization did not therefore receive any compensation. In contrast, victims who were sterilized by force for political, racial, or religious reasons were entitled to compensation according to the compensation law. The compensation office in Hamburg sought assistance in determining the Nazi motives by asking members of the criminal police, who had taken an active part in deporting Gypsies to camps.

In 1950, the Hamburg office personnel approached the criminal police to clarify the reasons for the Gypsies' deportation in May 1940. In September 1950 Otto Schmidt, at that time the head of the agency for collecting information about Gypsies (Zigeunernachrichtdienststelle) in Hamburg, replied: "As far as I remember, the resettlement of Gypsies in the Third Reich concerned prevention measures mainly intended against asocials."

In 1961, the Hamburg compensation office sought the opinion of Leo Karsten, who during the Third Reich had served as the head of the agency for Gypsy affairs (Dienststelle zur Zigeunerfragen) in the Reich's main office of criminal police (RKPA) in Berlin, an office that ceased to function after the defeat. Karsten also gave similar services to other compensation offices and to courts throughout Germany.[93] The written opinions that were prepared contained detailed personality evaluation and registration of previous convictions (if any), and clearly expressed a negative attitude toward Gypsies. Even in cases where the offenses had been very slight, such as fortune-telling (which was forbidden by the Nazis) and begging, the racial motive for persecution was denied to the claimant, and he was presented as an asocial and therefore not worthy of recognition as a victim. According to Hessdörfer, many written opinions contained the following sentence: "The racial persecution began only after the issuing of the Auschwitz decree [Auschwitz Erlass]" in January 1943. According to him, the vagrants' center *(Landfahrerzentrale)* in the Munich criminal police continued to submit such opinions until 1963.[94]

The recognition policy of the aid and compensation authorities in Germany toward the Gypsy victims of Nazism unfavorably discriminated against Gypsies from its first days, together with other groups of victims, which were not perceived as typical victims of Nazism. Since the Allies had stressed the racist nature of the Gypsies' persecution, the Gypsies' situation was better than the situation of other groups of victims, such as asocials, homosexuals, and others who were not recognized as victims at all. However, in comparison with other groups considered to be typical victims, Gypsies were discriminated against since special demands were placed on them as a condition for being recognized, demands that were not always relevant to the question of their eligibility. These demands derived from various reasons: sometimes from a rigid formalistic approach of the officials, which continued the tradition of the communal welfare policy in Germany and which did not take into consideration the Gypsies' unique problems; sometimes from Enlightened ideas, which sought to use the official recognition and the compensation money accompanying it as an incentive for the settlement and integration of Gypsies; and sometimes from a clear intention of the officials, which was supported by the former political prisoners, to limit and reduce the dimensions of recognition awarded to Gypsies, who were sweepingly regarded as asocial.

A rationalization was consolidated among the German officials, in which prejudice against Gypsies was entwined with a desire by officials to save government expenses for compensation payments. As long as Jewish senior officials operated in the FRG compensation authorities, they struggled against the German officials' position, both because they regarded it as inherently evil and because they regarded the attitude toward Gypsies as a possible criterion for future trends in the compensation policy toward Jews. After the retirement of these Jews in 1950, the attitude of the German officials prevailed, and the Gypsies' claims for compensation were rejected in most cases, leaving some Gypsies to turn to the courts in their pursuit of justice.

5

German Courts, Nazi Perpetrators, and Gypsy Victims

F ROM the late 1940s to the mid-1960s, the legal system of the Federal Republic of Germany (FRG) conducted an investigation into issues related to the Nazi persecution of Gypsies, in particular, the appeals for compensation by Gypsy survivors of Nazi persecution. In dealing with these questions, the courts often ruled in favor of the state, relying on a single Nazi document as the legal underpinning for its decisions.

Known as the Auschwitz decree (Auschwitz Erlass), this document (which was promulgated by the Reichsführer of the SS and the head of the German police, Heinrich Himmler, on 29 January 1943) ordered the deportation of most of the German Gypsies to the concentration camp at Auschwitz-Birkenau.[1] The postwar judicial system cited this decree in overruling the appeals of Gypsies who had been persecuted before January 1943. The document also was cited in dismissing the investigation conducted by the prosecution against the two most prominent "Experts on Gypsy Matters" in the Third Reich, Robert Ritter and his assistant Eva Justin.

AUSCHWITZ DECREE AND COMPENSATION OF GYPSY VICTIMS

The compensation laws enacted in Germany after 1945 recognized eligibility only for victims whose persecution derived from political, racial, or religious motives. Allegedly, then, Gypsies persecuted before the Auschwitz decree was published were not persecuted for these motives, so the compensation authorities did not recognize them as actual victims of Nazism. In trials conducted from 1950 to 1953, the courts concurred with the opinion of the compensation authorities and maintained that prior to the issuing of the Auschwitz decree the Nazi state did not take racially motivated measures against Gypsies. The racial nature of Himmler's decree has never been contested in court sentencing.[2] Some of the first commentaries on the Federal Compensation Law (BEG) supported a restrictive (nonracial) interpretation of earlier persecution of Gypsies prior to the Auschwitz decree. Two of the authors of these commentaries, Hans Wilden and Otto Küster, both senior officials in the compensation system of the FRG, had previous experience in this field. Their section about Gypsies in the 1955 commentary to the BEG began thus: "Since the beginning of time, Gypsies have been regarded by Western civilized nations *[Kulturvölker]* as a state plague *[Landplage]*. No one can claim that actions taken against them before 1933 constituted racial persecution. Gypsies' characters (antisocial behavior, crime, the wandering drive) were occasion for combating them."[3]

This declaration accepted at face value the Nazi regime's formal excuse for persecuting Gypsies. Basing their argument on the precedent of maltreatment of German Gypsies before 1933, Wilden and Küster argued that the decision to send those people to concentration and death camps was not racially inspired before 1943. Turning back Gypsy appeals in the 1950s against the authorities' refusal to recognize them as victims of Nazism, the courts repeatedly concluded that their racial persecution began only with the issuance of the Auschwitz decree.[4]

The facts show otherwise. Antecedents in German maltreatment of Gypsies notwithstanding, "racial" motives were interwoven with official Nazi policy toward Gypsies as early as 1936, when the commentary to the Nuremberg Laws was published and when racial motives were explicitly expressed by various decrees of the criminal police.[5] In the 1950s, the judicial system of the FRG acknowledged that the massive deportation of Gypsy families from Germany to Auschwitz beginning in 1943 was the result of racial motives. Among the German police experts and compensation authorities a more extremist interpretation was widespread: even after 1943, a few experts maintained, the persecution of Gypsies was not based on racial motives.[6]

The claim that the Nazi racial persecution of Gypsies actually began in 1943 was neither asserted nor mentioned in the 1950 discussions of the compensation authorities in the Federal Republic on the eligibility of Gypsies for compensation. The available evidence suggests that this argument had been raised for the first time between 1948 and 1950, during the prosecution investigation of Ritter. This claim subsequently appeared in a 1951 police newspaper article written by Rudolf Uschold, a Bavarian police expert on Gypsies.[7] Uschold had specialized in this field during the Third Reich, and, from 1946 to 1951, he remained active in the area as a member of the information agency concerning Gypsies (Nachrichtenstelle über Zigeuner) in Munich police headquarters. From 1950 to 1953 he appeared as an expert witness both during the Ritter investigation and in numerous eligibility appeals of Gypsies against the compensation authorities.[8] Uschold's view was not accepted by all of the police experts on Gypsy matters. As I have indicated, some of them even suggested that the whole persecution of Gypsies during the Third Reich was not racial at all.

The "post-1943" formula, then, occupied a middle ground between those who denied that Gypsies were persecuted on racial grounds and those who regarded Nazi treatment of Gypsies as analogous in motive to Nazi persecution of Jews. Senior Jewish officials among the compensation authorities of the FRG took the latter position. Constituting a compromise view between the police experts and the Jewish officials, the Auschwitz decree thus served as a watershed criterion to determine the eligibility of Gypsies for recognition as victims of Nazism. Thus, the survivors of the first deportation of German Gypsies to the Government-General of Poland in May 1940 (there were 2,330 Gypsies, only half of whom survived) were deprived of such status. By 1956, this approach was also adopted by the federal supreme court *(Bundesgerichthof;* BGH) of the FRG.

The court did not hesitate to apply this stricture in rejecting the appeal of a Gypsy who had been deported to Poland in May 1940. The man had challenged the compensation office for its refusal to recognize his confinement in Polish ghettoes and camps as racial persecution. In their verdict, the judges gave a strict interpretation of the Nazi terms, especially "resettlement" *(Umsiedlung),* thereby echoing the common position of the compensation authorities. Further, no attempt was made by the court to verify the squalid circumstances in which Gypsies deported to Poland had lived during this period (for example, by summoning witnesses who could describe the reality of life there).

The part of the written verdict that might have given rise to any perception of prejudice by the judges against Gypsies seemed carefully formulated to shield them from accusations of racism. Presented as an objective review of the historical and social background of the persecution of Gypsies in Germany, the ruling began with a description of the circumstances in which the image of Gypsies was consolidated within German culture, determining that the Gypsies' vagrant lifestyle was perceived by the settled society as unstable *(unstetes Leben).* This way of life, the verdict indicated, was associated with occupations such as palm reading, entertainment, and play, which "did not always enjoy much appreciation in the surrounding society." The judges emphasized that their finding did not constitute a moral criticism of Gypsies but, rather, was a mere reflection of public perception.

At a certain point, the ruling shifted from summarizing public opinion to citing pseudoscientific explanations from the racial-criminological literature, condemning Gypsies: "As most Gypsies opposed quitting their nomadic life and being integrated into the settled population, they were perceived as asocial. As experience shows, they tended toward crime, especially theft and fraud. They totally lack the moral instinct to respect the property of others, because as primitive people they are governed by unrestrained dominating instinct."[9] This verdict denied any possibility of granting compensation to Gypsies who had been persecuted before 1943.

In the face of this decision, Dr. Kurt May, a Jew who headed the central office of the United Restitution Organization (URO) in Frankfurt, was one of the few people in the FRG who worked intensively to revise the court's ruling. May regarded the ruling as a gross mistake, and he acted on several levels to correct it. He encouraged Hans Buchheim, a historian at the Institute for Contemporary History (IfZ) in Munich, to investigate the May 1940 Gypsy deportation to Poland and even assisted him in doing so. May sent letters and had discussions with representatives of the compensation bureau and with members of the political and the judicial systems.

Furthermore, he asked his friend, Franz Calvelli-Adorno, the president of the senate of the district court (*Oberlandesgericht;* OLG) in Frankfurt, to publish an article on the issue, a move that turned out to be of paramount importance.[10] May understood that to generate a revision in the supreme court ruling, he needed to recruit a member of the judicial system whose pro-Gypsy stance would not be based on self-interest, or what might perceived as such.

This was not the first time in post-1945 Germany that Jews had defended the rights of Gypsies to be compensated as victims of Nazi persecution. In 1950, Marcel Frenkel and Philip Auerbach, both senior officials in the compensation office in the FRG, protested against the position of their German colleagues in the coordination committee in denying eligibility for compensation to Gypsies. Their non-Jewish colleagues maintained that Gypsies had been persecuted not for racial motives but for asocial behavior *(Asozialität)* and crime. It was not incidental that the Jews, rather than the non-Jewish officials who dealt with these questions, demonstrated more sensitivity for the injustice done to Gypsies.

Without gainsaying moral concern, Jewish involvement with and concern for the discrimination against Gypsies seems to have derived largely

Jewish lawyer Dr. Kurt May, the director of the URO office in Frankfurt. (Tom Gross.)

from practical considerations, at least in the early 1950s. Auerbach worried that the denial of compensation for Gypsies on the pretext that their persecution by the Nazis was a legitimate action to eradicate crime, not a result of racial factors, might serve as a precedent to deny Jews compensation for the persecution they had suffered.[11] By the late 1950s this fear had dissipated, and May apparently acted primarily out of identification with Gypsies and in outrage against the injustice inflicted on them by the judicial system of the FRG.

In 1961 and under the advice of May, Calvelli-Adorno published a sharp criticism of the BGH's verdict, in which he invalidated the acceptability of the commonly advanced argument predicated on the perceived antisocial behavior of Gypsies. Calvelli-Adorno criticized the "anticipated collective identification" of Gypsies, based on "fixed and unchangeable racial properties," that "Gypsies are identical to asocials. . . . The injustice done to Gypsies must be defined as racial persecution. The individual Gypsy was treated as asocial only because he belonged to the Gypsy race. The membership was enough to differentiate him from the rest of the population and to subordinate him without investigation to illegal and cruel treatment."[12]

Publication of this article was an important contribution to the German discourse on Nazi persecution of Gypsies, a discourse that had been gaining momentum in the FRG press since the end of the 1950s.[13]

Moreover, it influenced the BGH's judges to revise their ruling. On 23 May 1963, reversing verdicts of the Cologne district court, the BGH ruled on the appeals of Gypsies who had fled Germany in 1939 after they had been examined by members of Robert Ritter's institute. The plaintiffs argued that the research conducted by Ritter and his subordinates should be regarded as racial persecution and that Gypsies were entitled to compensation. The supreme court accepted their arguments, and, for the first time, the German judicial system recognized Ritter's pseudoscientific activity as Nazi persecution. The court, two members of which had been judges in 1956, revised its previous decision that racial persecution of Gypsies began only in 1943 and ruled that its actual origins were in 1938.[14] Unfortunately, some of those who should have benefited from the revised ruling were no longer alive.

AUSCHWITZ DECREE AND THE PERSECUTORS

The offices of the public prosecutor *(Staatsanwaltschaft)* in the FRG initiated criminal investigation procedures against dozens of policemen, officials, and scientists, who had participated in the Nazi persecution of Gypsies during the Third Reich, but did not find it proper to bring most of them to trial.[15] Accordingly, let us now examine the investigation procedures employed in connection with two individuals who held key positions within the Nazi system, dealing with Gypsies: Robert Ritter and Eva Justin.

Ritter and Justin were scientists in the field of racial hygiene, known in English as "eugenics." This pseudoscientific discipline was internationally recognized by as a legitimate field of inquiry by the end of the nineteenth century, long before the Nazis came to power. Although neither Ritter nor Justin was a member of the National Socialist Party, their racial consciousness supplied the basis for their solid and enthusiastic cooperation with the regime.[16] Furthermore, they were integrated into the bureaucratic machinery of the Nazi state through their efforts to translate these radical racial ideas into the social policies of the Third Reich. Like the technocrats who consolidated the final solution to the "Jewish problem," the thinkers and designers of the final solution to the Gypsy problem *(die endgültige Lösung der Zigeunerfrage)* were "desk criminals" *(Schreibtischtäter)*, who themselves took no part in murdering or sterilizing Gypsies.

All of the racial researchers worked within the framework of the Racial Hygiene and Demographic Biology Research Unit (Rassenhygienische und Bevölkerungsbiologische Forschungsstelle), which operated from 1937 to 1944 under Ritter's direction in the health office of the Reich.[17] This unit cooperated closely with the Reich's criminal police department (RKPA) under the command of Arthur Nebe and with criminal police stations throughout Nazi Germany. Ritter and his assistants collected data from police files and church archives about Gypsies, as well as anthropological and genealogical data from the Gypsies themselves. The Gypsies did not respond willingly to these examinations of the racial researchers. Ritter and his colleagues tried to overcome their resistance with incentives, and also reportedly with threats and the exercise of brute force, under the protection of policemen who accompanied them.

The data collected by Ritter's team enabled the purported experts to prepare racial hygiene opinions about each of the approximately 24,000 Gypsies examined by mobile teams. The opinions that classified the extent of the Gypsies' "racial purity" were then submitted to the criminal police. Ritter had already argued in 1935 that experience showed that, in contrast to racially pure *(reinrassige)* Gypsies, Gypsy Mischlinge were clearly inclined toward crime and asociality. At that time, the only solution Ritter had foreseen for the Mischlinge population was mass sterilization and incarceration; however, it was not long before such a sentence for thousands of Mischlinge men, women, and children led directly to confinement in concentration camps and consequently to death by starvation, disease, and gas.

The decisions of the public prosecutor in Frankfurt to terminate the investigation procedures conducted against Ritter in 1950 and against Justin in 1960, and not to bring them to trial, were part of a broader pattern. The two educated defendants were regarded as people who had been thrown into an extreme situation by circumstances and who involuntarily had carried out their duties. Put another way, some German courts did not adjudge such crimes perpetrated during the Nazi period as having been committed out of free will but, rather, as actions forced upon the actors by a dictatorship. Therefore, no personal responsibility for their deeds was adduced, and no accountability was imposed.

Their Gypsy victims, however, faced quite a different attitude from the FRG's justice system. Gypsies who had agreed to be sterilized (a term some testified that they had not fully understood), under threat of deportation to the concentration camps, were regarded as responsible for their own sterilization.[18]

In addition to his work at the Reich's health office, beginning in 1942 Ritter also headed the Institute for Criminal Biology of the security police *(Sicherheitspolizei)*. There he helped design (and I believe that the evidence shows that he did so enthusiastically) the Gypsy policy of the Third Reich and thus played a central role in the Gypsies' fate.

His future assistant, Eva Justin, was a nurse in the children's ward of the psychiatric clinic of Tübingen University, where Ritter served as a psychiatrist and where he met her in 1934. When Ritter was appointed

Robert Ritter, with Eva Justin helping him, taking a blood sample from a Gypsy, late 1930s.
(BA Koblenz.)

in 1936 to head the racial hygiene research unit of the Reich's health office in Berlin, he brought Justin and some other Tübingen colleagues along with him In 1943, Ritter helped Justin earn a Ph.D. from Humboldt University in Berlin.[19] Justin took anthropological measurements and blood samples from Gypsies. She also signed for the criminal police hundreds of racial opinions, in which she determined that many Gypsies were Mischlinge and thus sealed their fate of sterilization or deportation to concentration camps. In her doctoral thesis she recommended the sterilization of all Gypsy children who were removed from their parents' homes and had received a German education since she thought that they were hopeless and could not be improved.[20] In so doing, Justin had a hand in the fate of many Gypsies.

In October 1948, the public prosecutor in Frankfurt initiated an investigation of Ritter who, since having undergone the denazification process in 1947, had served as the principal youth physician in the city's municipal health service. The investigation was opened after a complaint was filed by the state commissar for those been persecuted for political, racial, and religious reasons in Bavaria. The basis of this complaint was evidence provided by German Gypsies who had come to know Ritter in the course of his activity during the Third Reich.[21] The principal claim against Ritter was that his research and other actions had been instrumental in the compulsory sterilization of a large number of Gypsies and, similarly, had been instrumental in the deportation of thousands to concentration camps during the war, making him partially responsible for their deaths.

Other sections charged Ritter with physically injuring the Gypsies he examined for research purposes and with showing cruelty toward them. He also was accused of concealing during his denazification information on his alleged membership in the SS. The investigation lasted for almost two years, during which time dozens of witnesses were interviewed throughout Germany. In August 1950, the chief prosecutor in Frankfurt, Dr. Kosterlitz, decided to terminate the investigation and close the file; in his opinion, the results did not warrant preparing an indictment of Ritter.[22]

A few years after Ritter's death in 1950, the investigation file was officially destroyed. Of the entire file, only the summary of the investigation and the decision of the chief attorney to close it remained, so that it absolutely was no longer possible to examine in full either the prosecutor's evidence or Ritter's statement. However, it is possible that a copy of the file survived, in that in the summary of the investigation of Eva Justin, conducted in 1959, it is implied that the prosecutors were familiar with the evidence in the Ritter file.[23]

In February 1959, less than nine years after the investigation of Ritter had been terminated, the pattern repeated itself when the chief prosecutor

Eva Justin taking anthropological measurements from an old Gypsy woman, late 1930s. (BA Koblenz.)

in Frankfurt opened a criminal investigation against Eva Justin on the charge of abetting mass murder. Since her completion of the denazification process in 1948, Justin had worked in the health services office in Frankfurt as a psychologist for children and youth.[24] In late 1958, Sigmund S. Wolf, a linguist and the compiler of a Romany dictionary, attacked Justin for the work she had done during the Third Reich. The most severe accusation was that she conducted research and catalogued, for the Reich's main security office (RSHA), the personal data of about 20,000 Gypsies, with the aim of physically eliminating them. She was also charged with spreading the notion of the advisability of sterilizing Gypsies, pressuring Gypsies to accept voluntary sterilization, and falsely testifying in Ritter's denazification procedure.[25]

The resolution that the racial persecution of Gypsies began in 1943, the year that Himmler published the Auschwitz decree, heavily influenced the decision of the public prosecutor in Frankfurt to terminate investigations of Ritter and Justin. In each case, prosecutors adopted the defendant's claim of innocence on the basis that Ritter and his team completed their research on the Gypsy issue before 1943, thereby making it possible to argue that their activity should not be regarded as racial persecution.[26] This is a false claim. Today we know of many of Ritter's racial opinions that were written after 1943.

Ritter had argued that he did not know to what extent, if any, the research material he collected was used in the framework of the grand deportation of German Gypsies to Auschwitz-Birkenau that had begun in March 1943, and thus he strongly denied having anything to do with that deportation. The prosecution also accepted the formalistic claim that since the criminal police did not publish the Auschwitz decree, Ritter could not have known about its existence. He further asserted that he had become aware of the deportations to Auschwitz only after the war.[27]

It is worth stressing, too, that ten years later the same argument was instrumental in terminating the investigation of Justin. The prosecutor concluded that the racial-biological opinions about Gypsies, which Ritter and his team prepared until 1942, had served as the basis of the Law concerning the Gypsies *(Zigeunergesetz)*, which was to be enacted together with the Law concerning Asocials.[28] The prosecutor's assertion that the law's intent was to regulate the lives of Gypsies in the Reich in order to prevent additional mixing of blood distinctly proved the researcher's awareness of the racial nature of this law, which was not different from the 1935 Law for the Protection of German Blood and Honor, one of the Nuremberg Laws.

With this legal formalism the prosecution ignored the illegal nature of the Law concerning the Gypsies. It also determined that Justin could not have known, when preparing the opinions for Gypsies, that they would serve as a basis for illegal actions within the framework of Himmler's subsequent 1943 Auschwitz decree, thus inflicting death and sterilization on many Gypsies.[29] In accord with this formalistic approach, the prosecution excluded Ritter and his institute from the list of criminal organizations that shaped the "Gypsy policy" of the Third Reich.

In the course of the investigation of Justin, more than 20,000 personal files of Gypsies were collected from the various branches of the criminal police throughout the FRG.[30] Had these files been examined during the investigation of Ritter, his opinions, written after the publication of the Auschwitz decree, would have surfaced. However, according to the prosecution, not even one file containing racial opinions signed by Justin was located. Today we know that Justin signed hundreds of racial opinions *(gutachtliche Äusserungen)* on Gypsies.[31]

PERPETRATORS AS ANTI-NAZI FIGHTERS

An apologetic composition that Ritter wrote in 1947, when he applied for a post in the municipal health service in Frankfurt, can help us reconstruct his lost statement of defense. In this essay Ritter presented his own version of the Nazi persecution of Gypsies, as well as his part in designing the Reich's Gypsy policy.

This document also helps clarify the context and meaning of various assertions in the investigation's summary. For example, in the summary, in addition to the reference to the head of the criminal police, Arthur Nebe, the prosecutor mentioned that Nebe was executed for complicity in the 20 July 1944 attempt on Hitler's life.[32] Prima facie, this information is irrelevant to the issue in the summary of Ritter's investigation. The emphasis on Nebe's opposition to Hitler, while ignoring his murderous role as the commander of Einsatzgruppe B, sought to explain that both Nebe's and Ritter's treatments of the Gypsy problem should be regarded as an integral part of their opposition to Hitler and Nazism.

The prosecutor accepted Ritter's main rejoinder that he should not be held responsible for the fate of Gypsies in the Third Reich and that the fields in which he engaged, racial hygiene and criminal biology, were legitimate scientific areas that had no connection to the racial ideology of Nazism.[33] In short, Ritter's defense presented him as a persistent opponent to Nazism, even before Hitler came to power. By 1947, when Ritter attended his denazification in Frankfurt, he presented two genuine notes he had written for a local newspaper in Cologne, which had published them in 1931. In these notes he criticized Nazism from a conservative rightist viewpoint, accusing it of mobilizing youth by means of hatred, terror, and murder.[34] Ritter claimed as well that in early 1932 he had sent President Paul von Hindenburg a letter warning him against Hitler.

Ritter insisted that out of a sense of political responsibility as a psychiatrist, he had tried to bring to the attention of the Reich president Hitler's "doubtful nature, his resistance to orderly work, his susceptibility to mood swings, his ruthlessness and the unfair conspiracies deriving from this restlessness."[35] No copy of this alleged letter to Hindenburg survives.

Ritter tied his positions and recommendations on the Gypsy issue in the Third Reich to his alleged opposition to Nazism. An important layer in his defense was his own evidence that in the first International Congress for Population Science, which had convened in Berlin in 1935, he had already heard that the SS planned "to solve the Gypsy problem in one blow."[36] Ritter added later that the speakers, whose names he did not mention, belonged to the SS offices of racial policy *(die rassenpolitischen Ämter)* and that they referred to a plan to put all Gypsies on a ship and sink it in the Mediterranean. Ritter recounted this story in a letter written during the period of investigation.[37] This argument that as early as 1935 the intention of the SS was to murder all Gypsies enabled Ritter to present his own recommendations in the above-mentioned congress to sterilize and incarcerate in family camps the asocials among Gypsies and the Gypsy Mischlinge (these two groups were allegedly inclined to become criminals and constituted, according to his earlier research, more than 90 percent of Gypsies in Germany), as a humanistic and anti-Nazi attempt to frustrate the murderous conspiracy and to solve the problem in a fair way. He personally spoke in the congress about reducing the Gypsy population.[38]

Ritter argued that when he heard of these murderous intentions he decided to do everything he could to prevent any unfair and inhumane treatment of Gypsies. The prosecutor's office accepted this argument, as well as Ritter's implied claim that his and Nebe's actions concerning the Gypsy issue in the Third Reich were important aspects of their opposition to Hitler's regime. A few books were published after the war by former Gestapo members who were stung by being presented as bloodthirsty and brutal barbarians. In their search for legitimization, Nebe served as an antithesis to the negative image of the Gestapo and other "law and order" organs of the Nazi state. He was presented as a professional policeman, who contributed to the modernization of criminal investigation techniques in Germany and as an opponent of Nazism.[39]

Ritter was attentive to the need prevailing among the majority of the German public, and apparently also among the members of the prosecutor's office, to believe that the Nazi system included some decent people, too. According to his version of the story, after meeting Nebe, Ritter felt that Nebe was open to human concerns and that the police official could be of assistance in preventing brutal actions against Gypsies. According to Ritter, he laid before Nebe his fears of the "fanatics," and the latter responded approvingly, apparently proposing that Ritter conspire with him against those who wanted to exterminate all Gypsies.[40]

The prosecution accepted Ritter's argument that Nebe was the one who initiated the recording, registration, and collection of data on all Gypsies and vagrants inside the Reich. Ritter's own correspondence from 1935 onward with the German Research Community (Deutsche Forschung Gemeinschaft; DFG) implies that he supported this action; correspondence from 1939, if not earlier, expressed that support openly.[41]

VICTIMS AND PERPETRATORS AT GERMAN COURTS

The way the Frankfurt chief prosecutors handled the investigation files against Ritter and Justin, despite the decade that lay between them, was virtually identical. First, they rejected the respondents' responsibilities for the direct implications of their deeds. Instead, the accountability for persecution of Gypsies was fully attributed to Himmler, who promulgated the Auschwitz decree in early 1943, as well as to anonymous figures defined as "fanatic SS people," who wanted to brutally exterminate all Gypsies in Germany. Some charges leveled against Ritter and Justin attributed blame to their colleagues and to individuals high in the Nazi hierarchy who already were dead at the time of the investigation. Some of the Gypsy accusations about Ritter's brutality were thought more properly to be actions attributable to his former colleague, Karl Moravek, who was killed in the war. Later, Justin's alleged role in the dissemination of the notion of sterilization of Gypsies was attributed to Ritter, who had died several years earlier.[42]

The respondents themselves were presented as scientists who tried to legitimately solve a difficult social problem. After the prosecution examined Ritter's writings about Gypsies, it accepted his nonverifiable and impudent assertion that his scientific publications constituted proof of his revulsion with any radical racial doctrine of the Nazi regime.[43] The prosecution's position ignored Ritter's explicit writings, however, as well as the basic racial assumptions that were interwoven in his theories about Gypsies. Moreover, their position reveals their uncritical opinion of the whole notion of racial hygiene and the "solutions" its experts recommended for Gypsies and other fringe groups in German society. In both investigations, the prosecution preferred the evidence of Ritter and Justin, their colleagues in the institute, and the criminal police over that of the Gypsy victims.

In Ritter's investigation, the prosecution even questioned the possibility of reaching a verdict on the basis of Gypsy-supported evidence, a position based on the learned opinion of the accused himself. As evidence that Gypsies were unreasonable, the prosecutor presented one Gypsy man's claim that Ritter had beaten up his brother-inlaw, as well as the testimony of a Gypsy woman that Ritter addressed her in a vulgar and humiliating manner: "It is hard to believe that an educated man like the defendant was able to resort to such ill-treatment."[44]

Ritter built his case around "scientific" literature, published before the Nazis came to power, and which was thus considered to be free of racism. His position, furthermore, was supported by Rudolf Uschold, the policeman who not only shared Ritter's perceptions but also expressed them publicly in magazines on police issues.[45]

The summary of the public prosecutor's argument implied, too, that he accepted Ritter's contention that Gypsies, most of whom were illiterate, could not distinguish between reality and imagination and that the asocials among Gypsies believed wrongly that Ritter was responsible for the death of their family members in the concentration camps and therefore were prepared to accuse him falsely. Ritter submitted to the prosecutor racial heredity opinions about the families of some of the witnesses that had been prepared by people from his own institute during the Nazi regime.

In the end, the evidence of several Gypsy witnesses, including family members who initiated the investigation, was disqualified by the prosecution on the grounds of their criminal past.[46]

The policy of the legal system toward the Nazi persecution of Gypsies was strongly influenced by the negative image of this minority, an image rooted in German culture. A collection of citations from literature on Gypsies (very possibly compiled by an assistant on orders of the compensation board [Entschädigungskammer] in the Munich court in 1951 in a claim by a Gypsy woman against the state of Bavaria), revealed the hostile attitude toward Gypsies that prevailed in the judicial system. This collection, which to all appearances was oriented toward and prepared in accordance with the jurist instructions, looked to contemporary as well as classic literature and, not surprisingly, found "scientific" support for the argument that Gypsies were asocial and deeply involved in crime. Most of the citations, in fact, came from criminological literature that had been influenced by the racial ideas of the Third Reich. Amazingly, one of them was an article by Robert Ritter.

Citing Heinrich Grellmann's classic 1787 work on Gypsies, the anonymous collector chose the parts that reflected negative attitudes toward Gypsies. In the spirit of the Enlightenment, however, Grellmann called for integrating Gypsies into the state and making them useful citizens. By contrast, only a few lines from Martin Block's less biased book, a nonracist (although paternalistic) study, were cited.[47] Thus it was not just the Nazis who preferred racial explanations for the Gypsy phenomenon; these ideas preceded Nazism and were widely popular in German culture, and the entries on Gypsies in the German encyclopedias since the time of Weimar supply irrefutable proof for this claim.

STERILIZING GYPSIES AS AN UNPUNISHABLE ACT

During the investigation of Ritter and Justin, the prosecution apparently intentionally obscured the significant difference between the illegal sterilization of Gypsies during the Third Reich and the sterilization performed according to the 1933 Law for Prevention of Offspring from People Suffering with Hereditary Illnesses (Gesetz für Verhütung erbkranken Nachwuchses).[48]

The related judicial decisions that were consolidated in postwar Germany determined that the above-mentioned law was not a typical Nazi law but should be understood in light of the perceptions that already guided German legislators before 1933, as well as of parallel legislation in other countries. This ruling ignored the fact that since 1924 Hitler had adopted the principles of racial hygiene theory and made them an integral part of Nazi ideology. It also denied that the majority of Weimar legislators who tried to initiate legislation in the spirit of 1933 law were primarily members of the National Socialist Party or other radical rightist parties.[49] This ruling further dismissed any possibility of indicting physicians who were involved in carrying out this law. The British Martial Law and the Governing Council of the Allies did not cancel it, but the courts for hereditary health, which were the relevant ruling bodies, were not reestablished after 1945, and so decrees of sterilization were no longer issued in Germany.

The legal situation regarding compulsory sterilization of Gypsies and Jews for racial motives, however, was entirely different. Doctors who participated in compulsory sterilization on racial grounds were severely punished by the Allies for crimes against humanity and for causing injury to their victims. The prosecutors accepted Ritter's claim that he supported sterilization only in accordance with the law; in so doing, they obscured the inherently illegal nature of the sterilization of Gypsies. The legal authorities of the Third Reich already knew that applying the law for the prevention of hereditary diseases to the sterilization of Gypsies was illegal.[50] In cases when sterilization of Gypsies was performed under the authority of that law and in some measures of accord with the procedure defined therein, there was a substantial deviation from the provisions of the law because Gypsies did not voluntarily agree to the sterilization but succumbed to coercion, threats, and sometimes even force.[51] Likewise, the sterilizations were not performed to prevent hereditary illnesses, according to the provisions of the law, but were undertaken from racial considerations. The very classification of a person as Mischling labeled him as inclining toward criminal behavior and brought with it a sentence of sterilization.

The prosecution chose not to comply with the above distinction, the ruling made in Germany at the time, between these two categories of sterilization during the Third Reich, and regarded the sterilization of Gypsies as a legal act. The prosecution argued that as long as Ritter sought to implement this law for the sake of preventing crime by asocials and asocial Mischlinge, his perceptions should be regarded as legally sufficient and should not be denounced by any court. With this argument, the prosecution transformed what should have been an indictment of crimes against humanity, committed under the inspiration of a racial ideology, into a legal action that even amounted to a demonstration of humane responsibility toward future generations.

To repeat, then, the prosecution accepted Ritter's claim that resorting to sterilization during the Third Reich was a legitimate method of combating crime and that these methods allegedly were limited only to a group of Gypsy Mischlinge, who were inclined toward crime because of hereditary asocial characteristics these "defectives" had inherited from their non-Gypsy ancestors.[52] With their semantics, Ritter and the prosecution conveyed the impression that the target population for sterilization and confinement was only a minority of the Gypsies, while, according to Ritter's own classification, the asocial Mischlinge constituted more than 90 percent of Gypsies in the Reich. In 1947, Ritter wrote that the number of pure Gypsies in the territory of the Reich did not exceed 4,000.[53] All the remaining Gypsies in the Reich, more than 20,000 people, were intended for sterilization or incarceration in concentration camps. We need not quibble here over the mathematics of the few percentage points; the principle is clear enough.

During its investigation of Justin, the prosecution expressed a similar attitude toward the sterilization of Gypsies. In late 1943, Justin had submitted a report about a Gypsy who claimed that his 1941 classification by Ritter's institute was incorrect; he was not, he insisted, a Gypsy Mischling, and he objected to undergoing sterilization. Justin determined that there was no reason to change the designation. The prosecutor stated his opinion that Justin had indeed assisted in an attempt to cause severe physical injury, but he felt that no legal action should be taken against her, inasmuch as the expected punishment would be imprisonment for not more than six months. Moreover, because seventeen years had elapsed since the commission of the offense, it was entirely possible that even that punishment might be halved.

The prosecutor also found grounds for reducing the punishment on the basis of Justin's youth and inexperience (Justin was thirty-five years old in 1943) and the supposition that she was subject to the full influence of her teacher, Robert Ritter. Further, during the investigation she had disassociated herself from her previous conceptions.[54]

The prosecution accepted without reservation Justin's version of another one of her recommendations to sterilize a Gypsy Mischling woman who wanted to marry a German. Justin argued that there were three reasons to sterilize the woman. First, the sterilization was supposed to overcome the prohibition set by the Nuremberg Laws on marriages between Germans and non-Aryans. Second, since the girl had grown up among Germans, she could not go back to her original Gypsy family. Third, since the girl's relatives were asocial, it was possible that her descendants would also be asocial, and thus her sterilization should be regarded as a preventive measure. The prosecutor accepted Justin's arguments and concluded that without sterilization, the life and fate of this girl in the Third Reich would have been threatened. In this statement he sanctioned the implied argument of Ritter's investigation that, in recommending the sterilization of Gypsies, Ritter and Justin in fact protected the asocial among them from a much more brutal fate than that planned for them by the Nazis.[55]

The demonstrated attitude of the judicial system of the Federal Republic and in the prosecution of those responsible for persecuting and murdering Gypsies in the Third Reich reflected its general attitude with regard to all acts of genocide committed during the Nazi regime, including the extermination of the European Jewry.[56] In the 1950s and 1960s, the legal system of the FRG was an integral part of the civil service that remained from the Nazi regime, and it continued to function in the post-Nazi period without many significant changes in personnel.[57] During the Third Reich, these people played a central role in legitimizing the regime's criminal policy and, in effect, acted as accomplices to its crimes. According to Jörg Friedrich, the attitude of the postwar German judges and prosecutors toward their defendants reflected the attitude toward their own deeds in the Nazi regime, such that many of these bureaucrats identified with the defendants and the "problematic" situation in which they found themselves.

The decision to terminate the investigation of these two racial researchers reveals a conflict. On the one hand, there was the prosecutors' understanding of and perhaps even identification with the defendants and their situation. On the other, there was the need to disassociate themselves from the Nazi crimes brought upon them by the political culture in the FRG and their status as officials in the new democratic German state. The limited publication of their decisions, and the legal protection accorded their writers, almost afforded an "intimate" character to the rulings of the courts. In turn, this enabled bureaucrats, in their references to the Nazi crimes, to deviate from the rules of public expression on Nazism prescribed in the political culture of the FRG. The language of the rulings and the prosecution's decisions included many characteristics of the semipublic postwar German discourse on Nazi crimes, the public voicing of which was taboo and was usually conducted at home or in the pub.[58]

Yet Friedrich's explanation is only partial, as there was no substantial change in the attitude of the prosecution in the FRG toward racial researchers of the Third Reich, even in the 1980s, when the key positions in the system were largely transferred to a generation that had no personal responsibility for the system's activities during the Nazi regime. In 1985 the prosecution in Stuttgart terminated investigation procedures conducted against two of Ritter's colleagues, Prof. Sophie Ehrhardt and Dr. Adolf Würth, following a complaint submitted by the Gypsy organization, Union of German Sinti (Verband Deutscher Sinti). The two were accused of offenses similar in severity to those attributed to Justin.[59] Although legally it would have been difficult for the prosecution to prove that the opinion Ehrhardt and Würth prepared might prove their responsibility for assisting in murdering Gypsies, the way in which the investigation was terminated is reminiscent of the prosecutor's approach in Justin's case: the defendants were exempted from any guilt.

In the decision to terminate the investigation, the prosecutor argued that the defendants' participation in Ritter's research was a legitimate scientific activity.[60] The prosecutor further relied, without any reservation, on allegedly objective opinions of two anthropologists whose work can easily be read as racially biased. One, Hans Jürgens, even published a book in 1961 in which one perceives the spirit of racial hygiene; it dealt with asociality as a biological and sociobiological problem. (Under the influence of the denazification policy established by the Allies in occupied Germany, the term *Sozialbiologie* replaced the illegitimate term *Rassenbiologie*.) Obscuring that author's approach, the prosecutor emphasized that Jürgens's family was persecuted by the Third Reich.[61] In the decision to terminate the investigation, it would have been possible to relate in an entirely different way to the deeds of the accused, even if the prosecutor were unable, as he claimed, to bring them to trial. The prosecutor's opinion explicitly stated that there was a serious intention in the 1930s to prevent the biological production of Gypsies, and to do so by sterilization (leading inevitably to their collective extinction),[62] which was clearly an illegal intention. In Ritter's file in the DFG, published not later than 1984, as well as in some of his articles, evidence indicated that the aim of the research on Gypsies, in which Würth and Ehrhardt took part, was to give scientific legitimization to the idea of using sterilization for solving the problem of the asocials.[63]

All of Ritter's partners in the Gypsy research project were familiar with his scientific work and knew that Ritter believed that asociality was a direct consequence of intermingling of races. They must also have been aware that Gypsies classified as Mischlinge, through information extracted from those individuals, were intended for sterilization. In light of the preceding discussion, it is hard to see how anyone could doubt that Würth and Ehrhardt knowingly participated in acts that were designed to carry out a criminal plan for mass sterilization of the German Gypsies.

One possible conclusion is that the prosecution in effect lent itself to the acquittal of accomplices to what others would call crime. It also expressed a myth that in time became part of collective German memory. According to this myth, the Nazi upper ranks alone initiated the crimes, and the SS hangmen alone performed them. In this way, the army, the public administration, the scientific community, and, of course, the wider public had little or nothing to do with the Nazi crimes. This myth was generated in the political culture of postwar Germany under the inspiration of the Allies' reeducation policy and in face of the psychological difficulty of coping with the scope of the crimes and the extent of civil involvement in their initiation. The attitude of the system's bureaucrats revealed some of the denial mechanisms through which postwar German society coped with the wide dimensions of public collaboration in the crimes of the Nazi regime.

This myth also made it easier for Germans to endure the guilt the Allies' propaganda mechanisms threw at them during the short period of denazification. While it could be argued that all Germans were collectively responsible for the horrors, the myth created a partition between the Nazi regime and civil society.

The politicians and the bureaucrats of the Federal Republic of Germany believed, in contrast to the Allies' denazification policy, that the normal functioning of the new state apparatus depended not on the purging without compromise of all officials who took part in the Nazi crimes but, rather, on obscuring the deep involvement of officials and civil servants in planning and organizing the crimes.[64] Transforming this myth into a collective memory of the German consciousness ensured that it became entrenched in the next generation.

6

Effect of Nazism and Denazification on Attitudes toward Gypsies

ATTITUDE OF GERMAN SOCIETY TOWARD GYPSIES AFTER 1945

THE mass murder of Gypsies by the Nazis did not lead to any substantial change in attitudes toward them by ordinary Germans after 1945. Nor were the Allies' military governments particularly interested in the attitude of the German population toward Gypsies. The denazification policy they established concentrated mainly on uprooting antisemitism and racism in general from public discourse, and it did not deal specifically with the antigypsyism that was then prevalent in Germany. The explicit failure on the part of the Allied military governments in occupied Germany to refer to the Gypsy persecution in the crucial years when the new political culture was being consolidated in Germany contributed to the fact that persecution of Gypsies, in contrast to the Jewish Holocaust, was not perceived by the German public as a political issue.

While the attitude toward Jews became a central criterion for measuring the state of democracy in the FRG,[1] the question of attitudes toward the Gypsies remained in the margins. Only gradually, from the late 1950s on, did recognition of the Gypsy as a victim of Nazism begin to penetrate the consciousness of the enlightened strata in Germany, and only then did the victim motif become a part of the Gypsy image. Meanwhile, antigypsyism and the romanticizing of Gypsies, with their varied layers, continued to exist. The most salient expressions of Gypsy romanticization in German popular culture during the 1950s and 1960s were pictures of Gypsy women dressed in a Spanish style and communicating eroticism, which were sold in the picture departments of large department stores and were even named by the public after one of them, "Die Karstadtzigeunerin." These pictures were particularly popular with the lower middle class, which used them to decorate their apartments. Also, Günter Grass hints at this phenomenon in his novel *The Tin Drum (Die Blechtrommel),* as he describes the artist Kuchen, who "was from the successful and well-sold Gypsy period" and whose only motif was the "black Gypsy."[2]

One of the most popular and successful musical hits in the FRG in 1967 was the song "Gypsy Boy" ("Zigeunerjunge"), as recorded by Alexandra (Doris Treitz-Nefedov). This song concentrated all the romantic motifs and stereotypes associated with Gypsies, which, along with its sentimental tune, contributed to its popularity. The Gypsies are described in this song in a nostalgic manner, according to the traditional romantic stereotypes, as happy, colorful, figures, who play, laugh, and dance around the bonfire at night. The song brings in the first person a story about a woman who, as a girl, fell in love with a young Gypsy who had come to town with a Gypsy caravan. The song ends by her discovering after a few days that the Gypsies left town.

> Zigeunerjunge, Zigeunerjunge
> Wo bist Du, Wo sind eure Wagen,
> Doch es blieb alles leer
> Und Mein Herz wurde schwer.[3]
>
> [Gypsy boy, Gypsy boy
> Where are you, Where are your wagons,
> Yet everything remained empty
> And my heart broke.]

With these lines, songwriter Hans Blum aimed to express a disappointed childhood love. There was certainly no hint of this romantic longing at Auschwitz.

Romantic motifs also appeared in German film adaptations of Gypsy musicals in the 1950s, and some scenes in films of the 1970s also included Gypsy figures such as *The Girl from Hof (Das Mädchen vom Hof)* and *The Large Flutter (Die grosse Flatter).*[4]

However, both the traditional romantic motifs and the antigypsy motifs remained. The old stereotypes were sometimes updated to fit in with the period, but they did not change in substance. The only limits placed were on blatant antigypsy expressions that were associated with the Nazi murder. An article in the *Frankfurter Rundschau* dealt with the Gypsies: "Today they no longer engage in the horse trade, but nevertheless they

Typical Gypsy woman, the so-called *Karstadtzigeunerin*.

have stayed in horse power; namely, they frequently appear as dealers of used cars and go on behaving according to their motto, 'Make new of the old,' as in the past, when they dealt with horses, when a limping worthless horse would within a few hours become full of energy."[5] There is still evidence that blatant antigypsy attitudes, similar to the parallel antisemitism, were voiced openly and explicitly not only around the regular customers' table *(Stammtisch)* in the pub. However, unlike the antisemitic discourse, these attitudes were expressed also in semipublic forums, which were closed to the wider public and the media, such as Landtag committees or government and local authority offices. Due to the delegitimization of these attitudes after denazification, these opinions were not publicly expressed and were probably even censored out of the minutes when they were too blatant.[6]

A comparison between the attitude expressed toward Gypsies in closed discussions on the vagrants law in the Bavarian Landtag committees in the early 1950s and the open debate on the issue that took place in the Landtag plenary session indicates the existence of different patterns of discourse about Gypsies within these two frameworks. While the committees held an intimate discourse, which expressed the authentic attitudes and even racist opinions toward Gypsies, the plenary session, which was open to the media and the public reflected the internalization of the prohibitions imposed by the Allies on the expression of racist and antisemitic views, and the beginning of making discriminating expressions toward Gypsies taboo in the political culture of the FRG. In the Landtag committee, Karl Weishäupl, the Social Democrat member who sought to settle the Gypsies and integrate them into society, still did not refrain from defaming them. He labeled them rabble *(Gesindel)* and portrayed all Gypsies as a delinquent group, supporting itself by theft, begging, and compensation *(Wiedergutmachung)* payments as victims of Nazi persecution.[7] Not one of the committee members protested against the pejorative comments about Gypsies because within the context of that closed forum they were perceived as legitimate.

The government's representatives also expressed themselves even more blatantly. Arthur Kääb, from the Bavarian Ministry of the Interior, explicitly stated in the committee that Gypsies were asocial, like work shys, and that their official occupations in trade were only a cover for criminal activity.[8] This defamation was also voiced without anyone protesting. In contrast, in the discussions of the bill in the Landtag plenary session, no such discriminatory expressions were heard. The process of making the public expression of discrimination against the Gypsies taboo within the political culture of the FRG, therefore, had already begun in the early 1950s. However, this taboo was only a pale reflection of that imposed in postwar Germany—one against any discrimination or discriminating statement against Jews.

The American military government conducted public opinion polls in occupied Germany. These polls aimed at measuring antisemitic, racist, and non-democratic trends in Germany. Since OMGUS did not attach much importance to German attitudes about Gypsies, it did not examine this question in its polls, and, until the 1990s, the German research institutes, which continued to follow up German prejudices against foreigners, also ignored the question of German attitudes toward Gypsies.

Public opinion polls conducted in Germany after 1945 that did deal with Gypsies concentrated on the question of the German willingness to live in a neighborhood with Gypsies. Their results indicate a high degree of constancy in the German population's attitudes toward Gypsies, as reflected in complaints to the authorities and letters to the local press, during the second half of the nineteenth century up until the Third Reich.[9] Apparently, despite the far-reaching political and social changes that took place during this period among both Germans and Gypsies, no substantial change occurred in the attitude of the German population toward Gypsies, who remained outcasts and a rejected group.

PUBLIC OPINION POLLS ON GYPSIES AND "FOREIGNERS"

The first public opinion poll on the attitude of the German public toward Gypsies was conducted by Lukrezia Jochimsen in Hildesheim in the early 1960s.[10] This primary study was based on too small a sample to constitute a representative pattern of the whole population of the FRG, but its results do accord with the results of larger public opinion polls that have been conducted in Germany with great frequency since 1990, when a wave of Eastern European Roma began to arrive.

Opinion polls about Gypsies that were taken from the early 1960s through the mid-1990s unanimously reveal that Gypsies are the people the Germans most wish to reject. In Jochimsen's first public opinion poll in the early 1960s, about 65 percent of the 177 respondents said they did not want Gypsies residing in their country. A substantial gap was revealed between the rates of rejection with regard to Gypsies and the next category, "blacks" (about 30 percent). Italians were rejected by about 30 percent, Indians by 23 percent, and the French by about 20 percent. The rate of rejection concerning Jews was 21 percent. Only slightly fewer than 10 percent of the respondents said they had no reservations about Gypsies.[11]

A further poll conducted by Jochimsen in 1966 yielded similar results. More than 80 percent of the 160 adult respondents rejected Gypsies, while only 10 percent were free of any negative attitude toward them. About 83 percent of the respondents supported a total isolation of Gypsies. With regard to rejection by the respondents, the Gypsies occupied the first place, before blacks and Italians.[12]

Only since 1990 have public opinion institutes in Germany begun to examine these opinions more carefully. The results of a public opinion poll conducted by the Emnid Research Insitute at the end of 1990, in both parts of the newly reunited Germany, were published in the *Spiegel Spezial* magazine. Germans were required to rate their opinions of eight other peoples, on a scale ranging from +5 to −5; the Gypsies received the most negative rating (−1.5), just ahead of the Turks (−0.8) and the Poles (−0.4). These were the only nations with regard to which there was a national consensus among the citizens of both former German states. (Jews received 1.3 in the East and 0.4 in the West).[13] Some 17 percent of the respondents in East Germany and 9 percent in West Germany defined their attitude toward Gypsies by the maximal negative value (−5), which is almost twice the rate of respondents who so defined their attitude toward Turks. In East Germany, the enmity toward Gypsies was even greater than that toward Africans living there, suggesting that the Gypsies' dark complexion was not the main cause of the negative attitude toward them.[14]

Two further polls conducted after 1990 again emphasized that former East Germans were more hostile to Gypsies than were West Germans, although the number of Gypsies in the GDR had been very small. A poll conducted in 1992 by the institute in Allensbach (Institut für Demoskopie Allensbach), which investigated the preferences of the German population concerning the identity of its neighbors, indicated a gap of 5 percent between the rate of rejection in West Germany toward the Gypsies (63 percent) and their rejection in East Germany (68 percent); this gap prevailed in three of the four age groups of the respondents. In the youngest age group (sixteen–twenty-nine), the gap reached 14 percent (67 percent in the East and 53 percent in the West).[15] The gap between the West and the East is also substantial concerning two groups of foreigners that are disliked in Germany: the Turks and the Poles. The Emnid Institute researchers explained this phenomenon by both the provincial and the closed nature of the GDR, which did not encourage openness toward foreigners, and by the economic and identity crisis of the society in the East after the collapse of the Communist regime in 1989, which encouraged the channeling of frustration toward foreigners. This phenomenon was especially salient among youngsters, who were in the stage of consolidating their identity.[16]

This trend was revealed again in a poll that Wuppertal University researcher Manfred Bursten conducted among 1,342 students in various German universities, concerning prejudice against ethnic and foreign minorities. Some 60.4 percent of the students from the former GDR admitted that they held no sympathy for Gypsies, while only 37.7 percent of the old FRG students admitted this. A similar gap was revealed between former GDR students and students from the old FRG concerning the lack of sympathy for Turks (27.2 percent from the GDR and 7.5 percent from the old FRG).[17] Further polls revealed similar results. The general gap between the attitudes of the students and those of the wider public can be explained by the fact that the students represent the educated and enlightened layer of German society, which also tends to a lesser extent to expose its true attitudes in public polls.

The gap between students from the former GDR and those from the old FRG may be explained, as the Emnid Research Institute's staff did, by reasoning that the Germans of the old FRG are more open and enlightened than the former GDR's citizens in their attitude toward foreigners. Alternatively, the gap can be explained by the differences that derive from the different political cultures in which the students' concepts and rules of communicating opinions concerning foreigners evolved. The students from the old FRG were more exposed in their youth to foreigners and to the restraints imposed by the political correctness prevalent in educated circles in the FRG. The number of foreigners then living in the GDR was only about 90,000, and, in general, they lived and worked separate from the German population.[18] Under these conditions, no friction at all was created between the German majority and the foreigners, and there was no need to curb antiforeigner expressions, as there had been in the political culture of the FRG in the late 1970s and 1980s. If this assumption is correct, the students' attitudes reflect not only the German attitude toward the Gypsies but also the fact that the rules of communicating about them were different from those about other foreigners' groups and totally different from the communicating rules concerning Jews.[19] This phenomenon might derive from the fact that antigypsy views were tolerated not only in private but also in public, as long as they were not clearly associated with Nazism. Therefore, the public did not feel the need to hide its hostility toward them.

A poll conducted by the Emnid Research Institute in January 1992 for the weekly *Der Spiegel* investigated the relation between antisemitic attitudes and hostility toward other minorities in the FRG.[20] The poll results support the findings of Panahi's study—namely, that individuals with antisemitic attitudes will tend to reveal greater hostility toward foreigners, too.[21] At least 77 percent of the German citizens holding significant antisemitic attitudes (constituting 13 percent of the whole German population) revealed hostility toward Gypsies. But the results show that rejection of Gypsies was not the exclusive property of antisemitic circles, who are close in their worldview to the extreme rightist circles. Rejection of Gypsies was also revealed by a substantial proportion of Germans who do not hold antisemitic attitudes (a group constituting 48 percent of the whole population): 44 percent of the respondents evaluated the extent of rejection they felt toward the Gypsies by values ranging from −1 to −5 on a scale from +5 to −5.[22] Another noteworthy phenomenon deriving from the poll is that there is an antisemitic group, albeit small, that is not hostile toward Gypsies. This phenomenon is possibly the successor attitude to the romanticizing of

Gypsies in the Heritage of the German Ancestors (Deutsche Ahnenerbe) of the SS.

The poll conducted in 1992 by the demoscopic institute of Allensbach concerning the preferences of the adult German population for their neighbors' identity also inquired about ethnic, religious, and political differences, along with differences in sexual preference. Some 64 percent of the German public said they would not like to have Gypsies as neighbors. A much higher rejection rate was recorded for Gypsies than for other ethnic, religious, and racial categories (Muslim, 17 percent; Hindu, 14 percent; foreign laborers, 12 percent; dark-skinned, 8 percent; Jews, 7 percent) and is equal only to the rejection rates for drug addicts (66 percent), drunkards (64 percent), and leftist extremists (62 percent). The rejection the public feels for the last three categories derives primarily from a fear of violence.[23] It seems, therefore, that Gypsies are perceived by the German public as violent offenders. Similar attitudes characterize police reports on crimes committed by Gypsies. Such reports were uncritically accepted and published by the German press.[24]

Similar public opinion polls conducted in several European countries reveal that there, too, Gypsies are the most rejected minority. In the following countries the rate of rejection of Gypsies is higher than the 63 percent rate of rejection in the FRG: Britain (65 percent), Lithuania (77 percent), Latvia (68 percent), Estonia (68 percent), Hungary (76 percent), Poland (73 percent), Czechoslovakia (85 percent). In the following countries the rate is lower than in Germany: Russia (48 percent), Ukraine (52 percent), Belarus (49 percent), Austria (45 percent).[25]

A poll conducted by the Emnid Research Institute in early 1994 revealed that 68 percent of the respondents would not like to live near Gypsies.[26] Contrary to the questions asked by the Allensbach Institute, the Emnid Institute poll categories explicitly referred to the national origins of the neighbors, except for one category that referred to the neighbors' continent of origin, Africa. It might be that the use of these categories is the explanation for the received rates of rejection. Those were significantly higher than the Allensbach poll's results conducted two years earlier. The category of dark complexion was apparently pictured in the eyes of the respondents—contrary to Africa, which was perceived as a geographic location—as a significant expression of racism; therefore, about 30 percent of the respondents avoided revealing their true attitude (37 percent objected to being neighbors of Africans, compared with 8 percent who objected to being neighbors of dark-skinned people).

A similar gap exists between other questions in the two polls: 47 percent objected to living in a neighborhood with Arabs, and 36 percent objected to living in a neighborhood with Turks, compared with 17 percent who objected to living in a neighborhood with Muslims in Allensbach's poll. (This last category might refer also to nationals of the former Yugoslavia.) However, the significant gap between the two poll results concerning objection to living in neighborhoods with Jews (22 percent, as compared with only 7 percent in Allensbach's poll) raises doubts about the reliability of Allensbach's methods.[27]

Another important datum provided by the Emnid Institute poll was the rate of rejection of Poles (39 percent), which was a little higher than the rate of those who answered rejection of Africans. This datum reinforces the findings of Jochimsen's poll from the 1960s and the poll of 1990, and it indicates that rejection of Gypsies derives more from their traditional image as thieves and asocials than from significant racist motives or prejudices based on their physical appearance.

A further question that the poll sought to explore was whether the way in which the various ethnic minorities were perceived to behave might encourage hostility against them. The rate of those who answered "yes" was the highest with regard to Gypsies, at 40 percent, and the rate of those who answered "no" for Gypsies was the lowest, at 41 percent. For Arabs, 18 percent said "yes" and 56 percent said "no," and for Poles, 20 percent said "yes" and 58 percent said "no."[28]

Perhaps most disturbing is that the public opinion polls from the early 1960s on indicate a constant, unchanging trend of rejection toward Gypsies. The poll results also demonstrate that the attitude of Germans toward Gypsies lacks the inhibitions typical of the attitude toward Jews and other foreigners after 1945. This phenomenon derives not just from the fact that the Gypsies are the least liked people for the Germans but also from the fact that the taboo imposed in postwar German political culture on expressions of pejorative and hostile statements about Gypsies was weak, and the attempts made in the 1980s to equalize the expressions toward the Gypsies also failed. The negative expressions toward Gypsies were not perceived by the public as illegitimate but, rather, as a legitimate belief based on the experience of many years of contact with Gypsies.

LIMITED INFLUENCE OF DENAZIFICATION ON RACIST ATTITUDES TOWARD GYPSIES IN THE FRG

Even if the German rejection of Gypsies did not derive solely from racism, racist and racial hygiene perceptions of German Gypsies continued to occupy an important place in German attitudes to Gypsies after the defeat of Nazism, as it had before. This phenomenon is not unique to Gypsies but is typical of the characterization of the non-European "other" in German discourse. It is mainly a cultural rather than a political phenomenon, one that apparently preceded Nazism; however, during the course of the Third Reich, due to the popularity of Gypsy research, further "characteristics" were added to the treasury of public knowledge about these people. The fact that many of the theories developed by Ritter and others became embedded in public consciousness does not necessarily indicate support for the murderous conclusions that the Nazis themselves inferred from these data, however.

The tracks of some of these theories can also be located in leftist and liberal circles, the worldview of which theoretically denies racism. An article in the radical leftist newspaper, *Konkret,* in 1970 bore the title, "Gypsies—A Portrait of a Displaced Race." The title and the captions that accompanied the pictures in the article reveal the racist patterns that were still prevalent in the attitude of leftist circles toward Gypsies in post-1945 Germany. The use of such patterns with regard to Jews was taboo. One of the picture captions introduced an anti-Nazi argument against the extermination of the Gypsies, while at the same time it used arguments from the domain of racial romanticism: "The Nazis almost exterminated them totally, although they were more racially pure than Himmler's blond SS heroes: the Gypsies, deported many hundreds of years ago from India, are the purest race of Indo-Germans *[die reinrassigsten Indogermanen].*"[29] Already, back in 1980, the liberal daily *Süddeutsche Zeitung* referred to India's diplomatic action on behalf of the Gypsies: "The Roma . . . are in fact Mischlinge; however, they are the authentic descendants of the Indian peoples."[30]

When the use of racist terminology continued to prevail in circles that, after 1945, were supposed to express ideological reservation before expressing any racist thinking, it is not surprising that the more conservative circles in German society continued to hold such perceptions. Racist expressions were not perceived as illegitimate in substance after 1945, only when they appeared in contexts perceived as political in Germany. Every racist attack on Jews was clearly regarded as having a political context, as such context also appeared clearly in the racist propaganda of the Third Reich, and the Allies concentrated on this issue in the reeducation policy that they established in occupied Germany. In contrast, the racial character of the Nazi persecution of the Gypsies was not perceived in public as a wider political issue but as an internal issue of the state's struggle against asociality and crime. For their part, the Allies failed to show any interest in the issue and therefore did not make the public aware of the need to change their attitude toward Gypsies.

Most entries concerning Gypsies in encyclopedias published in the FRG, which can be taken as a good indication of the attitudes of the central streams in German society, contained terminology and concepts taken from the racist and racial hygiene vocabulary. The entries of the editions published after 1945 were rewritten. Certain sections were copied from previous editions, dating from the Nazi period or before, but in other parts, harsh racist terms were substituted by neutral terms, untarnished by illegitimacy after the Holocaust. The entry for "Gypsies" in the 1950 edition of the *Der Kleine Brockhaus* states that anthropologically the Gypsies belong to a mix of Indian peoples *(Völkergemisch)*. An identical sentence in the 1938 edition of *Der Neue Brockhaus* reveals that the original term was a mix of races *(Rassengemisch)*. The 1950 edition of *Der Kleine Brockhaus* stated as well Ritter's theory that "the vagrant tent Gypsies were preserved in the purest manner, while many other parts [of the Gypsies] mixed with foreign asocial elements."[31]

In the entry for "Gypsies" of the 1950 edition of *Der Neue Herder,* the mixture of Gypsies with foreign elements is mentioned twice. In editions published during the Third Reich, the German elements with which the Gypsies mixed were defined as asocials; in the 1950 edition, the editor chose to substitute this expression by "those who belong to parts of the nation who are not permanently settled" *(Angehörige nichtseßhafter Volksteile).*[32] The bibliography connected to some of the entries included studies made under the auspices of the Nazi regime, including Justin's.[33]

A comparison between entries in encyclopedias published in the FRG with foreign encyclopedias indicates that the taboo on engaging in race questions in the FRG was, in fact, quite limited. All over the world, the horrors of Nazism resulted in the delegitimization of engaging in physical anthropology, an area which during the first decades of the twentieth century had still constituted an integral part of the encyclopedic information about nations. Encyclopedias published in the GDR and in all other European countries after 1945 did not include this subject at all in entries about Gypsies.[34] The delegitimation process that the rest of the world had accepted passed by the FRG. The editors and authors of encyclopedias there not only continued to allocate substantial parts of the entries about Gypsies to discussing their physical traits and defining them from a racist and racial hygiene viewpoint but also usually placed these issues at the very beginning of the entry "Gypsy." Even the 1979 edition of *Meyers Enzyklopaedisches Lexikon* stated that "notwithstanding their Hindu-Germanic language, the Gypsies belong to the pre-Hindu-Germanic population of India. Their racial type *[Rassentypus]* is influenced by their mixing with people of all the countries through which they had passed. In part of the groups, the mixing is so strong that they do not reveal any characteristics of an Indian type."[35] The 1974 edition of *Die Brockhaus Enzyklopaedie* also still placed an emphasis on physical characteristics: "The Gypsies present many racial characteristics which enable us to identify India as their homeland. Where they remained pure, they have black eyes, their hair is very black, and their skin color is of various degrees, from brown to light. They are short, the men's height about 160–165 cm, the women 140–154 cm."[36] Different racial Gypsy types are also described in the entry. Such racist themes disappeared only in the last edition of *Die Brockhaus Encyclopaedie,* in 1993.

German interest in the physical characteristics of Gypsies has also been expressed in the press and in films. Almost every report of Gypsies that was published in the West German media from the late 1940s to the late 1960s mentions their dark complexion or their black hair or eyes.[37] In an only partly conscious manner, the physical and anthropological data were perceived by many Germans as external revelations of the innate and unchanged essence and properties of the Gypsy. The lack of German sensibility toward such a typically racist concept derived from the fact that racism preceded Nazism and had already taken root in German culture at the end of the nineteenth century. Racism enjoyed an image of being scientifically based and was not perceived at all as a political position. The race issue became a central component of the German attitude toward exotic nations and nature peoples *(Naturvölker),* a category into which the Gypsies were also classified. In this allegedly nonpolitical context, such racist attitudes were also entwined in the German collective consciousness. Racism became so well rooted and obvious as a general viewpoint that even denazification did not succeed in undermining its legitimacy outside clear political contexts, mainly the Jewish one.

The attention focused on the Gypsies' dark complexion was perceived in German discourse not as a neutral statement but as a critical one. The physical characteristics of the "other" are frequently perceived in the German culture, even to this day, as an expression of mental and moral inferiority, in view of the racist hypothesis about the hierarchy that prevails among races in the world. For example, casting the actors for the TV thriller *Poor Nanosh (Armer Nanosh),* written by Martin Walser and Asta Scheib, in 1989, demonstrates this argument about the hidden mental and moral significance of physical appearance in German culture. The Gypsy protagonist of the thriller, Valentin Sander (Nanosh, by his Gypsy name), and his German wife have two sons: Moritz and Georg. Like his father, the young Georg has a Gypsy name: Titi. Moritz, the eldest, stands by his betrayed mother and is reserved toward his father, who has left home after an affair with another, younger, woman. Moritz is dressed decently, his hair is blond, like his mother's, and he speaks German with his father. In contrast to his brother, Georg-Titi represents the essence of the Gypsy genes he inherited from his father: he has black hair and dark eyes, like his father's, and he is hot-tempered, violent, and plays the guitar very well. Georg speaks not only German but Romany with his father.[38]

In the late 1950s, the widespread inclination to attribute mental inferiority to people with dark appearance caused several German writers, who were aware of the racist character of the discourse and held a certain degree of sympathy for Gypsies, to avoid any reference to the Gypsies' appearance. Wolfdietrich Schnurre was the first author who, in his work "Jenö Was My Friend" ("Jenö war mein Freund"), avoided mentioning the Gypsy protagonist's appearance. Johanes Bobrowski followed suit in respect to his Gypsy figures in his novel *Levin's Mill (Levins Mühle)*, as did Enno Podehl in his play *Hermann* in the late 1980s.[39] These authors believed that focusing on the Gypsies' appearance was not right. In a very limited way, this viewpoint also penetrated the West German press, where various solutions were found. In 1957, the daily *Frankfurter Rundschau* chose to contradict the racist interpretation for the different appearance of Gypsies by a using slogan that would later characterize the African American struggle in the United States: "Black Is Beautiful." This presentation expressed pride in external characteristics that were otherwise perceived in German culture to be expressions of ugliness and evidence of mental inferiority. The newspaper featured a picture of a small Gypsy girl, with the caption "Touching sincerity": "Why do you photograph me and not the blond, white-skinned children who used to taunt me, who throw sand and rocks at me, who do not want to play with me, pull my long black curls, and call me Gypsy. But all this does not upset me, and I laugh about it. My mother said I should be proud to be a Gypsy. I inherited my brown skin from my Indian forefathers. . . . We have our own language, our own religion, a clan patriarch, and a Gypsy mother *[Zigeunermutter]* who maintains the clan's morality."[40] Although the author's aim was no doubt to undermine the prejudices against the dark complexion of the Gypsies, his decision to counteract the prejudice by emphasizing the difference in the color of the skin, the eyes, and the hair between many Germans and Gypsies only emphasizes the importance granted to these external characteristics in German culture.

This attitude was exceptional and without parallel in the German press in later years. More typical was the attempt to find new codes for describing the physical difference of the Gypsies, ones that were not contaminated with Nazism. This attempt created several ludicrous terms, including, among others, "the richly pigmented skin of the refugees" *(die starke Hautpigmentierung der Flüchtlinge)*.[41] The harsh contradiction between the dogmatic avoidance, on the one hand, of explicit reference to the Gypsies' brown skin (as the very mention of skin color was perceived to smack of racist attitude) and, on the other hand, the inability to totally avoid referring to the different appearance of Gypsies, which had become such a clear characteristic of the Gypsies in German culture (in many folk songs the Gypsy is labeled "black Gypsy" *[schwarze Zigeuner]*) expresses a wider phenomenon that has been termed by the historian Dan Diner "contraphobia." This is typical of certain circles of the radical left in Germany, who sought to adopt antiracist attitudes that would constitute a polar contradiction to the Nazi worldview so they might escape any compulsory repetition of the past. However, their infatiguable efforts, in fact, exposed exactly what they were trying to escape.[42] The prohibition imposed on expressions perceived as racist was bypassed by using a semantic parallel, exactly as the Bavarian political establishment used the word vagrant in order to get around the restrictions imposed by the constitution of the FRG on discrimination and denial of basic human rights of Gypsies.

Ritter's perceptions of the Nazi era gained much appreciation among FRG police as they dealt with the Gypsy question. At the opening of a lecture given in April 1954 by the consultant for criminal issues in the federal criminal police office, Dr. Ochs, to the heads of the criminal police offices of the regional states of the FRG, Ochs mentioned Ritter's "scientific" theory—that only about 10 percent of those called Gypsies are indeed "pure race" Gypsies and that the other 90 percent are mixed with German blood, mainly with German vagrants known as Jenische.[43]

Following their use by the Nazis, such racial theories were delegitimized all over the world, but in Germany itself the legitimacy of this field was not undermined and was recognized as a respected scientific discipline right up to the 1980s. Even the greatest supporter of the Gypsies in the FRG, the priest Georg Althaus (1898–1974) of Braunschweig, an anti-Nazi, continued to hold romantic racial perceptions and attitudes from the domain of racial hygiene concerning Gypsies. In 1935 Althaus held an intercession prayer for the persecuted Jews ("Gott schütz das gehetzte arme Volk der Juden") and forbade his confirmation pupils to use the "Heil Hitler" salute. In 1936 he was sentenced to six months' imprisonment.[44]

Althaus presented the Gypsies as a racially mixed nation *(Mischvolk)* that derived from a light-skinned Aryan element from the north of India and a Dravidian dark-skinned element from the south of India; however, he opposed the racist perception that regarded the mixing of races as a cause of mental and physical degeneration. Althaus described the Gypsies, in the manner typical of racial romanticism, as noble savages, pure and uncorrupted, who reveal more zeal and strictness about morals than the Germans. He emphasized their strict moral laws that are intended to eliminate all evil from Gypsy society, especially the keeping of sexual purity.[45] As a romantic racist, Althaus believed that this lifestyle expressed the Gypsies' racial substance, and he therefore also accepted Ritter's racial hygiene concept that crime among the Gypsies was not the result of social and environmental circumstances but provided evidence of the existence of inherent inclination. Althaus argued that "pure Gypsies" did not commit crimes and that "if Gypsies were convicted of crimes they committed, it means they are not pure Gypsies but Mischlinge, born to

Gypsies and German asocials, thus inheriting the inclination toward crime from the non-Gypsy blood." According to him, "these couplings generated many criminals, whores, retarded people, and anomalies."[46] On several occasions Althaus publicly repeated Ritter's concept concerning "the Gypsy blood contaminated [*verseucht*] by criminal elements," especially of the Jenische.[47] Althaus ended one of his lectures on Gypsies by a paraphrase of the infamous antisemitic saying of the historian Heinrich von Treitschke: "The Jenische and other German asocials are the misfortune [*Unglück*] of the German Gypsies."[48]

The first people who were sensitive to the fact that the field of the racial hygiene in political culture was being delegitimized, and who adjusted their attitude to Gypsies accordingly, were the scientists who engaged in this field. To overcome the trend toward delegitimization, they implemented semantic disguises to cover their racist concepts, similar to those that also served the political and cultural establishment in Germany. These racial hygiene researchers adapted a social terminology that substituted the explicitly racist terminology: the term "racial hygiene" (*Rassenhygiene*) was substituted by the term "social hygiene" (*Sozialhygiene*).[49]

In a document in 1947 that reviewed his scientific and public activity during the Nazi era, Robert Ritter, the central figure in the domain of racial hygiene, expressed his explicit reservation about Nazi racism and the murder of Gypsies.[50] But even during the investigation against him, Ritter did not retract his support of the sterilization of the asocials among the Gypsies and their incarceration in camps during the Third Reich. He denied the racist terminology and arguments that had characterized his dealings with Gypsies during the Nazi period, and he presented his work as a legitimate scientific method for dealing with the problem of asociality, methods that had been acknowledged outside of Germany, too, and which were, apparently, not associated with the illegitimate Nazi racial theories that resulted in the murder of Gypsies.[51]

Typically, Ritter totally ignored the research on Jews and Jewish Mischlinge who "had penetrated the body of the German people," which had been conducted by his subordinates in his racial hygiene institute, because, contrary to dealing with the Gypsies, which was not considered to be a political act and was not therefore yet tainted with delegitimation, any such dealing with Jews might have incriminated Ritter.[52] The open conducting of racial studies about Jews was terminated in Germany after 1945; however, racial studies about Gypsies, based on data collected by Ritter, continued not only to be performed openly but even to be published in the FRG, adjusting the attitudes from the Nazi period to patterns perceived as legitimate in the political culture of the "new Germany."

From the late 1950s to the 1980s, Hermann Arnold, Ritter's most prominent follower in the FRG, was a consultant on Gypsy issues to the federal authorities and to volunteer welfare organizations. He presented himself as a social physician *(Sozialmediziner)* rather than a racial hygienist.[53] Contrary to Ritter's attitude in the late 1940s, Arnold did not express in his writings any support of the Gypsies' compulsory sterilization in the Third Reich, even for those labeled as asocials, and he tried to argue that Ritter had also objected to such measures.[54]

However, Arnold did not abandon the old views but expressed them only in intimate settings. In 1962, he published an article in an ethnology magazine in Braunschweig. In this article, which was based on Ritter's work, Arnold explained how we can identify Gypsies by using the standards of racial hygiene.[55] In other, more widely distributed publications, which might have reached more critical readers, Arnold refrained from expressing these views so explicitly. In his book of 1958, Arnold wrote on the question of the Gypsies and Mischlinge race and quoted Ritter's thesis and data on crime among Gypsies; but he avoided mentioning explicitly that he investigated the issue using the tools of racial hygiene, and he also tried to blur the part that Ritter had played in the Gypsy policy of the Third Reich.[56] He noted that Ritter headed the Gypsy unit *(Zigeunerstelle)* in the framework of the Reich's Ministry of Health, and he ignored Ritter's consulting role for the criminal police (RKPA) and the main office for the Reich's security (RSHA).[57]

The shadow of illegitimacy that Auschwitz had imposed on this field, and his wish as a scientist to be acknowledged by the international research community,[58] led Arnold to adjust his own views to the social concepts which by the 1960s had become dominant, even in Germany. In a lecture he gave at an international convention entitled "Help for the Gypsies" ("Hilfe für Zigeuner") held in 1966 in Hildesheim, Germany, Arnold did not disclose his racist views. Arnold reviewed the difficulties of integrating Gypsies into society and the way to overcome them.[59] He mentioned the German population's hatred of and envy toward the Gypsies,[60] an issue that was also central to the study of the German sociologist Lukrezia Johimsen, who participated at the convention.[61] Arnold established that care should be taken to ensure that the occupations for which the Gypsies would be trained would afford them adequate wages to sustain their families, so that their wives would not have to beg or steal.[62]

Arnold therefore explained stealing not by the Gypsies being poacher-gatherers *(Wildbeuter)* in substance, as he explained in his article "Who Is a Gypsy?" but by a social explanation that perceived crime to be the result of distress.[63] Although Arnold adjusted his attitudes to the spirit of the period, certain parts of his beliefs—the heritage of racial hygiene, for example—continued to deny Gypsies' intellectual skills. Arnold recommended that the Gypsies be trained only for the simplest technical

work (sewing machine repair, oven cleaning, shoe shining, sewage cleaning, lawn mowing, and so on).[64] He implied that they were not capable
of anything more, that they would have to be satisfied forever with simple
manual work. Arnold finished by arguing that if the Gypsies were not
integrated into the circle of productive society, their persecution might
be renewed in the not too distant future. In other words, he again implied
that the Gypsies' persecution did not derive from the racist nature of the
Nazi regime but from the problematic Gypsy lifestyle, which was continuing to remain unchanged in the democratic reality of the FRG and which
might constitute an objective reason for their persecution in the FRG,
too.[65]

Arnold felt the need to introduce an apology in the foreword of his
1958 book, reflecting an updating of his attitude, so that he would be
consistent with the enlightened circles in the FRG in the late 1950s. But
it was an apology that Arnold omitted from articles he wrote for more
closed audiences. The apology read: "It should be mentioned that the
author does not in any way defame individuals or groups: as he allows
each animal and each plant to maintain its unique lifestyle and does not
wish them to change, he refers in the same manner to people who are
exceptional with relation to the frameworks of the conventional bourgeois lifestyle."[66]

The public legitimization that Arnold's racial hygienic studies and his
public engagements in Gypsy matters in general enjoyed was totally undermined in the early 1980s when the Gypsies themselves, joined by the
Society for the Threatened Peoples, denounced him as a Nazi and his
publications as Nazi-like.[67] The Society's campaign for Gypsies determined new standards for communicating about Gypsies in the German
political culture and contributed to a new public awareness of the illegitimacy of the use of any discriminating pejorative or racist terminology.[68]

Notwithstanding this trend of political correctness, discriminatory
and even racist opinions about Gypsies are still occasionally heard in
various forums, sometimes under not too subtle disguise, sometimes more
blatantly. Such comments might indicate that the decrease in discriminatory statements derived more from a fear of being branded as racist, an
incriminating label in Germany, where racism is immediately associated
with the Nazi murders, than from any genuine internalization of antiracist conviction.

7

Public Debate on Nazi
Persecution of Gypsies

[handwritten margin note: Focus on MOTIVE]

THE debate among Germans about the Gypsy persecution has focused more on the motives of the Nazis than on the fate of the
victims. Opinion has been divided sharply between those who
share the Allies' views and those whose views are more in line with the
defeated Nazis. The Allies, who first received details about the Gypsy
persecution as early as 1942, perceived it as a racist crime against an
innocent victim. By contrast, from 1936 onward, the Nazi regime presented their actions against Gypsies as part of a legitimate and integral
struggle against crime.

These differences of opinion are reflected in three narratives found in
the German discourse about the Gypsy persecution. Two are contradictory narratives, each expressing one of the two interpretations of the
Gypsy persecution, and the third is syncretic and reconciliatory, combining elements of the other two narratives. The first of these I shall refer
to as the Nazi Narrative, because of its shared viewpoints with Nazism.
The second narrative (perceiving the Gypsy persecution as a crime against
innocent victims) is borrowed from Western consciousness. It was generated in 1942 in England, just after the first news from German-occupied
Europe about the persecution and murder of Gypsies, and it copied the
narrative about the persecution of Jews that had preceded it.[1] For this
reason I term it the Jewish-like Narrative.

The third narrative, which I term the Syncretic Narrative, adopted
the element of blaming the victim for his fate from the Nazi Narrative,
when it accused Gypsies of being at least in part responsible for their
own persecution due to their behavior. At the same time, it also adopted

the moral attitude of the Allies, who denounced the Gypsy persecution as an evil crime. This narrative expressed the attitude of much of federal and local government and of many of the central streams in German society for most of the postwar period, until the 1980s. These narratives, passed from one generation to the next, were processed in the German consciousness to become collective memories.

NAZI NARRATIVE

Als man dies in Dorf erfuhr
War von Trauer keine spur.

[In the village, when word went out
There was no mourning, not even a pout.].[2]

The postwar Nazi Narrative has been widely expressed among the German public, bureaucracy, and political establishment. It was based on the interpretation that the Nazi regime provided for its Gypsy policy and on the common image, engraved on the German collective memory over many centuries, of Gypsies as thieves and asocials. Government officials also provided support for this interpretation by citing original Nazi documents, which stated that Gypsies were dealt with because most of them were found to be asocials and criminals who endangered public safety. This narrative linked the Gypsy persecution with that aspect of Nazi policy which many Germans, even after 1945, perceived as positive: the regime's struggle against crime.

The Nazis had promised to provide law and order for respectable citizens and to deport to concentration camps the criminals and asocials who disturbed the peace.[3] The most extreme adherents of this narrative presented death as the appropriate way to punish Gypsies for their evil deeds. However, its more moderate proponents ignored the criminal aims of the persecution—as if the mass murder of Gypsies was not an integral part of Nazi persecution—and ended the narrative with the supposedly "legitimate incarceration" of Gypsies in concentration camps.

As this revealed a certain identification with one of the criminal aspects of Nazism, the political culture consolidated under the auspices of the Allies in post-1945 Germany imposed a taboo on the public voicing of the narrative, and its expressions in the media or in writing were rare. While only neo-Nazis dared to completely violate the taboo and express the narrative in its crudest and most direct form, in more moderate and seemingly decent circles it was expressed more subtly, using codes that could be easily understood by others.

As far as is known, the only German politician who publicly aired this narrative in a political forum in the postwar period was Joseph

Vogt, a Christian Democrat member of the local parliament of Baden-Württemberg. In 1956 Vogt requested that the Bavarian vagrancy law of 1953 also be adopted by Baden-Württemberg, in order to "protect" the population from "vagrants" *(Landfahrer)*, which was from the late 1940s on a euphemism for "Gypsies." In the course of his speech to parliament, Vogt took care to use this euphemism: "There are people affected by the vagrant plague *[Landfahrerplage]* who say that in the Third Reich this was dealt with more simply and thoroughly. I am of the opinion that what happened there was unjust, at least in that it went so far that the foreigners *[Ausländer]* have conceded to those who shared their fate in the concentration camps certain prerogatives that no longer do them any good today. We now want to put this back in the proper order *[Wir wollen das ja nun wieder in die rechte Ordnung bringen]*."⁴ Vogt was deliberately ambiguous.⁵ Although his words implied clear support for Nazi persecution policy, he did not go as far as to support extermination. Further, he refrained from presenting the argument as his own and instead chose to present it as the position of anonymous involved persons.

There is a contradiction in his words. On the one hand, Vogt concluded that this problem had been simply and thoroughly dealt with under the Nazis (and all present knew what the Nazi treatment implied), yet, on the other hand, he expressed reservations about their persecution, while stating that once more, today, it was necessary to bring order. The whole context of his words clarified his intention to all present. In the harshest part of his sentence, Vogt chose to blur the fact that Gypsies were murdered in concentration camps, and he referred to them as foreigners—even though many of the persecuted Sinti were German citizens, the descendants of those who had lived on German soil for hundreds of years. The use of this term out of context seemed to be a substitute for a Nazi term, probably for members of a foreign race *(Fremdrassige)*.

While the Jewish-like Narrative about the Nazi persecution of Gypsies concentrated on its criminal conclusion and contained a clear element of empathy toward the Gypsy victim, Vogt concentrated on the supposed causes of the persecution, regarding it as protective measure aimed at defending the true victim, the German public, from Gypsies. The attitude of Vogt (who was referred to by Detlev Peukert and Ulrich Herbert as "the little man") and his associates was a reminder of the alleged personal safety that citizens enjoyed during the Third Reich. This was achieved, so to speak, thanks to the severe policy of the regime and through the existence of the concentration camps.⁶

The expression of this narrative among the circles Vogt represented exposed a layer in their collective memory derived from the Third Reich, which was, more often than not, hidden in published opinion and historic research. This layer was not the exclusive property of radical rightists but was shared by many members of the ruling CDU, a mainstream party. The understanding shown for Nazi positions by representatives of the main political streams, which theoretically should have been committed to democratic and anti-Nazi values, is only one expression of a general phenomenon.

This phenomenon, which is not unique to Germany, has been termed "extremism of the center" by the sociologist Seymour Lipset. (Contrary to Lipset, who perceived fascism to be a revelation of extremism of the center, the term here is used to denote extremism about certain aspects of social life, which are not necessarily anchored in a consolidated fascist worldview.) In Germany, as elsewhere after 1945, this phenomenon led basically nonradical circles to support very radical approaches to the fringe groups in society who were stigmatized as asocials.[7] It resembles the willingness to support the Bavarian Law for Combating Gypsies and Work Shys of 1926 and the Hessian Law for Combating Gypsies of 1929 (described in chapter 3 of this volume). In both cases, these laws won the approval of a wide and varied coalition, from the radical right through the conservatives to elements of the antifascist left.

In the circles where this narrative prevailed, honoring the civil rights of asocials and Gypsies by the democratic regime after 1945 was perceived as an expression of society's helplessness, if not outright cowardice, against criminals. And the brutal nature of the concentration camps was thought to have been an appropriate response to the disrespect the criminals allegedly displayed toward the legal authorities and the conventional punishment imposed on them.[8] Lacking a consolidated humanistic view, democrats, too, might have at times adopted (especially after friction with Gypsies) the Nazi Narrative. This allegedly nonpolitical narrative argued that the Gypsy persecution should be examined not solely from the side of "winners" and "victims" but also from the viewpoint of the German population, the legitimate needs of which these measures of the regime came to protect.[9]

Verbal expressions in praise of the Third Reich's policies against crime were fairly common after 1945.[10] A letter written in December 1953 by Mr. Lotz, a high official in the Braunschweig municipal administration, to the welfare department of the German mayors' conference *(Deutscher Städtetag)*, reads: "Whenever the Gypsy problem is under discussion, may it be among the public, in official committees, or in the municipal administration, expressions shockingly similar to those common in the Third Reich are loudly voiced."[11] However, opinions voiced in public forums were often censored in the press and official minutes and proceedings, and there is not much by way of written documentation for such expressions.

What documented support there is for Gypsy persecution was usually aired by neo-Nazis. In 1990, Wilhelm Schmidt, a member of the local parliament in Bremen for the extreme right-wing party DVU (Deutsche Volksunion; German People's Union), said in response to a reference to the extermination of half a million Gypsies: "Not more? A pity!"[12] Such a blatant outburst in full view of the media was unacceptable to most on the far right in the FRG, who, contrary to the neo-Nazis, de jure respected the FRG's constitution and the rules of democracy.

The response of the *Deutsche National Zeitung,* the newspaper owned by DVU leader Dr. Gerhardt Frey, to the murder of Gypsies revealed certain similarities to its attitude toward the Jewish Holocaust. The roles of victim and perpetrator were reversed. On the one hand, that Gypsies were murdered at all was denied and was presented as a libel intended to extort money from Germany; on the other hand, the very same article portrayed all Gypsies as frauds and delinquents and suggested that concentration camps were probably the best place for them. Apparently, some readers understood from these insinuations that it was also appropriate to exterminate them.[13]

Gypsies were now presented not only as thieves and frauds but also as violent criminals harming defenseless Germans. The first such article in the paper was a large report in November 1979 that was probably in reaction to the launch of a public campaign in favor of Gypsies in the FRG. The newspaper emphasized that Gypsies were sent to concentration camps in the framework of actions against asocials and that there was no plan to exterminate them, and indeed they were not exterminated.

The report included a photograph from 1978, taken during a Gypsy demonstration against a convention of SS veterans in Würzburg. The photograph showed two Gypsies, armed with sticks, pursuing two elderly SS veterans. The caption didn't mention the "soldiers" had been in the SS. It simply said they had to escape from Gypsies. It then read: "And after this the Gypsies still argue they are the 'victims' *[Opfer]* and that the attacked men were the 'persecutors' *[Täter].* This photograph helps to reveal the truth."[14] Further newspaper articles in 1980 also emphasized that the real victims were the Germans, while the Gypsies were the perpetrators.

While the readers of the *Deutsche National Zeitung* became familiar with this message, elsewhere explicit versions of the Nazi Narrative were voiced only in closed forums. When such opinions did appear in the press, they were attributed to speakers who were drunk or had got into a fight with Gypsies, when emotions were said to be overflowing and self-restraint was weakened. For example, a report in the weekly *Die Zeit* from 1964 quoted a drunk carpenter as having said in a Hamburg pub: "The whole world thanks us because Hitler has reduced their [the Gypsies'] numbers a little." A citizen of Bad-Hersfeld expressed himself when sober in a similar manner toward his Gypsy neighbor: "Hitler has forgotten to gas you!" (In German this is a play on words—"Hitler hat vergessen dich zu vergasen").[15]

The Nazi treatment of Gypsies did not just gain post facto understanding in neo-Nazi circles. By the 1990s, a process of sanctification also began to take place. In contrast to the attitudes of the National Socialist Party before it assumed power, today Nazi-type atrocities are coming to be regarded as an integral part of the neo-Nazi program for treating this problematic and hated population in the future. For example, a report published in 1991 in *Der Spiegel* about complaints made by Germans living in the Karolinen quarter in Hamburg against the Roma inhabitants of the quarter, who had recently arrived from Eastern Europe, quoted the words of the local supermarket manager: "Thoughts are free. What can I do if, when I see Gypsy children, thoughts about gas chambers come to my mind?"[16]

JEWISH-LIKE NARRATIVE

This narrative, expressed mainly in West German media reports from the late 1950s on, shaped the Gypsy victim of Nazism in the image of the Jewish victim. It was reflected for the first time in June 1942, when a short news report by the Reuters agency was carried in the *Times* of London and elsewhere. Citing a reporter of the Swedish Social Democratic Party in Berlin, and concerning oppressive measures taken against German Gypsies, the report shows that this primary information was already being interpreted in the West within the context of the Nazi persecution of German Jewry. The measures against Gypsies were described as a criminal assault on innocent and helpless victims: "Gypsies may be obliged to wear a distinguishing mark on their clothing, like Jews, and be forced to work in settlements. There are about 20,000 Gypsies in Germany, 80 percent being according to Nazis anti-social and degenerate. Until now Gypsies were treated better than Jews, although in practice the Nazi authorities banned marriages between Gypsies and Aryans."[17]

Another article, published in London in March 1943 in *Die Zeitung*, an anti-Nazi newspaper run by German refugees, said: "It is already a long time that Jews and Gypsies have been placed on the same level by the racial evaluation."[18] The article stated that 262,000 Romanian Gypsies had been brought to the east of Poland, in accordance with Nazi instructions, and murdered there like Jews. It was written that deportation and extermination awaited another 300,000 Romanian Gypsies and that the Nazis were planning to prepare a similar fate for the 300,000 Gypsies in Hungary. Fortunately, after the war it became clear that these fears had been greatly exaggerated, and, in fact, only about 9,000

Romanian Gypsies had been killed or perished during their deportation in Transnistria.[19]

The existence of such reports shows that the information about Gypsies that reached the West was interpreted according to the information the West already possessed at that time about the extermination of Jews. This narrative continued to spread in the West after the war ended, especially in Jewish publications in the English-speaking world. Its publication in Britain and the United States shaped the collective memory of the Gypsy persecution in the whole Western consciousness.[20]

This narrative was imported into Germany within the framework of the denazification policy established by the Allies. Some of the articles about Nazi persecution (published in the first years after the war in the British press) voiced this narrative and were translated into German and published in Germany.[21] In 1948 a Catholic magazine in Germany published an article by Fredrick Cowles. Cowles was affiliated with the Gypsy Lore Society, and he believed that Gypsies were the most ancient race in the world. His article contributed not only to spreading the Jewish-like Narrative within the German discourse about Gypsy persecution but also to its manipulative use as a disguised protest against the special status afforded to Jews in the postwar era, a use that would become important in German public discourse about Gypsy victims. Cowles wrote that "the Nazis regarded Gypsies as an asocial plague and treated them more harshly than Jews. Lacking citizenship, Gypsies had no rights, and they were tortured and murdered in the concentration camps."[22]

Articles about Gypsies began appearing in the German press in 1947. However, up to the end of the 1950s they usually refrained from referring to their fate in the war.[23] Although after 1945 the German press did not totally ignore the Gypsy destiny under the swastika, references to the issue were rare; only in the 1960s did articles about it begin to appear regularly. The short time that had elapsed since the genocidal crimes were committed by the Nazis had made it harder for German society, which felt guilty and responsible for the horrors, to confront them. There were a few exceptions from one or two outstanding journalists. S. Roberts, for example, presented the Gypsy as a victim as early as the late 1940s, when he asserted that the state had "much to compensate [*wiedergutzumachen*] the survivor for": "It is not the fault of the Gypsies but, rather, of those barbarian acts of the [German state] who wanted to degrade this little people with fire and sword, concentration camps, and starvation."[24]

The painter Otto Pankok also played an important role in West Germany in spreading the Jewish-like Narrative. In 1947, after he was reunited with those Gypsy friends of his who had survived the persecution, he displayed an exhibition of his drawings of Gypsies in Düsseldorf and

Otto Pankok with the Kreutz family in Düsseldorf, 1948. (Otto Pankok Museum Haus Esselt, Hünxe-Drevenack.)

published an album of these drawings, in the text of which he referred to the Nazi persecution of Gypsies.[25]

Over the course of the ensuing years, Pankok was interviewed in the media about the fate of Gypsies and their condition after the war, and he also wrote several articles himself.[26] His interest in Gypsies did not stem from their persecution but from the romantic opinion he had developed in the early 1930s. For him, their authentic and free lifestyle was in marked contrast to the materialism of the bourgeoisie.[27] Pankok not only compared the Nazi persecution of Gypsies to the Jewish Holocaust, but he also linked the Gypsies' fate throughout the Third Reich with the Jewish fate. In his album of Gypsy drawings published in 1947, he wrote: "Here [in the Gypsy camps] the SS boots began the brutal trampling, even before the synagogues were burned. Gypsy families were incarcerated behind barbed wire fences, in order to later take part in the Jewish fate in the death camps of the East."[28]

Institutions, as well as private individuals, also voiced this narrative. The 1950 edition of *Der Kleine Brockhaus* encyclopedia established that the Nazis persecuted Gypsies as they did Jews: Most of them were exterminated, though some escaped.[29]

Public discourse about the Gypsy persecution was conducted at the fringes of the discourse about the Holocaust. Memoirs and artistic works by Jewish Holocaust victims and survivors, published in German, awakened and fertilized public discourse about the Holocaust, especially in the second half of the 1950s. Publication of the diary of Anne Frank in 1955 was a prime example of this.[30] In contrast, Gypsies did not document their persecution and were not capable of initiating public discourse about their tragedy. Many of them were illiterate, and their limited mastery of the German language left the horrible and unique experience they went through largely unknown to the German public.

In general, the literature about concentration camps referred very little to the fate of Gypsies, although one or two books, such as that by Egon Kogon, linked the persecution of Gypsies with the persecution of Jews.[31] Only in the late 1950s was an autobiographical book published in the FRG describing the Gypsy persecution. The book, by Martha Adler, a German woman who was married to a Gypsy, was published in 1957. It gave a more personal dimension to the Gypsy victim and his suffering under Hitler, but held no great resonance among the general public.[32]

The story of the Gypsy victim reached the public's consciousness primarily through the press, although it was rare for German journalists in the 1950s and 1960s to actually know Gypsies or to familiarize themselves with their story. In 1953, the daily newspaper *Frankfurter Rundschau* published a true story by Godo Remszhardt about a Gypsy who went with his family after the war to thank an old German who had protected his parents from the police in the Nazi period. The story ended with the old man's reply: "I only did my human duty." This sentence was probably interpreted as a message of reproach among the German public, most of which did not fulfill its "human duty."[33]

The first time an extensive account of the Gypsies' fate under the Nazis appeared in the press was in 1954, in the conservative newspaper *Frankfurter Allgemeine Zeitung*. This article included a passage under the title "Had Been Killed in Auschwitz" ("In Auschwitz umgekommen"), which said that from 1943 Gypsies also shared in the Jewish fate ("auch die Zigeuner haben . . . an das Schicksal der Juden geteilt"): "A tribe which had been naturalized in Germany for 500 years, was almost totally exterminated. Those who did not die a 'natural' death by hard labor, hunger or illness, as was especially the fate of children, were exterminated in another way." The article also referred, for the first time, to the traumatic implications of their persecution for the life of Gypsies in Germany after 1945. Notwithstanding these expressions of empathy, and maybe because of them, the writer felt he had to end his words in an apologetic tone, explaining why, after all, Gypsies did not deserve to be exterminated: "Most Gypsy children in Germany are no older than six years. Perhaps today some of them were made hostile by their fate, but they are not a corrupted race [*verdorbene Rasse*]. Gypsies did not take part in serious crime."[34]

Now the Gypsy victim of Nazism was portrayed to the West German public as mute and anonymous; his image was copied from the image of the Jewish victim of Nazism. As was the case for the Jews, the German public's image of the Gypsy victim often lacked the features of his individual persecution or identity. In articles published by the press in the late 1950s, one can detect an empathy with the Gypsy fate and the traumatic implications of their persecution for the survivors: "When asked about their Indian origin, they do not know where India is; but they know one thing: their father was murdered in Auschwitz, their mother in a gas chamber in Mauthausen."[35]

At the same time, this empathy was all too often accompanied by attempts to play down the Jewish Holocaust, as well as to deny that the central thrust of Nazi ideology, policy, and action was aimed against Jews. In 1962, the first major article in the German press on the persecution of Gypsies was published by the Berlin newspaper *Der Tagesspiegel*. It was published to mark the occasion of Fraternity Week (Woche der Brüderlichkeit), which was originally intended as a remembrance of the Jewish victims of the Holocaust, and the entwining of the persecution of Gypsies with the persecution of Jews was emphasized in the article: "It is not well known that the Nazi racial policy was applied to Gypsies as well," the newspaper said. "As their persecution has not yet been investigated scientifically, we feel it is our special duty to refer to this nation's martyrdom in the framework of Fraternity Week."

The article related the story of a Gypsy survivor of the concentration camp at Majdaneck, Poland. The Gypsy in question is anonymous, and except for his status as a victim no personal or individual aspects are given. A study of the details strongly suggests that the reporter provided a fictitious story built mainly on the description of the Jewish fate in Majdaneck. The article describes how the young Gypsy was suddenly removed from school in May 1940 and taken to a place where Gypsies were concentrated. From there, he was deported by train to Majdaneck with the others. In reality, however, the camp at Majdaneck only became functional in September 1942. Gypsies who were deported to the Government-General in Poland in May 1940 were concentrated in ghettos and small camps; some were later taken to concentration camps, while others lived in hiding and survived the war.

The article reflects one of the manipulative and hidden motives that some who adopted the Jewish-like Narrative held. The points in common between the persecution of Gypsies and that of Jews enabled the Gypsies' fate in the Third Reich to be used as a tool to undermine the primacy awarded the Jewish victim in German political culture and as a tool for taunting Jews. The reporter even went so far as to consider the Jewish victims as collaborators in the prejudice of German society against Gypsies: "The Nuremberg Laws were the first step of their persecution and that of Jews, who were integrated into German life. Jews, too, wondered why they and Gypsies were put in the same category. Even Jews have been obliged to regard this as a slander against their integration in Germany."[36]

The reporter deliberately claimed that, in the context of persecution, German Jews shared German society's prejudice against Gypsies—a prejudice that, according to this article, eventually led to mass murder. The reporter's motives stemmed from a German need to ease the guilt focused on the image of the Jewish victim. The absolutely false presentation of other Nazi persecutions as identical by their nature and totality with the Jewish Holocaust was one method of achieving this goal.

Such manipulative use of the Gypsy victim was also common in religious circles in the 1950s. A familiar feature of their approach was to reverse the historical truth and claim that the persecution of Gypsies by the Nazis was more severe than that of Jews. On some occasions, it was suggested that Jews gained recognition in public opinion not because they bore the vast brunt of the humiliation, persecution, murder, and torture but because of their financial power and international influence.[37] An example of this is a letter written to the liberal magazine *Der Spiegel* in April 1958 by Probst (Prior) Heinrich Grüber, a former member of the Confessing Church (Bekennende Kirche)—a group within the Protestant Church who opposed Nazism on theological and moral grounds. During the Third Reich Grüber and the Confessing Church helped non-Aryan Christians escape Germany.[38] He wrote: "It is well known that the Gypsies made a greater bloody sacrifice, and withstood a harder martyrdom, than people Hitler called 'Jews.' "[39] Grüber said no more about Gypsies, which for him only served as a new tool by which to attack Jews. The persecution of Gypsies, whom he apparently regarded as Christians, he defined as a martyrdom, but the murder of Jews was perceived by him as an altogether different phenomenon. In 1961, Grüber finally made his views known clearly: "It was the will of God to send Adolf Hitler in order to exterminate European Jewry," he said.[40] Grüber wished to integrate the Holocaust into the history of Christian redemption *(Heilgeschichte);* he regarded Hitler as a kind of whip of God, who was taking out revenge on the Jews for not acknowledging Jesus, if not even for his crucifixion.

By contrast, Georg Althaus, the so-called Gypsies' priest *(Zigeuner-pastor)* from Braunschweig, interpreted both the Jewish Holocaust and the murder of Gypsies in light of the history of redemption. Althaus's humanism prevented him from blaming the victims for their fate—and from exempting the German public from its liability. Althaus did not regard Gypsies as Christians but as pagans who adopted external signs of Christianity, and he claimed that the Germans had been guilty of not doing enough to bring these two non-Christian peoples to believe in Christ.[41]

There have also been two other phenomena: of hinting (completely falsely) that it was somehow the fault of the Jews that the Gypsy suffering was not properly documented; and the use of formulations and terminology taken from the policies to exterminate European Jewry to describe the Gypsy fate. These are discernible in the introduction to a review of two books dealing with Gypsies, published in the liberal weekly *Die Zeit*:

> It seems that many among us have not paid attention at all, or have successfully repressed the fact that Nazi Germany sentenced Gypsies, too, to a final solution, beginning with sterilization and terminating in the gas chambers. A comprehensive and decisive extermination, so that for some families who survived and the rest of the tribe, one cannot speak any more about the Gypsy people in Central Europe. The Gypsy world was always so isolated and its relations with the surroundings so limited that the persecuted could not expect help from anyone, not even recognition of the injustice done to them; they could not hope to be saved even in small numbers from extermination. The Nazis succeeded in what nobody else had succeeded in doing in hundreds of years. How helpless and left to their fate were these people is shown by the fact that there is no Gypsy evidence about their fate in the camps. They disappeared without being able to document their suffering, and apparently those around them did not find it worthwhile to do it for them.[42]

Using the Gypsies' inability to document their suffering as an indication of the Gypsies being defenseless and in the hands of their fate is designed to invite a hidden comparison with the Jewish fate, which, due to the Jew's documenting ability, was supposedly better than the fate of the Gypsies. The repetition in secular circles of this manipulative use of the Gypsy victim as a tool against Jews indicates that the central status of the Jewish victim in the FRG's political culture—a direct outcome of Hitler's choice to turn the Jew into Germany's declared enemy and its designated victim—was interpreted even by the nonreligious in a typical Christian manner (albeit perhaps unconsciously) as a recognition of the Jews as God's chosen people.

From the late 1950s, the way the Jewish-like Narrative was voiced became more direct. Articles appearing in the press contained a more severe tone of accusation, both toward those who were directly responsible and toward the German public in general for ignoring its guilt and liability for the crimes. In 1958 a children's story, "Jenö Was My Friend" ("Jenö war mein Freund"), by Wolfdietrich Schnurre appeared for the first time. The author remembers with nostalgia his childhood friend and the colorful and special lifestyle of his extended family before they were taken away by the Nazis. The story moderately criticizes German society for its passive cooperation with the Nazi persecution of Gypsies.[43] Another article stated: "The German Gypsies are haunted by memories of the past and realize that the German public failed to cope with it."[44] In 1959, the conservative *Frankfurter Allgemeine Zeitung* published an article concentrating on the part played by German Tsiganologie in the persecution of Gypsies and determined that racism destroyed this field of scientific inquiry when Ritter suggested exterminating Gypsies by sterilization. "Whoever deals in Tsiganologie after 1945," the author wrote, "is standing in the shade of Ritter and Justin."[45] A few years later, Hermann Langbein, himself a former political prisoner in Auschwitz, harshly attacked German attitudes toward Gypsy survivors. Langbein, who had reviewed the Auschwitz trial in Frankfurt in the early 1960s, wrote: "Only when they recognize the human dignity of the most despised people will they overcome the Nazi poison. And if you see a man whose forearm is tattooed with the letter Z, then look for a word which is more than a phrase!"[46]

The response of the West German public to the events of February 1959 reflects the shaping power of the Jewish-like Narrative in the consciousness of certain sectors of German society. In February 1959, the frontier guards of the FRG in Büchen, a small place in Schleswig-Holstein, discovered over 300 Polish Gypsies who had illegally boarded a train. The train had passed from Poland through the GDR and on to the FRG. It was carrying ethnic Germans from the former German territories incorporated into Poland after 1945, who wished to emigrate to the FRG. The frontier guard forbade the Gypsies to get off the train, and the authorities decided that they should be deported back to Poland. As the FRG had no diplomatic relations with Poland, negotiations with the Polish authorities were conducted through mediators. As the talks dragged on, the incident began to attract wide media attention, both in Germany and abroad. Eventually, the German authorities surrendered and agreed not to deport the Gypsies.[47]

During the negotiations, which took place between 18 and 28 February, about thirty German citizens sent letters and telegrams to Chancellor Konrad Adenauer and Minster of the Interior Dr. Gerhard Schröder, expressing their feelings on the issue. Opinions were split. Most of those who supported granting asylum to the "Büchen Gypsies" argued that the Germans owed a moral debt to Gypsies for the crimes committed against them during the Nazi regime, an argument that can clearly be attributed to the Jewish-like Narrative. Pastor Luckhardt, a priest from Bad Rehburg, wrote: "Thousands of Gypsies were murdered by Germans. We owe a big debt to these Gypsies."[48] The Gypsies' benefactor, the priest

Georg Althaus of Braunschweig, also called on the Minister of the Interior and on the chancellor to accept Gypsies in the name of the Wiedergutmachung ("correcting the wrong") debt the German people owed Gypsies.[49] Perhaps more significantly, others, too, all over the FRG, supported granting asylum to Gypsies, demonstrating that the Jewish-like Narrative, which in the late 1940s was the property of the few who had relations with Gypsies, had a decade later been absorbed into a wider stratum of society.[50]

Alternatively, others wrote to oppose giving Gypsies asylum. They accused Gypsies of being a rabble *(Gesindel)* living at the expense of the public. Two anonymous letters calling for the Gypsies' deportation contained arguments, typical of the extreme right, that the Schleswig-Holstein authorities' decision not to deport Gypsies back to Poland was associated with compensation policy, although the writers provided no evidence to back up these claims. They said that enough compensation had been paid to the state of Israel to atone for Nazi crimes.[51] Such a linkage between attitudes toward Gypsies and compensation policy with regard to the Jewish state suggests that by the late 1950s, the Jewish-like Narrative was also influential—albeit in negative ways—in German extreme-right circles. These radical rightists chose to regard the Nazi persecution of Gypsies from the perspective of how the Jewish Holocaust had been dealt with, rather than how the West German compensation authorities dealt with the Nazi persecution of Gypsies: as a legitimate persecution of criminals and asocials.

In 1963, an article in *Der Spiegel* on the persecution of Gypsies in the Third Reich expressed the Jewish-like Narrative in the clearest manner published in the German press until that time. Gypsies were presented as innocent victims of a criminal and racist regime, and it was reported that 500,000 of Europe's 2 million Gypsies had been murdered by the Nazis. This was the first time since the magazine was founded in 1947 that it had dealt with the Gypsy issue and with the question of the discrimination against Gypsies in the FRG.[52] The description of postwar careers of the late Robert Ritter and, especially, of his former assistant, the psychologist Eva Justin, in the municipal health office in Frankfurt elicited a scandal in the municipal council (Magistrat) and raised the demands of Gypsy citizens and city politicians to remove her from her office, especially from taking care of Gypsy children in the caravan camp Bonames. Unfortunately, these demands were only partially implemented, and Justin was never compelled to resign from her post. She died of cancer three years later.[53]

The change that occurred in the public discourse between 1945 and 1965 about the mass murder of Gypsies in many ways resembles Germany's coming to terms with the Jewish Holocaust. From an almost complete repression of the issue in the media and in literature in the first years after the war, a public discourse about the Gypsy fate in the Third Reich gradually developed in the second half of the 1950s, on the fringes of the ever expanding public discourse about the Holocaust.[54] From the late 1950s, the image of the Gypsy victim was molded in the press and elsewhere, based on the image of the Jewish victim. As a result, the "victim of Nazism motif" turned into a central element in attitudes toward Gypsies in general, at least in liberal circles. This was true even when the point of discussion was not their persecution by the Nazis. But as the German debate on the Gypsy victim became more forceful, hidden expressions of protest against Jews also became more numerous. Accompanying the discourse was an accusatory tone that was pointed toward the German public for its responsibility for the Gypsy persecution. Nevertheless, even when in the 1960s public awareness of the Gypsy persecution was enhanced, no corresponding phenomenon to the philosemitism generated among large sections of the German public by the Holocaust and the reeducation policy of the Allies developed.[55]

A significant indication of the way in which the Jewish-like Narrative had penetrated into the mainstream of German consciousness during the 1960s is contained in two important German encyclopedias in the 1970s. The 1974 edition of *Die Brockhaus Enzyklopaedie* carried a new entry about Gypsies, which stated that Gypsies had incurred heavy losses, assessed between a quarter million and a half million people, at the hands of the Nazis. Some milestones in the persecution of the German Gypsies until their deportation to Auschwitz in 1943 were also included, similar to the description of the persecution of Jews given in these encyclopedias.[56] This new edition excluded Justin's book from its bibliography. The 1979 edition of the *Meyers Enzyklopaedisches Lexikon* took a less reserved tack, stating that the repression and persecution of Gypsies reached its peak under the Nazis, when it developed into a racial genocide.[57]

This phenomenon shows that even before the Society for the Threatened Peoples launched its campaign in favor of Gypsies in 1979 (which is outlined in the next chapter), their recognition as victims of the Third Reich had already spread within the West German cultural elites. Despite the dominance of the Jewish-like Narrative, however, until November 1985 the German political establishment had not yet held any official ceremony to honor the Gypsy victims of the Nazi regime. Apparently, the universal perceptions imparted by the Allies' reeducation policy influenced German political culture and especially the press more than it influenced public opinion and the German consciousness in general.

THE SYNCRETIC NARRATIVE

After 1945, a further narrative, of a syncretic nature, developed in Germany, combining elements of the other two narratives. It presented the persecuted Gypsies as dubious people rather than as innocent victims, a view that bore some similarity to the Nazi Narrative; like the Jewish-like Narrative, however, this Syncretic Narrative also denounced the persecution and murder of Gypsies as a crime. This attitude was intended to reconcile the commitment to universal values contained in the Allies' denazification and reeducation policy with the identification with German national heritage, which necessarily included a certain understanding of Nazism and its motives. The paradoxical combination expresses the somewhat schizophrenic condition of the German consciousness after 1945, not only concerning Gypsies but also concerning Jews and other problematic issues from the Nazi past.

The Syncretic Narrative suggested, albeit in a slightly more moderate way than the Nazi Narrative, that the victim had by his behavior and acts brought disaster upon himself. This belief mirrored the wide consensus prevalent in German society. It expressed the German attempt to mitigate liability for the crimes committed against Gypsies and to reduce the responsibility that society and the state now owed to the Gypsy victims and their descendants.

The most practical way this narrative was expressed was the denial—in the media up until the 1960s, and in the political establishments of both West and East Germany up to 1985—of unconditional recognition that Gypsies were victims of Nazism. In 1985 the political establishment in the two German states substituted this narrative with the Jewish-like one (the events of that year are outlined in the next chapter), but after a short period, the Syncretic Narrative returned in fact in a more subtle and sophisticated form.

As the Gypsy issue in general did not occupy an important place on the public agenda in postwar Germany, this narrative was rarely explicitly presented in public. However, while there were no official pronouncements in West Germany in support of the Syncretic Narrative, it was expressed at least implicitly by various government officials, as well as in reference books and encyclopedias; this expression is an indication of the mood of mainstream post-1945 West German society.

Up until the late 1950s, both highbrow and popular literature, the cinema and the press, dealt with Gypsy issues in the same way as they had done before 1945, sometimes to the point of completely ignoring the Nazi persecution. For example, in both the 1957 edition of *Der Grosse Brockhaus* encyclopedia and the 1968 edition of *Der Neue Brockhaus* encyclopedia, the description of Gypsy history ends with the attempts to settle them in the eighteenth century.[58] However, the editors took the trouble to update the bibliography of this edition of *Der Grosse Brockhaus* to include the 1943 Ph.D. dissertation by Justin, in which she presented her racist credo regarding the alleged hopelessness of educating Gypsy children due to the supposed impossibility of "correcting" them. Justin concluded by recommending the sterilization of all Gypsy children who were raised in a German educational framework, in order to prevent crime and the transfer of inherent defects.[59]

This silence about the Nazi past has been defined by the philosopher Karl Jaspers as "aggressive."[60] The inclusion by the encyclopedia editors of a significant Nazi work in an updated bibliography was a subtle way of expressing the belief that Gypsies were responsible for their fate. Sometimes the truth was blurred. The 1950 edition of *Der Neue Herder* stated that "in the Nazi state, part of the Gypsies were deported to Poland or exterminated."[61] This version left it to the reader to decide between the two possibilities. The 1956 edition of *Der Grosse Herder* was more accurate: it clearly stated that Gypsies were deported to Poland and exterminated. However, this fate was put down to Gypsy problematics, deriving from the fact that "being vagrants, they found it difficult to integrate into the settled culture of the host nations."[62]

The suppression of the truth by the German media and public after 1945 did not derive mostly from guilt and shame (which were important factors in why the Germans ignored and were silent about the murder of Jews) but much more from the fear of explicitly expressing a Nazi attitude, which the Allies had deemed illegitimate. Even Ritter was quick to adopt this narrative. In his apologetic essay of 1947, Ritter expressed his reservations about the Gypsy murders, which he presented as a consequence of racism and attributed to "Nazi fanatics." At the same time, he justified the incarceration and the "prevention of proliferation" of the asocials among Gypsies as a solution for the problem of asociality. Ritter claimed this was not in any way a racist solution,[63] but, of course, this was a lie because previously Ritter had claimed that the so-called asociality of Gypsies was a result of their racial origin.

Ritter's disciple in the racial hygiene research of Gypsies, Herman Arnold, adopted a Jewish-like Narrative. In 1961, he wrote: "The Gypsies living in Germany were severely injured by the mass murder in concentration camps in 1942–1944. To compensate them financially is not enough; we must also act so that the hostility and contempt toward them will be undermined and substituted by understanding and appreciation of the otherness of these people."[64]

In contrast to the lack of official government statements in the FRG, in East Germany the totalitarian regime dominated the kind of publications that were in private hands in the West, and therefore they officially

Sinti caravans near Ludwigslust (GDR), ca. 1960. (Reimar Gilsenbach.)

expressed the Syncretic Narrative. For example, a booklet on women in-mates at the concentration camp at Ravensbrück, published by the com-mittee of the resistance fighters of the GDR, included the two components of the Syncretic Narrative blaming the victim for his fate, while at the same time denouncing the murder: "This people [the Gypsies], who, ac-cording to their tradition, are difficult to settle, were classified by the illiterate and barbaric theory of German fascism as 'racially inferior.' The fascists decided upon their total extermination."[65]

Accusations against Gypsies had a Marxist flavor in the GDR. Marx-ism was influenced through the Enlightenment by the physiocratic percep-tion, so that in Marxism Gypsies were perceived to constitute a parasitic, unproductive element and therefore were also considered socially back-ward and politically reactionary. However, Enlightenment ideas also led Marxists to perceive Gypsies as a target for "civic correction" *(bürger-liche Besserung)* through education and work. Such a concept, which could be found throughout the Communist block, was based on the En-lightened tradition common among government officials in Central Eu-rope since the nineteenth century.

The first encyclopedia in the GDR was the *Meyers Neues Lexikon,* appeared in Leipzig in 1964. The entry for "Gypsies" again suggested Gypsies were responsible for their fate, although it was presented in a subtle way, within a paragraph describing the occupations and character of traditional Gypsy society and the changes made to it by the Socialist regimes. The entry explained that in the capitalist system Gypsies were peddlers, musicians, small craftsmen, and cattle traders, which implied that the Marxist world regarded these as parasitic occupations. Then it was stated that Maria Theresa had failed to force Gypsies to settle permanently (hinting that this was at least in part the fault of the victim). After that, a short and minimalist sentence, seemingly describing the consequence of the failure, read: "Thousands [of Gypsies] were murdered in the fascist-Hitler concentration camps." Thereafter, many Gypsy *kolkhoses* (cooperative agricultural units) in the former Soviet Union were mentioned, giving the impression that in the Socialist world Gypsies became laborers and farmers, occupations recognized in German culture from the time of the Enlightenment as productive. The social aspect of the traditional Gypsy lifestyle was also described negatively. It was said that in the past Gypsy social life had been characterized by strong patriarchal features and a despotic rule of the camp elders and family heads. It was suggested that Socialism liberated Gypsies from these evils.[66]

The East German Communist regime also put into practice this ideological perspective. The authorities forced Gypsies from Thuringia to abandon their caravans and traditional lifestyle and to settle permanently and work in a stable job. Some Gypsies who refused to comply with these new dictates were imprisoned as asocials.[67] But, as in the West, the Communist version of the Syncretic Narrative did not ignore the criminal nature of the Nazi persecution, and, like the Jewish-like Narrative, it used motifs that were borrowed from the Holocaust, such as the call for total extermination in gas chambers according to a predetermined intention. Contrary to the manipulative use of the Gypsy victim as a means of attacking the Jewish victim, which was common within West German political culture, this phenomenon was absent in the GDR from both official and unofficial publications on the Gypsy persecution. This was because in the political culture of the Communist state, the Jew did not function as the representative victim of Nazism, as was the case in the West. Neither the Soviet occupiers nor the Communist leadership in the GDR that followed fostered among their citizens awareness of guilt or the feeling of collective liability toward the Jew, as the reeducation, and denazification and later a certain trend in the public discourse, in the West had done.[68]

The Communist oligarchy of the GDR felt a need for national reconciliation between, on the one hand, the victims and resistance fighters of fascism (whose tradition they aspired to and in many cases did, in fact, represent), and, on the other hand, the past records of many of their citizens, who had served as soldiers in the Nazi army. To achieve this purpose, the East German regime had chosen exactly as their Western opponent to regard the German soldiers who fell in the war while serving Hitler as victims of Nazism.

A symbolic expression of this was given at a ceremony in 1969 at the memorial site for the victims of fascism and militarism that had been established in 1960 in the New Guard (Neue Wache) monument in central Berlin. At the ceremony, the remains of an unknown concentration camp prisoner and of an unknown soldier were buried together. The remains were covered with soil brought from the concentration camps at Buchenwald and Mauthausen and from the battlefields of Stalingrad, El Alamein, and Monte Casino. This symbolic ceremony commemorated both the Wehrmacht fallen soldiers and those who had fallen in the fight against fascism as victims of Nazism and war.[69] In the early 1990s, following German reunification, the government, headed by Conservative Chancellor Helmut Kohl, adopted the Communist concept of the memory of the Wehrmacht's fallen soldiers, which had been a widespread national German concept since 1945. Kohl turned the New Guard into the principal memorial site in Germany in memory of the victims of war and dictatorship *(Gewaltherrschaft),* thus continuing to nurture the idea of reconciliation between the persecutors and their victims, including the Gypsies.

Analysis of the way the Gypsy persecution has been presented in German discourse shows that there is no unified German consciousness about this issue. In the several different schools of thought, certain thinking overlaps (for example, "blaming the victim" in both the Nazi and Syncretic Narratives); in other areas, the schools are in complete contradiction. This is because the groups who created these narratives were not ideologically consolidated or homogeneous. One cannot attribute a certain narrative to a certain political party, for example.

The individuals who participated in their creation and preservation also played a role in interpreting other historic events from the Nazi past and in consolidating them into collective memories, although the way they brought together these other events did not necessarily correspond with the various narratives about the Gypsy persecution. As we shall see in the next chapter, the dominance of the Jewish-like Narrative (or elements from it) in the German political culture of the 1980s did not necessarily derive from a deep identification with the contents and values embedded within it but, rather, from various constraints dictated by political, social, cultural, and psychological factors, which were, and generally still are, of a subconscious nature.

8

"Discovery" of the Gypsy Victim of Nazism

AWAKENING GERMANS TO NAZI PERSECUTION OF GYPSIES AND ITS MOTIVES

ALTHOUGH a public discourse on the Nazi persecution of Gypsies had begun in Germany in 1945, the issue was not properly placed on the public agenda until March 1979, when the Society for the Threatened Peoples (Gesellschaft für bedrohte Völker), a German human rights organization, initiated a public campaign in favor of West German Gypsies.

The timing of this campaign in favor of Gypsies was linked to the greater German confrontation with the Nazi past and in particular with the Jewish victim, after the American TV miniseries *Holocaust* was broadcast in the FRG in late January 1979. Watching this program proved to be a traumatic event for German society, as it was confronted on a mass public level with the darkest aspects of its recent past, which the German consciousness had done much to repress after 1945. Following from their living room armchairs the story of the tragic persecution of the German Jewish Weiss family, about 20 million German viewers were exposed, probably for the first time, to the concrete meaning of the extermination of the European Jewry. The narrative strategy of the series dragged many Germans into identifying with the Jewish victims, thus creating an unprecedented emotional conflict in Germany.[1] Many of the viewers were torn between their identification with the victims' suffering and their belonging to and identification with the national collective from which the murderers came.

The *Holocaust* broadcast led to an intense public discourse, which continued for many weeks after the program aired. The public's responses to watching the series were varied. For example, over the course of several weeks, *Der Spiegel* published letters by readers who said they had been shocked into feelings of guilt and shame. Others reacted with anger, resistance, and, in certain cases, even denial.[2] These angry responses came not only from people who were close to the Nazi war criminals and their political supporters on the German nationalistic right but also from people in the new German left.

The *Pflasterstrand,* a biweekly magazine published in Frankfurt and edited by Daniel Cohn-Bendit, printed an article about the TV series by an anonymous author, who claimed that its broadcast on German television was part of a conspiracy designed by capitalistic interests and zionist ideology, to relativize in public opinion the crimes committed by the Americans in Vietnam and to increase the public support for zionism and for Israel.[3] Such a response shows that, despite their political differences with the Nationalist right, the new German left also found it difficult to cope with the feelings of guilt caused by the murder of Jews, which now affected them like other segments of the German society. Furthermore, the patterns of arguments of these leftists did not differ greatly from that of those on the radical right.[4] This might support Dan Diner's claim that many Germans in the postwar period turned to the left mainly because of the desire to avoid too great a biographical proximity to the criminal past.[5]

In contrast with these direct responses to *Holocaust,* the concerns of the Society for the Threatened Peoples did not bear any direct relation to the TV series. Until 1979, the society had not dealt publicly with Gypsies, although it had collected some material on the issue since the early 1970s. But in March 1979, about six weeks after *Holocaust* was broadcast, the society held a convention in Göttingen entitled "Holocaust Means Also the Extermination of 500,000 Gypsies in the Third Reich."[6] The organization's chairman, Tilman Zülch, opened the convention by establishing that the Holocaust was perceived in the public consciousness as constituting Nazi crimes performed against Jews and that it had been forgotten that another group had been exterminated by the Nazis for racist reasons.[7] The very use by Zülch of the term "Holocaust" derived from the projection of the American series; this term had not been used previously in Germany to mark the Nazi murder of Jews.[8] Raising the issue of the Gypsy victim at a time of unprecedented preoccupation in the FRG with the fate of Jewish victims of Nazism had a certain similarity to the response in the *Pflasterstrand:* the decision was to avoid directly coping with the Holocaust and to escape confrontation with Jewish victims by concentrating on other crimes and alternative victims.

In fact, this pattern had been entwined with the organization's activity and publications since the society's establishment in Hamburg in 1970. Like most of the cofounders, Zülch, the main spirit of the organization, was a member of a German family who had been expelled or had escaped from the German territories in the East in 1945 or 1946. These people are commonly referred to as expellees *(Heimatvertriebene)*. Zülch's awareness of and deep identification with the suffering of the German expellees, which appears repeatedly in his writing, molded his political conviction. Zülch claims that the Red Army either murdered or caused the death of about 2 million German men, women, and children by forsaking them to cold and hunger at the end of the war as they escaped to the West and again after the war during the mass expulsion westward of Germans from the occupied German territories in Eastern Europe. Zülch claims that the victimization of Jews in Auschwitz, terrible as it was, could not reduce the gravity of this crime, which he perceived as genocide *(Völkermord)* committed on helpless victims. Zülch also accuses the democratic Allies, who agreed at the Potsdam convention to the deportation of the German inhabitants of the East, as being an accomplice to genocide.[9] In the radical circles of the student movement into which Zülch and his colleagues had been integrated in the late 1960s, this attitude might have been perceived as an illegitimate expression of nationalism and what was then defined in Communist jargon as *Revenchism.*

Zülch expressed his feeling of being a victim in a somewhat odd way, by identifying with Third World minorities who had been persecuted for racist, ethnic, and religious reasons. On occasion, he pointed at the former Allies who had fought Nazi Germany and held them responsible for these persecutions.[10] Although the society said that it had arrived at this conclusion from the lessons it had learned from the Nazi crimes, it might have seemed that, in fact, the lessons had been drawn from the "Allies' crimes." The name of the organization's publication, *Pogrom,* a term associated in the Western collective consciousness with the persecution of Jews, was now used in favor of Third World peoples and expressed Zülch's own tendency to project from the reality of Jews suffered by the Third Reich onto the reality of the Third World.[11] From the beginning, the organization focused attention on minorities who had been victims of genocide or who, according to them, were in danger of becoming extinct. The organization dealt with the peoples of Biafra, southern Sudan, eastern Bengal, and Kurdistan, among others, most of whom were perceived in Germany to be nature peoples *(Naturvölker)*.[12] The society organized several events related to the fate of Gypsies in the Third Reich and after, which were intended to raise awareness among the German public of Gypsy persecution.

In 1981, regarding the German "discovery" of another "Holocaust" (namely, the Gypsy persecution), the ethnologist Bernhard Streck pointed out that, rather than increase feelings of guilt, the preoccupation with multiple cases of genocide might mollify the Holocaust's unperceivable horror by minimizing it. Streck raised the possibility that because of this, "the German press accepted with prominent willingness the 'second genocide' and did not challenge the number of 500,000 victims."[13] The "discovery" of the Gypsy victim so close to the opening of German discourse on the Holocaust was not an isolated phenomenon. In 1979 and the early 1980s, other victim groups of Nazism were "discovered" and placed on the public agenda in the FRG, becoming known as the "forgotten" victims *(die Vergessene Opfer):* homosexuals, asocials, victims of euthanasia, victims of the forced sterilization, and forced laborers.[14]

While the confrontation with the murder of Jews after 1945 had enhanced in some Germans the interest in Jewish victims and their world, others, who for various reasons found it difficult to cope with the guilt that this debate had stimulated, probably preferred to run away from the confrontation with the Holocaust and Jewish victims.[15] The German preoccupation with "forgotten" victims in the early 1980s was one of the legitimate escape routes from the confrontation as a result of the public discourse initiated by the TV series. Focusing on these victims met the wishes of those Germans, who for emotional reasons sought, on the one hand, to run away from confronting the Holocaust, but, on the other hand, found it difficult to ignore it altogether.

Certain aspects of the public preoccupation with forgotten victims went beyond the mere hint of a protest against the status of Jewish victims in the political culture of the FRG and rallied openly and blatantly against Jews. The German discussion about compensation for forgotten victims was characterized by antisemitic tones: in a complete reversal of the truth, Jews and their representatives who had been involved in consolidating the compensation policy for the victims of Nazism in the FRG were accused of putting Jewish interests first and of depriving the forgotten victims of compensation.[16]

Not only the timing of the "discovery" of the Gypsy victim but also the nature of the German preoccupation with this subject might support Streck's argument and that made even more forcibly by Dan Diner, a few years later, about awakening German interest in the forgotten victims. Diner called the phenomenon "covering memory" *(Deckerinnerung)* because he saw it as an expression of what he defined as a new historical desire *(Geschichtesbeflissenheit)* to come closer to the events of the Nazi period, while at the same time avoiding coping with the main guilt-causing factor the Nazi past evoked in the German consciousness—the Jewish Holocaust. Diner and Streck believed that the motive for shifting the emphasis to other victims of Nazism was primarily to circumvent

the German impression that the extermination of Jews had a special significance.[17] They implied that the German preoccupation with the persecution of Gypsies was manipulative, intended in part to relativize the
Holocaust. However, not everyone dealing with the issue was aware of
this. The society's activists sought not only to shift German public opinion from focusing on the Jewish victim but also to bring a substantial
change in the way and patterns in which Germans coped with the Holocaust and Nazi atrocities in general. This coping was characterized by
natural feelings of guilt and shame, and these characteristics were widely
presented in the public discourse after the broadcast of *Holocaust*. Effectively, the society's prominent activists tried to free the Germans from
their feelings of guilt and shame regarding the Holocaust.

Fritz Greußing was the central activist of the society. An Austrian, he
later became the secretary general of the Sinti organization, the Central
Committee of German Sinti and Roma (Zentralrat deutscher Sinti und
Roma). In one of the society's early publications on the Gypsy issue,
Greußing argued that "the way in which the society's members coped
with the Nazi past *[Vergangenheitsbewältigung]* should be understood
neither as an anti-German conjuration of the German collective guilt nor
as a moral and generalizing accusation of the older generation by us, who
were born later."[18]

Greußing is younger than Zülch; he was born in 1948 and came from
a different background. Although he claimed his mother was of Jewish
origin and his father had been an anti-Nazi,[19] his and Zülch's thinking
had an ideological affinity. Greußing argued that "even though most Germans and Austrians followed the Führer, many of the executioners of the
Nazi period were members of other European nations," which he assumed could reduce the central liability of the Germans for planning and
carrying out the Holocaust and other mass murders in Europe. To
weaken the sense of German collective guilt, Greußing was not satisfied
with this argument, which blurred the identity of the executors, so he
added a complementary argument to also blur the identity of the victims:
"Among the victims of Nazism were also German Jews, German Sinti,
German Socialists, Communists, Christians, trade union members, officers, homosexuals, and handicapped people," as if their simply being
German made them victims of Nazism.[20] Greußing's arguments break the
German extermination system into apparently isolated acts of murder,
while the blurring of the executioners' and the victims' identities gives
them an arbitrary nature, also blurring the German feelings of guilt and
making it easier for those who feel guilty.

Choosing to preoccupy the German political culture in the 1980s with
the Gypsies, asocials, and homosexuals and not with Jews or citizens of
the Soviet Union who formed the major groups of victims of the Nazi

regime may also have had a manipulative nature. It raises the question of whether the concern was really motivated by a sincere desire to salvage these victims of Nazism from oblivion. The forgotten victims were mostly Germans,[21] and their persecution was not perceived by wide circles of the German public as a crime of the type perpetrated against Jews. Many Germans did not even regard Gypsies, asocials, or homosexuals as victims but as delinquents who were rightly persecuted in the Third Reich. Remembering these persecutions and their victims did not involve the kind of feelings of guilt that were evoked by the memory of Jewish victims and the Holocaust.

Notwithstanding the above, the German preoccupation with the forgotten victims was characterized by the "Jewification" of these victims. Terminology and concepts from the total and unrelenting context of the Nazi extermination of European Jewry were borrowed for describing the often more sporadic persecution of the forgotten victims under Nazism, even though, at least in part, the aim of these persecutions, unlike the Holocaust, had not been the total annihilation of the entire group of marked victims.[22] The emotional confrontation with the murder of Jews that was forced on the population by the broadcast of *Holocaust* appears to have undermined the hidden comparison the society had been trying to make between the Holocaust and crimes against minorities in the Third World.

Undermining this ideological foundation after broadcast of the TV series in 1979 required proximity to the Nazi past and finding an alternative victim whose persecution would be more like that of Jews. The Gypsy victim was selected as a "substitute" for the Jewish victim, partly because his fate in the Third Reich did not evoke heavy guilt feeling among the German public. No less important, Gypsies were perceived by the German public as mute victims, like the other repressed ethnic minorities of the Third World with which the society dealt. Zülch and his colleagues unconsciously chose a group of victims whose supposed muteness would enable them to speak on their behalf and to voice as if from their own mouths. But what was said certainly did not express the feelings of many Gypsy victims and their descendants toward the Germans.

This silence of the Gypsy victim was only illusory. The Gypsy victims—especially their children who were born after the war—authentically expressed their feelings toward Germans, without taking into consideration the positioning Greußing and his colleagues would have liked them to address. Melanie Spitta, for example, opened her film *The Lie (Das falsche Wort)* with a piercing monologue on the German collective guilt: "My brothers and all our children were murdered and died in agony. For this you Germans demonstrated courage; however, most of you did not have the courage to assume liability for [the way] in which this murder was made possible and was realized. Of us, only a few survived, because among you, so many Nazis *[Hackenkreuzler]* remained, who knew how to deny us compensation."[23] Spitta's monologue was criticized in 1989 in a statement published by the Hessian branch of the Verband Deutscher Sinti, the organization of Sinti in the FRG. The paper's position was similar to Greußing's opinion of the issue of German guilt: "There was a serious mistake in the film, in that Mrs. Spitta distinguished in "you Germans" between those who allegedly carried the meaningless collective guilt, who persecuted us and denied us compensation, and "we the Gypsies," who now again appear as strangers to most of the [German] population and are beyond its understanding."[24]

Among the Sinti there are indeed some individuals who oppose Spitta's expressing feelings that were prevalent among them toward the Germans, but this is not because of their ideological opposition to perceiving German society as collectively guilty of persecuting Sinti in the Third Reich. It derives from their desire not to antagonize further German feelings toward Sinti. The consciousness of the Sinti in the FRG was shaped under the influence of the traditional animosity toward them, and later the Nazi persecution that was inflicted on them and by the further rejection and discrimination they experienced after the war. From the Sinti perspective, German society is indeed collectively to blame for their fate in the Third Reich and for denial of their eligibility for compensation afterward.

The Sinti organization's statement expresses a typical German attitude rather than a Sinti one; it also reveals a great degree of similarity to Greußing's view of the issue of collective guilt; therefore, it is not improbable that the publication of this statement had something to do with Greußing's capacity as secretary general of the Central Committee of German Sinti and Roma, the Sinti principal organization in the FRG. He might have tried to impart through it to the Sinti "correct" patterns of viewing the Nazi past, which were consistent with the coping patterns of their German "benefactors."

The benefactors were not shy to criticize and denounce the victims' descendants, who dared to express an opinion that differed from that of the descendants of the Nazi murderers' generation. Greussing sought to give the Germans preoccupied with the Gypsy persecution a reconciliatory and nonaccusatory expression that not only would help ease the German sense of guilt but also would preserve the status of the German "benefactors" as superior to their "protegees."

For Zülch, Greussing, and others, Gypsies acted as a kind of bridge from the Third World back to Germany and the preoccupation with the Nazi past. This return from the Third World to the Third Reich signifies the beginning of the process of "return to the nation" *(zurück zur Na-*

tion), which was to become a prevalent phenomenon in Germany more than a decade later. The Society for the Threatened Peoples' preoccupation with Gypsies, although highlighting "the half million Sinti and Roma murdered all over Europe by the Nazis" (a number that is much higher than that given in all credible research assessments and seems to have been plucked out of the air, possibly to serve their purposes), focused mainly on the German Sinti rather than on the Roma of Eastern Europe, although the number of Roma victims exceeded the number of Sinti victims.

Zülch identified with the Sinti as German victims, and he presented them as mistreated Germans rather than as foreigners. Although Zülch associated the Gypsy persecution with the Jewish Holocaust, it is not clear whether he identified with the Sinti because they were victims of Nazism or because he perceived them to be an integral part of the German victims persecuted by the Red Army. Zülch emphasized the common fate of the Sinti from the German territories in the East and the German expellees (such as himself), who had suffered Communist repression, were uprooted from their homes, and underwent other hardships.[25] He presented Gypsies as Germans and linked them with the German victim of what he termed "the crimes of Stalinism."

In the 1980s the German focus on the Gypsy victim primarily criticized the seniority status the Jewish victim supposedly enjoyed in the German consciousness. Toward the end of 1979, a collection of articles edited by Zülch was published under the title *In Auschwitz Gassed, until This Day Persecuted* (*In Auschwitz vergast, bis heute verfolgt*), and this became the slogan of the public civil rights campaign in favor of Gypsies that the society launched at the same time. This slogan implicitly summarized the essence of the society's message: protest against what seemed to them hypocritical in German society, which concentrated all its efforts on compensation and atonement toward the Jewish victims, while causing the public to forget the Gypsy victims, whose fate in the Third Reich, they claimed, was identical to the Jewish fate. In various public settings they argued strongly that the Nazi persecution of Gypsies was identical in motives, nature, and schedule with the persecution of European Jewry. They also implied that, although the persecution of Jews ended with the defeat of Nazism, the racist persecution of Gypsies continued in the Federal Republic and was not substantially different from their persecution under Nazism.

Zülch chose to open the collection with a short article by the Jewish German philosopher Ernst Tugendhat, an active member of the society. Tugendhat discussed the different fates of Jews and Gypsies, who, he said, were "brothers in fate for centuries in Europe; however, after Auschwitz their paths separated." Tugendhat claimed that while assimilating

Jews like himself felt quite comfortable in Germany, the Gypsies' nightmare had not disappeared after Auschwitz, and they were still treated as subhumans *(Untermenschen)*, although they were no longer targeted for extermination. Tugendhat explained that Germans can more readily identify with Jews, whose lifestyle does not substantially differ from their own, than with Gypsies. Tugendhat "confessed," as a German Jew, that the German Jews also shared the German non-Jews' prejudices toward Gypsies, and thus he positioned the former Nazi victims alongside their German persecutors.[26]

As not only Nazi racism but any racism was associated by the German left wing as leading to Auschwitz, the exposure of the Jews' "racism" in this article and in various speeches and articles by Tugendhat[27] enabled many Germans to read between the lines he had written; they found a message that helped them cope with their guilt over the Holocaust. From Tugendhat's writing the German reader could gather that Jewish victims were no less racist than their Nazi persecutors were, and they might even conclude that it could have been only accidental that Germans were the persecutors and Jews the victims.

Although Tugendhat had not intended that his writing would be interpreted this way, publication of his short article coincided with Zülch's exposure of the "hypocrisy" of the winning superpowers who had presented their war against Nazi Germany as a moral war of the good against the evil, while claiming that "the war crimes" of the Allies who stood by the Jews against the Germans were no less grave than Nazi crimes.[28] Zülch's decision to open the collection with an article by a Jew rather than one of his own essays probably stemmed from a desire to introduce arguments that were perceived to be illegitimate when they were presented by a German according to the existing communication rules of the political culture of the FRG.[29]

Other protests against the unique status of the Jewish victim in the political culture of FRG were made in the historical literature published in Germany in the 1980s. For example, the late Joachim Hohmann compared the Gypsy and Jewish victim in the FRG after 1945. After previously publishing several books on homosexuality, Hohmann, a social pedagogue, apparently started to deal with the question of Gypsies after the society had started to address this issue in 1979, and he participated in this activity.[30] Hohmann noted that after 1945 public attention was turned toward the Jews' suffering, and the extermination of Gypsies remained unknown.[31] He quoted from Fredrick Cawles's 1948 article that "the Gypsies had been more gravely persecuted than Jews, as lacking citizenship they had no rights, they were tortured and murdered in concentration camps," and then he added some baseless arguments of his own: "The escape possibilities [from Germany] open to them [the Gyp-

[handwritten marginalia: "use g Gypsies to create new narrative"]

sies] were much more limited than were those for many Jews and Communist intellectuals."[32] Clearly, undermining the central role of the Jewish victim at the hands of the Nazis was a target of concern, no less than was the salvation of the Gypsy victim from oblivion.

In the writings of the late Detlev Peukert (1950–1990), too, the Gypsy victim served as a device for deemphasizing and downplaying the Jewish victim. Peukert was the first German historian who put the Nazi persecution of Gypsies, together with that of homosexuals and asocials, in the context of a historiographic discussion of Nazi racism and mass extermination. His book *Volksgenossen und Geminschaftsfremde* (the English title is *Inside Nazi Germany*), published in 1982, dealt with the social history of the Third Reich from the perspective of "history from below." In the chapter on racism as a social policy in the Third Reich, Peukert presented a monocausal explanation for the Nazi mass extermination policy, placing the persecution of Gypsies at the center of this policy, while also mentioning asocials and homosexuals. In this book he dedicated only one page to Jewish victims.[33] In his article "Everyday and Barbarism" ("Alltag und Barbarei"), which he wrote in 1987, following what is known as the historians' debate *(Historikerstreit)* of 1986, Peukert outlined the ideological considerations that guided his choice to push the Holocaust of the European Jewry out from the central place it formerly held in the historiography on Nazism and in the FRG.

Peukert's considerations are moralistic in substance. According to him, the concentration of German public consciousness on the Jewish Holocaust was a means of repressing in the German collective memory the millions of other victims of the Nazis, including the Gypsies. Peukert defined this process as a "renewed selection of victims." The use of this term, which was borrowed from the Nazi jargon of the final solution, was intended to imply that emphasizing the Jewish fate while apparently ignoring the other victims was as racist as Nazism itself. On the basis of this analysis, Peukert argued that the thesis regarding the uniqueness or singularity of the (Jewish) Holocaust should be rejected, because it created a hierarchy of victims, while the extermination measures and goals of the Nazis were multiple and never reduced to Jews alone.[34] Perhaps for the purpose of weakening the arguments of his adversaries, Peukert confused a moral hierarchy of the various Nazi persecutions, according to which the persecution of Gypsies and the other "forgotten" victims was allegedly less evil than that of Jews, with the hierarchy of the various victims of Nazism in the German collective consciousness. As part of this discussion, he also interpolated the focusing of the historic research on extermination of European Jewry rather than on Gypsy persecution.

From a purely moral point of view, it is not possible to scale on different levels of evil the mass murders the Nazis committed on different groups, according to their numbers or the extent of totality in which they were persecuted. However, by its very nature human consciousness is selective and unequal. It tends to classify the impressions it absorbs according to the significance it attributes to them. The persecution of Jews occupied a higher status than that of Gypsies in the German consciousness because of the unique significance that was attributed to the Holocaust of the European Jewry, known as the Shoah. This uniqueness had two dimensions: one objective and realistic, and the other subjective and metaphysical.

The objective dimension stemmed from the unique nature of the persecution of Jews, which was the most total of all the persecutions undertaken by the Nazi regime and occupied a central place in the public consciousness of the Third Reich's, as well as on Nazi agenda. As such, the Nazi persecution of Jews was engraved on the German collective memory. The circumstances of the Cold War have intensified this memory, as it repressed from the Western consciousness the memory of the 16 million civil victims of the Nazi annihilation war conducted against the Soviet Union. At these circumstances the 6 million Jewish victims became the largest group of victims of Nazi Germany, and hence the Jewish victim was also regarded in the Western consciousness as a representative victim of Nazism. By contrast, the Gypsy persecution was at the bottom of the national agenda in the Third Reich from 1933 on, and the impressions of the Gypsy persecution are not analogous in their intensity to the impression on the German consciousness made by the Shoah. The different stages of the persecution of Jews from 1933 to 1945 were later interpreted, under the influence of the reeducation policy of the Allies, as being a complex of preliminary stages that led to murder. The notion of singularity of the Shoah in the German consciousness was intensified by the active involvement of considerable sections of the German population at the preliminary stages of the Nazi persecution of the Jews. Some of the most famous events were the boycott of 1 April 1933, and in the Reichskristallnacht of 9 November 1938. This public involvement was presented in Nazi propaganda as an authentic expression of the popular wrath *(Volkszorn)* of the German people toward the Jews. This active participation of the German public in the persecution of the Jews and later in the looting of their property gave this persecution a national character, which had no parallelism either in the Nazi persecution of the Gypsies or in any other Nazi persecution. All other persecutions were and are therefore remembered as having been perpetrated by the Nazi regime and not by the German people.

The subjective dimension of this uniqueness involves the metaphysical significance attributed only to the murder of Jews in the German consciousness, which is essentially a Christian one. It did not derive directly from the impression left on the German consciousness by concrete perse-cution of Jews in the Third Reich but, rather, from the interpretation given to this persecution in view of the centrality that Jews and Judaism held in the German consciousness. The Jew occupies a central place in all the layers of German historical memory: from the myth of crucifying Jesus; through the Christian myths and the Medieval blood libels; through the integration of "the other" in Christian society, an issue which first came up during the Enlightenment; to the modern and secularized myths as racism. This centrality of the Jewish other in the German self-understanding, engraved with a Christian seal, contributed to the Nazi selection of the Jew as a victim and the desire to "redeem" Germany and the whole of humanity from the "destructive influences" of the Jewish spirit. In the earliest years of the Third Reich, Otto Pankok painted the image of Christ as other (he used Gypsy models, but they were perceived as Jewish), an image that became prevalent in antifascist circles in Ger-many. After 1945, this symbolic interpretation became even more com-mon, and many Germans interpreted this negative choice of the Jew by the Nazis in light of the Christian metaphysical choice of Jews over all Gentiles. Auschwitz, therefore, was perceived as the crucifixion of Jews.

As early as the late 1940s, the Gypsy victim served as a tool for ex-pressing protest, especially by Christian religious figures, who resisted such interpretation of the murder of Jews. While it was apparently based on humanistic principles of justice and equality to all victims, in fact, Peukert's argument may be an unconscious attempt to provide a secular rationalization to the Christian protest against what some interpreted as choosing Jews. It seems that this protest was mixed with a yearning to be released from the feelings of guilt that had been evoked in the Germans by the Jewish victim, and it may even have been motivated by a subcon-scious resentment toward Jews.

This thesis is reinforced by the other educational-practical argument beside the moral one, which Peukert brought. Peukert claimed that the thesis of the uniqueness of the Holocaust enabled the German public to avoid responsibility for the atrocities of the Third Reich by isolating as an unperceivable horror the barbaric murderousness of the Third Reich from the everyday normalcy of the "little man" during Nazi rule.[35] He implied that the texture in which the system of terror and normalcy were embedded in the Third Reich could only be exposed through highlighting the persecution of the non-Jewish victims. He conveniently ignored the persecution that Jews had had to undergo in public in Germany, which was overt and widely known to the German population, many of whom participated in looting of Jewish property.[36] The German public, Peukert asserted, made it easy for itself by concentrating on the Jewish victim, as it chose to atone for crimes against a group which, he said, was removed after the Nazi crimes from the vision field of the Germans. The hard way, argued Peukert, would have been to express regret with regard to crimes against groups of victims; according to him, these victims continue to exist at the top of the public agenda in Germany, namely: Gypsies, homosexuals, mental patients and handicapped, those who were forcibly sterilized, and asocials.[37] Peukert's argument shows inconsistency. He ignored Jews who remained on German soil after 1945, whose number in fact exceeded that of Gypsies, and the persistence of both overt and latent antisemitism in postwar German society.[38] While all the groups persecuted by the Nazis, such as Gypsies, homosexuals, and others, remained for him a part of the German reality, as far as he was concerned, the Jews remaining on German soil had no part in the German homeland.

This shifting of the emphasis from the Holocaust of European Jewry to the fate of Gypsies as part of the "forgotten" victims found its expression especially in the leftist-alternative section of the political culture in the FRG. It has been reflected as well in the fringe of the artistic work of these circles during the 1980s. In 1982, in the spirit of the period, a new short play dealing with the Gypsy fate in the Third Reich, *Hermann,* by Enno Podehl, was shown by Podehl Puppet Theater in Germany. On the stage, the Gypsy victim replaced the Jewish one. The Gypsy victim remained anonymous, and except for its name there is no expression of its individuality. The protagonist Hermann's monologue also reveals the softened nature of the way the Germans dealt with the Gypsy persecution, namely avoiding the heavy weight of guilt that was involved in the German dealing with the Holocaust. Hermann is an old German man, who in the Nazi period lived with Johanna, a Gypsy woman, who bore him a daughter. Herman loved his daughter very much and took good care of her. Then Johanna and their little daughter are deported by train to an unknown destination. The deportation and its circumstances are not described in the play at all but are only implied from Hermann's words. About six months after the deportation, Hermann heard for the first time about concentration camps and tried to find out what happened to his family: "Whenever he told me this story he always asked himself again why he had let the child go just like that."[39]

On an unconscious level at least, the playwright wanted to ease the guilt that oppressed the German protagonist, with the well-used argument of not knowing. Surprisingly, Hermann's feeling of guilt is concentrated on his daughter alone, his own flesh and blood, and there is no indication of the existence of any similar feeling with regard to Johanna. The playwright says of Hermann's attitude toward Johanna: "She must have been very significant to him."[40] Similarly to the German public who does not feel guilt toward the Gypsies, the playwright also seems not to feel obliged to express the German protagonist's guilt toward his Gypsy wife.

POLITICIZATION OF THE GYPSY ISSUE DURING
THE EARLY 1980S

The campaign launched by the Society for the Threatened Peoples in the FRG strengthened the delegitimization of the discrimination of Gypsies and obviated this trend that had begun in 1945 as part of the political culture consolidated in Germany after the defeat of Nazism. The goal of the society's campaign was to make the discrimination toward Gypsies as badly thought of as that toward Jews.

As the Gypsy issue, in contrast to the "Jewish issue," was not regarded in post-Auschwitz Germany as a political issue, Zülch and his colleagues, who had sharp political instincts, were aware of the urgent need for politicizing the Gypsy issue in the German political culture. Therefore, the society initiated several well-publicized public events that were intended to increase sympathy toward Gypsies among the general public.

The first event was a ceremony in memory of Gypsy victims of Nazism held at the site of the concentration camp in Bergen-Belsen on 27 October 1979. Simone Weil, the president of the European parliament and herself a Jewish survivor of Belsen, was present, together with political and municipal representatives and German church officials. The Christian Democratic (CDU) opposition leaders were not among the federal political representatives who attended the ceremony, nor did they send any congratulatory telegrams.[41] Supporting the public struggle of Gypsies was still perceived at that time as an expression of an allegedly liberal leftist attitude, damaging the FRG's reputation and not appropriate for the CDU. Simone Weil's presence turned the ceremony into an international event and gained attention from the German and foreign media. The media proliferated the society's message concerning the Gypsies' fate in the Third Reich and their condition in the Federal Republic.

The remnants of the New Left, including the Green Party (who in 1983 entered the Bundestag as a political party), voiced their support for the Gypsy issue, even though some of them did not accept all of the society's perceptions, and some even regarded the society's ideas as reactionary.[42]

Taking up the issue of Gypsies enabled various circles of the alternative left to free themselves from identifying with the Jewish victims of Hitler. This commitment derived from their antifascist stance. The need to identify with Jews and their suffering was oppressive for them, because of the feeling of guilt involved and apparently also because of antisemitic sentiments in their consciousness, although most of them were not aware of these sentiments. Unlike Jews, Gypsies fit into their social and political attitudes not only with regard to the Nazi past but also with regard

Simone Weil, president of the European Parliaments, speaks in the memorial ceremony at the site of the former concentration camp at Bergen-Belsen, 1979. (Axel Gruenwald.)

to other contemporary issues preoccupying them. The prevailing anti-Americanism and anti-imperialism added to the trend of romanticizing those perceived of as "natural peoples," a trend which had deep roots in all European cultures. Defining Jews as agents of capitalism, an action also common in leftist circles, made it easier for these groups to alienate themselves from the Jews, following old leftist antisemitic traditions.

Unlike Jews, Gypsies were perceived not only as victims of Nazism but also as victims of capitalism and modernization, both in the past and in the present, which had sentenced the traditional Gypsy lifestyle to destruction. This perception was well integrated into the romantic ecologist approach of these circles, continuing the romantic traditions about Gypsies that had prevailed since the early twentieth century. A stereotypical perception of Gypsies and their lifestyle was common among these alternative circles, who viewed it as an antithesis to the bourgeois lifestyle. Some even regarded the Gypsy stereotype as a model of an alternative culture, an issue that very much preoccupied what has been termed the 1968 generation.

In a speech she gave at the memorial ceremony for Gypsies at Bergen-Belsen in 1979, the Green Party's representative in Bremen, Delphin Brox, projected the Greens' worldview on Gypsies. Her speech implied that she still regarded Gypsies as a nomadic people and that she was not aware of the profound changes that they had undergone since 1945. Most of them had now settled permanently, and their lifestyle did not differ substantially from that of the rest of the German public. Brox also viewed the goals of the Gypsy struggle to be the preservation of their natural lifestyle and the ideal of primeval communism, while, in fact, Gypsies were striving to gain equal rights as citizens in Germany in the spirit of the bourgeois tradition: "You Gypsies fight with much effort for a right which all of us human beings once possessed, to wander across the land freely, for the land belongs to everyone, to wander from place to place, and to remain where we feel good, to gather the land's fruits, to hunt its animals, and graze the herds. Against this [right] stood those whom settlement turned into the majority. Everywhere concrete cities and streets, roundabouts, fences, barbed wire, private property, barriers, authorities, offices, walls." She then referred to the Gypsies' incarceration and murder, and so presented this in the context of, or perhaps as a result of, permanent settlement of the majority, materialism and modernization, in the spirit of the interpretation typical among her circles, that Nazism was a form of capitalism: "We, the Greens . . . as we perceive life to be threatened, are your friends. . . . We do not want to be enclosed by concrete, neither in our everyday environment nor in the political scenery."[43] As modernization continued, the Greens, who genuinely believed themselves threatened by modernization, were able to feel they were victims, too, and as such to identify with the victimization of Gypsies.

In contrast, certain radical left circles regarded Gypsies as part of the proletariat, similar to their perception of Third World nations. In reality, however, the Gypsy lifestyle is usually patriarchal and conservative, and very far from the antiauthoritarian and antibourgeois views of the New Left and the mythical image of the proletariat nurtured by German radical circles. In a meeting of the radical scene in Hamburg in 1988, the physician and thinker Karl Heinz Roth, a highly important figure on the German radical left, argued that racism is mainly a tool used by the ruling classes against the proletariat, to which Gypsies belong. Therefore, he said, "in their struggle for emancipation the Gypsies deserve the support of the radical circles."[44]

The second event the society organized in cooperation with Gypsy organizations in 1980 led to a profound change in the political culture of the FRG, not only by expanding support for the Gypsy cause to the political right but also by politicizing the Gypsy issue. In April 1980, thirteen Sinti held a hunger strike at the site of the concentration camp in Dachau. This resulted in the SPD's adopting, first in Bavaria and later on a federal level, the society's positions about the Gypsy issue in the framework of the political struggle in Bavaria against the CSU. In neighboring

Hunger strike of Sinti and Roma activists at the site of the former concentration camp at Dachau, 1980. (GfBV-Archiv. Photo by Wolfgang Radtke.)

Baden-Württemberg, another political party, the small liberal faction FDP (Freie Demokratische Partei), also adopted the Gypsy cause.[45]

The hunger strikers' demands concerned not only the Nazi persecution of Gypsies but also the postwar discrimination against Gypsies. They demanded that the Bavarian Minister of the Interior, Gerold Tandler, rehabilitate Gypsies and apologize for enactment of the Landfahrerordnung (Law concerning Vagrancy) by the Bavarian Landtag in 1953. Tandler refused, claiming he could not distance himself from the Landtag's and authorities' legitimate decisions.[46] Tandler's opposition, along with the journalistic cover of the strikers, led Jürgen Böddrich, the deputy head of the SPD faction in the Bavarian Landtag, to come to the aid of the Gypsy cause. In a move without precedent in German politics, Böddrich demanded that Tandler stop playing with decrees against Gypsies and that the Bavarian government consider ways in which to accept the Sinti's justified claims for rehabilitation. Böddrich's intervention turned the issue into a controversial topic between the CSU coalition and the oppositional SPD. Tandler responded by saying that Böddrich's accusations were tasteless and motivated by party interests; he emphasized that the initiator of the Law concerning Vagrancy in 1953 had been an SPD member, the then Minister of Interior, Dr. Wilhelm Hoegner. Böddrich wrote a short article in response, which was published in newspapers all over the FRG, claiming that it was in fact Tandler who was trying to turn the topic into a party issue.[47]

A few days after the hunger strike had begun, the SPD faction agreed to the strikers' demands. The faction's chairman, Karl-Heinz Hiersemann, and another of its members, Joachim Schmolke, who was involved in the contacts between the Sinti and the Bavarian government's representatives, published an official statement on behalf of the SPD, in which they distanced themselves from the Law concerning Vagrancy and from the activity of the Vagrants' Center that had operated at the police headquarters in Munich.[48] The Federal Minister of Justice for the SPD, Hans-Jochen Vogel, who had been Hoegner's assistant in the 1950s, also came to Dachau to visit the strikers and expressed his support and appreciation for their struggle against discrimination and prejudice.[49] When the strike ended, the SPD faction's members brought up in several committees of the Landtag the question of Gypsy discrimination by the Bavarian authorities, along with the Sinti's demand that a culture and documentation center be established in Dachau. When the majority CSU faction in the Landtag rejected the SPD's demands, the SPD faction brought up the issue for discussion in the Landtag plenary. Two of the speeches made in the Landtag expressed the new status Gypsies had meanwhile gained in the political culture of the FRG.

SPD member Schmolke adopted most of the views of the Society for the Threatened Peoples and sought to undermine the legitimacy of the discriminating policy toward Gypsies in the FRG. Trying to defend Hoegner and his predecessors in the SPD faction, he stated that enactment of the Law concerning Vagrancy was unjust, although he said that the legislators had not actually intended to discriminate against Gypsies. Schmolke also complained about the policy of the postwar compensation authorities, and he brought some examples to demonstrate that the police submitted to the compensation authorities information collected about Gypsies during the Nazi regime in order to deny the Gypsies' eligibility for compensation. Schmolke presented the Nazi persecution, as well as the continuing discrimination and prejudice, as being responsible for the faulty education of Gypsy children and the backwardness of Gypsies in the FRG. In conclusion, he presented the Sinti's demand that the government set up and finance the culture and documentation center for the Gypsy culture and history at Dachau.

On behalf of the CSU faction, Dr. Alois Hundhammer responded to Schmolke's speech. He began with a statement, which had not been heard in the Landtag's discussions about the Law concerning Vagrancy in the early 1950s. "There is no one in the Landtag," he said, "who does not regard what was done to the Gypsies in the Third Reich as a terrible injustice." He expressed his concern that the Sinti's hunger strike might create the impression that there is a link between the horrible injustice in the Third Reich and prejudice against them prevalent after 1945, an attitude which the Sinti speakers indeed voiced. Immediately thereafter, he again apologized, emphasizing that his father had been imprisoned at Dachau because of his opposition to Nazism. However, Hundhammer did not abandon the traditional position, for he also expressed sympathy for the Syncratic Narrative about the Gypsy persecution in the Third Reich, which emphasized that Gypsies were not innocent victims like Jews.

Hundhammer presented Schmolke as a spineless politician who had accepted without criticism the Sinti's attitude as it was expressed. "We will not allow [this] to mark us as guilty," he raised his voice, and added that Schmolke's words imply that "the Gypsies are angels and we are guilty." As if quoting the conclusions of some scientific research, Hundhammer argued that as long as the Gypsies did not give up their devious perception of law, their discrimination could not be prevented. The SPD faction's leader, Hiersemann interjected angrily against him, but Hundhammer declared that despite Sinti activist Romani Rose's presence, he did not fear declaring that he did not want to identify with the Sinti and Gypsies, but at the same time he would not refrain from helping them with the difficult problems involved in coping with prejudices and discrimination. These words awarded Hundhammer the support of his faction. He determined that the name Gypsy (Zigeuner) is not a pejorative term (as Romani Rose had argued). He opposed Schmolke's depiction of Gypsies as victims of German society, instead saying that the German discrimination was historically an outcome of the Gypsies' refusal to adopt the acceptable lifestyle of the settled population namely, it was their own fault.

Using the argument, which is only formally true, that Gypsies were awarded compensation in Germany when they met the criteria determined by the compensation laws, Hundhammer avoided dealing with the existence of special and discriminating criteria for Gypsies, and he rejected all the Gypsies' claims that they were discriminated against by the compensation authorities. Hundhammer regarded the Gypsy parents as being responsible for the deficient education of their children, as according to him they did not ensure that their children attended school regularly. The authorities, he said, "should not have to establish a mobile educational system to follow the vagrant Gypsies." In conclusion, he opposed the establishment of a cultural center at Dachau and determined that Gypsies had no special tie to Dachau, as according to him Gypsy prisoners in the Third Reich were not brought to Dachau but to other camps.[50]

The legitimacy of his claims, even those that were not based merely on prejudice and the denial of reality, was largely undermined in the face of the generous media coverage awarded to the Gypsies' representatives. Hundhammer himself complained that some Gypsies denounced as "Nazi" certain beliefs he and others shared regarding them. The speeches of Schmolke and Hundhammer and especially the apologetic tones and expressions that were embedded in both of them emphasized the collapse of the legitimacy of the Syncretic Narrative on the persecution of the Gypsies, and of using derogatory expressions against them, in the German political culture. The media exposure caused the German public to be acquainted with the Gypsy victim, who in the past had been mute and anonymous. The Gypsies' representatives, primarily Romani Rose, who headed the Sinti organization (Verband Deutscher Sinti), became "darlings" of the German media, and the Society for the Threatened Peoples was content to let them come to the foreground.

The last communicative event the society organized for Gypsies was the convention of the World Gypsy Congress in Göttingen in 1981. Thereafter Romani Rose's Sinti organization continued to act on its own. Two of the society's activists, Fritz Greußing and Herbert Heuß, joined Rose and held managing and organizing roles in his organization, so that some of the society's precepts were stated in proclamations published by the Sinti organization.

Gypsies and their German supporters sought to adopt the style of public activity that Jews had undertaken in post-1945 Germany. In 1982 Rose established the Central Council of German Sinti and Roma (Zentralrat Deutscher Sinti und Roma), which was similar to the name of the central Jewish organization in the FRG: Zentralrat der Juden in Deutschland. The new body was in fact identical to that headed by Rose (Verband Deutscher Sinti). The change of name was intended to give Rose's organization the image of a body representing all the Gypsies in Germany, although, in fact, the Roma were not represented on its board, and neither were many Sinti. The organization's demands were also inspired by the financial and political achievements of the Jewish organizations. The central committee demanded that the federal government award Gypsies global compensation, like the "shilumim" awarded to the government of Israel. It also acted to apply the prohibitions on antisemitic expressions in the political culture of the FRG to negative comments on Gypsies.

The Gypsy leaders active in the 1950s and 1960s—such as Walter Strauss and Rudolf Karway of the Roma and the Bamberger and Rose families who stood out among the Sinti—expressed a willingness to be integrated into German society and meet its demands of Gypsies and even, to a certain degree, hide their Gypsy identity.[51] In contrast, the next generation of leaders emphasized their Gypsy identity, encouraged by the

Society for the Threatened Peoples and in the spirit of emancipation of Third World nations from Western cultural imperialism. They demanded that the German political establishment not only award them unconditional equal rights, but at the same time respect their ethnic difference and allocate them special resources for cultivating their uniqueness. The German demand for assimilation and integration, accepted at least theoretically by the old leaders' generation, was denounced as a wish to exterminate a unique culture. For example, Lolotz Birkenfelder, of the Sinti young leadership, expressed the new line of thinking:

> You have stolen my essence
> destroyed my consciousness
> muted my tongue
> in order to repress me and separate me
> from the others,
> you wanted to bury my culture
> and change my way of life,
> so that eventually I would not know
> who I am.

> Ihr habt mein Wesen gestohlen,
> mir mein Bewußtsein vernichtet
> und meine Zunge gelähmt,
> um mich zu demütigen und von
> den anderen zu trennen.
> Meine Kultur wolt ihr begraben,
> Meine Lebensweise bestimmen,
> so dass ich schließlich nicht mehr weiß,
> wer bin ich.[52]

Contrary to their predecessors, who viewed it as important to demonstrate bourgeois respectability, the protest style of the young leaders adopted external features from the 1968 students' movement. The provocative character of their actions enraged many Germans. The young leaders presented themselves in the media by their Gypsy names, which their predecessors had not exposed to the German public at all.[53] In the spirit of respecting self-identification, the *Süddeutsche Zeitung* was the first newspaper to publicly introduce (since the hunger strike at Dachau) the term *Sinti and Roma* as the politically correct one for Gypsies in the German language. *Zigeuner,* the name given to Gypsies by non-Gypsies, was presented as a pejorative term and an abbreviation for thief *(ziehnde Gauner)*. The *Süddeutsche Zeitung* was followed by the German media in general, except for *Der Spiegel,* which continues persistently to use the term *Zigeuner* even today, at the beginning of the new millenium.[54]

The liberal media, especially the leftist circles, were enchanted by the charisma and exoticism of the Gypsy leaders. For the radical leftist circles,

Gypsy speakers such as Romani Rose and Rudko Kawczynski were examples of proletariat leaders. However, the image they projected in their public appearances was not of workers' leaders but was a popular variation of the Jewish intellectual, who sharply, and sometimes even wittingly, criticizes German society and its culture. Rose and Kawczynski, especially, with his sharp tongue, publicly denounced different aspects of German society, even on issues that did not explicitly concern Gypsies.

Rose, the Sinti representative, criticized the materialism of Germany's consumer society from a traditional romantic perspective that concealed an apologetic tone: "We still do not dump our elders in old people's homes. . . . Our nation is not a consumer society that strives to endlessly increase our standard of living. We only strive to meet basic necessities."[55] Kawszynski, the Roma representative, had no romantic perspective at all; his criticism is much more blunt and critical than that of Rose. In a press interview in 1993, Kawczynski criticized German government policy on the issue of granting political asylum to refugees, claiming it reflects a Nazi mentality. He also criticized the demonstrations against the violent wave of attacks on asylum seekers' hostels in Germany in the early 1990s, which were organized by liberals and leftists, the churches, and other organizations. He defined the demonstrations as a deed similar to the verdict of Pontius Pilate, the only purpose of which was to purge the Germans of their liability for the violence against foreign refugees.[56]

From the 1980s on, television allowed Gypsies to present to the German public, sometimes in their own langauge, their personal stories and experiences of persecution, and thus the Gypsy victim ceased to be an anonymous mute figure.[57] By the 1980s the argument over the Gypsies' status as victims was mainly over, and the debate now focused on the civil rights campaign. The victim component now became the main motif of the Gypsy image in German political culture. Valentin Sander, the Gypsy protagonist in the plot of the thriller *Armer Nanosh,* written by Martin Walser and Asta Scheib in 1989, is a survivor of deportation to Auschwitz, and he plays the role of a victim rather than of a criminal, unlike earlier Gypsy figures in thrillers and films.[58] In later years this trend became an expression of political correctness in forums of the leftist circles in the FRG, and any diversion from it, although legitimate, was denounced by Romani Rose and his German allies as a pejorative expression that might denote racist prejudice.[59]

The media resonance gained by the Gypsy issue in the early 1980s caused Chancellor Helmut Schmidt in 1982 to meet with the Central Committee's representatives, headed by Romani Rose. The chancellor publicly expressed his wish to morally correct the wrong done *(moralische Wiedergutmachung)* toward Gypsies. He indicated that the Nazi dictatorship had persecuted them for racist motives.[60] Several days after the meeting with Schmidt, Rose and his colleagues met with the leader of the oppositive Christian Democratic Party, Helmut Kohl. This encounter was the first sign that the opposition did not intend to leave the issue of taking care of Gypsies solely to the left parties and that Kohl regarded it as a national matter. Following these contacts with the government, the Central Committee of the German Sinti and Roma turned from being an oppositional organization representing only part of the Sinti families in the FRG into being the official representative of the Gypsy minority in Germany. From 1983 onward, the federal government helped finance the organization's office in Heidelberg, and, on behalf of the Gypsy community in the FRG, the organization controlled the budgets flowing to it from the public treasury.[61]

In 1983 the *Frankfurter Allgemeine Zeitung* carried an editorial protesting inclusion of the Gypsy issue in the election campaign by members of the SPD, arguing that they were using this sensitive issue to avoid publicly discussing the important issues of the day.[62] In effect, this was the last expression of protest made by conservatives in the FRG against the "fashionable" new way Gypsy issues were being handled. In the following two years, for the most part, it was representatives of the left parties who dealt with the Gypsies' discrimination and their deprivation within the framework of compensation to victims of Nazism and their demand to be recognized as a national minority in Germany. However, the financing of the Central Committee of German Sinti and Roma came from the federal government, which passed to CDU leadership.

In 1985, the public campaign, started by the Society for the Threatened Peoples six years earlier, reaped its biggest success. The political establishments in both the FRG and the GDR expressed at an official ceremony their recognition of the Gypsy victim and the wrong done to him. This ceremony awarded the Gypsy victim an equal status to that of the Jewish victim in the FRG political culture.

THE ADOPTION OF THE JEWISH-LIKE NARRATIVE BY THE POLITICAL ESTABLISHMENT

Official adoption of the Jewish-like Narrative by the political establishments of the two German states occurred in the same year.

The timing and ways the political establishments in both East and West Germany had chosen for ceremonial recognition of Sinti and Roma as victims of evil Nazi persecution frequently gave rise to an uneasy impression that these morally appropriate and just steps, which finally had been taken after a delay that had lasted four decades, stemmed from more than the result of pragmatic motives and an unconscious urge to ease latent feelings of guilt than out of any real deep conviction or desire to atone for Nazi crimes.

The motives of the Communist establishment of the GDR for this adoption apparently derived from the desire to use the Gypsy issue for propaganda against the FRG. The change in the political establishment of the FRG, in contrast, might have been an implicit reaction to the Jewish protest against the official visit of Chancellor Kohl and the American president Ronald Reagan at Bitburg Cemetery where fallen SS soldiers are buried. On a deeper level, it reflected the needs of many in the FRG to ease the burden of German guilt that was concentrated on the Jewish victim. By publicly recognizing the Gypsy victim, the political establishment in the FRG adopted the patterns of coping with the Nazi past that had been created by the Society for the Threatened Peoples.

In March 1985, Reimer Gilsenbach, a journalist and a supporter of the Sinti in the GDR, submitted a letter to Erich Honecker, in which he raised several requests for the Sinti's status in the GDR. Among others, he requested that a memorial for the Sinti be erected on the site of the former Gypsy camp at Marzahn on the outskirts of Berlin, where Gypsies had been forced to live from 1936 until they were deported to Auschwitz. That Honecker agreed to this request was apparently one outcome of the public campaign in the FRG, initiated by the Society for the Threatened Peoples in the early 1980s, to which the GDR also was exposed. This was the first monument anywhere in Germany to be erected in memory of the Gypsy victim. Later that year a presentation board dedicated to Gypsy prisoners was erected at the museum on the site of the concentration camp at Buchenwald.[63]

During the final years of the GDR, the official press there showed a tendency to adopt not only the Jewish-like Narrative, which emphasized that the Gypsy was an innocent victim, but also the perceptions of the Society for the Threatened Peoples toward Gypsies, which had previously been perceived by the Communist regime as a reactionary approach. In 1986 and 1988, *Junge Welt,* the newsletter of the youth movement of the ruling party of the GDR, Freie Deutsche Jugend (FDJ), published two long articles about Gypsies, hinting at these changes. One of the articles reported sympathetically about the occupations of Gypsies in the GDR: "Most preserve their ancestors' traditional occupations, as wandering scissors sharpeners, or are roaming the roads with fair equipment. The actors from Reideburg, near Halle, for example, and the Sinti Swing-Sextet of Berlin, enjoy a good reputation."[64]

The Communist apparatus of the GDR recognized the propagandistic potential of the Gypsy issue as a means for attacking the democratic regime of the FRG and presenting it as the successor of the Nazi state. The information published during the campaign started by the Society for

Memorial stone for the Sinti victims in Berlin-Marzahn, erected by the GDR in 1985.
(Reimar Gilsenbach. Photo by Vicar Peter Leu.)

the Threatened Peoples caused the Communist government to change its propaganda and forsake its former ideological perceptions toward Gypsies and to adopt the society's positions. They claimed, therefore, that in contrast to the capitalistic West, which eliminated the traditional Gypsy occupation, the GDR had enabled Gypsies to preserve their traditions.[65] *Junge Welt* also argued that the social relationships prevailing in the GDR, which awarded a fatherland *(Heimat)* to everyone, regardless of origin, belief, or opinion, enabled Gypsies also to enjoy rights equal to those of any other citizen: "Even the weak ones, who could not build a decent existence for themselves anywhere else, who were excommunicated and isolated, found their home in the German farmers' and laborers' country, which offered them the opportunity. The humanistic spirit of Socialism appreciates the Sinti," the paper wrote.[66]

It was further argued, in the spirit of Marxist dogma, that the change of social relationships also changed the public's attitude toward Gypsies. This argument, as we have seen, had no basis in reality.

In the FRG, too, there was finally recognition that Gypsies were victims of German society before, during, and after the Third Reich. In May 1985, on the occasion of a Bundestag plenary session marking the fortieth anniversary of the end of the war, President von Weizsäcker included in an official speech an explicit reference to the fact that Sinti and Roma constituted part of the victims of Nazism. This was the first such direct reference.

However, placing Gypsies on the list of victims left a lot to be desired. Jews were mentioned first, then Slavs. Next German victims who died as soldiers, who had been killed as civilians in air raids, or who had been captured or deported were mentioned. Only then were the Gypsy victims recalled, quickly followed by homosexuals, mental patients, and political and religious victims.[67] Placing Gypsies with the homosexuals left them in the same category they occupied in the 1950s, victims who wide circles of Germans perceived as not entirely innocent, if not questioned their very victimization.

In November 1985, a few months after the infamous ceremony at Bitburg cemetery, where Chancellor Kohl attempted a symbolic reconciliation between the representative of Nazism's most decisive enemy, the president of the United States, and the dead warriors of the SS.[68] He took an initiative that ended the exclusivity of the left parties in caring for the Gypsy interest and turned the issue into a national question. The ruling coalition parties, the CDU and the FDP, added their suggestion for the agenda to those previously submitted by the Greens and the SPD on the issue of the Gypsies' condition. The discussions took place in the Bundestag on 7 November, in a far from accidental proximity to the anniversary of the Reich's *Krystallnacht,* commemorating the pogrom the Nazi re-

gime initiated against the German Jews on 9 November 1938, in retalia-
tion for the assassination of a German diplomat in Paris by a young Jew,
Hershel Grinschpan. The commemoration of the Jewish victim of 9 November 1985 had been shadowed in the political culture of the FRG by
the Gypsy victim. Now Gypsies were officially recognized as victims of
Nazism and were awarded equal status with Jewish victims. During the
discussions in the Bundestag, the representatives of all the factions headed
by Chancellor Kohl (including the representative of the Bavarian CSU),
expressed their commitment to Gypsies, admitting the wrong done to
them not only under the Third Reich, but also in the Federal Republic.
Commitments were made to generously solve the problem of compensation for the Gypsy victims of Nazism and to terminate their discrimination by the police and the welfare authorities. "We sought in the Republic
a chance for reconciliation *[Versöhnung]* with those who suffered under
the Nazi dictatorship," said Chancellor Kohl, "and in the first place
reconciliation *[Aussöhnung]* toward Jews and Israel." He then said that
with regard to Gypsies this was not done after 1945, and he expressed
his hope that the errors could still be corrected. The chancellor also
emphasized that the government was aware of the special responsibility
(besondere Verantwortung) it bore toward Gypsies.[69] The context and
the identical terminology compared the Gypsy victim with the Jewish
victim.

Since coming to power in 1982, Kohl's public expressions on the Nazi
past had been characterized by ambivalence that was typical of the positions of the Federal administration since the early 1950s when the features of the people's mourning day (Volkstrauertag) for the victims of
War and dictatorship and for the fallen soldiers of both world wars had
consolidated.[70] On the one hand, Kohl, a historian by training, again expressed an unequivocal reservation about Nazism as both a regime and
an ideology, and he revealed his own identification with and commitment
to the victims of Nazism. On the other hand, Kohl had expressed on
several occasions, both verbally and nonverbally, his aspiration to "normalization" and reconciliation of Germans with their Nazi past. This reconciliation was at the expense of the feeling and collective memory of
the victims and their descendants, and was therefore perceived especially
by member of the Jewish collective as a compulsory reconciliation.[71]

German political culture is profoundly influenced by the Christian
character of its society. Its ceremonial patterns are significantly Christian.
In a series of gestures and ceremonies in which Kohl participated, he expressed his intention to reconcile Germany with its past in a Christian
spirit, and by this contributed to a shaping of German historic memory,
in which the Nazi period is reflected from the perspective of the German
collective memory rather than from the accusing perspective in which it

was reflected in the Jewish collective memory and the Western consciousness. These last perspectives have penetrated the German political culture since the late 1950s, mostly thanks to the German media, which has constantly been preoccupied with the Nazi destruction of European Jewry and has emphasized its singularity.

Since the late 1960s the (Jewish) victim's and the (Allied) triumphant party's perspectives have challenged the dominance of the official German mourning and commemoration concept in the political culture of the FRG. This concept in Germany had been crystallized since 1945. It mourned and commemorated together all the German victims of both world wars and Nazi dictatorship *(Opfer von Krieg und Gewahltherrschaft)*. This German concept regards all dead as victims: German Jews, as well as fallen German soldiers who might have participated in the murder of the former. Its ultimate public demonstration of this concept has taken place in the FRG every year since 1952, in the celebrations of the *Volkstrauertag* (the people's mourning day) every November. Basically, Kohl attempted to restore this German concept. His sole innovation was the expansion of the ceremonial category of victims of Nazism. In the past it has not pertained to the "forgotten" victims. Now also these victims were ceremonially commemorated.

The Jewish representatives in both Israel and the Diaspora stubbornly refused to be morally and ceremonially reconciled with Germany (in spite of the political reconciliation of the state of Israel with Germany). In the German Christian consciousness such a reconciliation would mean the awarding of a pardon by the heirs of the Jewish victims to the heirs of the Nazi persecutors; this prevented Kohl's goal of achieving a Christian reconciliation between the two sides. The official German recognition of the Gypsy victim, and especially its timing might be viewed, therefore, as a subversive attempt on the part of the chancellor, who was angry about the angry Jewish reactions to the Bitburg reconciliation ceremony. He might even have regarded his official act as a challenge to the exclusivity the Jewish victim of Nazism had enjoyed as the sole representative victim of Nazism in the political culture of the FRG.

Beside this motive, which may be seen as an important factor in Kohl's decision to officially recognize Gypsies as victims in the Third Reich, there were moral and political considerations to take into account. Kohl aimed to check protests by the Gypsy community that they were being discriminated against, claims that gained much media coverage in Germany and abroad, harmed Germany's image in the West, and played into the hands of Communist propagandists in the East. The surprising turn in the status of the Gypsy victim in the West German political culture in the 1980s was also the result of climate changes in the political culture of the FRG that had been inaugurated by the idealistic 1968 generation. The ideas that blossomed in the late 1960s helped both to delegitimize expressions of prejudice against Gypsies and to turn the Gypsy figure into one with which German political culture could positively identify.

The political establishment's recognition of Gypsies as victims was accompanied by various commemorative services, copied from gestures toward Jews, which gave the recognition a ceremonial dimension. On the same day that the Bundestag recognized Gypsies as victims, two ceremonial events took place: Richard von Weizsäcker, the republic's president, received Romani Rose, the chairman of the Central Council of the German Sinti and Roma, for an official meeting, and in the Bundestag building an exhibition was opened, entitled "Sinti and Roma—in Germany since 600 Years ago."[72] Public opinion was also carefully prepared for these events in Bonn. In the days before the Bundestag session, Germany's premiere TV network, ARD, screened Lea Rosh's documentary film about the persecution of Gypsies by the Nazis and the discrimination against them in the FRG.[73] The events in the Bundestag were widely reviewed by the German media, providing an official validity to the revolution that had been taking place in the German preoccupation with Gypsies since the early 1980s. Among the most politically correct circles in Germany, almost every public reminder of the Holocaust or the Jewish victim of Nazism was accompanied in the second half of the 1980s by a reminder of the Gypsy victim. In 1990 the federal government granted the Gypsies' claim, first made in the early 1980s, that in addition to receiving personal compensation they be awarded global compensation, similar to the Shilumin given to the government of Israel. Financed by the federal government, a culture and documentation center of the Sinti and Roma was established in Heidelberg.[74]

In a lecture he gave in 1961 to students at Frankfurt University, the Israeli journalist Joel Brand said: "An upheaval in the German thinking will occur only when they remember the Gypsy tragedy, as Gypsies have no press or public opinion."[75] Apparently, one can perceive the enlisting of German public figures and politicians to the Gypsy cause, and the change that then followed it in the official attitude of the political system in the FRG toward Gypsies in the early 1980s, as such an upheaval; however, the trend in the two German states to recognize Gypsies as an innocent victim, like Jews, did not fully develop. Following the collapse of the Berlin wall in 1989, the GDR disintegrated and was rapidly swallowed up into the FRG. For their part, the political establishment in the West found it hard to draw the full conclusions deriving from the adoption of the Jewish-like Narrative as the official narrative of the state.

It seems that the ascendancy the Gypsy victim enjoyed in the hierarchy of victims of Nazism in the political culture of the FRG during the 1980s derived mainly from the manipulative use needed to downplay the tragedy of the Jewish victim, on whom the German guilt feelings were concentrated. This need underwent a considerable decline following the "return to the nation" atmosphere that spread rapidly in Germany after its unification in the early 1990s, when it became again much more legitimate in the German political culture to remember the Nazi past from the German national point of view, and therefore the Jewish victim, who had symbolized the criminal character of this past and was perceived as concretization of German guilt, was now considered a less essential component in the representation of this past.

The central memorial for the victims of war and dictatorship *(Krieg-und Gewaltherrschaft)* in Germany, which was inaugurated in the site of the New Guard (Neue Wache) in Berlin in November 1993, significantly symbolizes and expressed these trends. It adopted the dominant German commemoration concept of the Victims of War and Dictatorship in the postwar era in both German states, the communist East and democratic West. During the Communist period the site served as "a memorial for the victims of fascism and militarism." The idea that all these dead were in fact victims, and the attempt of reconciling the persecutors and the persecuted was realized by a common burial on the site of the remains of an anonymous prisoner of a Nazi concentration camp, and the remains of an anonymous soldier during the GDR period in 1969.

The renewed design of the site is full of Christian symbols of reconciliation. The center of the construction is occupied by a statue of a mother with her dead son by the socialist sculptress Käthe Kollwitz. (Kollwitz's own son, Peter, had fallen in the first World War.) Iconographically, this is the image of the Christian Pieta, symbolizing the virtue of grace and compassion sent to all the victims, including the German victims, and even the murderers.[76]

The writing on some of the wreaths placed on the site by private visitors indicates that there are some among the German public who regard dead Nazi murderers as victims of the war, too. After Ignaz Bubis, the chairman of the central committee of Jews in Germany, had protested to the chancellor about the comparison between the murderers and their victims, there was an attempt to appease him by introducing an explicit reference to the Jewish victim by adding a text on a bronze plaque at the front of the construction.[77] Officials in Chancellor Kohl's office chose to use as text a fragment of von Weizsäcker's speech to the Bundestag from May 1985, a speech that had been very much appreciated worldwide, as an expression of Germany having come to terms with its Nazi past. However, the officials in the chancellor's office edited the speech, adapting it to the spirit of the era following the reunification of Germany:

Mother with Her Dead Son, sculpture by Käthe Kollwitz, in the Central Memorial of the Federal Republic for the Victims of War and Dictatorship, Neue Wache, Berlin. (Bundesbild Dienststelle.)

> We remember the people who suffered from war
> We remember the citizens who were persecuted and lost their lives
> We remember the fallen soldiers in the world wars
> We remember the innocent people who were killed during the war
>   and its consequences at home, in captivity, or in exile.
>
> We remember the millions of Jews who were murdered
> We remember the murdered Sinti and Roma
> We remember all those who were killed due to their descent, their
>   homosexuality, or their sickness and weaknesses
> We remember all the murdered people whose right to live was denied
> . . . We remember the men and women who were persecuted and
>   killed since they had opposed the dictatorship after 1945.

The Jewish victim was taken down from his prestigious place at the top of the list and was placed in a secondary category, behind the German victims.

The concrete reference to the identity of the Soviet and Polish victims, which in the president's speech was cited in second place after the Jewish victim, was erased altogether. Thus, von Weizsäcker's lucid call for the

German remembrance of the people who suffered under the Germans in World War II *(die im Krieg gelitten haben)* and the sacrifice these people made, turned into a general call to remember all the people who suffered in the war *(die durch Krieg gelitten haben)*, which was also taken to refer to the German people. In the second category of victims were the "murdered Sinti and Roma" *(die ermordete Sinti und Roma)* in the second place after the Jewish victims and before the homosexuals. Thereafter are two categories referring to the political and religious victims, and following them the category of the victims of the totalitarian dictatorship after 1945. The addition of this last category introduced into Nazi dictatorship also the GDR, thereby removing the Nazi atrocities from the specific historical position they had occupied in the original speech. This edited version completely twisted the meaning and context of von Weizsäcker's words. The text on the bronze plaque turned out to be a prominent example of compulsive reconciliation between the murderers and their victims in the spirit of the Bitburg gestures.

Placing the Gypsy victim of Nazism on the public agenda in the FRG served as a passage between an era of concentrating on the Jewish victim of Nazism, which started approximately in the 1960s, and a new era in which pre-1960s conceptions of official commemoration of the victims of war and dictatorship would be revived. As well, the downgrading of the status of the Jewish victim reduced the need to protest against him, a need that had contributed to the increase in the status of the Gypsy victim in the political culture of the FRG in the 1980s.

The wave of Roma immigrants from Eastern Europe, especially from Romania, to Germany, which began in 1989 when the Communist regimes were undermined, also contributed to a change of attitude. The fear in the German government that the moral commitment expressed by the chancellor toward the Sinti and Roma in his speech of 1985 might raise claims that the federal government would be obliged to absorb in a multitude of Gypsy refugees, led the German authorities to take a cautious line. In its reply to a query submitted by a Party of Democratic Socialism member of the Bundestag, Ursula Jelpke, in April 1991, concerning the arrangements of the right of stateless Roma refugees to remain in the FRG, the government avoided stating that they shared her attitude that the FRG bore a special responsibility toward the Roma people. The government merely replied that it had already stated on several occasions in the past that the Nazi dictatorship had inflicted tremendous injustice on the Sinti and Roma.[78]

A reduction in the Gypsies' status in the political culture of the FRG was also evident in the media. In the 1990s there was a waning of the victim motif as a central component of the Gypsy image in the FRG and a renewed legitimization of public expressions of hostility toward

Gypsies, in view of the problems that accompanied the adjustment of the Roma immigration from Eastern Europe. This phenomenon was expressed even among the circles of the New Left, which in the past had expressed a historic commitment toward Gypsies. Hoki Heck, a member of the Green Party and the head of the local office *(Ortsamt)* in Bremen, spoke to the leftist daily *Tageszeitung* in August 1990 against providing the right of asylum in Bremen and in Germany in general to Roma fleeing the former Yugoslavia. He told the newspaper: "What infuriates me is the false and fanatic way of people who now come with bombastic humanism, liberals from here to eternity, and say: they [Roma asylum seeker] should stay [in the FRG] because of the German guilt of the past. With all the best intentions, I wish to have nothing to do with this matter. I am not responsible for Christ's crucifixion, and I also do not feel myself guilty for what happened between 1933 and 1945."[79] This isolated expression from the left might reflect the attitude of many who did not dare to express themselves so bitingly. Nevertheless, despite reflecting continuity in German attitudes toward Gypsies, such expressions represent only one side of the status of Sinti and Roma in the political culture of the federal republic during the late 1990s.

In retrospect, since 1979 the strategy of the campaign for German Sinti and Roma, launched by the Society for the Threatened Peoples and by Gypsy organizations, has proved highly effective in the German political culture, as well as in international forums. Only recently the editorial of the *New York Times* reaffirmed the Jewish-like Narrative: "Gypsies and Jews were the only two groups that the Nazi regime sought to exterminate completely. . . . Perhaps half of Europe's million Gypsies were murdered."[80] In a relatively short period, the Jewish-like claim that the persecution of Gypsies was identical to the Jewish Holocaust became widely accepted. The ultimate expression of its adoption by the German political establishment was the announcement of the president of the Federal Republic, Roman Herzog, on 16 March 1997 at the opening of the Documentation and Culture Center of the German Sinti and Roma in Heidelberg, an institution operated by the Central Council of German Sinti and Roma: "The genocide inflicted upon the Sinti and Roma was conducted out of the same motive of the racial madness and [was pursued] with the same intention and with the same will for systematic and final extermination as that of Jews."[81] The notion that these two Nazi persecutions were identical, and yet only one of them, the Jewish Holocaust, underwent historical examination, led several German and foreign historians (among them the author of this book) to embark on systematic research of Nazi persecution of Gypsies. At that time it was a relatively unknown field of research.

However, paradoxically, the results of these researches did not substantiate the claim of identity between the two Nazi persecutions. In 1996 Michael Zimmermann's book *Rassenutopie und Genozid* (Racial utopia and genocide) appeared.[82] This comprehensive study shed new light on Nazi persecution and mass murder of European Gypsies. He drew a highly complex picture of Nazi persecution, which was not initiated by Hitler, and which occupied only a marginal place on the Nazi agenda. Yet it resulted in genocide, even though genocide had not been its designated goal at the outset. Implicitly, Zimmermann's book challenges two basic arguments of the Society for the Threatened Peoples and the Central Council of German Sinti and Roma: the actual parallelism between the persecution of Gypsies and the Holocaust of European Jewry, and the figure of half a million Gypsy victims of the Nazi persecution. This number appeared in the German press in the early 1960s, and since 1979 has been used by the society and the Gypsy organizations.

A little later Zimmermann's implicit conclusions found their way to the German press,[83] and the indignant response of the Central Council was quick to follow. From August to October 1997, Romani Rose, the chairman of the Central Council, launched a slander campaign attempting to discredit Zimmermann's reputation. He tried in vain to prevent Zimmermann from participating in a conference that was to take place at the site of the former concentration camp in Buchenwald, by appealing to the board of the Buchenwald Memorial and to Thuringian Minister of Science Gerhard Schuchardt (SPD). Absurdly, Rose accused Zimmermann of denying the Nazi genocide of Sinti and Roma and accepting Nazi propaganda. Then he charged him with "relativizing in his researches the number of Gypsy victims without relativizing the very genocide [committed against them]."[84] The chairman of the scientific board of the Buchenwald Memorial, the renowned German historian, Eberhard Jäckel, was resolute in his rejection of Rose's claims and demands. He insisted that the board protest against the defamation of serious research by an interest groupe *(Interessengruppe)*. Jäckel emphasized that "the board rejected that an interest group, enjoying the status of a competent [instance] on victims of crime, force its own historical picture *[Geschichtsbild],* upon the Buchenwald Memorial." He stated that Rose wished "to inflict censorship on the critical engagement *[Auseinandersetzung]* in the history of the camp at Buchenwald."[85]

In June 2000 Jäckel embarked on a public attack on the Jewish-like strategy of two groups, the homosexuals and Gypsies. He published a long polemic article in the cultural supplement of the conservative *Frankfurter Allgemeine Zeitung.* In his review of the most up-to-date studies on these two persecutions, he referred to Günter Lewy's *The Nazi Persecution of the Gypsies,* at that time a new book not yet translated into German. Lewy went farther than Zimmermann. In contrast to

Zimmermann, who insisted on the genocidal character of this persecution, Lewy rejected the very definition of the Nazi persecution, which resulted in the killing of thousands of men, women, and children as a genocide, since according to him it does not meet all the conditions required to such a definition. Jäckel accused the organizations of homosexuals and of Gypsies of proliferating historical legends that contradict the historical truth to further their political interests as deprived groups in German society.[86] As was only to be expected, the Central Council's representatives hurried to send letters of protest. While Romani Rose only likened Jäckel to Holocaust deniers of German far right circles, Fritz Greußing was not averse to calling him a forger and Holocaust denier.[87]

Such unacceptable reactions to a highly respected and prestigous historian could not win many sympathizers in German society. Only sworn supporters of the Central Council might view it as proper, but there are very few of them in German society. The long-term influence of Norman Finkelstein's book *The Holocaust Industry: Reflections on the Exploitation of Jewish Suffering,* might harm the public status of the Central Council of German Sinti and Roma. Finkelstein blames Jewish organizations of cynically employing the Holocaust in order to press the German government to pay them more money.[88] I assume that Finkelstein's sharp denouncement of Günter Lewy's central thesis in his book ("Gypsies didn't suffer like Jews—indeed, didn't even suffer a genocide—during World War II"),[89] would attract much less attention among the German public than his provocative claim that Jewish organizations "made improper use of the monies originally earmarked by the German government for Holocaust victims." This claim might be applied in Germany to the Central Council, as this organization has always imitated Jewish organizational patterns of action.

What would be the implication of this undermining of the very historicity of the Jewish-like Narrative on the persecution of Gypsies for the status of the Gypsy organizations and the German Gypsies in the political culture of Germany?

Fifty-seven years after Nazi persecution of Gypsies was terminated, this story has not yet become the past. The German relationship with German Gypsies still carries the consequences of the Nazi persecution. It is an ongoing story that probably will continue to engage the German society well into the twenty-first century.

Epilogue

THE CONFRONTATION between Joseph Vogt and Emmi Diemer-Nicolaus in parliament in Stuttgart on 9 January 1957, which set the opening scene of this book, is highly representative of the German discourse on Gypsies in the aftermath of Auschwitz. Strange as it might sound, each speaker, the conservative bigot and the enlightened liberal, represents a contradictory and yet dominant "German position" in postwar Germany toward Gypsies and their persecution by the Nazis. These two viewpoints have shaped policies toward Gypsies to the present day.

Vogt expressed the traditional antigypsy view, to which he added a certain measure of his own bigotry. This approach regarded the Gypsies as criminals and aimed at legally limiting their freedoms by using the precedents of discrimination that had been set by some German states during the Weimar Republic. In another appearance before the local parliament in Stuttgart, Vogt even went so far as to express a certain understanding of the motives of the Nazis in persecuting Gypsies.[1]

By contrast, Diemer-Nicolaus's position reflects a brand-new reformist trend in the German Gypsy policy *(Zigeunerpolitik)* that appeared in Germany only after the defeat of Nazism. Reformists of her kind regarded Gypsies as equal citizens of the Federal Republic, deserving of the same civil rights as all other citizens. Opposing special laws against Gypsies was one of the lessons liberals in Germany drew from the Nazi experience. They believed that the power of the state to violate fundamental civil rights of the individual, including Gypsies, should be limited as much as possible. They were reluctant to accept that the Nazi persecution of Gypsies was simply part of some legitimate struggle the German state waged against crime during the Third Reich, as many argued. In general, they recognized the Nazi persecution as a racial crime of such proportions that it could only be compared with the Holocaust of European Jewry.

In contrast to the clear-cut division between the positions of Dimmer-Nikolaus and Vogt in the Stuttgart confrontation, German policies and attitudes toward Gypsies in the postwar era were much more complex, and the distinction became somewhat blurred. Usually, policies and attitudes combined elements of the two contradictory approaches.

Vogt's antigypsyism was not the only traditional viewpoint that influenced policies and attitudes toward Gypsies in postwar Germany. The "Enlightened" view of "civic correction" of Gypsies (in contrast to the "enlightened" notion of "civic improvement" of Jews) was also influential. Despite its paternalistic character and its attempts to coerce and repress Gypsy identity and culture, this Enlightened view still opposed traditional antigypsyism and Nazism. It sought to permanently settle Gypsies and find them steady work to "correct" them and integrate them as useful and productive citizens into German society. This is quite different from traditional antigypsyism that ignored the Gypsies' distress and regarded them as foreign rabble, believing that, if it was not possible to get rid of the rabble, the rabble should be restricted. Some German officials shared Dimmer-Nikolaus's opposition to antigypsy legislation but wholeheartedly believed that the state should compel Gypsies to settle permanently.

Despite the stark ideological differences between the democratic regime in the FRG and the communist regime in the GDR, an analysis of governmental approaches and policies toward Gypsies and their Nazi persecution reveals a high degree of similarity between the two ideologically rival states. In both countries, the perceptions of the political establishments and the bureaucracy were deeply rooted in traditional German antigypsy policy. In both regimes, the enlightened concept of civic correction merged with the antigypsy approach. In the West as in the East, Gypsies were basically regarded as asocials and a threat to public safety.

In regard to the Nazi persecution, both East and West have evinced a halfhearted recognition of Gypsies, like Jews, as innocent victims of a supremely criminal regime. This view was characterized by unequivocal denunciation of genocidal Nazi policies, paradoxically combined with a certain understanding for the reasons behind the persecution. Not surprisingly, such "understanding" resulted in a reluctance to exercise justice on behalf of these victims on either an individual or a collective basis.

Because they were influenced by traditional approaches and were backed by some politicians, West German bureaucrats, especially in local Ministries of the Interior and in police departments, sought to restore the traditional policies toward Gypsies that preceded Nazism and were therefore deemed to be legal. However, usually they found it quite impossible to officially restore the old antigipsy legislation and policies of the Wilhelminian and Weimar periods as they wished. They faced the opposition of officials of the Ministries of Justice, as well as of politicians like Emmi Diemer-Nicolaus. These latter officials and politicians opposed these attempts because they contradicted the liberal principles of the Basic Law *(Grundgesetz)* of the Federal Republic, which guaranteed basic human rights to German Gypsy citizens. It did not prevent the bureaucracy of police and the Ministries of the Interior from attempting to bypass constitutional limitations on antigypsy measures they wished to take. In not a few cases, the bureaucracy succeeded.

Although the departments of the Reich's Ministry of the Interior, which were directly involved in the Nazi persecution of Gypsies until 1945, collapsed with the defeat of the Nazi regime, only in the Soviet occupation zone were they, as well as the criminal police departments of the regional states *(Länder),* reorganized and their personnel replaced. These departments continued their routine activity in which some of the officials had been engaged as long as before the Weimar Republic. In conducting the research for this book, I actually came across official files, such as "Combating the Gypsy Nuisance," which was filed in the state archive in Bremen. One of these files had been opened during the Wilhelminian period, had continued during the Weimar Republic and was closed during the Third Reich. Another had been opened during the Weimar Republic and was still open in the early 1990s, several years after the reunification of Germany.

These decentralized departments, which de jure conducted an independent Gypsy policy, had already operated in coordination before the Nazi regime came into power. Their coordination also endured after Nazism collapsed.

One expression of continuity from the Nazi period was the composition of the staff who dealt with Gypsy affairs in the criminal police and the Ministries of the Interior after 1945. As stated, some of these officials and experts had served in similar positions during the Nazi regime. Several of them had played major roles in persecuting Gypsies in the Third Reich, and they remained in office after 1945. Others who had been dismissed from their positions in 1945–1946 returned to manage Gypsy concerns after the denazification policy failed.

German Gypsies could only regard the presence of these officials in the civil service of the Federal Republic as a clear sign of unbroken continuity from the Nazi period. Despite the personal continuity of these officials' careers and the harassment to which they had subjected the German Gypsies, however, they did not apply Nazi policy toward Gypsies after 1945.

After the defeat of the Nazis in 1945, Germany discarded collective incarceration, murder, and sterilization of Gypsies as possibilities for solving the "Gypsy problem." In contrast to several Scandinavian states, where, in fact, eugenic nonracial sterilization continued until the early 1970s, and where it was an integral component of welfare policy, in postwar Germany the Nazi past placed a taboo on such practices.

The taboo on using racial terms and concepts—which was imposed by the conquering Allies and also was based on the new German legislation—was enforced mainly in the political postwar culture. As Gypsy themes, in contrast to Jewish ones, were not considered to be a political issue in Germany, the use of racist terms regarding Gypsies in nonpolitical contexts was not perceived as an expression of Nazi concepts and ideas. Accordingly, the legitimacy of racial discourse on Gypsies in a nonpolitical context was not questioned until the 1980s. Officials and politicians did not hesitate to use such terminology in closed forums, even though they avoided this practice in public. Most of these expressions and concepts did precede Nazism and were quite common in the Weimar Republic, but they become popular during the Third Reich. Just after 1945 this thinking was identified with Nazism by only a minority of the German public, but this identification gradually penetrated the German political culture. Since the 1980s apparently no one has argued against it in the mainstream political culture of the FRG. Two other points might also be seen as expressions of continuity from the Nazi period: first, the uncritical acceptance by officials in the postwar compensation and legal agencies, as well as by politicians, of arguments adduced by the Nazis to legitimize the Gypsy persecution; and, second, furtherance of these arguments as premises of legitimate anticrime policy during the 1950s.

However, the phenomenon of continuity basically seems to reflect the bureaucratic behavior patterns and antigypsy mentality that had prevailed in Germany well before Nazism. In spite of their being pejorative and degrading, this behavior and this mentality are not typically Nazi manifestations. As noted, hatred for and negative feeling toward Gypsies did not begin with the Nazi ascent to power. The German Gypsies remained a rejected and despised minority in the postwar period, as they had been for the previous five centuries. They were still perceived by too many of their fellow Germans to constitute a foreign element on German soil. The terrible suffering inflicted during the Nazi period on Gypsies by Germans, many of whom were not even active Nazi party members, failed to evoke much sympathy from ordinary Germans after the war. Even former German political prisoners who had also been persecuted at the hands of the Nazis were not generally supportive.

Perversely, the stigmatization of Gypsies as asocials, which had condemned them to be victims of the criminal messianic vision of the Nazis, also adversely affected their prospect of being officially recognized as victims of Nazism after the war. For many years after 1945, such stereotypes deterred the "new" German authorities from any radical rethinking of the state's traditional discriminatory policies toward Gypsies.

Nevertheless, alongside the continuity of discriminatory attitudes and behavior to Gypsies, after 1945 new attitudes and new patterns of public conduct in regard to this minority also penetrated the German political culture. Indeed, such patterns had never existed in Germany, and their introduction in the German political culture was indeed an innovation. This development was one of the side effects of the Allies' denazification policy. The military governments overlooked Gypsies and showed no special interest in their rehabilitation. But the taboo the Allies placed on racism and racist discourse left a very profound imprint on the German public discourse on Gypsies in the German political culture. It exists to the present day.

While German political culture, and society as a whole, absorbed certain liberal principles that were thrust on them by the victorious Allies' reeducation policy, they still have retained discriminatory patterns and even certain racist elements. To this day, attitudes in Germany toward Gypsies are certainly less encumbered with guilt and political considerations than feelings arising out of the Jewish Holocaust. Yet, to some extent, these views have been influenced by patterns regarding Jews, which were crystallized in German political culture after the war.

Later in the postwar period another phenomenon appeared. As the German collective memory was concentrated on the Jewish Holocaust, the subjectively less burdened character of the persecution of Gypsies enabled some individuals and groups in Germany to manipulate the situation. They used the relative inattention to the Nazi persecution of Gypsies as a pretext to attack German preoccupation with the Jewish Holocaust. By this means certain religious and secular Christian circles could protest against the alleged unique status Jews enjoyed in postwar German political culture.

When various important changes were finally introduced into the compensation policy of the FRG in the early 1960s, awarding Gypsies some measure of justice, these often proved too little, too late. Some survivors had died; for others, the increased suffering they had endured in the postwar period had meant that, by then, it was hard to achieve a modicum of justice.

Application of the concept of "Wiedergutmachung" (correction of the wrong done), for Gypsies at least, has been a bitter failure. They were neither provided with adequate compensation nor properly helped to rehabilitate their lives. To this day, they have not been integrated as a distinct but wholeheartedly accepted part of German society. That so little has been done in this respect makes it difficult to concur with arguments advanced by those on the German New Right in recent years that West Germany has coped fully and frankly with the Nazi past.

Notes
Bibliography
Archival Sources
Secondary Sources
Index

Notes

PREFACE AND ACKNOWLEDGMENTS

1. HSTH Stuttgart, EA 2/303, Bü 332/1 Minutes of the Administration and Construction Committee of the local parliament of Baden-Württemberg (Protokoll der Sitzung des Verwaltungs und Wohnungsbauausschusses des Landtags von Baden-Württemberg) (9 Jan. 1957), Bl. 30.

2. Berghoff 1998.

3. Giordano 1987.

4. Kittel 1993. See also Maislinger 1990.

5. Allemann 1956.

6. Huster 1972, 120.

7. Kocka 1979. See also Klessmann 1990, 159–178; Klessmann 1986, 135–145; Schildt and Sywottek 1997, 413–440, esp. 415: " 'Modernisation under a conservative guardianship'—this formulation may ultimately best summarize the Adenauer era."

8. Geigges and Wette 1979; Zülch 1979; Hohmann 1980c; Hohmann 1981.

9. Hohmann 1981, 182; Hohmann 1980c, 85ff.; Tugendhat 1979, 9.

10. Rose 1979, 257.

11. Hoffman 1960.

12. Wodak 1990.

13. Wodak 1990.

CHAPTER 1. IMAGES AND IMPRESSIONS OF GYPSIES IN THE GERMAN COLLECTIVE MEMORY

1. Fraser 1992, 20ff., 25–26, 43–44; Block 1964, 514.

2. Rüdiger 1782; Grellmann 1787; Ruch 1986.

3. Weltzel 1938, 105.

4. Oliner and Hallum 1978.

5. Wittich 1911, 287–288.
6. Fricke 1991, 76ff., 145.
7. Crabb 1832, 99ff.; Pischel 1894, 9.
8. Jochimsen 1963, 9–10.
9. Archiv der Otto Pankok-Gesellschaft (Hünxe-Drevenack): Die Zigeuner in heutigen Deutschland (undated manuscript).
10. Familienministerium: Zwei Drittel der Sinti bekommen Sozialhilfe, *Süddeutsche Zeitung* (26 Apr. 1980); Rose (1987, 11) estimates the Gypsy population of the FRG to be 60,000; Hundsalz (1982, 139) estimates the Gypsy population of the FRG to be 45,000; Gilsenbach (1993, 276) estimates the Gypsy population in the former GDR to be in the few hundreds; Central Council of German Sintiad Romaled, Minority Protection for Sinti and Roma within the framework of the Council of Europe, the CSCE and the UNO, Heidelberg (1994, 85).
11. Assmann 1992, 46–56; Zuckermann 1993, 16.
12. Gronemeyer 1987, 15–33; Ebhardt 1928, 14–21.
13. Gronemeyer 1987, 15, 18, 25, 49.
14. Ebhardt 1928, 20ff.
15. Gronemeyer 1987, 88ff.; Ebhardt 1928, 33–36.
16. Gronemeyer 1987, 34ff.
17. Hehmann 1987, 44; Kenrick and Puxon 1981, 23; Gilman 1992, 24–25.
18. Ebhardt 1928, 33; Rakelmann 1988, 21; Rakelmann 1991, 145ff.; Labourie 1990. On the demand for the Gypsies' supernatural powers in Modern Germany, see Margalit 1996, 11 n. 4.
19. Ebhardt 1928, 32–33; Leblon 1985, 163ff.
20. Luther 1883, 613, ll.19–24.
21. Fricke 1991, 19; Ebhardt 1928, 26ff.; Avé Lallement 1858, 8–9.
22. Berger 1972, 182; Briel 1989, 84–99.
23. Jütte 1980, 121.
24. Erk and Böhme 1893–1894.
25. Ebhardt 1928, 113.
26. Goethe 1982, 220ff.; Friedrichsmeyer 1997.
27. Deutsche Volksliedarchiv: B 43842, Wir arbeiten nicht und verdienen doch; A 99419, Zick Zack Zigeunerpack.
28. Margalit 1996, 3ff.; Diner 1993, 37.
29. Hanau, *Frankfurter Rundschau* (17 Sept. 1965).
30. Hinton 1993, 71–72, 79; Jones 1990, 102–103, 106–107, 110–111.
31. Partos 1980.
32. Fricke 1991, 152ff., 158, 202; Hehmann 1987, 184–214.
33. StA Frankfurt a.M.: StK, municipal council file (Magistrat Akte) 2203, vol. 1, Citizens' Committee to the Municipal Council of Frankfurt a.M. (Bürger Ausschuss e.V. an den Magistrat der Stadt Frankfurt a.M.) (19 Sept. 1930).
34. Bobrach 1984, 334; Report on the interior political situation 9 (Bericht zu innenpolitischen Lage), vol. 1, *1930–1946,* no.1 (9 Oct. 1939).
35. Jochimsen 1963, 87–88.
36. Jochimsen 1963, 81.
37. Dennler 1910, 63ff., 71.

38. Roda 1960.
39. Hohmann 1980a, 216–217; Hohmann 1980b, 108ff.
40. Hundt-Radowsky 1819, 4ff.; Tetzner 1835, 57ff.
41. Wahrmund 1887, 84, 94; Mosse 1978, 115–116.
42. Urban 1913.
43. Mayall 1988, 73ff.
44. Chamberlain 1906, 2:1165 n.1; 2:1168.
45. Zigeuner 1909.
46. Luschan 1922, 78–79.
47. Günther 1929, 91–92.
48. Zigeuner 1935a; Zigeuner 1935b; Zigeuner 1938.
49. IfZ Archiv: Presse-Dienst NRG Romantik der Landstrasse: Das Volk ohne Vaterland (26 Aug. 1935); Die Leute ohne Vaterland, *Süddeutsche Sonntagspost,* Nr. 29 (undated).
50. *Mittag,* 27–28 Jul. 1936, in Zigeuner ein arischer Stamm? *Das Schwarze Korps* (6 Aug. 1936), 14.
51. Nawrocki 1937.
52. Römer 1934, 112–113; Römer 1936, 88–95.
53. Ritter 1941; IfZ Archiv: Pressedienst für Reportage und Feuilleton, Carl Otto Hamann RDKN Berlin: Ein Sippenarchiv der "Nomaden der Landstrasse" (1 Mar. 1941); Bestandsaufnahme der Zigeuner und Zigeunermischlinge, *Stuttgarter Neues Tageblatt* 50 (21 Feb. 1941); Deutschland zählt 30,000 Zigeuner, *Neues Wiener Tagblatt* (25 Feb. 1941); Zigeuner erhalten ein Sippenarchiv, *Stuttgarter NS-Kurier* 74 (6 Mar. 1941); Die Nomaden der Landstrasse: Falsche Romantik um asoziale und erbminderwertige Elemente: Unsere Tageskasten, *Völkische Beobachter* (10 Nov. 1941).
54. Asoziale 1928; Asoziale 1966.
55. Mosse 1978, 83–87.
56. Ritter 1937; see also n. 54.
57. Nawrocki 1937, no. 223 (18 Aug. 1937); Weltzel 1938, 33.
58. Eichberg 1981, 451.
59. Berger 1972, 186; Briel 1989, 62–69.
60. Avé Lallement 1858; Liebich 1863.
61. Berger 1972, 189.
62. Hesse 1968, 103.
63. Hesse 1974.
64. Yates and Picton 1951, 81–83.
65. *Die Czardasch Fürstin* (1934), film by Georg Jacoby, Universum Film (UFA) A.G.
66. *Tiefland* (1954), film by Leni Riefenstahl; Riefenstahl 1987, 359ff.; Hinton 1978, 89–106; Krass 1983; *Die Macht der Bilder: Leni Riefenstahl* (1992), film by Ray Müller; letter from Fritz Hippler to the author (7 Mar. 1992).
67. Die Nomaden der Landstrasse: Falsche Romantik um asoziale und erbminderwertige Elemente." Unsere Tageskasten, *Völkische Beobachter* (10 Nov. 1941).
68. Nawrocki 1937, no. 225 (20 Aug. 1937).

CHAPTER 2. POLICY TOWARD GYPSIES UNTIL THE COLLAPSE OF THE THIRD REICH

1. Gronemeyer 1987, 15ff., 34–36; Fraser 1992, 68; Mode and Wölffling 1968, 145, 147.
2. Mode and Wölffling 1968, 147; Gronemayer 1987, 88–90; Arnold 1965, 37.
3. Arend 1990, 77–83.
4. Fricke 1996, 17–23; Mode and Wölffling 1968, 153; Arnold 1965, 38ff.; Sibeth 1985, 7.
5. Arnold 1965, 44, 47; Mode and Wölffling 1968, 156ff.; Sibeth 1985, 6, 9.
6. Arnold 1965, 48ff.; Sibeth 1985, 9, 12.
7. Fricke 1991, 30ff.
8. Mode and Wölffling 1968, 161–163.
9. Jochimsen 1963, 8; Grellmann 1787, 188; Fricke 1991, 40.
10. Fricke 1991, 37ff., 42–43, 48ff.; Hehmann 1987, 245ff.
11. Fricke 1991, 39, 46ff., 59.
12. Hehmann 1987, 249–251, 277, 279.
13. Fricke 1991, 70; Hehmann 1987, 258; 278.
14. Fricke 1991, 182; Hehmann 1987, 265–266, 281.
15. Strauss 1986, 41.
16. Hehmann 1987, 270–271, 284–285, 293; STA Bremen, 4,13/1–P.1.a, no. 10, Bekämpfung des Zigeunerwesens; Bayer. Staatsministerium des Innern (18 Mar. 1933 and 8 May 1933), Bl. 22.
17. Hehmann 1987, 328; Strauss 1986, 59.
18. Bay. HSTA: StK-GuV 911, Gesetz zur Bekämpfung von Zigeunern, Landfahrern und Arbeitsscheuenunwesens = Landfahrer Ordnung (22 Dec. 1953); Law for combating Gypsy vagrants and work shys, (Gesetz zur Bekämpfung von Zigeunern Landfahrern und Arbeitsscheuen) GVBl. no. 17 (22 Jul. 1926).
19. Gesetz zur Bekämpfung des Zigeunerunwesens (Law for combating the Gypsy nuisance) (3 Apr. 1929).
20. Zimmermann 1996, 79–162.
21. StA Frankfurt a.M.: Stadt Kanzlei, municipal council file (Magistrat Akte) 2203, vol. 1, letter from the residents of Ginnheim to the city mayor (Oberbürgermeister) of Frankfurt (14 Jul. 1933), and letter from the Bürgermeister of Frankfurt A.M. to the NSDAP Gauleitung, Hessen-Nassau (31 Mar. 1934).
22. Bay. JM: Az 4726, vol. 1–542/52 (20 Mar. 1952).
23. Combating the Gypsy Plague, a circular of the Reich and Prussian Ministry of the Interior (Bekämpfung der Zigeunerplage, RdErl.d. RuPrMDJ), RMBliV (1936) no. 27, Bl. 785 (6 Jun. 1936).
24. Zimmermann 1996, 93–100.
25. Milton 1991, 378; Milton 1992, 3–4; Fings and Sparing 1992, 32.
26. Zimmermann 1996, 89–90.
27. BA Berlin: R 73/13620, Robert Ritter, short report to the hands of Dr. Blome (Robert Ritter Kurzbericht zu Hd. von Dr. Blome) (19 Jun. 1941); Milton 1995, 125; Zimmermann 1996, 88.
28. Zimmermann 1996, 156ff.

29. BA Berlin: R 73/14005, the Head of the Security Police and SD [Security Service] to the DFG, care of the Reich Minister for Science, Education, and People's Culture (Der Chef der Sicherheitpolizei und des SD an die DFG durch die Hand der Reichsministers für Wissenschaft, Erziehung und Volksbildung) (6 Jan. 1940).

30. Zimmermann 1996, 372–373; Nawrocki 1937, no. 223 (18 Aug. 1937).

31. Combating the Gypsy Plague, a circular of the Reichsführer SS and the Head of the German Police (Bekämpfung der Zigeunerplage, RdErl. d. RFSSuCdDtPol.) (8 Dec. 1938), RMBliV (1938), Bl. 2105.

32. Ritter 1938b, 77.

33. Ritter 1936, 713ff.; HSTA Düsseldorf: Rep. 231, no. 1535, Bl. 32–33.

34. Bock 1986, 361ff.; esp. 363–364; Zimmermann 1996, 86ff.

35. Ritter 1938a, 84; StA Frankfurt: PA Dr. Ritter Robert sig. 18.576, Explanation to our Asocial and Gypsy research (Erläuterungen zu unseren Asozialen- und Zigeunerforschung) (20 May 1947), Bl. 40.

36. BA Berlin: R 73/14005, Ritter's file in the DFG report or lecture, 27; Ritter 1938a, 77; Ritter 1938b, 425–426; Günter 1929, 91–92; Luschan 1922, 77ff.; Zimmermann 1989, 30.

37. Ritter 1938a; Justin 1943, 21–22.

38. Peukert 1989, 71ff.

39. Luschan 1922, 79.

40. Müller-Hill 1984, 60ff.

41. Roth and Aly 1984, 114–115.

42. StA Frankfurt: PA Dr. Ritter Robert sig. 18.576, Erläuterungen zu unseren Asozialen- und Zigeunerforschungen (20 May 1947), Bl. 40; HSTA Düsseldorf: Rep. 231, no. 1535, Bl. 22; Arnold 1989, 9; letter from Ritter to Arnold (28 Apr. 1949); 62; Müller-Hill 1984.

43. Heiden 1939, 148–149; Breitman 1991, 56–59.

44. Hohmann 1991, 92; a letter of Schreiben Günther Panckes, head of the SS Race and Settlement Office (Schreiben Günther Panckes, chef der Rasse- und Siedlungsamt-SS) (19 Dec. 1938); Zimmermann 1996, 167–169; Döring 1959, 420, 425.

45. Zimmermann 1996, 186.

46. Hohmann 1991, 93–94; BA Berlin: R 73/14005, Ritter's report to the DFG (6 Jan. 1940), 7.

47. Zimmermann 1989, 57; Zimmermann 1996, 362.

48. Hohmann 1991, 107ff.

49. Roth and Aly 1984, 114, 139.

50. Wippermann 1997, 150–152.

51. Zimmermann 1996, 161.

52. Winter 1999, 68.

53. Krausnick 1987, 96; Zimmermann 1996, 197; Krausnick 1990, 30; Rose 1987, 70, 72.

54. Zimmermann 1996, 195–198.

55. Winter 1999, 29–34, esp. 33.

56. Steiner and von Cornberg 1998, 168–187; Noakes 1989, 328–336.

57. Krausnick 1987, 96; BA Berlin: R 6/34a folder 1-82, Bericht no. 39, Bl. 2 (3 Oct. 1941).

58. Deutschland zählt 30,000 Zigeuner. *Neues Wiener Tagblatt* (25 Feb. 1941); Zigeuner erhalten ein Sippenarchiv. *Stuttgarter NS-Kurier* no. 74 (16 Mar. 1941).

59. Wüst 1942, 37; Zimmermann 1996, 297; Kater 1974, 206–207.

60. Ritter 1938a, 73–74; Ritter 1941, 477.

61. Mosse 1978, 46.

62. Zigeuner, ein arischer Stamm? *Das Schwarze Korps* (6 Aug. 1936): 14.

63. Fahrendes Volk: Die Bekämpfung der Zigeunerplage auf neuen Wegen. *NS-Rechtspiegel* (21 Feb. 1939), 7.

64. Zimmermann 1996, 250ff.

65. Zimmermann 1996, 259ff.

66. Zimmermann 1996, 260.

67. Ogorreck 1996.

68. Zimmermann 1996, 260; Himmler 1999, 195 n.14. Today, there are doubts whether Himmler really had given such orders in Minsk on 15 August 1941.

69. Dieckmann 1998, 292–306, esp. 299.

70. Zimmermann 1996, 262–264.

71. Zimmermann 1996, 261.

72. International Military Trial at Nuremberg (IMG 1947 IV), 528–551.

73. Streim 1987.

74. Zimmermann 1996, 267–271.

75. Zimmermann 1996, 203.

76. Himmler 1999, 405.

77. Zimmermann 2000, 45ff.

78. Manoschek 1995, 178; Manoschek 1998, 228–230, 233.

79. Tsentr Khraneniya Istoriko-Dokumentalnykh Kollektsii (Special Archive), Moscow: R-1323-2-363, 93. I am very grateful to Dr. Dieter Pohl from the Institut für Zeitgeschichte in Munich, who drew my attention to this document.

80. Zimmermann 1996, 259–276.

81. Zimmermann 1996, 283.

82. STA Nürnberg: NOKW-802, Circular of the Commander Deputy General in Serbia to all the Field and Region Commanders (Rundschreiben des bevollmächtigen kommandierenden Generals in Serbien an alle Feld- und Kreiskommandaturen) (26 Oct. 1941).

83. Peukert 1989, 74.

84. Hohmann 1991, 110–111; Zimmermann 1996, 299.

85. Arnold 1965, 268; StA Frankfurt: PA Dr. Ritter Robert sig. 18.576, Explanation to our asocial and Gypsy research (Erläuterungen zu unseren Asozialen- und Zigeunerforschungen) (20 May 1947), Bl. 41ff.

86. Gilsenbach 1993, 149–150.

87. Höß 1978, 108; Zimmermann 1996, 301.

88. IfZ Archiv: MA 3 (9/91), letter of Martin Bormann to Heinrich Himmler (3 Dec. 1942).

89. Zimmermann 1996, 300.

90. Hohmann 1991, 115ff.

91. Bacharach 1985, 82 n. 32.

92. Mommsen 1983.

93. Höß 1978, 108; Broad 1969, 73–74; Zimmermann 1996, 305–315, Kenrick and Puxon 1981, 76.

94. Höß 1978, 108; Broad 1969, 73.

95. Yad Vashem Archive, Jerusalem: Testimony of John Heinrich, 033/1119, 99, 103; Höß 1978, 109.

96. Yad Vashem Archive: Testimony of John Heinrich, 033/1119, 92, and Testimony of Alter Feinsilber, 033/429 (13 Apr. 1945); Streck 1981a, 82ff.; Kielar 1979, 253–256; Kenrick and Puxon 1981, 110.

97. Wanda Pranden in *Es ging Tag und Nacht liebes Kind: Zigeuner (Sinti) in Auschwitz* (1982), film by Katrin Seibold and Melanie Spitta, Zweites Deutsches Ferensehen (ZDF).

98. Höß 1978, 109; Szymanski, Szymanska, and Snieszko 1987, 206; Lifton 1986, 323; Czech 1989, 837–838; Zimmermann 1996, 340ff.

99. Zimmermann 1996, 340 ff.; Höß 1978, 108; Streck 1981a, 81ff.; Czech 1989, 774–775; Lewy 2000, 162–166.

100. Kulka 1984, 315–330; Bauer 1994, 448; Lewy 2000, 152–153.

101. Zimmermann 1996, 347; interview with Otto H., who had served in this unit in Oldenburg (26 Aug. 1992); Krausnick 1990, 15; Winter 1999, 79–82. On Dirlewanger's unit, see Auerbach 1962, 250–263; Lewy 2000, 179–180.

102. Müller-Hill 1984, 63.

103. Kenrick and Puxon 1981, 135.

104. Vetter (1963) cited the passage directly from the article "So arisch," *Der Spiegel*, no. 17 (24 Apr. 1963), 48.

105. Arnold 1989, 30–39.

106. Zimmermann 1996, 284–292; Zimmermann 1997; Lewy 2000, 221–222.

107. Zimmermann 2000, 45.

CHAPTER 3. POLICY TOWARD GYPSIES IN THE SHADOW OF AUSCHWITZ

1. Arnold 1989, 32; How the Gypsies Were Persecuted, *Vienna Library Bulletin* 4(3–4) (May–July 1950): 18. (The source of the bulletin was an article that allegedly had been published in the newspaper *Neue Zeitung* on 15 Mar. 1950.)

2. Fings and Sparing 1992, 34. Also from the author's interviews with Harald Heller, Frankfurt a.M. (27 Jun. 1992); Mrs. Berta Weiss, Hannover (18 Aug. 1992); and Karl Wagner, Oldenburg (26 Aug. 1992).

3. Pankok 1950.

4. STA Hamburg: Polizeibehörde II 446, letter from Senator Alfred Höhlein to the commander of the defense police (2 Aug. 1945), 4; Niedersachsen (Lower Saxon) HSTA Hannover: Nds. C 100 Acc. 60/55, no. 1103, letter from the inspector of the order police for Hannover province and the Braunschweig and Oldenburg lands to the Oberpräsidenten of Hannover (17 Oct. 1945); Hess. MInn: Dept. 3, 22 e 30, letter from the police president to the Minister of the Interior (15 Aug. 1946); HSTA Stuttgart: MIN EA 2/303, Bü 332/1, letter from the County Police (Landespolizei) of Württemberg to the Minister of the Interior (11 Jun. 1947), 5; Der Senator für Inners und Sport, Bremen, P.1.a., no. 281,

letter from the police chief to the Senator for Interior Administration (Senator für innere Verwaltung) (19 Apr. 1948).

5. Pankok 1950.

6. Protest gegen "Asoziale," *Abendpost* (1 Jul. 1951); StA Frankfurt a.M.: Stadt Kanzlei municipal council file (Magistat Akte) 2203: vol. 1: Die Bekämpfung des Zigeunerplage, Citizens' Committee Inc. to the Municipal Council of Frankfurt (Bürger Ausschuss e.V. to the Magistrat of Frankfurt a.M.) (19 Sept. 1930), letter from the residents of Ginnheim to the Mayor (Oberbürgermeister) of Frankfurt (14 Jul. 1933), and letter from the NSDAP Gau Hessen-Nassau Ortsgruppe Obermain the region Great Frankfurt to the region's leadership of the Nazi Party (Kreis Gross Frankfurt to the Kreisleitung der NSDAP) (19 Mar. 1936); vol. 2: Combating the Gypsy Plague (Die Bekämpfung des Zigeunerplage) (1950–1954), letter from Dr. Otto Friecke, help organization of the Protestant Church in Hesseal Nassan to the Mayor of Frankfurt (Hilfwerk der Evangelischen Kirche in Hessen und Nassau, to the Oberbürgermeister of Frankfurt) (17 Aug. 1951).

7. Hess. MInn: Dept. 3, 22 e 30, from Dept. 3b to Dept. 3, Öffentliche Sicherheit (10 Nov. 1947).

8. Hessian Ministry of the Interior: Dept. 3, 22 e 30, letter from the local administration's president (Regierungspräsident) in Kassel to the Minister of the Interior (7 Nov. 1946); HSTA Stuttgart: MIN EA 2/303, Bü 332/1, letter from the president of the country region Baden Department of the Interior Administration (Präsident des Landesbezirks Baden Dept. innere Verwaltung), Karlsruhe (22 Jul. 1947), 7; Hess. MInn: Dept. 3, 22 e 30, letter from the local administration's president Darmstadt (Regierungspräsident Darmstadt) to the Minister of the Interior, Dept. 3 (12 Nov. 1947).

9. HSTA Stuttgart: MIN EA 2/303, Bü 332/1, letter from the Bürgermeister of the community Laufen am Kocher to the Country Council at Backnang (Gemeinde Laufen a. K. to the Herrn Landrat in Backnang) (6 Jan. 1946), Bl. 2.

10. STA Hamburg: Polizeibehörde II 446, 101, report of the Polizei Revier (30 Jun. 1945), 2.

11. Hess. MInn: Dept. 3, 22 e 30, letter from the Commando of the Constabulary (Kommando der Gendermerie) to the chief of police of Gross-Hessen state (9 Jul. 1946); Niedersachsen (Lower Saxon) HSTA Hannover: Nds. C 100 Acc. 60/55, no. 1103, letter from the Local Administration's President at Lüxembourg (RegierungsPräsident Lüneburg) to the Herrn Oberpräsidenten of Hannover (15 Nov. 1945).

12. Niedersachsen (Lower Saxon) HSTA Hannover: Nds. C 100 Acc. 60/55, no. 1103, letter from the British military government at Lüneburg to the local German administration (Nov. 1945).

13. Niedersachsen (Lower Saxon) HSTA Hannover: Nds. C 100 Acc. 60/55, no. 1103, letter from the British military government at Lüneburg to the local German administration (Nov. 1945).

14. Hess. MInn: Dept. 3, 22 e 30, letters from Zinnkann to the Office of Military Government (20 Sept. 1946 and 22 Nov. 1946); National Archives, Washington, D.C., RG 260, OMGUS OMG Hesse, Legal Division, Legislation Branch, #17/211-2, folder 4, box 923, 7/57/34/7.

15. STA Munich: RA 77636, Determination and Reporting of Nationalities (16 Nov. 1945); National Archives, Washington, D.C.: RG 260, OMGUS OMG Hesse, Legal Division, Legislation Branch, #17/211-2, folder 4, box 923, 7/57/34/7; Hess. MIN Dept. 22 e 30 (3 Mar. 1947); Hess. MJ: Az. 4726: vol. 1: Zigeunerwesen (20 Mar. 1947), 1.

16. National Archives, Washington, D.C.: RG 260, OMGUS OMG Hesse, Legal Division, Legislation Branch, #17/211-2, folder 4, box 923, 7/57/34/7.

17. Law no. 1, Military Government Gazette Germany, U.S. Area of Control, OMGUS (1949), 3–4.

18. Niedersachsen (Lower Saxon) HSTA Hannover: Nds. C 100 Acc. 60/55, no. 1103 (7 Oct. 1945) and Criminal Headquarters (Kriminal Direktion) Hannover (6 Dec. 1945).

19. STA Hamburg: Polizeibehörde II 446 (12 Jul. 1945), 3, and (25 Sept. 1945), 19; HSTA Stuttgart: MInn EA 2/303, Bü 332/1, letter from the president of the country district Baden, Department Interior Administration (Landesbezirks Baden, Dept. Innere Verwaltung) to the Minister of the Interior of Stuttgart (22 Jul. 1947), 7ff.

20. Hess. MInn: Dept. 3, 22 e 30, the President of the Police (Der Polizei-Präsident) (15 Aug. 1946).

21. Hess. MInn: Dept. 3, 22 e 30, from Dept. 3b to Dept. 3, Public Security (Öffentliche Sicherheit) (10 Nov. 1947).

22. Law on Combating Gypsies, vagrants, and work shys (Gesetz zur Bekämpfung von Zigeunern, Landfahrern und Arbeitsscheuen), Gesetz und Vevordnungsblatt (Laws and Decrees Bulletin; GVBl.) 17 (22 Jul. 1926); Bay. HSTA: RG OMGBy, 17/175–3/19, Murray Van Wagoner Land Director to the Minister President of Bavaria (28 Nov. 1947); Bay. HSTA: OMGUS Legal Division, box 9, folder 1345, OMGUS Legal Division Berlin, Whitney R. Harris to the director of the OMGBY (25 Mar. 1948); Bay. HSTA: RG OMGBy, 17/175–3/27, John J. Raymond Prisons Branch to Legal Advice and Legislation Branch (10 Nov. 1947).

23. Bay. HSTA: RG OMGBy, 17/175–3/19, Murray Van Wagoner Land Director to the Minister President of Bavaria (28 Nov. 1947).

24. Gesetz no. 14 der OMGUS GVBl. (1949), 78.

25. Bay. GV Bl. 19 (1947), 247; Bay. HSTA: RG OMGBy, 17/175–3/19, Dr. Ehard to OMGBy Legal Division, Legislation Branch (1 Mar. 1948).

26. STA Munich: Pol. Dir. München 11219, Organization of the Department of Criminal Investigations (Organisation der Kriminaluntersuchungsabteilung) (14 Oct. 1947).

27. Bay. HSTA: MInn 86363, A proposal for supplementing the existing decree on the establishing of an office for identification in Bavaria (Vorschlag zur Ergänzung des bestehenden Erlasses über die Errichtung des Landeserkennungsamtes Bayern) (no date), 6; STA Bremen: 4,13/1-P.1.a., no. 10, Bekämpfung des Zigeunerwesens; Bavarian Ministry of the Interior (Bay. Staatsministerium des Innern) (18 Mar. 1933); Proceedings of the Bavarian Landtag 9 Vote Period 1978/82 Stenographic report 9/66 (Verhandlungen des Bayerischen Landtags 9 Wahlperiode 1978/82 StenographischerBericht 9/66) (17 Jul. 1980), 4160.

28. Bavarian Public Prosecutor Office Munich (Bay. Staatsanwaltschaft

München) 1:2KLs 1/52, Mr. Koch of Bayerisches Hilfswerk to the Central Office for Criminological Identification and Police Statistics, Dept.of Gypsy Police for Mr. Uschold (Zentralamtes für Krim. Identifizierung und Polizeistatistik, Dept. Zigeunerpolizei, z. Hd. Herrn Uschold) (14 Jun. 1950); Bay. HSTA: MIN 86363, the Head of the Central Office for Criminological Identification and Police Statistics of the Bavarian State (Der Leiter des Zentralamtes für Krim, Identifizierung und Polizeistatistik des Landes Bayern) (19 Nov. 1951).

29. HSTA Düsseldorf: Rep. 231, no. 1535, 158–159; no. 1536, 214ff.; no. 1537, 564ff.

30. Rose 1987, 31–32; Berbüsse 1992, 117ff.; Feuerhelm 1988, 301ff.; Hohmann 1980c, 90–96.

31. Meixner 1948.

32. Hess. MInn: Dept. 3, 22 e 30, Dept. 6 to Dept. 3, Öffentliche Sicherheit (3 Oct. 1947).

33. Hess. MInn: Dept. 3, 22 e 30, memo from Dr. Epstein to the Minister for Political Liberation (25 Sept. 1947).

34. Hess. MInn: Dept. 3, 22 e 30, Betr: Initiativantrag der Fraktion der CDU (5 Mar. 1956), and the Minister for Political Liberation (Der Minister für politischen Befreiung) to Dept. 3 Public Security (Öffentliche Sicherheit) (25 Sept. 1947).

35. Hess. MInn: Dept. 3, 22 e 30, Local Administration's President (Regierungspräsident Darmstadt an) to Dept. 3 Public Security (Öffentliche Sicherheit) (21 Apr. 1948).

36. Hess. MInn: Dept. 3, 22 e 30, a notice (Aktenvermerk) (18 May 1949); Hess. JM: Az. 4726, vol. 1, Herr Canter, the Minister of Justice to the Minister of the Interior (15 Feb. 1950).

37. HSTA Stuttgart: MInn EA 2/303, Bü 332/1, Country Councils of the American Occupation Zone. The Coordination Office of the German Lands, minutes of the tenth meeting of the Committee for State and Administration legal questions (Länderrat des amerikanischen Besatzungsgebiets. Koordinierungsbüro der Länder Niederschrift über die zehnte Sitzung des Ausschusses für staats- und verwaltungsrechtliche Fragen) (14–15 Dec. 1948), 49.

38. HSTA Stuttgart: MInn EA 2/303, Bü 332/1, Country Councils of the American Occupation Zone. The Co-ordination Office of the Lands, minutes of the sixteenth meeting of the Committee for State and Administration legal questions (Länderrat des amerikanischen Besatzungsgebiets. Koordinierungsbüro der Länder Protokoll über die vierzehnte Sitzung des Ausschusses für staats- und verwaltungsrechtliche Fragen) (5–6 Jul. 1949), 52.

39. The Designing Authorities for Registration and Inventory of the Population (Planungsbehörde für Registrierung und Bestandsaufnahme der Bevölkerung) to the Local Administration's President (Regierungspräsidenten) (23 Jun. 1949).

40. HSTA Stuttgart: MInn EA 2/303, Bü 332/1, Preliminary remark (Vorbemerkung) (27 Sept. 1949), 53.

41. HSTA Stuttgart: MInn EA 2/303, Bü 332/1, work group of the Ministries of Interior of the Federal State, Stuttgart minutes of the sixteenth meeting of the work group of the Ministries of the Interior of the Federal States (Arbeit-

gemeinschaft der Innenministerien der Bundesländer Stuttgart, Protokoll über die 16. Sitzung der Arbeitsgemeinschaft der Innenministerien der Bundesländer) (27–28 Oct. 1949).

42. HSTA Düsseldorf: NW 59/106 (6 Apr. 1962), Criminal Police Office of the State North Rhine–Westphalia (LKA Nordrhein-Westfalen) to all Regional Police (alle Kreispolizei) belonging to the lands of North-Rhine–Westphalia; STA Hamburg: Polizeibehörde 2, 439.

43. Münzel (1983), 234ff.

44. Hess. MInn: Dept. 3, 22 e 30, an excerpt of the minutes of the thirty-sixth meeting of the Parliamentary Council of the Committee for Fundamental Questions (Auszug aus dem Protokoll über die 36. Sitzung des Parlamentarischen Rats des Ausschusses für Grundsatzfragen) (27 Jan. 1949).

45. Proceedings of the Bavarian Landtag 2nd Legislation Period 4, convening 1949–1950, Munich, 1951, vol. 4, supplements, supplement 683, Bavarian Landtag Committee for Social-Political Affairs, 25th Meeting (2. Legislaturperiode 4, Tagung 1949–1950, München, 1951, vol. 4, Beilagen, Beilage 683, Bayerischer Landtag-Ausschuss für Sozialpolitische Angelegenheiten, 25. Sitzung) (22 Sept. 1952), 3–4; Proceedings of the Bavarian Landtag Supplement 986 (Verhandlungen des Bayerischen landtags, Verhandlungen des Bayerischen Landtags, Beilage 986); Bay. HStA: StK-GuV 911, Gesetz zur Bekämpfung des Landfahrer und Arbeitsscheuenunwesens = Landfahrer Ordnung (22 Dec. 1953).

46. Bay. HSTA: StK-GuV 911, no. 12806 (5 Jul. 1951).

47. Basic Law (GG) Art. 3—Equality before the Law, Sec. 3 (Gleichheit vor dem Gesetz, Abs. 3), 1; Bay. HSTA: StK-GuV 911, Begründung, 3.

48. Laws and Decrees Bulletin of the Free Bavarian State (GVBl. für den Freistaat Bayern), no. 17 (22 Jul. 1926), 361.

49. Bavarian Landtag Committee for Social-Political Affairs, twenty-sixth Meeting (Bayerischer Landtag-Ausschus für Sozialpolitische Angelegenheiten 26. Sitzung) (2 Oct. 1952), 8.

50. Bay. HSTA: StK-GuV 911, letter from Dr. Koch of the Bavarian Ministry of Justice to the Bavarian Ministry of the Interior (18 Mar. 1952), 6; Basic Law (GG) Art. 3—Equality before the Law, Sec. 3 (Gleichheit vor dem Gesetz, Abs. 3), 1.

51. Bay. JM: Az. 4726, vol. 1 (6 May 1952).

52. Bay. JM: Az. 4726, vol. 1, letter of the Federal Ministry of Justice in Bonn, (1 Aug. 1952).

53. Bay. JM: Az. 4726, vol. 1, letter of Dr. Hoegner, the Minister of the Interior to the Bavarian Ministry of Justice (4 Sept. 1952); Bay. HSTA: StK-GuV 911, Dr. Hoegner's letter to the Bavarian prime minister (30 Apr. 1952), and preliminary remarks for convening the Council of Ministern, Proceedings of the Bavarian Landtag, 2 (Vormerkung für den Ministerrat, Verhandlungen des Bayerischen Landtags, 2 Tagung) (1951–1952), vol. 3, Munich 1952, Suppl. (Beil.) 2979.

54. Bavarian Landtag Committee for Social-Political Affairs, twenty-fifth meeting (Bayerischer Landtag-Ausschus für Sozialpolitische Angelegenheiten, 25. Sitzung) (22 Sept. 1952), 1ff., 24; proceedings of the Bavarian Landtag 3rd convening (Verhandlungen des Bayerischen Landtags, 3 Tagung) 1952/53, vol. 4, Munich 1953, 127th Meeting (Sitzung) (10 Feb. 1953), 743.

55. Bay. HSTA: StK-GuV 912, Dr. Hoegner's letter to the Bavarian prime minister (29 Apr. 1953); Vagrants Order (Landfahrerordnung) (22 Dec. 1953), Bay. GVBl. no. 27/1953, 197.

56. Bavarian Landtag Committee for Social-Political Affairs twenty-fifth Meeting (Bayerischer Landtag-Ausschuss für Sozialpolitische Angelegenheiten 25. Sitzung) (22 Sept. 1952), 15–16, 27.

57. Hess. MInn: Dept. 3, 22 e 30, Minister of the Interior of Dept. 3 to the Local Administration Presidents (Regierungspräsidenten) (7 May 1953). Interview with Harald Heller, Frankfurt (27 Jun. 1992). Heller's family and four other Roma families left Munich in 1952, where they had settled in 1947, after harassment of the "Gypsy police," including Rudolf Uschold, who took away their German passports. They settled in Frankfurt and Cologne.

58. Hess. MInn: Dept. 3, 22 e 30, letter to the Hessian Local Administration (Regierungs) president (7 May 1953).

59. Hess. MInn: Dept. 3, 22 e 30; Hessian State's Criminal Office Identification Service (Hess. LKA Landeserkennungsdienst) to the Federal Criminal Office (BKA) (2 Oct. 1953); STA Hamburg: Polizeibehörde 2, 447, BKA to the head of the LKA State Criminal Office Hamburg (1 Mar. 1954), 28.

60. HSTA Stuttgart: MIN EA 2/303, Bü 332/1, the Criminal Office of the State (Landeskriminalamt) Baden-Württemberg to the Minister of the Interior of Baden-Württemberg (12 Jan. 1954); STA Hamburg: Polizeibehörde 2, 447 (4 Mar. 1954), 30.

61. Hess. MInn 22 e 30 (6 Feb. 1954).

62. STA Hamburg: Polizeibehörde 2, 447, BKA (14 Apr. 1954).

63. Landesarchiv Berlin: Rep. 142/9, no. 0/713–14, Zigeuner, 57. Sitzung des Präsidiums in Düsseldorf (30 Jan. 1954), E 333, Dept. 4 to Dept. O, regarding Zigeunerunwesen (25 Feb. 1954); Landesarchiv Berlin: Rep. 142/9, no. 4/00-00-26, Protokolle des Sozialausschusses (24 Feb. 1954); Landesarchiv Berlin: Rep. 142/9, no. 0/713–14, Dr. Dellbrügge from Dept. 4 to Dept. O (22 Jun. 1954); Landesarchiv Berlin: Rep. 142/9, no. 0/713–14, letter from Dr. Grafe to the State Association of the German Conference of City Mayors (Landesverbände des Deutschen Städtetag) (24 Jul. 1954).

64. STA Hamburg: Polizeibehörde 2, 447, BKA, Guidelines for the Combating of Vagrant Nuisance (Richtlinien für die Bekämpfung des Landfahrerunwesens) (24 Jul. 1954), 36.

65. Hess. MInn: Dept. 3, 22 e 30, minutes of the Legal Comission of the Work Group (Rechtskommision des Arbeitskreis) 2 (26–27 Sept. 1955).

66. Bay. HSTA: StK-GuV 912, Proposals for Administration Simplification in the Field of Vagrants Law (Vorschläge zur Verwaltungsvereinfachung aus dem Bereich des Landfahrerrechts) (28 Jul. 1969).

67. Printed matter of the Hessian Landtag Third Election Period. Stenographic Report on the plenary meeting (Drucksachen des Hessischen Landtags, 3. Wahlperiode, Dept. 3, Stenographische Berichte über die Plenarsitzungen), vol. 2, Wiesbaden 1956, Twenty-third meeting (Sitzung) (7 Mar. 1956), 887–888.

68. Hessian Landtag, Committee for Communal-Political Affairs (Hessischer Landtag, Kommunalpolitischer Auschuss) (2 Nov. 1956), 1; printed matter of

the Hessian Landtag Third Election Period. Stenographic Reports on the plenary meeting (Drucksachen des Hessischen Landtags, 3. Wahlperiode, Dept. 3, Stenographische Berichte über die Plenarsitzungen), vol. 3, Wiesbaden 1957, thirty-ninth meeting (Sitzung) (6 Feb. 1957), 1430ff.

69. Hess. MInn: Dept. 3, 22 e 30, Mr. Keil to the Local Administrations Presidents (Regierungpräsidenten) (13 Sept. 1957) and Mr. Keil to the Working Group (Arbeitsgemeinschaft) of the Ministry of the Interior (9 Dec. 1954). In these letters Keil characterized this population as work shys and criminals.

70. Instructional pamphlet concerning the combating of criminal vagrants in the State of Hesse. Special supplement for the criminal paper of the State of Hesse (Merkblatt Betr. Bekämpfung der kriminellen Landfahrer im Lande Hessen, Sonderbeilage zum Landes-Kriminalblatt Hessen) no. 597 (27 Jun. 1957); instructional pamphlet for the combating of vagrant nuisance in Lower Saxony (Merkblatt für die Bekämpfung der Landfahrerunwesens in Niedersachsen).

71. Mangoldt 1953, 609–610; Klebe 1974, 61–63; Ott 1979.

72. Hess. MInn 22 e 30: The Minister of Interior of the State North Rhine–Westphalia (Der Innenminister des Landes Nordrhein–Westfalen Düsseldorf) (13 Jan. 1954).

73. HSTA Düsseldorf: Rep. 231, no. 1535, 101–102; Interview with Harald Heller, Frankfurt (27 Jun. 1992).

74. Interview with Paul Jochum, Cologne (27 Oct. 1992); Schlüssig Deutsche: Eine Sinti-Familie kämpft um Anerkennung und Pässe, *Die Zeit* (28 Nov. 1986).

75. Interview with Paul Jochum, Cologne (27 Oct. 1992).

76. Interview with Paul Jochum, Cologne (27 Oct. 1992).

77. Rose 1987, 136–144; Feuerhelm 1987, 139–151.

78. STA Hamburg: Polizeibehörde 2, 449, from the short minutes of the Twenty-eighth Working Meeting of the Heads of the State Criminal Offices with the Federal Criminal Office (aus dem Kurzprotokoll über die 28. Arbeitstagung-der Leiter der Landeskriminalämter mit dem Bundeskriminalamt) (28–29 Mar. 1960), 7.

CHAPTER 4. COMPENSATION POLICY TOWARD GYPSY VICTIMS OF NAZISM

1. HSTA Düsseldorf: NW 114/94, declaration of the defeat of Germany, Art. 6, no. 52 (6 May 1945), 250, and Control Proclamation no. 2 of the Allied Control Authorities (Kontrollproclamation no. 2 der alliierten Kontrollbehörde) (30 Sept. 1945), Art. 11, no. 42b.

2. IfZ Archiv: 3058/62, sentence of the BGH (23 May 1962), 4 ZR, 221/61 (OLG Cologne), and sentence of the BGH (23 May 1962), 4 ZR, 198/61 (OLG Cologne).

3. Gilsenbach 1993, 9, 266–267.

4. STA Munich: RA 77636, letter from the mayor (Bürgermeister) of community (Gemeinde) Geiselbullach to the Country Council Fürstenfeldbruck (Landrat Fürstenfeldbruck) (29 Jun. 1945).

5. HSTA Düsseldorf: NW 114/94, 141, guidelines for the help measures for

those who had been injured because of political stance (Richtlinien für die Hilfs-massnahmen für politisch Geschädigte) (1 Aug. 1945), 2.

6. Bay. HSTA: StK 113799.

7. Romey 1988, 226; Goschler 1992, 79. BA Berlin: DQ-2 3320, the President of the province Saxony (Der Präsident der Provinz Sachsen) (9 Sept. 1945) and Dr. Raff to Dr. Hoegner (4 Dec. 1945); Bay. HSTA: StK 113800; Bay. HSTA: MF 69409; Bavarian Law and Decrees Bulletin, Bay. GVBl 1947, 276.

8. BWMJ: 601 Organisation, the Office for Correcting theWrong Done and Its Tasks (Das Amt für Wiedergutmachung und seine Aufgaben) (9 Jan. 1946), Bl. 5; HSTA Düsseldorf NW: 114/94; Niedersachsen (Lower Saxon) HSTA Hannover: Nds. 50 Acc. 82/68, no. 100.

9. BA Berlin: DQ-2 3361, 751–752; The Main Committee Victim of Fascism (Hauptausschusses "Opfer des Faschismus") Ed. (1947) 2 Jahre "Opfer des Faschismus," Berlin, 8; BA Berlin: DQ-2 3377; Reuter and Hansel 1997, 71–89.

10. BA Berlin: DQ-2 3377, administration bulletin for the State of Thuringia (Regierungsblatt für das Land Thüringen), Part 1: Gesetzsamlung Ausgegeben in Weimar (12 Aug. 1946), and Gesetz über die Entschädigung für Freiheitsentziehung aus politischen, rassischen und religiösen Gründen (11 Feb. 1949) GW. NW. no. 10, Bl. 63.

11. Timm 1992, 125–138; Goschler 1993, 107; Groehler 1994, 283–302; Herf 1997, 80–83; Reuter and Hansel 1997, 82–84; Gilsenbach 1993, 9, 266–267.

12. Becker, Hüber, and Küster 1955; Blessin, Wilden, and Ehrig, 1954.

13. SPD und VVN, *SPD Nachrichten,* no. 10 (Aug. 1948); Reuter and Hansel 1997, 189–211; Schneider 1997, 26, 29ff.

14. VVN-Landesverband BW Archiv, Stuttgart: D2700, provisorische Richtlinien Stuttgart (26 May 1945).

15. IfZ Archiv: MF 260, OMGUS-WB (12/26–2/24), statistical reports from the VVN to the OMGWB (May 1947–Nov. 1947); Archiv der Otto Pankok-Gesellschaft (Hünxe-Drevenack), Akte Zigeuner, letter of the VVN State Association (Landesverband) North Rhine–Westfalia to Pankok (24 Jun. 1948) in recognition of those persecuted for racial motives (Gypsies) (Betr: Anerkennung von rass. Verfolgten [Zigeuner]).

16. Archiv der Otto Pankok-Gesellschaft (Hünxe-Drevenack): Akte Zigeuner, letter from the Minister of the Interior to Pankok (19 Jul. 1950).

17. VVN-Landesverband BW Archiv, Stuttgart: D2701, D2702.

18. VVN-Landesverband BW Archiv, Stuttgart: D2704; Bay. HSTA: RG 260 OMGBy, 10/130–1/3; Wetzel 1987, 37–41.

19. National Archives: RG 260, OMGUS OMG Hesse, Legal Division, Legislation Branch, #17/211-2, folder 4, box 923, 7/57/34/7.

20. "How the Gypsies Were Persecuted," *Vienna Library Bulletin* 4 (3–4), (May–July 1950): 18.

21. Bay. HStA: StK 113799.

22. Control Proclamation no. 2 of the Allied Control Authorities (Kontrollproclamation no. 2 der Alliierten Kontrollbehörden) (20 Sept. 1945), Art. 11, 42b.

23. Romey 1988, 226.

24. HSTA Düsseldorf: NW 114/94, from the official bulletin of the country

district Kirchheim-Bolanden (Aus dem Amtsblatt für den Landkreis Kirchheim-Bolanden), no. 4 (26 Jan. 1946), Bl. 206 and Bl. 196.

25. Giessler 1981, 13: "Moral offenders, pimps, vagrants . . . work shys . . . the so-called asocial, were not truly opponents of Nazism" (my translation).

26. Erker 1988, 96.

27. IfZ Archiv, MF 260, OMGUS-WB (12/26–2/24). Karl Hauff, memo on the situation of the political, racial, and religious persecutees of the Nazi regime (Denkschrift über die Lage der vom Naziregime politisch, rassisch und religiös Verfolgten) (5 Feb. 1947); Ayass 1987, 43; Goschler 1992, 87–90.

28. Hess. HSTA Wiesbaden 659/902; IfZ Archiv: RG 260, OMGBy (13/41–1/1).

29. HSTA Düsseldorf: NW 114/94, The Municipality of Cologne (Stadtverwaltung Köln) to the Oberpräsidenten der Nort Rhein Province, Department of Public Welfare, Aug. 17, 1945, 219.

30. VVN-Landesverband BW Archiv, Stuttgart: D2701.

31. HSTA Düsseldorf: NW 114/259, the Regierungspräsident (Local Administration official) Minden to the Social Misistry (Dept.) 3- D -Dr. F[renkel] (8 May 1947), 218. Similar accusations can be found in testimonies of political prisoners, e.g. Streck 1981a, 82.

32. HSTA Düsseldorf: NW 114/258, letter from Dr. Frenkel to the Local Adminstration President Detmold, the Minden Office (Regierungspräsidenten Detmold, Geschäftsstelle Minden) (25 Oct. 1946), 201.

33. HSTA Düsseldorf: NW 114/258, letter from Dr. Frenkel to the Local Administration President Detmold, the Minden office (Regierungspräsidenten Detmold, Geschäftsstelle Minden) (21 May 1948), Bl. 232 and (24 Jan. 1948), Bl. 132; Mit Molari bei den Zigeunern. *Freiheit* no. 7 (23 Jan. 1948).

34. BWMJ: 202 Entschädigungsgesetz, Dr. Beyerle the Württemberg Ministry of Justice dept. Composition to the Bavarian State Ministry for Justice (württembergischen Justizministerium Dept. Wiedergutmachung an das Bayerische Staatsministerium für Justiz) (26 Aug. 1947), Bl. 91.

35. Law no. 951 (Gesetz Nr. 951), for correcting the wrong done by the Nazis (Zur Wiedergutmachung nationalsozialistischen Unrechts) (16 Aug. 1949), administration bulletin of the Administration of Württemberg-Baden (Regierungsblatt der Regierung Württemberg-Baden), no. 20, Art. 50; law for correcting the wrong done by the Nazis (compensation law) (Gesetz zur Wiedergutmachung nationalsozialistischen Unrechts) (Entschädigungsgesetz) (12 Aug. 1949), Bayer. GVBl. no. 20/1949, 195ff.

36. Information through the Federal Administration, Report of the Federal Administration on correcting the wrong done and compensation for Nazi wrong as on the situation of Sinti, Roma, and related groups. (Unterichtung durch die Bundesregierung. Bericht der Bundesregierung über Wiedergutmachung und Entschädigung für nationalsozialistisches Unrecht sowie über die Lage der Sinti, Roma und verwandter Gruppen). German Bundestag tenth voting period (Deutscher Bundestag 10 Wahlperiode), printed matter (Drucksache) 10/6287 (31 Oct. 1986), 39ff.; interview with Karlo Hessdörfer, former president of the Bavarian Compensation Office, Munich (24 Jul. 1991).

37. Romey 1988, 226. BWMJ: 601 Organisation, guidelines for the care for

political persecutees of the Nazi regime (Richtlinien für die Betreuung der politisch Verfolgten des Naziregimes) (21 Mar. 1946), 36/3; IfZ Archiv: RG 260, OMGBy (13/141–1/1). Dr. Philipp Auerbach to OMGBy Public Welfare Branch Att. Mr. Miniclier (6 May 1947); BA Berlin: DQ-2 3375 and DQ-2 3376.

38. Rose 1987, 31ff., 53.

39. Mit Molari bei den Zigeunern. *Freiheit* no. 7 (23 Jan. 1948): 3; Roberts 1949.

40. E.g., BWMJ: 601 Organisation, Ministry of the Interior, office for Correcting the Wrong Done in Consequence of Nazi Terror (Innenministerium Amt für Wiedergutmachung der Folgen des Naziterrors), Stuttgart (9 Jan. 1946), Bl. 5; HSTA Düsseldorf: NW 114/94 (1946), Bl. 205, guidelines for immediate help in correcting the wrong done for political injuries (Richtlienien zur Soforthilfe bei Wiedergutmachung politischer Schädigungen).

41. BWMJ: 601 Organisation, guidelines for the care for political persecutees of the Nazi regime in the region of the state office Württemberg-Baden, Stuttgart (Richtlinien für die Betreuung der politisch Verfolgten des Naziregimes im Gebiet der Landesstelle Württemberg-Baden, Stuttgart), (21 Mar. 1946).

42. BA Berlin: DQ–2 3320, Bl. 117 (Art.7).

43. Hess. HSTA Wiesbaden: 502/2773a (27 Nov. 1946), guidelines for carrying out the decree on the formation and prodecure of the care office in Hesse (Richtlinien zur Durchführung der Verordnung über die Bildung und das Verfahren der Betreuungsstellen in Hessen).

44. BA Berlin: DQ-2 3320, Bl. 97–99.

45. VVN-Landesverband BW Archiv, Stuttgart: D2700, the VVN's directions for official recognition of victims persecuted by the Nazis (1 Jun. 1947).

46. Bulletin of the state committee for political persecutees in Bavaria (Mitteilungsblatt des Landesausschusses der politisch Verfolgten in Bayern), Munich (1 Feb. 1947); HSTA Düsseldorf: NW 114/259 (24 Apr. 1947), 230, a draft of guidelines for the recognition of political and racial persecutees (Entwurf Richtlinien für die Anerkennung politisch und rassisch Verfolgter).

47. Interview with Alfred Hauser, Stuttgart (7 Dec. 1992).

48. Jochimsen 1963, 8; HSTA Düsseldorf: NW 114/94, guidelines for the help measures for the politically injured peoples' welfare, Düsseldorf (Richtlinien für die Hilfsmassnahmen für politisch Geschädigte Volkswohlfahrt, Düsseldorf) (1 Aug. 1945).

49. BWMJ: 601 Organisation, Ministry of the Interior, office for correcting the consequences of Nazi terror, Stuttgart (Innenministerium, Amt für Wiedergutmachung der Folgen des Naziterrors, Stuttgart) (9 Jan. 1946), 5.

50. STA Munich: RA 77636.

51. HSTA Düsseldorf: NW 114/259 (8 May 1947), 218.

52. Zigeuner und VVN. *VVN Nachrichten* no. 6 (2 Feb. 1948).

53. Law bulletin of the GDR (Gesetzblatt der DDR) no. 14 (18 Feb. 1950), 93; Reimer Gilsenbach. "One lie more on Sinti." Unpublished (Eine Lüge mehr über die Sinti. Msc.) (23 Jun. 1991).

54. Hehmann 1987, 252.

55. IfZ Archiv: MF 260, OMGUS-WB (26 Dec.–24 Feb.). Karl Hauff, memo on the situation of the persecutees of the Nazi regime for political, racial, and

religious motives (Denkschrift über die Lage der vom Naziregime politisch, rassisch und religiös Verfolgten) (5 Feb. 1947); VVN demonstriert vor dem bayerischen Landtag. *Süddentshe Zeitung* (10 Mar. 1950).

56. STA Bremen: 4,54-11-30/6, Zigeuner, 56. Zimmermann (1996, 176–184) describes the desperate situation of the deported Gypsies in Poland.

57. STA Bremen: 4,54-11-30/6, Zigeuner, 53ff.; IfZ Archiv: Micro. MA-21, the Senator for the Finance Bremen (der Senator für die Finanzen Bremen) (29 Jun. 1951), 1–2; BWMJ: 202 Entschädigungsgesetz, letter from Auerbach to Dr. Küster (17 Jan. 1950), 1171; STA Bremen: 4, 54-11-30/6, Zigeuner, 61–62; VVN (Vereinigung der Verfolgten des Naziregimes) Hamburg (8 Feb. 1950).

58. STA Bremen: 4,54-11-30/6, Zigeuner, 53ff.; IfZ Archiv: Micro. MA-21, the Senator for the Finance Bremen (der Senator für die Finanzen Bremen) (29 Jun. 1951), 1–2; BWMJ: 202 Entschädigungsgesetz, letter from Auerbach to Dr. Küster (17 Jan. 1950), 1171; STA Bremen: 4,54-11-30/6, Zigeuner, 61–62; VVN (Vereinigung der Verfolgten des Naziregimes) Hamburg (8 Feb. 1950); HSTA Düsseldorf: NW 114/25, 29/2.

59. STA Bremen: 4,54-11-00/1 (26 Jan. 1950).

60. HSTA Düsseldorf: NW 114/25 (4 Feb. 1950), 42, compensation for confinement for Gypsies (Haftentschädigung für Zigeuner).

61. HSTA Düsseldorf: NW 114/272, 1–12.

62. HSTA Düsseldorf: NW 114/25, 26–28.

63. BWMJ: 202 Entschädigungsgesetz (20 Jan. 1950), 1222.

64. BWMJ: 202 Entschädigungsgesetz (20 Jan. 1950), 1222.

65. Bay. HSTA: MIN 86364; Bay. HSTA: MIN 86369, an excerpt from the report on activity and success of the Bavarian State Criminal Office for the year 1962, in a supplement to the Bavarian state criminal bulletin no. 36 (Auszug aus dem Tätigkeits- und Erfolgsbericht des Bayerischen Landeskriminalamtes für das Jahr 1962, in Beilage zum Bayer. Landeskriminalblatt no. 36) (31 May 1963).

66. STA Munich: Pol. Dir. München 11219, a survey on the distribution of the activity tasks (Übersicht über die Verteilung der Geschäftsaufgaben) since 1 Apr. 1953.

67. BWMJ: 202 Entschädigungsgesetz (3 Feb. 1950), 1222–1223.

68. BWMJ: 202 Entschädigungsgesetz (16 Feb. 1950), 1284.

69. BWMJ: 202 Entschädigungsgesetz (22 Feb. 1950), 1330.

70. BWMJ: 202 Entschädigungsgesetz (22 Feb. 1950), 1330.

71. Küster 1953.

72. Bay. MJ: 1091-I SA, no. 416/50, a circular from the president of the Bavarian state compensation office (Bay. LEA Der Präsident, Rundschreiben).

73. BWMJ: 202 Entschädigungsgesetz, minutes of the meeting (Protokoll über die Sitzung) (17 Mar. 1950), vol. 12, Bl. 1486, 46–47.

74. HSTA Düsseldorf: NW 114/25 (18 Jan. 1950), 29, report on the care and recognition of Gypsies (Bericht über die Betreuung und Anerkennung der Zigeuner).

75. BWMJ 202 Entschädigungsgesetz, vol. 12, 1486, minutes of the meeting (Protokoll über die Sitzung) (17 Mar. 1950), 47ff.

76. BWMJ: 202 Entschädigungsgesetz, vol. 12, 1486, minutes of the meeting (Protokoll über die Sitzung) (17 Mar. 1950), 47–49.

77. IfZ Archiv: Micro. MA 21, decision of the Entschädigungskammer (Beschluss EK 2/51 Guttenberger gegen Freistaat Bayern) (7 Nov. 1951), 3.

78. Niedersachsen (Lower Saxon) HSTA Hannover: Nds. 110 W Acc. 106/89, Liste 60, no. 17, 8, district special help committee city of Braunschweig (Kreis-Sonderhilfausschuss Braunschweig-Stadt) to the president of Lower Saxon administrative district Braunschweig (Nieder. Verw. Bezirks, Braunschweig) (5 Dec. 1950).

79. Central State Archive Stuttgart Ministry of Justice Baden-Württenberg Dept. of Compensation (HSTA Stuttgart MJBW Dept. Wiedg. EA/4/202, 9).

80. "The Administrative Director Epstein Withdraws from His Office" (Regierungs direktor Epstein scheidet ans seimem Amt aus) *Frankfurter Rundschau* (17 Feb. 1950). Horst E. Scholz, "The Dismissal of Dr. Epstein" (Dr. Epstein Entlassung) *Frankfurter Rundschau* (18 Feb. 1950).

81. HSTA Düsseldorf: NW-Pe 7251I, PA Dr. Marcel Frenkel; Schneider 1997, 51.

82. Hüttenberger 1973, 481–482.

83. Goschler 1989, 78.

84. Goschler 1989, 89–90.

85. Goschler 1989, 89ff.

86. Goschler 1992, 165–167.

87. IfZ Archiv: Micro. MA-21, WG 2, 193 (2 Jan. 1951).

88. BWMJ: 202 Entschädigungsgesetz (11 Jul. 1951), Bl. 2757.

89. BWMJ: 701 Sterilisierung, 141ff.

90. STA Bremen: 4,54-11-30/6, Zigeuner (2 Jun. 1953), 66ff.

91. Interview with Paul Jochum, Cologne (27 Oct. 1992); interview with Karlo Hessdörfer, Munich (24 Jul. 1991).

92. Neukamp 1950; letter from Eva Justin to Bayer, Bavarian State compensation office (Landesentschädigungsamt, or LEA) (18 Sept. 1956).

93. HSTA Düsseldorf: Rep. 231, no.1535 (13 Mar. 1959), 103, proceedings against Dr. Hans Maly and others, police presidency Ludwigshafen on the Rhine (Polizeipräsidium Ludwigshafen am Rhein).

94. Interview with Karlo Hessdörfer, Munich (24 Jul. 1991); Karlo Hessdörfer, "Sinti und Roma," podium discussion (Podiumsdiskussion) (15 Apr. 1989).

CHAPTER 5. GERMAN COURTS, NAZI PERPETRATORS, AND GYPSY VICTIMS

1. Quick letter of the Reich Central Security office (Schnellbrief des RSHA) (29 Jan. 1943) V A 2, no. 59/43 (known as the "Auschwitz decree"); Zimmermann 1989, 61ff.; Becker, Hüber, and Küster 1955, 50; Calvelli-Adorno 1961, 529ff.; Spitta 1989, 385ff.

2. A list of sentences of German courts in which the appeals of German Gypsies against the compensation authorities were rejected: Becker, Hüber, and Küster 1955, 50.

3. Becker, Huber, and Küster 1955, 48.

4. See n. 2.

5. Zimmermann 1989, 20, 24.

6. Eller 1954, 126: "A racial persecution against the Gypsies, in contrast to the persecution of the Jews, simply should be denied."

7. Uschold 1951, 60.

8. HSTA Düsseldorf: Rep. 231, no. 1535, process against Dr. Hans Maly and others, letter from Rudolf Uschold to Eva Justin (6 Jun. 1953), Bl. 35–36; STA Bremen: 4,54-11-30/6, Zigeuner, 12–13; OLG Munich EK 34/51 (21 Sept. 1951).

9. Verdict of the Supreme Court (BGH) 4 ZR 211/55 (7 Jan. 1956), 9.

10. Buchheim 1958; Hockerts 1989, 269ff.; Pross 1988, 105ff.

11. Bay. MJ: 1091-I SA, Beiakte zu den Generalakten, Wiedergutmachung nationalsoz. Unrecht auf vermögensrechtl. Ged., minutes of the meeting of the Coordination Committee of the Eleven States (Protokoll über die Sitzung des Koordinierungsausschusses der 11 Länder) (17 Mar. 1950), 46–50.

12. Calvelli-Adorno 1961, 532.

13. The first article of the respectable newspaper *Frankfurter Allgemeine Zeitung* on the Nazi persecution appeared in 1954: Zigeuner: Die Nomaden unter uns, *Frankfurter Allgemeine Zeitung* (16 Jan. 1954).

14. Pross 1988, 105–106; interview with Karlo Hessdörfer, former president of the Bavarian Compensation Office (Landesentschädigungsamt), Munich (24 Jul. 1991). IfZ Archiv: 3058/62, verdict of the BGH (23 May 1962), 4 ZR 198/61 (OLG Cologne) and 4 ZR 221/61 (OLG Cologne). This ruling only partly solved the problem of compensation for Gypsies who had been persecuted by the Nazi regime. See Stanicki 1968, 529ff.

15. A survey of the investigation's procedures and trials conducted in the Federal Republic against perpetrators who participated in the Gypsies' persecution during the Third Reich. The public prosecution (Staatanwaltschaft) Stuttgart 3 (19) Js 921/81, decision of investigation procedure against Prof. S. Ehrhardt and Dr. A. Würth (Beschluss des Ermittlungsverfahrens gegen Prof. S. Ehrhardt und Dr. A. Würth) (21 Nov. 1985), 3–5.

16. Ritter denied after 1945 that he had ever been a member of the Nazi party or any other Nazi organization. In 1949, after a document of the American military government in Germany (OMGUS) showed that Ritter had been a member of both the Nazi party and the SS, OMGUS initiated an investigation against him, accusing him of supplying false information in his denazification process. An inquiry in the Berlin Document Center dismissed the charges against Ritter. Ritter's investigation files: Hess. HSTA Wiesbaden: 501/1547, Riek-Ritt, and 520/F 7019; BA Berlin R73/14005. In a letter of recommendation for Ritter directed to the DFG of 16 Jun. 1937, written by the president of the Reich's health office, Hans Reiter, Ritter was defined as "one of the few young scholars who follows his research drive in an almost fanatic devotion and totally free of selfish consideration." See also Müller-Hill 1984, 153, 156.

17. Reiter 1939, 356.

18. Müller 1991, 249–250; HSTA Düsseldorf: Rep. 231, no.1535, Bl. 39, conclusion to suspend the judicial procedure against Ritter: "The attestations of the witnesses imply that they voluntarily [Freiwillig] agreed to undergo a sterilization. . . . Their statements make it clear that they agreed to undergo a sterilization

in order to prevent their deportation to Concentration Camp." HSTA Düsseldorf: Rep. 231, no. 1540, Bl. 856, resolution of the public prosecutor to suspend the judicial procedure against Justin: "The girl herself applied for the sterilization."

19. Gilsenbach 1993, 97–133.

20. Justin 1944, 121.

21. 55 Js 5582/48: HSTA Düsseldorf: Rep. 231, no. 1535, 21ff., resolution of the public prosecutor to suspend the judicial procedure against Ritter (28 Aug. 1950).

22. HSTA Düsseldorf: Rep. 231, no. 1535, Bl. 37–39.

23. Hess. HSTA Wiesbaden: 461/29090, registration of the destruction of Ritter's investigation file; HSTA Düsseldorf: Rep. 231, no. 1536, Bl. 287ff.

24. StA Frankfurt: PA Dr. Eva Justin sig. 92.546, Bl. 1ff.

25. Wolf 1960; HSTA Düsseldorf: Rep. 231, no. 1535, Bl. 6ff.

26. HSTA Düsseldorf: Rep. 231, no. 1535, Bl. 29, resolution of the public prosecutor to suspend the judicial process against Ritter, and no. 1540, Bl. 852–853, resolution of the public prosecutor to suspend the judicial process against Justin.

27. HSTA Düsseldorf: Rep. 231, no. 1535, Bl. 32ff; on Ritter's activity after 29 Jan. 1943 see Zimmermann 1996, 14,; 155.

28. HSTA Düsseldorf: Rep. 231, no. 1540, Bl. 852.

29. HSTA Düsseldorf: Rep. 231, no. 1540, Bl. 853.

30. HSTA Düsselforf: Rep. 231 no. 1540 Bl. 854; Bl. 329ff.: list of files.

31. HSTA Düsseldorf: Rep. 231, no. 1540, Bl. 854; Zimmermann 1996, 150.

32. StA Frankfurt: PA Dr. Robert Ritter sig. 18.576, Erläuterungen zu unseren Asozialen- und Zigeunerforschungen (20 May 1947), Bl. 41ff.; HSTA Düsseldorf: Rep. 231, no. 1535, Bl. 22.

33. HSTA Düsseldorf: Rep. 231, no. 1535, Bl. 32f.

34. Ritter 1931a, 1931b.

35. StA Frankfurt: PA Dr. Robert Ritter sig.18.576, Erläuterungen zu unseren Asozialen- und Zigeunerforschung (20 May 1947), Bl. 39.

36. StA Frankfurt: PA Dr. Robert Ritter sig.18.576, Erläuterungen zu unseren Asozialen- und Zigeunerforschung (20 May 1947), Bl. 40.

37. HSTA Düsseldorf: Rep. 231, no. 1535, Bl. 22; Arnold 1989, 9, letter from Ritter (28 Apr. 1949).

38. Ritter 1936.

39. Schlabrendorff 1946, 49.; Giesevius 1946, 1:217.

40. StA Frankfurt: PA Dr. Robert Ritter sig.18.576, Erläuterungen zu unseren Asozialen- und Zigeunerforschung (20 May 1947), Bl. 41.

41. BA Berlin: R 73/14005. In his letter to the Deutsche Notgemeinschaft of 12 Feb. 1935, Ritter emphasized that the results of his research on the Gypsies would have great significance for the policy of the criminal police and for the state's activity in the field of racial hygiene.

42. Hohmann 1991, 271–275. A survey of Moravek's research activities is found in HSTA Düsseldorf: Rep. 231, no. 1535, Bl. 37, and no. 1540, Bl. 855.

43. HSTA Düsseldorf: Rep. 231, no. 1535, Bl. 33.

44. HSTA Düsseldorf: Rep. 231, no. 1535, Bl. 35ff.

45. Uschold 1951.

46. HSTA Düsseldorf: Rep. 231, no. 1535, Bl. 25, 29, 36, 37.

47. IfZ Archiv: Micro. MA-21, State Court Munich 1 (Landgericht Munich 1) (13 Oct. 1951[?], date is not clear); Grellmann 1787; Block 1936.

48. Zimmermann 1989, 57–60.

49. Bock 1986, 24ff., 79.

50. Neukamp 1950, 773–774.

51. Zimmermann 1989, 57–58. HSTA Düsseldorf: Rep. 231, no. 1536, Bl. 301–302: Martha Adler's testimony on the pressure put on her husband by the racial hygiene reseacher and the police in order that he will agree to undergo a sterilization.

52. HSTA Düsseldorf: Rep. 231, no. 1535, Bl. 32ff.

53. StA Frankfurt: PA Dr. Robert Ritter sig.18.576, Erläuterungen zu unseren Asozialen- und Zigeunerforschung (20 May 1947), Bl. 41; BA Berlin: R 73/14005, Ritter's report on his research to the DFG (20 Jan. 1940), 5.

54. HSTA Düsseldorf: Rep. 231, no. 1540, Bl. 854–855.

55. HSTA Düsseldorf: Rep. 231, no. 1540, Bl. 851–852. After the appearance of an article on her Nazi past in *Der Spiegel* during the scandal at Frankfurt in 1963, Justin did not hesitate to publicly report on this apologetic argument. In contrast to the public prosecutor, the journalists regarded it as an immoral and criminal act. See Vetter 1963; see also chapter 7 herein.

56. Friedrich 1993, 57–77; Müller 1991, 249ff.

57. Friedrich 1993, 66.

58. Friedrich 1993, 66; Wodak et al. 1990, 210ff.

59. Staatanwaltschaft Stuttgart 3 (19) Js 921/81 (21 Nov. 1985), Beschluss des Ermittlungsverfahrens gegen Prof. S. Ehrhardt und Dr. A. Würth.

60. Staatanwaltschaft Stuttgart 3 (19) Js 921/81 (21 Nov. 1985), Beschluss des Ermittlungsverfahrens gegen Prof. S. Ehrhardt und Dr. A. Würth, 1.

61. Staatanwaltschaft Stuttgart 3 (19) Js 921/81 (21 Nov. 1985), Beschluss des Ermittlungsverfahrens gegen Prof. S. Ehrhardt und Dr. A. Würth, 7ff.; Jürgens 1961; Mazirel 1973, 149–150.

62. Staatanwaltschaft Stuttgart-3 (19) Js 921/81 v. 21.11.1985–Beschluss des Ermittlungsverfahrens gegen Prof. S. Ehrhardt und Dr. A. Würth, 6.

63. Roth and Aly 1984, 94. As far as I know, this was the earliest publishing of documents from Ritter's personal file in the DFG.

64. Frei 1996.

CHAPTER 6. EFFECT OF NAZISM AND DENAZIFICATION ON ATTITUDES TOWARD GYPSIES

1. Stern 1991, 264.

2. Grass 1962, 384–385.

3. Hans Blum, Zigeunerjunge (1967) on CD: Alexandra, *Mein Freund, der Baum* (Phonogram Hamburg); Boettcher 1998, 81–85; Port de la roi 1998, 50–61, 140.

4. The following film adaptations of Gypsy musicals were produced in Germany in the two first decades after the war: *Czardas der Herzen* (1951), directed by Alexander von Slatinay; *Die Czardasch Fürstin* (1951), directed by Georg

Jacoby; *Der Czardasch König* (1958), directed by Harald Philipp; *Der Zigeunerbaron* (1962), directed by Kurt Wilhelm, a collaboration between the BRD and France.

5. Dunkel wie ihre Haare ist ihre Geschichte, *Frankfurter Rundschau* (25 Jun. 1958).

6. Landesarchiv Berlin: Rep. 142/9, no. 0/713–14, Zigeuner, letter from Dept. 4 to Dept. O regarding Zigeunerunwesen (25 Feb. 1954).

7. Bavarian Landtag Committee for Social-Political Affairs twenty-fifth meeting (Bayerischer Landtag-Ausschus für Sozialpolitische Angelegenheiten 25. Sitzung) (22 Sept. 1952), Bl. 14, Bl. 17.

8. Bavarian Landtag committee for Social-Political Afffairs thirty-fourth meeting (Bayerischer Landtag-Ausschus für Sozialpolitische Angelegenheiten 34. Sitzung) (27 Jan. 1953), Bl. 7; on Kääb's career see Hess. MInn 86003.

9. See chapter 1, p. 14, and chapter 2, pp. 30, 33.

10. Jochimsen 1963, 95ff.

11. Jochimsen 1963, 95ff.

12. Niedersachsen (Lower Saxon) Ministry of Interior: 12 102, letter from Local Administration's President (Regierungspräsident) Hildesheim to the Lower Saxon Social Minister, conference "Help for gypsies" (Tagung "Hilfe für Zigeuner") (23 Jan. 1967).

13. Schubarth 1991, 47ff.

14. Schubarth 1991, 47ff.

15. Extremisten werden sozial geächtet, *Allensbacher Berichte* no. 1 (1993), 120, 124.

16. Schubarth 1991, 48–49.

17. German students resent Gypsies, *Romnews: An information of the Roma National Congress* no. 28 (2 Jan. 1995).

18. Schubarth 1991, 48–49.

19. Berbüsse 1987, 15–34, The cartoon on p. 18 summarizes the essence of the whole article. It shows a young man polling an older man at his doorstep. The caption reads, "After we finish filling in the forms, I will share with you my private opinion on Jews."

20. "Mehr verdrängt als bewältigt," In Juden und Deutsche, *Spiegel Spezial* no. 2 (1992), 71.

21. Panahi 1980, 103ff.

22. Mehr verdrängt als bewältigt (1992), 71.

23. Extremisten werden sozial geächtet (1993).

24. Bohn et al. 1995.

25. Golub 1993, 6; Golub and Cohen 1991, 16–17; Gudkov and Levinson 1994; Golub and Cohen 1995, 14.

26. Emnic Institute's public opinion poll (Emnid Umfrage) 1994.

27. Bergmann and Erb 1991, 149–150. Similar polls conducted in 1975–1988 point out a much higher objection rate than the Allensbach's poll (11 percent–16 percent).

28. Emnid Institute's public opinion poll (Emnid Umfrage) 1994.

29. Jochimsen 1970, 29.

30. Stetter 1980.

31. Zigeuner 1950a; Zigeuner 1938.

32. Zigeuner 1950b.

33. Justin 1944; Zigeuner 1957.

34. Zigeuner 1964; Zigeuner 1977; Gypsy 1962; Tsiganes 1968; Tsigane ou Tzigane 1964; Cyganie 1962; Gypsies 1978; Gypsy 1980. I found only one non-German encyclopedia with an entry that contained racial references regarding the Gypsies: Zingari 1950.

35. Zigeuner 1979.

36. Zigeuner 1974.

37. Kauck 1962; "Zigeuner-Romantik mit Mercedes, Champagner und sehr viel Trubel," *Kasseler Stadtausgabe* (2 Dec. 1949); *Frankfurter Rundschau* (25 Jun. 1958).

38. *Armer Nanosh-Tatort,*1989, film by Stanislav Barabas, Nord deutscheu Rundfunk (NDR).

39. Schnurre 1958; Bobrowski 1964; Enno Podehl (1982), Hermann-Erzählertext (Unpublished ms.).

40. Ergreifend Ernst, *Frankfurter Rundschau* (28 Jun. 1957).

41. Hermann 1964.

42. Diner 1995, 95ff., esp. 102.

43. StA Hamburg: Polizeibehörde 2, 447, BKA (14 Apr 1954); Hohmann 1980c, 89–96.

44. Margalit 2000a.

45. Landeskirchliches Archiv, Braunschweig: Georg Althaus, Dienst an Israel und den Zigeunern, no. 4, der Zigeuner und seine Welt–Heute (11 Apr. 1961), 1. Similar remarks by Althaus also appeared in interviews he had made to the German press: Der Zigeunerpastor von Braunschweig, *Stuttgarter Zeitung* (8 Nov. 1958); Beschützer der Zigeuner, *Frankfurter Rundschau* (4 Oct. 1959).

46. Landeskirchliches Archiv, Braunschweig: Georg Althaus, Dienst an Israel und den Zigeunern, no. 18, Erfahrungen mit Zigeunern (Juni–Juli 1959), 2; Dienst an Israel und den Zigeunern, no. 4, Der Zigeuner und seine Welt–Heute (11 Apr. 1961), 8.

47. Landeskirchliches Archiv, Braunschweig: Georg Althaus, Dienst an Israel und den Zigeunern, no. 4, Der Zigeuner und seine Welt–Heute (11 Apr. 1961), 6; Beschützer der Zigeuner, *Frankfurter Rundschau* (4 Oct. 1959).

48. Landeskirchliches Archiv, Braunschweig: Georg Althaus, Dienst an Israel und den Zigeunern, no. 4, Der Zigeuner und seine Welt–Heute (11 Apr. 1961), 6. Treitschke's dictum reads, "the Jews are our misfortune."

49. Mazirel 1973, 149–150.

50. StA Frankfurt: PA Dr. Robert Ritter sig.18.576, Erläuterungen zu unseren Asozialen- und Zigeunerforschung (20 May 1947), 39ff.

51. HSTA Düsseldorf: Rep. 231, no. 1535, Bl. 32–33.

52. Reiter 1939, 356; BA Berlin R73/14005: letter from Ritter to the DFG (2 Feb. 1938). For reports on racial hygiene research conducted by Ritter's team on Eastern European Jews, see BA Berlin R73/14005: letter from Ritter to the DFG (20 Jan. 1940); letter from Ritter to the DFG (30 Jan. 1941).

53. Hennig 1959.

54. Arnold 1989, 27ff.

55. Arnold 1962.
56. Arnold 1958, 5.
57. Arnold 1958, 97 n. 1.
58. Hennig 1959.
59. Lower Saxon Ministry of the Interior: 12102 (Nieders. MIN: 12102), report on the conference "Help for Gypsies" (Bericht über die Tagung "Hilfe für Zigeuner") (10–13 Nov. 1966), 1:3ff.
60. Lower Saxon Ministry of the Interior: 12102 (Nieders. MIN: 12102), report on the conference "Help for Gypsies" (Bericht über die Tagung "Hilfe für Zigeuner") (10–13 Nov. 1966), 1:3–4.
61. Jochimsen 1963.
62. Lower Saxon Ministry of the Interior: 12102 (Nieders. MIN: 12102), report on the conference "Help for Gypsies" (Bericht über die Tagung "Hilfe für Zigeuner") (10–13 Nov. 1966), 1:7.
63. Arnold 1962, 115–116.
64. Lower Saxon Ministry of the Interior: 12102 (Nieders. MIN: 12102), the Local Administration President at Hildesheim (Der Regierungspräsident Hildesheim) (23 Jan. 1967), 1:2.
65. Lower Saxony Ministry of the Interior: 12102 (Nieders. MIN: 12102), the Local Administration President at Hildesheim (Der Regierungspräsident Hildesheim) (23 Jan. 1967), 1:2.
66. Arnold 1958, 1–2.
67. Hohmann 1980c, 99ff.; Hohmann 1991, 351ff.; Franz, Rose, and Brantner 1981, 163ff.
68. Zigeuner protestieren gegen ZDF-Fernsehfilm, *Süddentshe Zeitung* (28 Apr. 1981); Ich gehe nie mehr ins Theater, *Tageszeitung (TAZ)* (24 Feb. 1986); Ness 1989; Pai 1989; Heidi Schumacher in Report ARD (Arbeitsgemeinschaft der Rundfunkanstalten Deutschlands) (1 Aug. 1989).

CHAPTER 7. PUBLIC DEBATE ON NAZI PERSECUTION OF GYPSIES

1. The iconographic representation of this narrative about the persecution of the Jews used the crucifixion, which already in the nineteenth century had become a symbol to indicate a victim. Otto Pankok drew the Passion circle as a protest against the persecution of the Jews in the Third Reich during 1933–1934. Pankok depicted Jesus and Mary as dark, oriental types modeled after Sinti figures, and the Roman soldiers as Aryan figures. The SS bulletin criticized Pankok's Passion with a considerable amount of venom because Pankok's Christ looked very Jewish to them: Gotteslästerung 1936 *Das Schwarze Korps* (21 Jan. 1937). See also Pankok 1970; Zimmermann 1972, 45ff. Amishai-Maisels 1993, 178ff. This motif became common, and in 1938 Marc Chagall drew his "white crucifixion"—a crucified East-European Jewish figure "with his head covered, and a prayer shawl . . . to stress his Jewish identity."
2. Busch 1989, 66.
3. Bührer 1990. Bührer showed that the official statistics on crime in the Third Reich does not confirm the myth that the Nazis provided law and order

for respectable citizens. Bossmann (1977, 111–157, 280–334) shows that many German pupils believe in the myth. See also Herbert 1990, 487–488; Peukert 1987a, 56; Peukert 1982, 233ff.

4. Proceedings of the Baden-Württemberg Landtags second voting period 1956–1960, minutes, Stuttgart 1957, 1, thirteenth meething (*Verhandlungen des Landtags von Baden-Württemberg. 2. Wahlperiode 1956–1960, Protokoll,* Stuttgart 1957, 1, 13. Sitzung) (24 Oct. 1956), 527.

5. Wodak et al. 1990, 355.

6. See n. 2.

7. Lipset 1963; Lohmann 1994, 23–50; Margalit 1996, 13–16.

8. Bossmann 1977, 286: Max (age seventeen) said, "The convicts in jail today enjoy too many liberties." See similar attitudes from Bernard (age fifteen) and Eva (age fifteen), 296.

9. Mehr verdrängt als bewältigt (1992), 64: "42 percent of the Germans think that the Third Reich also had its good sides."

10. Distel 1990, 28–31, esp. 29.

11. Landesarchiv Berlin: Rep. 142/9, no. 0/713–14, Zigeuner, letter from Dept. 4 to Dept. O regarding Zigeunerunwesen (25 Feb. 1954).

12. Volksverhetzung: Stadtverordneter der DVU verurteilt, *Oldenburgische Volkszeitung* (7 Jul. 1990).

13. Margalit 1996, 18–19, discusses the attitude of the German extreme right toward the Nazi persecution of the Gypsies.

14. Wiedergutmachung für Zigeuner? Die Deutschen werden wieder zur Kasse gebeten, *Deutsche National Zeitung* no. 45 (2 Nov. 1979), 5; Wodak et al. 1990, 352.

15. Hermann 1964; Zülch 1979, 216.

16. Barth 1991.

17. Nazis now attacking Gypsies, *Times* (London) (20 Jun. 1942).

18. Ende der Zigeuner-Romantik, *Die Zeitung* (26 Mar. 1943); Press in Exile: German Anti-Nazi Periodicals 1933–1945, *The Wiener Library Bulletin,* 3(5–6) (1947): 31.

19. Zimmermann 1996, 288.

20. Erwin 1948; Yates 1949; How the Gypsies Were Persecuted 1950, 18; Friedman 1951.

21. Erwin 1947, 12.

22. Cowles 1948, 10. Originally appeared in England as *The Tablet* (22 Nov. 1947).

23. Most of the articles concerning the Gypsies in the German press of that period continued to proliferate the traditional dual image of the Gypsy: "Zigeuner-Romantik mit Mercedes, Champagner und sehr viel Trubel," *Kasseler Lokalausgabe* (2 Dec. 1949); Schulze 1950; Das Zigeunerdorf mit dem Blutrachegesetz, *Stuttgarter Nachrichten* (7 Feb. 1951).

24. Roberts 1949.

25. Pankok 1958, 7–8.

26. Pankok 1950; Otto Pankok Museum 1957.

27. Interview with Otto Pankok's daughter, Eva, at Haus Esselt in Drevenack (28 Aug. 1992): "Pankok had never painted bourgeois people. . . . The Gypsies

they could still laugh and cry, and were always genuine, they did not play roles and did not use masks."

28. Pankok 1958, 9.

29. Zigeuner 1950a.

30. Vollnhals 1992, 376–377; Bergmann 1992; Rabinbach 1988, 169–175.

31. Kogon 1946.

32. Adler 1957.

33. Remszhardt 1953.

34. Zigeuner: Die Nomaden unter uns (1954).

35. Hachmann 1960.

36. Cassel 1962.

37. Kraschutzki 1954.

38. Gerlach 1987, 256ff.

39. *Der Spiegel* (16 Apr. 1958).

40. Gerlach 1987, 258 n. 5.

41. Landeskirchliches Archiv, Braunschweig: Georg Althaus, Dienst an Israel und den Zigeunern, no. 17; Georg Althaus, Festpredigt-Erste Missionskonferenz der schweizerischen Zigeunermission in Zurich (6 Nov. 1955), 4; Althaus 1959, 1902. Althaus's attitude was not genuine. It expressed the traditional Christian attitude toward the Gypsies, as stated in, for example, Gronemeyer 1987, 34.

42. Cramer 1965.

43. Schnurre 1958, 208–212.

44. Weil 1961.

45. Hennig 1959.

46. Langbein 1964.

47. Zigeuner in Panick, *Hamburger Abendblatt* (18 Feb. 1959), 5; Zigeuner durften abreisen, *Bild am Sonntag* (21–22 Feb. 1959), 3; BA Koblenz: B 106 47 404, Bundesministerium des Innern, Behandlung eines Zigeuner Aussiedlungstransport aus Polen, letter from the Federal Interior Minister, Dr. Gerhard Schröder, to the Schleswig-Holstein Interior Minister, Dr. Lemke (11 Mar. 1959).

48. BA Koblenz: B 106 47 404, letter from Priest Luckhardt to the Federal Interior Minister (19 Feb. 1959).

49. BA Koblenz: B 106 47 404, letters from Priest Althaus to the Federal Interior Minister (18 Feb., Feb. 1959).

50. BA Koblenz: B 106 47 404, letter from Mr. Albrecht to the Federal Interior Minister (19 Feb. 1959), letter from Mrs. Neumark to the Federal Interior Minister (18 Feb. 1959), and letter from Josephine and Ingeborg Wehner to the Federal Interior Minister (18 Feb. 1959).

51. BA Koblenz: B 106 47 404, anonymous letters to the Federal Interior Minister.

52. So arisch (1963), 45.

53. Vetter 1963; Wieder Diskussionen über Eva Justin, *Frankfurter Allgemeine Zeitung* (22 Sept. 1964); Eva Justin gestorben. *Frankfurter Rundschau* (17 Sept. 1966).

54. Vollnhals 1992, 381ff.

55. Stern 1991, 241ff.

56. Zigeuner 1974, 687.

57. Zigeuner 1979, 714.
58. Zigeuner 1957, 698; Zigeuner 1968.
59. Zigeuner 1957, 699; Justin 1944, 121.
60. Jaspers 1986, 130, 204.
61. Zigeuner 1950b, 5017.
62. Zigeuner 1956.
63. StA Frankfurt a.M.: PA Dr. Robert Ritter sig.18.576, Erläuterungen zu unseren Asozialen- und Zigeunerforschung (20 May 1947), Bl. 39ff.
64. Arnold 1961, 206.
65. Kommitee der antifaschisten Widerstandskämpfer der DDR 1982, 40.
66. Zigeuner 1964.
67. Letter from Stefan Görlich, Jena, to the author (7 Oct. 1991). Gilsenbach 1993, 277ff.
68. Diner 1995, 79–95; Niethammer 1990, 121–122; Reichel 1995, 34–40; Herf 1997, 162ff.
69. Groehler 1992, 43; Mosse 1993, 211–212; Reichel 1995, 238–240; Combe 1992, 141.

CHAPTER 8. "DISCOVERY" OF THE GYPSY VICTIM OF NAZISM

1. Märthesheimer and Frenzel 1979; Herf 1980; Markovits and Hayden 1980; Zielinski 1980; Huyssen 1980; Broszat 1979.
2. Markovits and Hayden 1980, 81ff.; Zülch 1979, 19–20; *Der Spiegel* no. 5, (29 Jan. 1979), 7–8; reader's letters in *Der Spiegel* no. 6 (5 Feb. 1979), 7–12; *Der Spiegel* no. 7 (12 Feb. 1979), 7–14; *Der Spiegel* no. 8 (19 Feb. 1979), 7–10.
3. Herf 1980, 43ff.; Holocaust—deutsches verdrängen, *Pflasterstrand. Stadtzeitung für Frankfurt* no. 47 (15 Feb. 1979), 23–27.
4. E.g., Neuer Holocaust-Schinken in deutschen Kinos: Schindlers Liste-Märchen oder Dokumentation? *Deutsche Wochen-Zeitung* (11 Mar. 1994), 4. This extreme rightist newspaper claimed that Steven Spielberg's *Schindler's List* aimed to minimize atrocities that Jews commit today, such as those done to Palestinian citizens in Hebron who had been massacred while praying in a mosque by the Jewish fanatic Goldstein in 1994.
5. Diner 1995, 102.
6. Auf ewig ins Ghetto abgedrängt? *Göttinger Tagblatt* (19 Mar. 1979); Völklein 1979.
7. Auf ewig ins Ghetto abgedrängt? (1979); Zülch 1979, 12ff.
8. Frei 1992, 101.
9. Interview with Tilman Zülch, Berlin (13–15 Dec. 1993); Moeller 1996; Henke 1985; Foschepoth 1985, 101–102. Foschepoth estimates the number of Germans who died as consequence of their deportation between thousands and millions of people. The extreme rightist German press claims that the number of German victims is equal to the Jewish victims; see n. 6. Millionen ermordete Deutsche: Der Massenmord ohne Sühne, *Deutsche National-Zeitung* (1 Aug. 1980).
10. Zülch 1980.
11. Zülch and Greußing 1981, 9–10.

12. The Society for the Threatened Peoples Press Communiqué (Gesellschaft für bedrohte Völker-Pressemitteilung) (10 Apr. 1981) in *Pogrom,* no. 80/81: 4.

13. Streck 1981, 53.

14. Stümke and Finkler 1981; Geigges and Wette 1979; Hohmann 1980.

15. Brendler 1997, 54ff.: 65 percent of the young people in the FRG in 1989 had felt shame when the Holocaust was mentioned. 41 percent of the young Germans felt guilt concerning the Holocaust, although they did not personally participate in the Nazi atrocities.

16. Pross 1988, 21–23. The baseless claim that the amount of money Jewish victims received as compensation for their incarceration in Nazi concentration camps was double the amount Gypsy victims received is common among Sinti. However, German Sinti do not attribute the Jews with the responsibility for this alleged discrimination, as did Germans who raised the subject: Interview of the author with Berta Weiss (18 Aug. 1992); interview of the author with Karl Wagner (26 Aug. 1992); letter of Karlo Hessdoerfer, former president of the Bavarian State's compensation office, to the author (23 Sept. 1992).

17. Diner 1986, 14–15.

18. Greußing 1980.

19. Greußing 1979, 192.

20. Greußing 1980, 12–13.

21. Niethammer 1990, 115: "One may doubt whether all of us Germans really wish to remember and honor the Gypsies."

22. Bundestag member Christian Ströbele (Greens) in the German Bundestag, stenographic report, plenary minutes 10th voting period, 171st meeting (Christian Ströbele in Deutscher Bundestag, Stenographischer Bericht, Plenarprotokoll 10. Wahlperiode-171. Sitzung) (7 Nov. 1985), 12812. "Where SS men first let [Gypsies] to play their Gypsy music for the sake of leading 40,000 Sinti and Roma into the gas chambers and murdering them."

23. *Das falsche Wort: Wiedergutmachung an Zigeunern (Sinte) in Deutschland?* (1987), film by Melanie Spitta and Katrin Seibold.

24. Association of German Sinti and the State Association of Hesse communiqué (Verband Deutscher Sinti, Landesverband Hessen, Stellungnahme) on the film *The Lie (Das falsche Wort)* by Melanie Spitta and Katrin Seibold (28 Apr. 1989).

25. Zülch 1981, 399.

26. Tugendhat 1979, 9ff.

27. Tugendhat 1992, 11, 77, 80, 114.

28. Zülch 1985.

29. Tugendhat 1992, 77, 92. He claimed that many Germans share the critical opinions that he has toward Israel and Zionism, but they do not dare to express them as he (the Jew) himself does. Tugendhat's claim is very observant, and one may apply it to any German critique on Jews and their status after 1945.

30. Hohmann 1977; Hohmann 1979.

31. Hohmann 1981, 179.

32. Hohmann 1981, 180.

33. Peukert 1982, 247–248. On Peukert's contribution to the German social history, see Bajohr 1991; Nolan 1988.

34. Peukert 1987a, 54.

35. Peukert 1987a, 54; Peukert 1982, 233–245.

36. Bajohr 1997, 331–338; Friedlünder 1997.

37. Peukert 1987a, 54ff.

38. Bergmann 1997.

39. Podehl 1982.

40. Podehl 1982; Markgraf 1985.

41. Gesellschaft für bedrohte Völker, 1980; Bei Hitler waren wir wenigstens Deutsche, *Der Spiegel* no. 43 (1979): 99–126.

42. Interview with Tilman Zülch, Berlin (13–15 Dec. 1993).

43. Brox 1980, 95.

44. Matras 1989, 38.

45. The international press reported on the hunger strike: Dachau hunger strike by gypsies, *Times* (London) (27 Feb. 1980); Hunger strike staged in Dachau by gypsies, *Times* (London) (7 Apr. 1980); Gypsies at Dachau ignore pleas to end hunger strike, *Times* (London) (12 Apr. 1980); FDP will Discriminierung von Zigeunern stoppen, *Stuttgarter Zeitung* (3 Jul. 1980); Liberale wollen Förderprogramm für Zigeuner, *Südkurier* (19 Jul. 1980); Sinti setzen Hungerstreik in Dachau fort, *Frankfurter Allgemeine Zeitung* (8 Aug. 1980).

46. Kister 1980b.

47. Böddrich 1980.

48. Kister 1980a.

49. Politiker versprechen Sinti Unterstützung, *Mindener Tageblatt* (14 Apr. 1980).

50. Proceedings of the Bavarian landtags ninth voting period 1978/82 (Verhandlungen des Bayerischen Landtags: 9. Wahlperiode 1978/82), stenographic reports no. 65–84 (Stenographische Berichte no. 65–84), sixty-sixth meeting (66. Sitzung) (17 Jul. 1980), 4:4152ff.

51. Hermann 1964; Schrecklich ist das Zigeunerleben, *Süddentshe Zeitung* no. 104 (30 Apr. 1960).

52. Lolotz Birkenfelder in *Lustig war's das Zigeunerleben,* a film of Hans Karnick and Wolfgang Richter, ZDF 1981.

53. Oskar Rose presented himself in public in his Gypsy name, Romani, his friend Oscar Birkenfelder as Lolotz; Margalit 1997, 293ff.

54. E. G. Kister 1980a.

55. Rose 1979, 261.

56. Bozic 1993.

57. *Es ging Tag und Nacht, liebes Kind* (1982), film by Melanie Spitta and Katrin Seibold, ZDF ; *Geschichte und Gegenwart einer Verfolgung* (1982), film by Leonore Paurat, Arbeitsgemeinschaft der Rundfunkonistalten Deutschlands (ARD).

58. Walser and Scheib 1989. Compare this screenplay to the typical depiction of the Gypsy image in German and European films. One example is the film by Hans Karnick and Wolfgang Richter, *Lustig war's Zigeunerleben*, ZDF 1981; or *Der Zigeuner,* a part of the thriller series *Der Alte,* ZDF 1981. See also *Der ewig kriminelle Zigeuner? Süddentshe Zeitung* (15 May 1981); Zigeunerfreundlich? *Der Tagesspiegel* (16 May 1981).

59. For example the critical comments of Rose and Hohmann against Streck. Streck 1981, who had dared to claim that the Nazi persecuation of Gypsies was not moved by the same motives as the Jewish Holocaust: Rose 1982; Hohmann 1982.

60. Schmidt für moralische Wiedergutmachung an Zigeunern, *Der Tagess-piegel* (18 Mar. 1982); Sinti und Roma geht es um die Moral, *Die Welt* (19 Mar. 1982).

61. Heuß 1987.

62. Zigeuner und Wahlen, *Frankfurter Allgemeine Zeitung* (11 Jan. 1983), 1.

63. Gilsenbach 1993, 257, 277.

64. Scholz 1986.

65. *Unsere Zeit,* the organ of the Communist party (DKP) in the FRG, which was directed by the GDR propaganda apparatus, wrote in "Sinti und Roma stellten Ultimatum," 1983: "It is an evidence of the continuity of the persecution of Gypsies in the successor state of Nazism." See also Lemke 1993.

66. Nehring 1988.

67. Weizsäcker 1985, 2–3; Gill and Steffani 1986; Moller 1998, 25–28.

68. Hartman 1986; Levkov 1987; the entire issue of *New German Critique* no. 38 (spring/summer) 1986, is dedicated to the Bitburg Scandal; Kiderlen 1985; Rabinbach 1988, 180ff.; Moller 1998, 21–24.

69. German Bundestag stenographic report plenary minutes 10/171 (Deutscher Bundestag stenographischer Bericht Plenarprotokoll 10/171), 171. Seventeenth meeting (Sitzung) (7 Nov. 1985), 12808–12809; Kanzler: Verantwortung für Sinti und Roma, *Die Welt* (8 Nov. 1985); Bundestag will Lage der Sinti und Roma verbessern, *Berliner Morgenpost* (8 Nov. 1985).

70. Goschler 1992, 217–224.

71. Moller 1998. Die unendliche Geschichte, *Der Spiegel* no. 11 (14 Mar. 1994), 18. Chancellor Kohl: "The fact that others achieved their victory in a battle where tens of thousands of Germans were killed or suffered is not a reason for the German chancellor to celebrate"; Kiderlen, 1985.

72. Bannas 1985.

73. *Das lustige Zigeunerleben,* film by Lea Rosh, Sender Frei Berlin (SFB), transmitted on the German TV channel ARD (3 Nov. 1985).

74. Sinti und Roma bauen Informationszentrum, *Süddentshe Zeitung* (30 Jul. 1990).

75. Weil 1961.

76. Reichel 1995, 242–246; Moller 1998, 40–71.

77. Author's conversation with Michael Wolfsohn, Munich, 18 Feb. 1994; Segev 1993. Bubis told Segev that the initiative for the inscription of the section from Weizsäcker's speech pertaining to the various victims groups of Nazism on the commemoration plaque came from the SPD.

78. German Bundestag twelfth voting period, answer of the Federal Administration on the "small inquiry" of member of the Bundestag Ursula Jelpke and the group of the Party of Democratic Socialism/Leftist List. The right to stay (in Germany) regulations for for homeless Roma refugees in the FRG. Article 18, printed matter 12/394 (Deutscher Bundestag 12: Wahlperiode, Antwort der Bundesregierung auf Kleine Anfrage der Abg. Ursula Jelpke und der gruppe der

PDS/Linke Liste. Bleiberechtsreglungen für heimatlose Roma-Flüchtlinge in der Bundesrepublik Deutschland. Art. 18, Drucksache 12/394) (19 Apr. 1991).

79. Kein Kulturgut, das schützenswert ist, *TAZ* (6 Aug. 1990); Barth 1991, 118ff.

80. Gypsies and the Holocaust, *New York Times* (14 Aug. 2000).

81. Sandner 1998, 12

82. Zimmermann 1996; Frei 1997; Margalit 2000b.

83. Schulte 1997; Zimmermann 1997.

84. Rothbart 1997a; Rothbart 1997b; Müller 1997; Lewy 2000, 216–217.

85. Gedenkstatte Buchenwald übt scharfe Kritik an Sinti und Roma, Allgemeiner Deutscher Nachrichtendienst (3 Oct. 1997).

86. Jäckel 2000.

87. Rose 2000; Historiker Jäckel gegen Sinti und Roma: Vorwürfe der Geschichtsfälschung, *Fuldaer Zeitung* (1 Jul. 2000).

88. Finkelstein 2000b. The book and Finkelstein's article (Finkelstein 2000a) elicited a debate in the German press that started in August 2000: Maier 2000; Rürup 2000; Herbert 2000; Longerich 2000; Sznaider 2000.

89. Finkelstein 2000a.

EPILOGUE

1. Proceeding of the Landtag of Baden Württemberg, second voting period 1956–1960 (Verhandlungen des Landtags von Baden-Württemberg: 2. Wahlperiode 1956–1960). Minutes. vol. 1, Stuttgart 1957, thirteenth meeting (Sitzung) (24 Oct. 1956), 527.

Bibliography

ARCHIVAL SOURCES

Abbreviations

BA	Bundesarchiv / Federal archive
Bay.	Bayern; Bayerische / Bavaria; Bavarian
BGH	Bundesgerichtshof / Federal supreme court
BW	Baden-Württemberg (founded in 1952)
CDU	Christlich-Demokratische Union /Christian Democratic Union
CSU	Christlich-Soziale Union / Christian Social Union
DKP	Deutsche Kommunistische Partei / The (new) German Communist Party in the FRG (founded in 1968)
DP	Deutsche Partei / German Party
DVU	Deutsche Volksunion / The German People's Union
FDJ	Freie Deutsche Jugend / Free German Youth (the Communist youth movement in the GDR)
FDP	Freie Demokratische Partei Deutschlands / Free Democrat Party of Germany
FRG	Federal Republic of Germany
GDR	German Democratic Republic
Hess.	Hessen; Hessische / Hesse; Hessian
HSTA	Central (Hauptstaatsarchiv) State Archive
KPD	Kommunistische Partei Deutschlands / Communist Party of Germany (banned in the FRG in 1956)
MF	Ministry of Finance
MInn	Ministry of the Interior
JM	Ministry of Justice
Nds.	Niedersachsen / Lower Saxon
NRW	Nordrhein-Westfalen / North Rhine–Westphalia
OdF	Opfer des Faschismus / Victim of Fascism
OLG	Oberlandesgericht / Supreme State Court

Bibliography

OMGBy	Office of Military Government, Bavaria
OMGUS	Office of Military Government (U.S.) for Germany
OMGUS-WB	Office of Military Government (U.S.) for Germany, Württemberg-Baden
PA	Personalakten / Personal file
PDS	Partei des Demokratishen Sozialismus / Party of Democratic Socialism
SED	Sozialistische Einheits Partei Deutschlands / Socialist Unity Party of Germany
SPD	Sozialdemokratische Partei Deutschlands / Social Democratic Party of Germany
STA	Staatsarchiv / State archive
StA	Stadtarchiv / City archive
StK	Staatskanzlei / State Chancellery
VdN	Verfolgten des Naziregimes / Persecutees of Nazism
VVN	Vereinigung der Verfolgten des Naziregimes / Organization of the Persecutees of the Nazi Regime

Archiv der Otto Pankok-Gesellschaft (Hünxe-Drevenack).

Akte Zigeuner: Die Zigeuner in heutigen Deutschland (undated manuscript).
Wie wir leben: Interview with Otto Pankok, broad-custom "Gypsies," Westdeutscher Rundfunk (29 Nov. 1957).

Bay. HSTA (Bavarian Central State Archive), Munich.

MF 69409: Bayerisches Finanzministerium, Landesamt für Vermögensverwaltung und Wiedergutmachung, Bd. 1.
MInn 86003: Kaäb Arthur (11 Oct. 1890), Ministerialdirigent beim Bayer, Staatsministerium des Innern (1948–1970).
MInn 86363: Bayerisches Landeskriminalamt (Generalia), Bd. 1 (1945–1950).
MInn 86364: Bayerisches Landeskriminalamt (Generalia), Bd. 2 (1951–1958).
MInn 86369: Bayerisches Landeskriminalamt, Personal Spezialia (1945–1963).
OMGUS Legal Division, box 9, folder 1345.
RG 260 OMGBy: 10/130–1/3; 17/175–3/19; 17/175–3/27.
StK 113799: Fürsorge für rassisch, religiös und politisch Verfolgten, Bd. 1 (1945–1946).
StK 113800: Fürsorge für rassisch, religiös und politisch Verfolgten, Bd. 2 (1945–1947).
StK-GuV 911: Gesetz zur Bekämpfung des Landfahrer- und Arbeitsscheuenunwesens = Landfahrer Ordnung (22 Dec. 1953).
StK-GuV 912: Gesetz zur Bekämpfung des Landfahrer-und Arbeitsscheuenunwesens = Landfahrer Ordnung (22 Dec. 1953), Bd. 2.

Bay. JM (Bavarian Ministry of Justice), Munich.

Az. 4726: Vol. 1, Zigeunerwesen.
1091-I SA: Beiakte zu den Generalakten, Wiedergutmachung nationalsozialistische. Unrecht auf vermögensrechtliche Ged.

Archival Sources

Bay. Landtagsarchiv, Munich.

Verhandlungen des Bayerischen landtags 2. Legislaturperiode 4 Tagung 1949–1950, München, 1951, vol. 4, Beilagen.Verhandlungen des Bayerischen landtags 3. Tagung 1952/53, vol. 4, 1953.
Verhandlungen des Bayerischen Landtags 9 Wahlperiode 1978/82, Stenographischer Bericht No. 65–84, vol. 4, 66. Sitzung (17.7.1980)1982.
Bayerischen Landtag-Ausschuss für Sozial politische Angelegenheiten, 25. Sitzung, 22.9.1952.
Bayerischen Landtag-Ausschus für Sozialpolitische Angelegenheiten 34. Sitzung, 27.1.1953.

Bay. Staatsanwaltschaft München 1 (Bavarian Public Prosecutor, Munich 1).

2KLs 1/52: Prozess gegen Philip Auerbach und drei Andere.

BA (Bundesarchiv / Federal Archive), Berlin.

DQ-2 3320: Ministerium für Arbeit und Berufsausbildung, Richtlinien für die Anerkennung und Ausgabe der Ausweise Kämpfer des Faschismus und Opfer des Faschismus in der SBZ Deutschland, Sitzungs Protokolle des Hauptausschuses OdF (1946–1949).
DQ-2 3326: Ministerium für Arbeit und Gesundheitswesen HA Sozialfürsorge, Abt. Sozialfürsorge, Ref. VdN: Rechtliche und Finanzielle Sicherung der OdF (1948–1950).
DQ-2 3361: Ministerium für Arbeit, Abt. Sozialfürsorge, Ref.: Zielsetzung, Tätigkeiten und Anerkennung der OdF und VVN im zonalen, interzonalen, in DDR und in Internationalem Rahmen (1945–1950).
DQ-2 3375: Ministerium für Arbeit und Gesundheitswesen, Abt. Sozialfürsorge, Ref. VVN: Auskunft aus den Strafregister der Staatsanwaltschaften zur Anerkennung von VdN, Bd. 1, A–L.
DQ-2 3376: Ministerium für Arbeit und Gesundheitswesen, Abt. Sozialfürsorge, Ref. VVN: Auskunft aus den Strafregister der Staatsanwaltschaften zur Anerkennung von VdN, Bd. 2, M–Z.
DQ-2 3377: DVAS, Abt. Sozialfürsorge, Ref. OdF: Anerkennung, soziale Betreuung und Wiedergutmachung für die Opfer des Faschismus bzw. die Verfolgten des Naziregimes im Land Thüringen, Bd. 1 (1945–1947).
R 6/34a, folder 1-82: Reichsministerium für die besetzten Ostgebiete, Aufzeichnungen des persönlichen Referenten Rosenbergs, Dr. Werner Koeppen, Über Hitlers Tischgespräche (6 Sept.–6 Nov.1941).
R 73/13620: Robert Ritter Kurzbericht zu Hd. von Dr. Blome (19 Jun. 1941).
R 73/14005: Arbeitsberichte von Dr. Robert Ritter an die DFG.

Deutscher Bundestag—Archiv, Berlin.

Stenographischer Bericht, Plenarprotokoll 10. Wahlperiode -171. Sitzung, 7.11.1985.

12: Wahlperiode, Antwort der Bundesregierung auf Kleine Anfrage der Abg. Ursula Jelpke und der gruppe der PDS/Linke Liste. Bleiberechtsreglungen für heimatlose Roma-Flüchtlinge in der Bundesrepublik Deutschland Art. 18, Drucksache 12/394 (19.4.1991).

BA (Bundesarchiv), Koblenz.

B 106 47 404: Bundesministerium des Innern, Behandlung eines Zigeuner Aussiedlungstransport aus Polen.

BW Landtagsarchiv, Stuttgart

Verhandlungen des Landtags von Baden-Württemberg 2. Wahlperiode 1956–1960, Protokoll, vol. 1, Stuttgart 1957, 13. Sitzung (24.10.1956).

BWJM (Baden-Württemberg's Ministry of Justice), Stuttgart.

Abt. 6, Wiedergutmachung, Akterzeichen, 202 Entschädigungsgesetz; 601 Organisation; 701 Sterilisierung.

Deutsche Volksliedarchiv (German Folksong Archive), Freiburg.

A 99419: Zick Zack Zigeunerpack.
B 43842: Wir arbeiten nicht und verdienen doch.

Hess. JM (Hessian Ministry of Justice), Wiesbaden.

Az. 4726, Bd.1, Zigeunerwesen.

Hess. Landtagsarchiv, Wiesbaden.

Drucksachen des Hessischen. Landtags, 3. Wahlperiode, Abteilung 3, Stenographische Berichte über die Plenarsitzungen, vol. 2, Wiesbaden 1956, 23. Sitzung (7.3.1956).
Drucksachen des Hessischen. Landtags, 3. Wahlperiode, Abteilung 3, Stenographische Berichte über die Plenarsitzungen, vol. 3, Wiesbaden 1957.
Hessisches Lantag, Kommunalpolitischer Auschuss, 2.11.1956.

Hess. MInn (Hessian Ministry of the Interior), Wiesbaden.

Abt. 3-öffentliche Sicherheit, 22 e 30: Bekämpfung des Zigeunerwesen (1946–1955).

Hess. HSTA (Hessian Central State Archive), Wiesbaden.

Abt. 649 OMGH Civ. Adm/Publ. Welfare 8/66-2/1.
501/1547: Riek-Ritt.
502/2773a: Der Hessische Ministerpresident-StK, Wiedergutmachung des nationalsozialistischen Unrechts.
520/F 7019: Spruchkammerverfahren gegen Dr. Robert Ritter.

Archival Sources

HSTA Düsseldorf (Nordrhein-Westfalian Central State Archive).

Rep. 231, Nr. 1535–1542: Prozeß gegen Dr. Hans Maly und.

NW 59/106: Meldepflicht für Landfahrer (Zigeuner, Personen ohne festen Wohnsitz), (1953–1966).

NW 114/25: Anerkennung von Zigeunern.

NW 114/94: Wiedergutmachung (1945–1948).

NW 114/258: Anerkennung politisch und rassich Verfolgter.

NW 114/259: Anfragen privater und öffentlicher Stellen über Richtlinien für die Anerkennung der politisch, rassisch oder religiös Verfolgten (1947–1949).

NW 114/272: Übersicht der Haftentschädigungszahlungen an Zigeuner im Land NRW.

NW–Pe 7251I: PA Dr. Marcel Frenkel.

HSTA Stuttgart (Baden-Württemberg's Central State Archive).

BW MInn EA 2/303, Bü 332/1: Bekämpfung der Zigeuner.

IfZ Archiv (Institut für Zeitgeschichte / Institut for Contemporary History), Munich.

MA 3 (9/91): Micro. MA-21: Zigeuner in der Nachkrieg Zeit.

3058/62: Urteil des BGH vom 23. Mai 1962, 4 ZR 198/61 (OLG Köln) and 4 ZR 221/61 (OLG Köln).

MF 260, OMGUS-WB (26 Dec.–24 Feb.).

RG 260, OMGBy, 13/41-1/1.

Presse Archive-IFZ: Akte Zigeuner.

Landesarchiv Berlin.

Rep. 142/9, Deutscher Städtetag: Nr. 0/713–14, Zigeuner; Nr. 4/00-00-26, Protokolle des Sozialausschusses (1954)

Landeskirchliches Archiv, Braunschweig.

Georg Althaus: Pfarramt für den Dienst an Israel und den Zigeunern, Nr. 4; Nr. 17; Nr. 18

Mahn- und Gedenkstätte (Memorial for the Victims of Nazism), Düsseldorf.

Interviews with Düsseldorfer Sinti (21 Mar. 1990).

National Archives, Washington, D.C.

RG 260: OMGUS OMG Hesse, Legal Division, Legislation Branch, General, Correspondence, Selected Pages on Gypsies, no. 17/211-2, folder 4, box 923, 7/57/34/7.

Niedersachsen (Lower Saxon) HSTA Hannover (Central State Archive).

Nds. C 100 Acc. 60/55, Nr. 1103: Zigeuner Kriminalität (1945–1946).

Bibliography

Nds. 50 Acc. 82/68, Nr. 100.
Nds. 110 W Acc. 106/89, Liste 60, Nr. 17.

Niedersachsen (Lower Saxon) Ministry of the Interior.

12 102: Landfahrer.

Private NL Georg Althaus, Braunschweig.

Der Senator für Inners und Sport, Bremen.

P.1.a., Nr. 281: Akte betr. Bekämpfung des Bettlerunwesens (1 Feb. 1927).

STA (City Archive), Bremen.

P.1.a., Nr. 1146: Gesetz zum Schutze der Bevölkerung, Belästigung durch Zigeuner . . . (1933–1953).
4,13/1-P.1.a., Nr. 10: Bekämpfung des Zigeunerwesens (1886–1941).
4,54-11-30/6: Zigeuner.
4,54-11-00/1.

StA Frankfurt a.M.

StK, Magistrat Akte 2203. Die Bekämpfung des Zigeunerplage, Bd. 1 (1930–1946); Bd. 2 (1950–1954).
PA Dr. Eva Justin sig. 92.546.
PA Dr. Ritter Robert sig. 18.576.

STA Hamburg.

Polizeibehörde 2, 439: Sammlung von Material über Zigeuner durch die Landfahrer, Dienststelle bei Behörden und Privaten (1953, 1959–1966).
Polizeibehörde 2, 446: Verhalten und Behandlung der Zigeuner in der ersten Nachkriegszeit (1945–1946).
Polizeibehörde 2, 447: Behandlung der Landfahrer, Allgemeines (1953–1968).
Polizeibehörde 2, 449: Material zur Landfahrer–Kriminalität (1957–1959).

STA Munich.

Pol. Dir. München 11219: Organisation der Kriminalpolizei, Geschäftsaufgaben, Geschäftsgang (1933–1955).
RA 77636: Regierung von Oberbayern, Allgemeine Fürsorge: Unterstützung politisch, rassisch und religiös Verfolgter u.a. (1945–1946).

STA Nürnberg.

NOKW-802: Dokumente der Nürnberger Prozesse.

Tsentr Khraneniya Istoriko-Dokumentalnykh Kollektsii (Special Archive), Moscow.

R-1323-2-363, 93.

Secondary Sources

VVN-Landesverband BW (Baden-Württemberg) Archiv, Stuttgart.
D2700; D2701; D2702; D2704.

Yad Vashem Archive, Jerusalem.
Testimony of John Heinrich, 033/1119.
Testimony of Alter Feinsilber, 033/429.

SECONDARY SOURCES

Adler, Marta. 1957. *Mein Schicksal waren die Zigeuner: Ein Lebensbericht.* Bremen: Schünemann.
Allemann, Fritz Renne. 1956. *Bonn ist nicht Weimar.* Cologne: Kiebenheur and Witsch.
Althaus, Georg. 1959. Zigeuner Zigeunermission.In *Evangelisches Kirchenlexikon,* edited by Heinz Brunotte and Otto Weber, 1901–1902. Göttingen: Vandenhoeck and Ruprecht.
Amishai-Maisels, Ziva. 1993. *Depiction and Interpretation: The Influence of the Holocaust on the Visual Arts.* Oxford: Pergamon Press.
Arend, Stefan. 1990. Zigeuner und Zigeunergesetzgebung in Deutschland im 16. Jahrhundert. *Tsiganologische Studien* 2:71–87.
Arnold, Hermann. 1958. *Vaganten Komödianten Fieranten und Briganten.* Schriftenreihe aus dem Gebiete des Öffentlichen Gesundheitswesens, Heft 9. Stuttgart: Thieme.
Arnold, Hermann.1961. Brauchen wir eine Zigeunerfürsorge? *Gesundheitsfürsorge* 12 (11): 204–206.
Arnold, Hermann. 1962. Wer ist Zigeuner? *Zeitschrift für Ethnologie* 87:115–134.
Arnold, Hermann.1965. *Die Zigeuner: Herkunft und Leben der Stämme im deutschen Sprachgebiet.* Olten und Freiburg: Walter.
Arnold, Hermann.1989 *Die NS-Zigeunerverfolgung: Ihre Ausdeutung und Ausbeutung. Fakten, Mythos, Agitation, Kommerz.* Aschaffenburg: Karl Heinz Gerster.
Asoziale. 1928. *Der Grosse Brockhaus,* 1:751. Wiesbaden: Brockhaus.
Asoziale. 1966. *Brockhaus Enzyklopaedie,* 1:792. Wiesbaden: Brockhaus.
Assmann, Jan. 1992. *Das Kulturelle Gedächtnis: Schrift, Erinnerung und politische Identität in frühen Hochkulturen.* Munich: C. H. Beck.
Auerbach, Helmut. 1962. Die Einheit Dirlewanger. *Vierteljahrhefte für Zeitgeschichte,* 10:250–263.
Auf ewig ins Ghetto abgedrängt? 1979. *Göttinger Tagblatt* (19 Mar.).
Avé Lallement, Friedrich Christian. 1858. *Das deutsche Gaunerthum.* Leipzig: Brockhaus.
Ayaß, Wolfgang. 1987. Ein Gebot der nationalen Arbeitsdisziplin: Die Aktion "Arbeitsscheu Reich 1938." In *Beiträge zur nationalsozialistischen Gesundheits- und Sozialpolitik: Bd. 6. Feinderklärung und Prävention,* edited by Götz Aly, 43–74. Berlin: Rotbuch.

Bacharach, Zvi. 1985. *Racism—The Tool of Politics: From Monism toward Nazism.* Jerusalem: Magnes Press. (In Hebrew.)

Bajohr, Frank. 1991. Detlev Peukerts Beiträge zur Sozialgeschichte der Moderne. In *Zivilisation und Barbarei: Die widersprüchlichen Potentiale der Moderne,* edited by Frank Bajohr, Werner Johe, and Uwe Lohalm, 7–16. Hamburg: Christians.

Bajohr, Frank. 1997. *"Arisierung" in Hamburg: Die Verdrängung der jüdischen Unternehmer 1933–1945.* Hamburg: Christians.

Bannas, Gunter, 1985. Eine wichtige Woche für Romani Rose. *Frankfurter Allgemeine Zeitung* (8 Nov.).

Barth, Ariane. 1991. Hier steigt eine Giftsuppe auf. *Der Spiegel* 42 (14 Oct.): 118–134.

Bauer, Yehuda. 1994. Gypsies. In *Anatomy of the Auschwitz Death Camp,* edited by Yisrael Gutman and Michael Birenbaum, 441–455. Bloomington: Indiana University Press.

Becker, Ingeborg, Harald Huber, and Otto Kuester. 1955. *Bundesentschädigungsgesetze (BEG).* Berlin.

Bei Hitler waren wir wenigstens Deutsche. 1979. *Der Spiegel* no. 43, 99–126.

Berbüsse, Volker. 1987. Die "Eigentliche Wahrheit" als kulturelle Form. *Leo Beck Institut Bulletin* 78:15–34.

Berbüsse, Volker. 1992. Das Bild "der Zigeuner" in deutschsprachigen Kriminologischen Lehrbücher seit 1949. Eine erste Bestandsaufnahme. *Jahrbuch für Antisemitismusforschung* 1:117–151.

Berger, Heidi. 1972. *Das Zigeunerbild in der deutschen Literatur des 19 Jahrhundert.* Ph.D. diss., University of Waterloo, Ontario.

Berghoff, Hartmut. 1998. Zwischen Verdrängung und Aufarbeitung. *Geschichte in Wissenschaft und Unterict* 49:96–114.

Bergmann, Werner. 1992. Die Reaktion auf den Holocaust in Westdeutschland von 1945 bis 1989. *Geschichte in Wissenschaft und Unterict* 43:327–350.

Bergmann, Werner. 1997. *Antisemitismus im öffentlichen Konflikten: Kollektives Lernen in der politischen Kultur der Bundesrepublik 1949–1989.* Frankfurt a.M./New York: Campus.

Bergmann, Werner, and Rainer Erb. 1991. *Antisemitismus in der Bundesrepublik Deutschland: Ergebnisse der empirischen Forschung von 1946–1989.* Opladen: Westdeutscher Verlag.

Beschützer der Zigeuner. 1959. *Frankfurter Rundschau* (4 Oct.).

Blessin, Georg, Hans Wilden, and Georg Ehrig. 1954. *Bundesentschädigungsgesetz. Kommentar.* Berlin: C. H. Beck.

Block, Martin. 1936. *Zigeuner: Ihr Leben und ihre Seele.* Leipzig: Bibliographisches Institut.

Block, Martin. 1964. Die Literatur der Zigeuner. In *Kindler Litterature Lexikon,* vol. 7. Zurich: Kindler.

Boberach, Heinz. 1984. *Meldungen aus dem Reich 1938–1945.* Herrsching: Pawlak.

Bobrowski, Johannes. 1964. *Levins Mühle: 34 Sätze über meinen Grossvater.* Frankfurt a. M.: Fischer.

Bock, Gisela. 1986. *Zwangssterilisazion im Nationalsozialismus: Studien zur Rassenpolitik und Frauenpolitik*. Opladen: Westdeutscher Verlag.

Böddrich, Jürgen. 1980. Es ist beschämend . . . *Berliner Stimme* (12 Apr.).

Boettcher, Marc. 1998. *Alexandra: Ihr bewegtes Leben, ihre sehnsuchtsvollen Lieder, ihr tragischer Tod*. Munich: Knaur.

Bohn, Irina, Franz Hamburger, and Kerstin Rock. 1995. Polizei und Presse: Eine Untersuchung zum "staatliche genährten Rassismus" am Beispiel der berichterstattung über Roma und Sinti. *Jahrbuch für Antisemitismusforschung* 4:166–183.

Bossmann, Dieter (Ed.). 1977. *"Was ich über Adolf Hitler gehört habe . . .". Folgen eines Tabus: Auszüge aus Schüler/z—Aufsätzen von heute*. Frankfurt a.M.: Fischer.

Bozic, Ivo. 1993. Der Rassismus ist eine Geisteskrankheit die man unterdrücken muss. *Neues Deutschland* 13./14.2.1993.

Breitman, Richard. 1991. *The Architect of Genocide: Himmler and the Final Solution*. New York: Knopf.

Brendler, Konrad. 1997. Die NS-Geschichte als Sozialisationsfaktor und Identitätsballast der Enkelgeneration. In *"Da ist etwas kaputtgegeangen an den Wurzeln . . ." Identitätsformation deutscher und israrelischer Jugendlicher im Schaten des Holocaust*, edited by Dan Bar-On, Konrad Brendler and A. Paul Hare, 53–104. Frankfurt a.M. and New York: Campus.

Briel, Petra-Gabriele. 1989. *Lumpenkind und Traumprinzessin: Zur Sozialgestalt der Zigeuner in der Kinder—und Jugendliteratur seit dem 19. Jahrhundert*. Giessen: Focus.

Broad, Pery. 1969. *KZ-Auschwitz Aussage einem SS-Mann der politischen Abteilung im Konzentrationslager Auschwitz*. Auschwitz: Panstwowe Muzeum w Óswiecim.

Broszat, Martin. 1979. "Holocaust" und die Geschichtswissenschaft. In *Nach Hitler: Der schwierige Umgang mit unserer Geschichte*, 102–118. Munich: Deutscher Taschenbauch Verlag.

Brox, Delphine. 1980. Von Euch Zigeunern wollen wir lernen. *Sinti und Roma in ehemaligen KZ Bergen-Belsen am 27. Oktober 1979*, edited by Gesellschaft für bedrohte Völker, 95–96. Reihe *Pogrom* 76. Göttingen: GfBV.

Brucker-Boroujerdi, Ute, and Wolfgang Wippermann. 1987. "Das Zigeunerlager" Berlin-Marzahn 1936–1945. *Pogrom* 130: 77–80.

Buchheim, Hans. 1958. Die Zigeunerdeportation von Mai 1940 in *Frenkels Entschädigungsrecht Abhandlungen*, Bl. 136.

Bührer, Werner. 1990. Kriminalität im Dritten Reich. In *Legenden Lügen Vorurteile: Ein Lexikon zur Zeitgeschichte*, 132–134, edited by Wolfgang Benz. Munich: DTV.

Bundestag will Lage der Sinti und Roma verbessern. 1985. *Berliner Morgenpost* (8 Nov.).

Busch, Wilhelm. 1989. *Bildergeschichte—Max und Moritz*. Herrsching: Manfred Pawlak

Calvelli-Adorno, Franz. 1961. Die rassische Verfolgung der Zigeuner vor den 1 März 1943. *Rechtsprechung zur Wiedergutmachung* 12 (12): 529–537.

Cassel, Sara. 1962. Begegnung mit einem jungen Zigeuner. *Tagesspiegel* (14. Mar.).

Chamberlain, Houston Stewart. 1906. *Die Grundlagen des Neunzehnten Jahrhunderts.* 2 vols. Munich: F. Bruckmann.

Combe, Sonia. 1992. Gedenkfeiern zur Überwindung der Nazi-Vergangenheit. In *Die wiedergefundene Erinnerung: Verdrängte Geschichte in Osteuropa,* edited by Annette Leo, 137–158. Berlin: BasisDruck.

Cowles, Frederick. 1948. Das Schicksal der europäischen Zigeuner. *Katholischer Digest: Monatsrundschau* 2(5): 9–12.

Crabb, James. 1832. *The Gipsies Advocate.* London: Nisbet et al.

Cramer, Heinz von. 1965. Das Schicksal der Zigeuner. *Die Zeit* (15 Jan.).

Cyganie. 1962. *Wielka Encyklopedia Powszechna (PWN),* 2:648. Warsaw: Pánstwowe Wydawn.

Czech, Danuta 1989. *Kalendarium der Ereignisse im Konzentrationlager Auschwitz-Birkenau 1939–1945.* Hamburg: Rowohlt.

Dachau hunger strike by gypsies. 1980. *Times* (London) (27 Feb.).

Das Zigeunerdorf mit dem Blutrachegesetz. 1951. *Stuttgarter Nachrichten* (7 Feb.).

Der ewig kriminelle Zigeuner? 1981. *Süddeutsche Zeitung* (15 May).

Der Zigeunerpastor von Braunschweig. 1958. *Stuttgarter Zeitung* (8 Nov.).

Deutschland zählt 30,000 Zigeuner. 1941. *Neues Wiener Tagblatt* (25 Feb.).

Dieckmann, Christoph. 1998. Der Krieg und die Ermordung der litauischen Juden. In *Nationalsozialistische Vernichtungspolitik 1939–1945: Neue Forschungen und Kontroversen,* edited by Ulrich Herbert, 292–329. Frankfurt a.M.: Fischer.

Die Nomaden der Landstrasse: Falsche Romantik um asoziale und erbminderwertige Elemente. 1941. Unsere Tageskasten, *Völkische Beobachter* (10 Nov.).

Die unendliche Geschichte. 1994. *Der Spiegel* no. 11 (14 Mar.), 18.

Diner, Dan. 1986. Negative Symbiose. Deutsche und Juden nach Auschwitz. *Babylon* 1:9–20.

Diner, Dan. 1993. Nationalstaat und Migration: Zu Begriff und Geschichte. In *Schwierige Fremdheit: Über Integration und Ausgrenzung in Einwanderungsländern,* edited by Friedrich Balke et al., 21–40. Frankfurt a.M: Fischer.

Diner, Dan. 1995. *Kreisläufe: Nationalsozialismus und Gedächtnis.* Berlin: Rotbuch.

Distel, Barbara. 1990. Asoziale und Berufsverbrechen. In *Legenden Lügen Vorurteile: Ein Lexikon zur Zeitgeschichte,* edited by Wolfgang Benz, 28–31. Munich: Deutscher Taschenbuch Verlag.

Döring, Hans-Joachim. 1959. Die Motive der Zigeuner: Deportation vom Mai 1940. *Vierteljahrhefte für Zeitgeschichte,* 418–428.

Dunkel wie ihre Haare ist ihre Geschichte. 1958. *Frankfurter Rundschau* (25 Jun.).

Ebhardt, Wilhelm. 1928. *Die Zigeuner in der Hochdeutschen Literatur bis zu Goethe "Götz von Berlichingen."* Ph.D. diss., University of Göttingen.

Eichberg, Hennig. 1981. "Produktive" und "Parasiten." In *Zeitschrift für Kulturaustausch* 31(4): 451–454.

Eller, Hans.1954. Die Zigeuner: Ein Problem. *Kriminalistik* 8:124–126.

Ende der Zigeuner-Romantik. 1943. *Die Zeitung* (26 Mar.).

Ergreifend Ernst. 1957. *Frankfurter Rundschau* (28 Jun.)

Secondary Sources

Erk, Ludwig, and Franz M. Böhme. 1893–94. Zigeunerleben in *Deutscher Lie-derhort* Nr. 1585/86. Leipzig: Breitkopf und Härtel.

Erker, Paul. 1988. Solidarität und Selbsthilfe: Die Arbeiterschaft in der Ernähr-ungskrise. In *Neuanfang in Bayern 1945–1949. Politik und Gesellschaft in der Nachkriegszeit*, edited by Wolfgang Benz, 82–102. Munich: C. H. Beck.

Erwin, Terry. 1947. Das Parlament der Zigeuner. *DND in Bild, Illustrierte Wo-chenzeitschrift* 2 (31/32) Baden-Baden.

Erwin, Terry. 1948. Gypsies and World Politics. *New Statesman and Nation*, Feb. 41ff.

Eva Justin gestorben. 1966. *Frankfurter Rundschau* (17 Sept.).

Extremisten werden sozial geächtet. 1993. *Allensbacher Berichte* no. 1, 120, 124.

Fahrendes Volk: Die Bekämpfung der Zigeunerplage auf neuen Wegen. 1939. *NS-Rechtspiegel* (21 Feb.), 7.

Familienministerium: Zwei Drittel der Sinti bekommen Sozialhilfe. 1980. *Süd-dentsche Zeitung* (26 Apr.).

FDP will Discriminierung von Zigeunern stoppen. 1980. *Stuttgarter Zeitung* (3 Jul.).

Feuerhelm, Wolfgang.1987. *Polizei und "Zigeuner": Strategien, Handlungesmus-ter und Alltagstheorien im polizeilichen Umgang mit Sinti und Roma.* Stuttgart: Enke.

Feuerhelm, Wolfgang.1988. Die fortgesetzte "Bekämpfung des Landfahrerunwe-sens": Zur Struktur polizeilichen Umgangs mit Sinti und Roma. *Monatsschrift für Kriminologie und Strafrechtsreform* 71(5): 299–314.

Fings, Karola, and Frank Sparing. 1991a. *Nur wenige kamen zurück: Katalog zur Ausstellung Sinti und Roma im Nationalsozialismus.* Cologne: Landesverband deutscher Sinti und Roma NRW.

Fings, Karola, and Frank Sparing. 1991b. Zigeunerlager Bickendorf 1935–1958. *1999 Zeitschrift für Sozialgeschichte des 20. und 21. Jahrhundert* 6(3): 11–40.

Fings, Karola, and Frank Sparing. 1992. *"z. Zt. Zigeunerlager": Die Verfolgung der Düsseldorfer Sinti und Roma im Nationalsozialismus.* Cologne: Volksblatt.

Finkelstein, Norman G. 2000a. Geschäft mit dem Leid? Die Macht der Holo-caust–Industrie. *Süddeutsche Zeitung* (11 Aug.).

Finkelstein, Norman G. 2000b. *The Holocaust Industry: Reflections on the Ex-ploitation of Jewish Suffering.* London: Verso.

Foschepoth, Josef. 1985. Potsdam und danach: Die Westmächte, Adenauer und die Vertriebenen. In *Die Vertreibung der Deutschen aus dem Osten: Ursachen, Ereignisse Folgen*, edited by Wolfgang Benz, 86–113. Frankfurt a.M.: Fischer.

Franz, Anton, Romani Rose, and Ranco Brantner. 1981. Zigeuner Seelsorge und Rassenideologie. *Pogrom* 12:163–173.

Fraser, Angus. 1992. *The Gypsies.* Oxford: Blackwell.

Frei, Norbert. 1992. Auschwitz und Holocaust. Begriff und Historiographie. In *Holocaust: Die grenzen des Verstehens. Eine debatte über die Besetzung der Geschichte*, edited by Hanno Loewy, 101–109. Hamburg: Rowholt.

Frei, Norbert. 1996. *Vergangenheitspolitik: Die Anfänge der Bundesrepublik und die NS-Vergangenheit.* Munich: C. H. Beck.

Frei, Norbert. 1997. Ein anderer Genozid. *Die Zeit* (31 Jan.).

Fricke, Thomas. 1991. *Zwischen Erziehung und Ausgrenzung: Zur würtemberg- ischen Geschichte der Sinti und Roma im 19. Jahrhundert.* Frankfurt a.M.: Peter Lang.

Fricke, Thomas. 1996. *Zigeuner im Zeitalter des Absolotismus, Bilanz einer einseitigen Überlieferung: Eine sozialgeschichtliche Untersuchung anhand südwestdeutscher Quellen.* Pfaffenweiler: Centaurus.

Friedlünder, Saul. 1997. *Nazi Germany and the Jews: The Years of Persecution, 1933–1939.* New York: HarperCollins.

Friedman, Philip. 1951.The Extermination of the Gypsies. *Jewish Frontier.* (Jan.), 11–14.

Friedrich, Jörg. 1993. Confronting the Past: The Attitudes towards Nazi War Criminals in the Federal Republic. In *"Normal" Relations Israeli-German Re- lations,* edited by Moshe Zimmermann and Oded Heilbronner, 57–77. Jerusa- lem: Magnes Press.

Friedrichsmeyer, Sara. 1997. Romantic Nationalism: Achim von Arnim's Gypsy Princess Isabella. In *Gender and Germanness, Cultural Productions of Nation,* edited by Patricia Herminghouse and Magda Müller (51–65). Providence: Berghann Books.

Gedenkstatte Buchenwald übt scharfe Kritik an Sinti und Roma. 1977. Allge- meiner Deutscher Nachrichtendienst (3 Oct.).

Geigges, Anita, and Bernhard W. Wette 1979. *Zigeuner heute.* Bornheim-Merten: Lamuv.

Gerlach, Wolfgang. 1987. *Als die Zeugen schwiegen: Bekennende Kirche und die Juden.* Berlin: Institut Kirche und Judentum.

German Students resent Gypsies. 1995. *Romnews: An information of the Roma National Congress* no. 28 (2 Jan.).

Giesevius, Hans Bernd. 1946. *Bis zum bitterer Ende.* 2 vols. Zurich: Fretz and Wasmuth.

Giessler, Hans. 1981. Die Grundsatzbestimungen des Entschädigungsrechts. In *Das Bundesentschädigungsgesetz,* edited by Walter Brunn et al.,11-00. Mu- nich: C. H. Beck.

Gill, Ulrich, and Winfried Steffani (Eds.). 1986. *Eine Rede und Ihre Wirkung: Die Rede des Bundespresidänten Richard von Weizsäcker vom 8. Mai 1985.* Berlin: Rainer Röll.

Gilman, Sander L. 1992. *Rasse, Sexualität und Seuche: Stereotype aus der Innen- welt der westlichen Kultur.* Hamburg: Rowholt.

Gilsenbach, Raimar. 1993. *Oh Django, sing deinen Zorn: Sinti und Roma unter den Deutschen.* Berlin: BasisDruck.

Giordano, Ralf. 1987. *Die zweite Sculd oder von der Last Deutscher zu sein.* Hamburg: Knaur.

Goethe, Johann Wolfgang. 1982. *Johann Wolfgang Goethe Fruhes Theater,* ed- ited by Dieter Borchmeyer. Frankfurt a.M.: Insel.

Golub, Jenifer. 1993. British attitudes towards Jews and other Minorities. In *Working Papers on Contemporary Antisemitism.* New York: American Jewish Committee.

Golub, Jenifer, and Renae Cohen. 1991. Attitudes towards Jews and other Minor- ities in Poland, Hungary, and Czechoslovakia: A comparative study. In *Work-*

ing Papers on Contemporary Antisemitism. New York: American Jewish Committee.

Golub, Jenifer, and Renae Cohen. 1995. Current Austrian attitudes towards Jews and the Holocaust. In *Working Papers on Contemporary Antisemitism.* New York: American Jewish Committee.

Goschler, Constantin. 1989. Der Fall Philipp Auerbach: Wiedergutmachung in Bayern. In *Wiedergutmachung in der Bundesrepublik Deutschland,* edited by Ludolf Herbst and Constantin Goschler, 77–98. Munich: R. Oldenburg.

Goschler, Constantin. 1992. *Wiedergutmachung: Westdeutschland und die Verfolgten des Nationalsozialismus (1945–1954).* Munich: R. Oldenburg.

Goschler, Constantin. 1993. Paternalismus und Verweigerung: Die DDR und die Wiedergutmachung für jüdische Verfolgte des Nationalsozialismus. *Jahrbuch für Antisemitismusforschung* 2:93–117.

Grass, Gunther. 1962. Die Blechtrammel, München: Deutscher Taschenbuch Verlag.

Grellmann, Heinrich Moritz Gottlieb. 1787. *Historische Versuch über die Zigeuner, betreffend die Lebensart und Verfassung Sitten und Schicksale dieses Volkes seit seiner Erscheinung in Europa und dessen Ursprung.* Göttingen: Dieterich.

Greußing, Fritz. 1979. Das offizielle Verbrechen der zweiten Verfolgung. *In Auschwitz vergast, bis heute vervolgt: Zur Situation der Roma (Zigeuner) in Deutschland und Europa,* edited by Tilman Zülch, 192–198. Hamburg: Rowohlt.

Greußing, Fritz. 1980. Vergangenheitsbewältigung der Nachgeborenen. In *Sinti und Roma in ehemaligen KZ Bergen-Belsen am 27. Oktober 1979,* edited by Gesellschaft für bedrohte Völker. Reihe *Pogrom* 76:12–13. Göttingen: Gesellschaft für bedrohte Völker.

Groehler, Olaf. 1992. Der Holocaust in der Geschichtsschreibung der DDR. In *Zweierlei Bewältigung: Vier Beiträge über den Umgang mit der NS-Vergangenheit in den beiden deutschen Staaten,* edited by Ulrich Herbert and Olaf Groehler, 41–66. Hamburg: Ergebnisse.

Groehler, Olaf. 1994. SED, VVN und Juden in der sowjetischen Besatzungszone Deutschlands (1945–1949). *Jahrbuch für Antisemitismusforschung* 3:282–302.

Gronemeyer, Reimer. 1987. Zigeuner im Spiegel früher Chroniken und Abhandlungen. Quellen vom 15. bis zum 18. Jahrhundert. Giessen: Focus.

Gudkov, Lev, and Alex Levinson 1994. Attitudes toward Jews in the Commonwealth of Independent States. In *Working Papers on Contemporary Antisemitism.* New York: American Jewish Committee.

Günther, Hans, F. K. 1929. *Rassenkunde Europas.* Munich: J. F. Lehmann.

Gypsies. 1978. *Great Soviet Encyclopedia,* 28:437. New York and London: Macmillan.

Gypsies and the Holocaust. 2000. *New York Times* (14 Aug.).

Gypsies at Dachau ignore pleas to end hunger strike. 1980. *Times* (London) (12 Apr.).

Gypsy. 1962. *Encyclopaedia Britannica,* 10: 43–45. Chicago London and Toronto: William Benton.

Gypsy. 1980. *Encyclopedia Americana International Edition,* 13:646–651. Danbury: Grolier.

Hachmann, Horst. 1960. Das Glück ist ihr Fahrplan. *Frankfurter Rundschau* (20 Oct.).

Halbwachs, Maurice. 1968. *La Memoire Collective.* Paris: Presses Universitaires de France.

Hanau. 1965. *Frankfurter Rundschau* (17 Sept.)

Hartman, Geoffrey (Ed.). 1986. *Bittburg in Moral and Political Perspective.* Bloomington: Indiana University Press.

Hehmann, Rainer. 1987. *Die "Bekämpfung des Zigeunerunwessens" im Wilhelminischen Deutschland und in der Weimarer Republik 1871–1933.* Frankfurt a.M.: Haag + Herchen.

Heiden, Konrad. 1939. *The New Inquisition.* New York: Modern Age Books.

Henke, Klaus Dietmar. 1985. Der Weg nach Potsdam: Die Alliirten und die Vertreibung. In *Die Vertreibung der Deutschen aus dem Osten: Ursachen, Ereignisse Folgen,* edited by Wolfgang Benz, 49–69. Frankfurt a.M.: Fischer.

Hennig, K. M. 1959. Ein Volk voller Rätsel. *Frankfurter Allgemeine Zeitung* (2 Jun.).

Herbert, Ulrich. 1990. Traditionen des Rassismus. In *Bürgerliche Gesellschaft in Deutschland: Historische Einblicke, Fragen, Perspektiven,* edited by Lutz Niethammer et al., 472–488. Frankfurt a.M: Fischer.

Herbert, Ulrich. 2000. Vorschnelle Begeisterung. *Süddeutsche Zeitung* (18 Aug.).

Herf, Geffrey. 1980. The "Holocaust" Reception in West Germany: Right, Center and Left. *New German Critique* 19:30–52.

Herf, Geffrey. 1997. *Divided Memory: The Nazi Past in the Two Germanys.* Cambridge: Harvard University Press.

Hermann, Kai. 1964. Traurig ist das Zigeunerleben. *Die Zeit* (11 Dec.).

Hesse, Hermann. 1974. *Wandering.* Translated by James Wright. New York: Farrar, Strauss & Giroux.

Hesse, Hermann. 1968. *Narziß und Goldmund.* Frankfurt a.M.: Suhrkamp.

Heuß, Herbert. 1987. Für ein Kulturzentrum deutscher Sinti und Roma. *Pogrom* 130:2.

Himmler, Heinrich, 1999. *Der Dienstkalender Heinrich Himmlers 1941/1942.* Edited by Peter Witte et al. Hamburg: Christians.

Hinton, David B. 1978. *The Films of Leni Riefenstahl.* Metuchen, N. J.: Scarecrow Press.

Hinton, Perry R. 1993. *The Psychology of Interpersonal Perception.* New York: Routledge.

Historiker Jäckel gegen Sinti und Roma: Vorwürfe der Geschichtsfälschung. 2000. *Fuldaer Zeitung* (1 Jul.).

Hockerts, Hans Günter. 1989. Anwälte der Verfolgten: Die United Restitution Organisation. In *Wiedergutmachung in der Bundesrepublik Deutschland,* edited by Ludolf Herbst and Constantin Goschler, 251–271. Munich: R. Oldenburg.

Hoffmann, Volkmar. 1960. Sie wollen keine Bürger zweiter Klasse sein. *Frankfurter Rundschau* (15 Mar.).

Hohmann, Joachim S. 1977. *Der unterdrückte Sexus: Ein Kompendium wissenschaftlicher Beiträge zum Problemfeld Homosexualität.* Achenbach: Lollar.

Hohmann, Joachim S. 1979. *Der heimliche Sexus: Homoseualle Belletristik in Deutschland der Jahre 1920–1970.* Foerester.

Hohmann, Joachim S. 1980a. Geh mir ja nicht zu diesen Zigeunern! In *Zigeunerleben: Beiträge zur Sozialgeschichte einer Verfolgung,* edited by Joachim S. Hohmann and Roland Schopf, 213–226. Darmstadt: ms edition.

Hohmann, Joachim S. 1980b. Zigeunermythos und -vorurteile. In *Zigeunerleben: Beiträge zur Sozialgeschichte einer Verfolgung,* edited by Joachim S. Hohmann and Roland Schopf, 85–124. Darmstadt: ms edition.

Hohmann, Joachim S. 1980c. *Zigeuner und Zigeunerwissenschaft: Ein Beitrag Grundlagenforschung und Dokumentation des Völkermords im Dritten Reich.* Marburg/ Lahn: Guttandin and Hoppe.

Hohmann, Joachim S. 1981. *Geschichte der Zigeunerverfolgung in Deutschland.* New York: Campus.

Hohmann, Joachim S. 1982. Ihnen geschah Unrecht: Zigeunerverfolgung in Deutschland. *Tribüne* 21(82): 100–113.

Hohmann, Joachim S. 1991. *Robert Ritter und die Erben der Kriminalbiologie: "Zigeunerforschung" im Nationalsozialismus und in Westdeutschland im Zeichen des Rassismus.* Studien zur Tsiganologie und Folkloristik, vol. 4. Frankfurt a.M: Peter Lang.

Holocaust—deutsches verdrängen. 1979. *Pflasterstrand. Stadtzeitung für Frankfurt* no. 47 (15 Feb.), 23–27.

Höß, Rudolf. 1978. *Kommandant in Auschwitz: Autobiographische Aufzeichnungen des Rudolf Höß.* Edited by Martin Broszat. Munich: Deutscher Taschenbuch Verlag.

How the Gypsies Were Persecuted. 1950. *Vienna Library Bulletin* 4(3–4) (May–July), 18.

Hundsalz, Andreas. 1982 *Soziale Situation der Sinti in der Bundesrepublik Deutschland–Endbericht: Lebensverhältnisse Deutscher Sinti unter besonderer Berücksichtigung der eigenen Aussagen und Meinungen der Betroffenen.* Stuttgart: Kohlhammer.

Hundt-Radowsky, Hartwig, von. 1819. *Der Judenspiegel: Ein Schand- und Sittengemälde alter und neuer Zeit.*Würzburg: Schlagehart.

Hunger strike staged in Dachau by gypsies. 1980. *Times* (London) (7 Apr.).

Huster, Ernst-Ulrich, et al. 1972. *Determination der westdeutschen Restauration 1945–1949.* Frankfurt a.M.: Suhrkampf.

Hüttenberger, Peter. 1973. *Nordrhein-Westfalen und die Entstehung seiner parlamentarischen Demokrati.* Siegburg: Republica.

Huyssen, Andreas. 1980. The Politics of Identification: "Holocaust" and West German Drama. *New German Critique* 19:117–136.

Ich gehe nie mehr ins Theater. 1986. *Die Tageszeitung* (24 Feb.).

Jäckel, Eberhard. 2000. Wider zwei Legenden über den Holocaust: Plädoyer für Einzigartigkeit des Genozids, den die Nazis an den Juden verübten. *Frankfurter Allgemeini Zeitung* (30 Jun.).

Jaspers, Karl. 1986. *Erneuerung der Universität: Reden und Schriften 1945/1946.* Heidelberg: Schneider.

Jochimsen, Lukrezia. 1963. *Zigeuner Heute: Untersuchung einer Aussenseitergruppe in einer Deutschen Mittelstadt.* Stuttgart: Enke.

Jochimsen, Lukrezia. 1970. Zigeuner–Porträt einer entwurzelten Rasse. *Konkret* no. 2 (15 Jan.).

Jones, Eduard, E. 1990. *Interpersonal Perception.* New York: W. H. Freeman.

Jürgens, Hans, W. 1961. *Asozialität als biologisches und sozialbiologisches Problem.* Stuttgart: Enke.

Justin, Eva. 1943. Die Rom-Zigeuner. *Neues Volk* 11(5): 21–24.

Justin, Eva. 1944. *Lebensschicksale artfremd erzogener Zigeunerkinder und ihrer Nachkommen.* Veröffentlichungen aus dem Gebiete des Volksgesundheitsdienstes, Bd. 57, Heft 4. Berlin: Schoetz.

Jütte, Robert. 1980. Vagantentum und Bettlerwesen bei Hans Jacob Christoffel von Grimmelshausen. *Daphnis* 10:109–131.

Kanzler: Verantwortung für Sinti und Roma. 1985. *Die Welt* (8 Nov.).

Kater, Michael. 1974. *Das "Ahnenerbe" der SS 1935–1945: Ein Beitrag zur Kulturpolitik des Dritten Reiches.* Stuttgart: Deutsche Verlagsanstalt.

Kauck, Otmar. 1962. Am Ende der langen Wanderschaft. *Frankfurter Neue Presse* (17 Mar.).

Kein Kulturgut, das schützenswert ist. 1990. *Die Tageszeitung* (6 Aug.).

Kenrik, Donald, and Puxon, Grattan. 1972. *The Destiny of Europe's Gypsies.* London: Chatto and Heinemann.

Kenrik, Donald, and Puxon, Grattan. 1981. *Sinti und Roma: Die Vernichtung eines Volkes im NS Staat.* Göttingen: Gesellschaft für bedrohte Völker.

Kiderlen, Elisabeth (Ed.). 1985. *Deutsch-jüdische Normalität . . . Fassbinders Sprengsätze.* Frankfurt a.M.: Pfalsterstrand.

Kielar, Wieslaw. 1979. *Anus Mundi: Fünf Jahre Auschwitz.* Frankfurt a.M.: Fischer.

Kister, Kurt. 1980a. Die SPD zollt den Sinti Respekt. *Süddentsche Zeitung* (11 Apr.).

Kister, Kurt. 1980b. Gesundheitszustand verschlechtert. *Süddentsche Zeitung* (9 Apr.).

Kittel, Manfred. 1993. *Die Legende von der "Zweiten Schuld." Vergangenheitsbewältigung in der Ära Adenauer.* Frankfurt a.M.: Ullstein.

Klebe, Thomas. 1974. Staatsangehörigkeit: Unbekannt. *Nachrichtendienst des Deutschen Vereins für öffentliche und private Fürsorge* 54(3): 61–63.

Klessmann, Cristoph. 1986. Das Jahr 1945 in der Deutschen Geschichte. In *Deutschland und Polen von der nationalsozialistischen Machtergreifung bis zum Ende des Zweiten Weltkrieges.* Schrieftenreihe des Georg-Eckert-Instituts 22(9): 135–145.

Kocka, Jürgen. 1979. 1945—Neubeginn oder Restauration. In *Wendepunkte der deutschen Geschichte 1848–1945.* edited by Carola Stern and Henrich A. Winkler. Frankfurt a.M: Fischer-Taschenbuch-Verlag.

Kogon, Egon. 1946. *Der SS-Staat.* Frankfurt a.M.: Europäische Verlagsanstalt.

Kommitee der antifaschisten Widerstandskämpfer der DDR (Autorenkollektiv unter Leitung von G. Zörner), 1982. *Frauen KZ-Ravensbrück.* Berlin: Deutsche Verlag der Wissenschaft.

Kraschutzki, Heinz. 1954. Der Zigeuner. *Freiburger Rundbrief* Nr. 25/28:25–27.

Krass, Stephan. 1983. Tante Leni kann sich nicht erinnern. *Stuttgarter Zeitung* (21 Jun.).

Secondary Sources

Krausnick, Helmut. 1987. Hitler und die Befehle an die Einsatzgruppen in Sommer 1941. In *Der Mord an den Juden im Zweiten Weltkrieg*, edited by Eberhard Jäckel and Jürgen Rohwer, 88–106. Frankfurt a.M.: Fischer.

Krausnick, Michail. 1990. *Abfahrt Karlsruhe: Die Deportation in den Völkermord*. Karlsruhe: Verband der Sinti und Roma Karlsruhe e.V.

Kulka, Otto Dov. 1984.Ghetto in an Annihilation Camp: Jewish Social History in the Holocaust Period and Its Ultimate Limits in the Nazi Concentration Camps. *Proceedings of the Fourth Yad Vashem International Historical Conference*, Jerusalem, 315–330.

Küster, Otto. 1953. *Wiedergutmachung als elementare Rechtsaufgabe*. Frankfurt a.M.: Schulte–Bulmke.

Labouvie, Eva. 1990.Wider Wahrsagerei, Segnerei und Zauberei. In *Verbrechen, Strafen und soziale Kontrolle: Studien zur historischen Kulturforschung III*, edited by Richard van Dülmen, 15–55. Frankfurt a.M.: Fischer.

Langbein, Hermann. 1964. Der Leidensweg der Zigeuner. *Die Neue Presse* (2 Aug.).

Leblon, 1985. *Les Gitans d'Espagne: Le Prix de la différence*. Paris: Presses Universitaires de France.

Lemke, Michal. 1993. Kampagnen gegen Bonn: Die Systemkrise der DDR und die West-Propaganda der SED 1960–1963. *Vierteljahrhefte für Zeitgeschichte* 41:153–174.

Levkov, Ilya I. 1987. *Bitburg and Beyond: Encounter in American, German and Jewish History*. New York: Schapolsky.

Lewy, Guenter. 2000 *The Nazi Persecution of the Gypsies*. Oxford: Oxford University Press.

Liberale wollen Förderprogramm für Zigeuner. 1980. *Südkurier* (19 Jul.).

Liebich, Richard. 1863. *Die Zigeuner in ihrem Wesen und in ihrer Sprache*. Leipzig: Brockhaus.

Lifton, Robert. 1986. *Nazi Doctors*. London: Basic Books.

Lipset, Seymour M. 1963. *Political Man*. New York: Anchor Books.

Lohmann, Hans Martin. 1994. *Extremismus der Mitte: Vom rechten Verständis deutscher Nation*. Frankfurt a.M.: Fischer.

Longerich, Peter. 2000. Ein Mann sieht rot: Norman Finkelstein und seine "Holocaust-Industrie." *Frankfurter Rundschau* (22 Aug.).

Luschan, Felix von. 1922. *Völker, Rassen, Sprachen*. Berlin: Welt.

Luther, Martin. 1883. Vom Schem Hamphoras und von Geschlecht Christi. *Martin Luthers Werke. Kritische Gesamtausgabe*, 53:613.

Maier, Charles. 2000. Das Spiel finsterer Mächte? Eine Erwiderung auf Norman Finkelstein. *Süddeutsche Zeitung* (16 Aug.).

Maislinger, Andreas. 1990. "Vergangenheitsbewältigung" in der Bundesrepublik Deutschland, der DDR und Österreich. In *Die Schatten der Vergangenheit: Impulse zur Historisierung des Nationalsozialismus*, edited by Uwe Backes, Eckhard Jesse, and Rainer Zitelmann, 479–495. Frankfurt a.M.and Berlin: Ullstein.

Mangoldt, Hermann von. 1953. *Das Bonner Grundgesetz*. Berlin and Frankfurt a.M.: Vahlen.

Manoschek, Walter. 1998. Die Vernichtung der Juden in Serbien. In *National-*

sozialistische Vernichtungspolitik 1939–1945: Neue Forschungen und Kontroversen, edited by Ulrich Herbert, 209–234. Frankfurt a.M.: Fischer.

Manoschek, Walter. 1995. *"Serbien ist judenfrei!" Militärische Besatzungspolitik und Judenvernichtung in Serbien 1941/1942.* Munich: R. Oldenburg.

Margalit, Gilad. 1996. Antigypsyism in the Political Culture of the Federal Republic of Germany: A Parallel with Antisemitism? *Analysis of Current Trends in Antisemitism (ACTA)* 9. Jerusalem.

Margalit, Gilad. 1997. Sinte und andere Deutsche: Über ethnische Spigelungen. *Tel-Aviver Jahrbuch für deutsche Geschichte* 26:281–306.

Margalit, Gilad. 2000a. Liebe Gott, Ich danke Dir dass Du kleine schwarze Kinder gemacht hast. Der Zigeunerpastor, Georg Althaus. *Werkstatt Geschichte* 25:59–73.

Margalit, Gilad. 2000b. Review of Michael Zimmermann's *Romani Studies 5* 10(1): 84–89.

Markgraf, Hendrik. 1985. Stumm und doch beredt. *Frankfurter Allgemeine Zeitung* (20 Jun.).

Markovits, Andrei S., and Rebecca S. Hayden. 1980. "Holocaust" before and after the Event: Reactions in West Germany and Austria. *New German Critique* 19:53–80.

Märthesheimer, Peter, and Ivo Frenzel. 1979. *Im Kreuzfeuer: Der Fernsehfilm "Holocaust"—Eine Nation ist betroffen.* Frankfurt a.M.: Fischer.

Matras, Yaron. 1989. Der Antirassismus ist noch verkrampft: *Zwischen "Helfern" und "Patienten."* In *Über herrschende Mehrheit und nationale Minderheit,* edited by Yaron Matras, 35–40. Hamburg: author.

Mayall, David. 1988. *Gypsy Travellers in Nineteenth Century Society.* Cambridge: University of Cambridge Press.

Mazirel, Lau. 1973. Die Verfolgung der "Zigeuner" im Dritten Reich: Vorgeschichte ab 1870 und Fortsetzung bis heute. *Essays über Naziverbrechen, Simon Wiesenthal gewidmet,* 124–176. Vienna and Amsterdam: Wiesenthal Fonds.

Mehr verdrängt als bewältigt. 1992. In Juden und Deutsche, *Spiegel Spezial* no. 2, 71.

Meixner, Franz. 1948. Die nicht sesshaften Menschen. *Die neue Polizei* 3.

Milton, Sybil. 1991.Gypsies and the Holocaust. *History Teacher* 24(4): 375–387.

Milton, Sybil. 1992. Nazi Policies toward Roma and Sinti, 1933–1945. *Journal of the Gypsy Lore Society* 5(2): 1–18.

Milton, Sybil. 1995. Vorstufe zur Vernichtung: Die Zigeunerlager nach 1933. *Vierteljahrhefte für Zeitgeschichte* 43:115–130.

Mit Molari bei den Zigeunern. 1948. *Freiheit* no. 7 (23 Jan.): 3.

Mode, Heinz, and Wölffling, Siegfried. 1968 *Zigeuner: Der Weg eines Volks in Deutschland.* Leipzig: Köhler and Amelang.

Moeller, Robert G. 1996. War Stories: The Search for a Usable Past in the Federal Republic of Germany. *American Historical Review* 101(3–5): 1008–1048.

Moller, Sabine. 1998. *Die Entkonkretisierung der NS-Herrschaft in der Ära Kohl: Die Neue Wache—Das Denkmal für die ermordeten Juden Europas; Das Haus der Geschichte der Bundesrepublik Deutschland.* Hannover: Offizin.

Secondary Sources

Mommsen, Hans. 1983. Die Realisierung des Utopischen: Die "Endlösung der Judenfrage" im Dritten Reich. *Geschichte und Gesellschaft* 9:381–420.

Mosse, Georg L. 1978. *Toward the Final Solution: A History of European Racism.* Madison: University of Wisconsin Press.

Mosse, Georg L. 1993. *Fallen Soldiers: Reshaping the Memory of the World Wars.* Tel-Aviv: Am-Oved. (In Hebrew.)

Müller, Ingo. 1991. *Hitler's Justice: The Courts of the Third Reich.* Translated by Deborah Lucas Schneider. Cambridge: Harvard University Press.

Müller, Hanno. 1997. Streit zwischen Sinti und Roma und Buchenwald. *Thüringer Allgemeine* (1 Oct.).

Müller-Hill, Benno.1984. *Tödliche Wissenschaft: Die Aussonderung von Juden, Zigeunern und Geisteskranken 1933–1945.* Hamburg: Rowholt.

Münzel, Mark. 1983 "Zigeunerpolitik in Frankreich: Skizze ihrer Geschichte und ihrer Gedanken." In *Eigensinn und Hilfe: Zigeuner in der Sozialpolitik heutiger Leistungsgesellschaften,* edited by Reimer Gronemeyer, 184–278. Giessen: Focus.

Nawrocki, Georg. 1937. "Cintis in Hamburg: Grossstadt–Zigeuner Ohne Romantik." *Hamburger Tageblatt* 223–225 (18–20 Aug.).

Nazis now attacking Gypsies. 1942. *Times* (London) (20 Jun.).

Nehring, Almuth. 1988. Damals: Am Rande von Berlin. *Junge Welt* (2 Sept.).

Ness, Oliver. 1989. Ein "Tatort"—Krimi zwischen allen Stühlen. *Die Tageszeitung* (22 Jul.).

Neuer Holocaust-Schinken in deutschen Kinos: Schindlers Liste Märchen oder Dokumentation? 1994. *Deutsche Wochen-Zeitung* (11 Mar.).

Neukamp, Franz. 1950. Ist die Unfruchtbarmachung von Menschen immer strafbar? *Neue Juristische Wochenschrift* 3(20): 773–774.

Niethammer, Lutz. 1990. Juden und Russen im Gedächtnis der Deutschen. In *Der historisches Ort des Nationalsozialismus: Annährungen,* edited by Walter H. Pehle, 114–134. Frankfurt a.M.: Fischer.

Noakes, Jeremy. 1989. The Development of Nazi Policy towards the German-Jewish "*Mischlinge*" 1933–1945. *Leo Baeck Institute Year Book* 34:291–354.

Nolan, Mary. 1988. The Historikerstreit and Social History. *New German Critique* 44:51–80.

Ogorreck, Ralf. 1996. *Die Einsatzgruppen und die "Genesis der Endlösung."* Berlin: Metropol.

Oliner, Samuel P., and Ken Hallum. 1978. Minority Contempt for Oppressors: A Comparative Analysis of Jews and Gypsies. *California-Sociologist* (Winter): 41–57.

Ott, Sieghart. 1979. Die unwillkommenen Deutschen. In *In Auschwitz vergast, bis heute vervolgt: Zur Situation der Roma (Zigeuner) in Deutschland und Europa,* edited by Tilman Zülch, 227–240. Hamburg: Rowohlt.

Pai, Claudia. 1989. Aus der Räuberpistole geschossen. *Der Tagesspiegel* (11 Jul.).

Panahi, Badi. 1980. *Vorurteile: Rassismus, Antisemitismus, Nationalismus . . . in der Bundesrepublik heute—Eine empirische Untersuchung.* Frankfurt a.M.: Fischer.

Pankok, Otto. 1950. Zigeuner sind auch Menschen. *Zeitung ohne Namen,* Nr. 6 (23 Mar.): 10.

Bibliography

Pankok, Otto. 1958. *Zigeuner* (2nd ed.). Düsseldorf: Progress.

Pankok, Otto. 1970. *Die Passion* (new ed.). Gütersloh: Gutersloher Verlagshaus G. Mohn.

Partos, Ferenc. 1980. A cigany es nem cigany lakossag velemenye a fobb tarsadalompolitikai celkituzesekrol. *Szociologia* 1:1–17.

Peukert, Detlev J. K. 1982. *Volksgenossen und Gemeinschaftsfremde: Anpassung, Ausmerze und Aufbegehren unter dem Nationalsozialismus.* Cologne: Bund.

Peukert, Detlev J. K. 1987a. Alltag und Barbarei: Zur Normalität des Dritten Reiches. In *Ist der Nationalsozialismus Geschichte? Zu Historisierung und Historikerstreit,* edited by Dan Diner, 51–61. Frankfurt a.M.: Fischer.

Peukert, Detlev J. K. 1987b. *Die Weimarer Republik: Krisenjahre der klassischen Moderne.* Frankfurt a.M.: Suhrkamp.

Peukert, Detlev J. K. 1989. Rassismus und "Endlösungs"-Utopie: Thesen zur Entwicklung und struktur der national-sozialistischen Vernichtungspolitik. In *Nicht nur Hitlers Krieg: Der Zweite Weltkrieg und die Deutschen,* edited by Christoph Klessmann, 71–81. Düsseldorf: Droste.

Pischel, Richard. 1894. *Beiträge zur Kenntnis der Deutschen Zigeuner.* Halle: Max Niemeyer.

Podehl, Enno. 1982. Hermann-Erzählertext. Unpublished ms.

Politiker versprechen Sinti Unterstützung. 1980. *Mindener Tageblatt* (14 Apr.).

Port le roi, André. 1998. *Schläger lügen nicht: Deutscher Schlager und Politik in ihrer Zeit.* Essen: Klartext.

Press in Exile: German Anti-Nazi Periodicals 1933–1945. 1947. *Vienna Library Bulletin,* 3(5–6), 31.

Pross, Christian. 1988. *Wiedergutmachung: Der Kleinkrieg gegen die Opfer.* Frankfurt a.M: Atheäum.

Protest gegen "Asoziale." 1951. *Abendpost* (1 Jul.).

Rabinbach, Anson. 1988. The Jewish Question in the German Question. *New German Critique* 44: 159–191.

Rakelmann, Georgia A. 1988. *Interethnik-Beziehungen Zwischen Zigeuner und Nicht-Zigeuner.* Münster: Lit.

Rakelmann, Georgia A. 1991. Zigeunerweisheit. In *Weisheit: Archäologie der literarischen Kommunikation III,* edited by Aleida Assmann, 139-153. Munich: Fink.

Reichel, Peter. 1995. *Politik mit der Erinnerung: Gedächtnisorte im Streit um die nationalsozialistische Vergangenheit.* Munich and Vienna: Hanser.

Reiter, Hans. 1939. *Das Reichsgesundheitsamt. Sechs Jahre nationalsozialistischen Führung,* Berlin: Springer.

Remszhardt, Godo. 1953. Es war nur Menschenpflicht. *Frankfurter Rundschau* (28 Feb.).

Reuter, Elke, and Detlef Hansel. 1997. *Das kurze Leben der VVN von 1947 bis 1953: Die Geschichte der Vereinigung der Verfolgten des Naziregimes in der sowjetischen Besatzungszone und in der DDR.* Berlin: Edition Ost.

Riefenstahl, Leni. 1987. *Memoiren.* Munich and Hamburg: Knaus.

Ritter, Robert. 1931a. Mehr gegenseitige Achtung. *Kölnische Zeitung* (22 Jan.).

Ritter, Robert. 1931b. NS und Jugend. *Kölnische Zeitung* (8 Jan.).

Ritter, Robert. 1936. Erbbiologische Untersuchungen innerhalb eines Züchtungs-kreis Zigeunermischlingen und "asozialen Psychopathen." In *Bevölkerungsfragen,* edited by Hans Harmsen and Franz Lohse, 713–718. Munich: J.F. Lehmann.

Ritter, Robert. 1937. *Ein Menschenschlag.* Leipzig: Thieme.

Ritter, Robert. 1938a. Zigeuner und Landfahrer. In *Der nichtseßhafte Mensch,* 71–88. Munich: C. H. Beck.

Ritter, Robert. 1938b. Zur Frage der Rassenbiologie und Rassenpsychologie der Zigeuner in Deutschland. *Reichs-Gesundheitsblatt* 13(22): 425–426.

Ritter, Robert. 1941. Die Bestandsaufnahme der Zigeuner und Zigeunermisch-linge in Deutschland. *Der Öffentlichen Gesundheitsdienst* 6(21): 477–489.

Roberts, C. S. 1949. Der Kaiser zahlt Zigeunern Zins. *Rheinische Post* (28 May).

Roda, Alexander Roda. 1960. Zigeuner sind ehrlich. In *Die Streiche des Junkers Marius,* 7–11. Reinbek: Rowohlt.

Römer, Joachim. 1934. Zigeuner in Deutschland. *Volk und Rasse* 4:112–113.

Römer, Joachim. 1936. Fremdrassen in Deutschland. *Volk und Rasse* 3:88–95.

Romey, Stefan. 1988. Zu Recht verfolgt: Zur Geschichte der ausgebliebenen Ent-schädigung. In *Verachtet-verfolgt-vernichtet: Zu den "vergessenen" Opfer des NS-Regimes,* edited by Projektgruppe für die vergessenen Opfer des NS- Re-gimes, 220–246. Hamburg: VSA.

Rose, Oskar (Romani). 1979. "Wiedergutmachung nur den Starken?" *In Ausch-witz vergast, bis heute vervolgt: Zur Situation der Roma (Zigeuner) in Deutsch-land und Europa,* edited by Tilman Zülch, 257–261. Hamburg: Rowohlt.

Rose, Oskar (Romani). 1982. Die neue Generation und die alte Ideologie. Zigeunerforschung–Wie gehabt? *Tribüne* 21(81): 88–108.

Rose, Oskar (Romani). 1987. *Bürgerrechte für Sinti und Roma: Das Buch zum Rassismus in Deutschland.* Heidelberg: Zentralrat Deutscher Sinti und Roma.

Rose, Oskar (Romani). 2000. Von Eberhard Jäckel ignoriert. *Frankfurter Allge-meine Zeitung* (18.7.2000).

Roth, Karl Heinz, and Götz Aly. 1984. Das "Gesetz über die Sterbehilfe bei un-heilbar Kranken." In *Erfassung zur Vernichtung: Von der Sozialhygiene zum "Gesetz über Sterbehilfe,"* edited by Karl Heinz Roth 101–179. Berlin: Verlags-gesellschaft Gesundheit.

Rothbart, Thomas. 1997a. Differenzen um sicht auf die NS-Geschichte. *Thü-ringer Allgemeine* (21 Aug.).

Rothbart, Thomas. 1997b. Protest gegen Referenten in Buchenwald. *Thüringer Allgemeine* (19 Aug.).

Ruch, Martin. 1986. Zur Wissenschaftsgeschichte der deutschsprachigen "Zi-geunerforschung" von den Anfänge bis 1900. Ph.D. diss., Universität Freiburg.

Rüdiger, Johannn Ch. Ch. 1782. "Von der Sprache und Herkunft der Zigeuner aus Indien." *Neuster Zuwachs der teutschen, fremden und allgemeinen Sprach-kunde in eigenen Aufsätzen,* 37–84. Leipzig: Kummer.

Rürup, Reinhard. 2000. Ideologisierter Holocaust? Was Norman Finkelsteins Vorwurf für die deutschen Gedenkstätten bedeutet. *Die Zeit* Nr. 34 (17 Aug.).

Sandner, Peter. 1998. *Frankfurt. Auschwitz: Die nationalsozialistische Ver-folgung der Sinti und Roma in Frankfurt a.M.* Frankfurt a.M: Brandes & Apsel.

Schildt, Axel, and Arnold Sywottek. 1997. "Reconstruction" and "Modernization": West German Social History during the 1950s. In *West Germany under Construction: Politics, Society, and Culture in the Adenauer Era*, edited by Robert G. Moeller, 413–440. Ann Arbor: University of Michigan Press.

Schlabrendorff, Fabian von. 1946. *Offiziere gegen Hitler: Nach einem Erlebnisbericht.* Zurich: Europa.

Schlüssig Deutsche: Eine Sinti-Familie kämpft um Anerkennung und Pässe. 1986. *Die Zeit* (28 Nov.).

Schmidt für moralische Wiedergutmachung an Zigeunern. 1982. *Der Tagesspiegel* (18 Mar.).

Schneider, Ulrich. 1997. *Zukunftsentwurf Antifaschismus: 50 Jahre Wirken der VVN für "eine neue Welt des Friedens und der Freiheit."* Bonn: Pahl-Rugenstein.

Schnurre, Wolfdietrich. 1958. Jenö war mein Freund. In *Als Vaters Bart noch rot war*, 208–212. Zurich: Arche.

Scholz, Peter. 1986. Rom heisst Mensch. *Junge Welt* (12 Aug.).

Schrecklich ist das Zigeunerleben. 1960. *Süddentsche Zeitung* no. 104 (30 Apr.).

Schubarth, Wilfried. 1991. Fremde als Sündenböcke. In Das Profil der Deutschen: Was sie vereint, was sie trennt, *Spiegel Spezial* no. 1, 47ff.

Schulte, Bettina. 1997. Die Forschung fängt erst an. *Frankfurter Rundschau* (13 Feb.).

Schulze, K. 1950. Hier werden Ehefrauen getauscht. *Frankfurter Rundschau* (11 Nov.).

Segev, Tom. 1993. The Foreign Reporter—The column of Political Kitsch. Suddenly the Gypsies came (Heb.). *Haaretz* (15 Oct.).

6 Millionen ermordete Deutsche: Der Massenmord ohne Sühne. 1980. *Deutsche National-Zeitung* (1 Aug.).

Sibeth, Uwe. 1985. Verordnungen gegen Zigeuner in der Landschaft Hessen-Kassel in Zeitalter des früh-Absolutismus. *Giessener Hefte für Tsiganologie* 2(4): 3–15.

Sinti setzen Hungerstreik in Dachau fort. 1980. *Frankfurter Allgemeine Zeitung* (8 Aug.).

Sinti und Roma bauen Informationszentrum. 1990. *Stuttgarter Zeitung* (30 Jul.).

Sinti und Roma geht es um die Moral. 1982. *Die Welt* (19 Mar.).

Sinti und Roma stellten Ultimatum. 1983. *Unsere Zeit* (26 May).

So arisch. 1963. *Der Spiegel,* no. 17 (24 Apr.), 48.

SPD und VVN. 1948. *SPD Nachrichten,* no. 10 (Aug.).

Spitta, Arnold. 1989. Entschädigung für Zigeuner? Geschichte eines Vorurteil. In *Wiedergutmachung in der Bundesrepublik Deutschland*, edited by Ludolf Herbst and Constantin Goschler, 385–401. Munich: R. Oldenburg.

Stanicki, Henning. 1968. Zur Problematik der Ansprüche von Zigeuner nach dem BEG-Schlussgesetz. *Rechtsprechung zur Wiedergutmachung*, 529–535.

Steiner, John M., and Jobst Freiher von Cornberg. 1998. Wilkür in der Willkür: Befreiungen von den antisemitischen Nürnberger Gesetzen. *Vierteljahrhefte für Zeitgeschichte* 46:143–187.

Stern, Frank. 1991. *Im Anfang war Auschwitz: Antisemitismus und Philosemitismus in deutschen Nachkrieg.* Gerlingen: Bleicher.

Stetter, Regina. 1980. Die Feindseligkeit der Seßhaften gegen das "fahrende Volk." *Süddetsche Zeitung* (6 Feb.).

Strauss, Eva. 1986. Die Zigeunerverfolgung in Bayern 1885–1926. *Giessener Hefte für Tsiganologie* 3(1–4): 31–108.

Streck, Bernhard. 1981. Die nationalsozialistischen Methoden zur Lösung des Zigeunerproblems. *Tribüne* 20(78): 53–77.

Streck, Bernard. 1981a. Zigeuner in Auschwitz. Chronik des Lagers BIIe. In *Kumpania und Kontrolle. Moderne Behinderungen Zigennerischen Lebens,* edited by Mark Münzel and Bernhard Streck, 69–128. Gießen: Focus.

Streim, Alfred. 1987. "Zur Eröffnung des allgemeinen Judenvernichtungsbefehls gegenüber den Einsatzgruppen." In *Der Mord an den Juden im Zweiten Weltkrieg: Entschlussbildung und Verwirklichung,* edited by Eberhardt Jäckel and Jürgen Rohwer, 107–119. Frankfurt a.M: Fischer.

Stümke, Hans-Georg, and Rudi Finkler. 1981. *Homosexuelle und "Gesundes Volksempfinden" von Auschwitz bis heute.* Reinbek: Rowholt.

Sznaider, Natan. 2000. Wahl der Waffen: Norman Finkelstein und das Einrennen offener Türen. *Süddeutsche Zeitung* (24 Aug.).

Szymanski, Tadeusz, Danuta Szymanska, and Tadeusz Snieszko. 1987. Das "Spital" im Zigeuner-Familienlager in Auschwitz–Birkenau. *Die Auschwitz-Hefte 1,* edited by Hamburger Institut für Sozialforschung, 199–207. Weinheim and Basel: Beltz.

Tetzner, Theodor. 1835. *Geschichte der Zigeuner: Ihre Herkunft, Natur und Art.* Weimar and Ilmenau: Voigt.

Timm, Angelika. 1992. Der Streit um Restitution und Wiedergutmachung in der Sowjetischen Besazungszone Deutschland. *Babylon* 10–11:125–138.

Tsigane ou Tzigane. 1964. *Grand Larousse Encyclopedique,* 10:532. Paris: Librairie Larousse.

Tsiganes. 1968. *Encyclopaedia Universalis,* 16:355–358. Paris: Encyclopaedia Universalis.

Tugendhat, Ernst. 1979. Zigeuner und Juden (Vorwort). *In Auschwitz vergast, bis heute vervolgt: Zur Situation der Roma (Zigeuner) in Deutschland und Europa,* edited by Tilman Zülch, 9–11. Hamburg: Rowohlt.

Tugendhat, Ernst. 1992. *Ethik und Politik: Vorträge und Stellungnahmen aus den Jahren 1978–1991.* Frankfurt a.M.: Suhrkamp.

Urban, Reinhold. 1913. Zigeunermission *Realencyklopaedie für protestantische Theologie und Kirche:* 24:691–692. Leipzig: Hinrichs.

Uschold, Rudolf. 1951. Das Zigeunerproblem. *Die Neue Polizei* 5(3): 38–40; 5(4): 60–62.

Vetter, Lothar. 1963. Die Wandlung der Frau Dr. Justin. *Frankfurter Rundschau* (29 Apr.).

Völklein, Ulrich. 1979. Zigeuner in der Bundesrepublik 1979. Immer noch: Verstossen und verjagt. *Die Zeit* (16 Nov.).

Volksverhetzung: Stadtverordneter der DVU verurteilt. 1990. *Oldenburgische Volkszeitung* (7 Jul.).

Vollnhals, Clemens. 1992. Zwischen Verdrängung und Aufklärung: Die Auseinandersetzung mit dem Holocaust in der frühen Bundesrepublik. In *Die*

Deutschen und die Judenverfolgung im Dritten Reich, edited by Ursula Büttner, 376. Hamburg: Christians.

Vossen, Rüdiger. 1983. *Zigeuner: Roma, Sinti, Gitano—Gypsies zwischen Verfolgung und Romantisierung.* Frankfurt a.M.: Ullstein.

VVN demonstriert vor dem bayerischen Landtag. 1950. *Süddentsche Zeitung* (10 Mar.).

Wahrmund, Adolf. 1887. *Das Gesetz des Nomadenthums und die heutige Judenherrschaft.* Vienna: Kubasta and Voigt.

Walser, Martin, and Asta Scheib.1989. *Armer Nanosh: Drehbuch.* NDR.

Weil, Walter. 1961. Zigeuner heute–Romantik und Wirklichkeit. *Frankfurter neue Presse* (3 Jun.).

Weizsäcker, Richard von. 1985. *Zum 40. Jahrestag der Beendigung des Krieges in Europa und der nationalsozialistischen Gewaltherrschaft: Ansprache am 8. Mai 1985 in der Gedenkstunde im Plenarsaal des Deutschen Bundestages.* Bonn: Bundeszentrale für politische Bildung.

Weltzel, Hanns. 1938.The Gypsies in Central Germany. *Journal of Gypsy Lore Society,* Third Series 17: 9–24; 73–80; 30–38; 104–109.

Wetzel, Juliane. 1987. *Jüdisches Leben in München 1945–1951: Durchgangsstation oder Wiederaufbau?* Munich: Stadtarchiv.

Wieder Diskussionen über Eva Justin. 1964. *Frankfurter Allgemeine Zeitung* (22 Sept.).

Wiedergutmachung für Zigeuner? Die Deutschen werden wieder zur Kasse gebeten. 1979. *Deutsche National Zeitung* no. 45 (2 Nov.): 5.

Winter, Walter Stanoski. 1999. *WinterZeit: Erinnerungen eines deutschen Sinto, der Auschwitz überlebt hat,* edited by Thomas W. Neumann and Michael Zimmermann. Hamburg: Ergebnisse.

Wippermann, Wolfgang. 1997. *"Wie die Zigeuner": Antisemitismus und Antiziganismus im Vergleich.* Berlin: Elephanten Press.

Wittich, Engelbert. 1911. The Organisation of South German Gypsies. *Journal of Gypsy Lore Society,* New Series 4(4): 287–292.

Wodak, Ruth. 1990. Opfer der Opfer? Der "altägliche Antisemitismus" in Östreich: erste qualitative soziolinguistische Überlegung. In *Antisemitismus in der politischen Kultur nach 1945,* edited by Werner Bergmann and Rainer Erb, 292–318. Opladen: Westdeutscher Verlag.

Wodak, Ruth, et al. 1990. "Wir sind alle unschuldigeTäter!" *Diskurshistorische Studien zum Nachkriegsantisemitismus.* Frankfurt a.M: Suhrkamp.

Wolf, Siegmund A. 1960. *Grosses Wörterbuch der Zigeunersprache (romani tsiw),* Mannheim: Bibliographisches Instituit.

Wüst, Walther. 1942. Deutsche Frühzeit und arische Geistesgeschichte. In *Indogermanisches Bekenntnis: Sechs Reden,* 33–50. Berlin: Ahnenerbe Stieftung.

Yates, Dora E. 1949. Hitler and the Gypsies. The Fate of Europe's Oldest Aryans. *Commentary* (Nov.): 455–459.

Yates, Dora, and Aenid Picton. 1951. Otto Müller: The Gypsy Artist. *Journal of Gypsy Lore Society,* 3rd Series, 30(3–4): 81–83.

Zielinski, Siegfried. 1980. History as Entertainment and Provocation: The TV Series "Holocaust" in West Germany. *New German Critique* 19:81–96.

Zigeuner. 1909. *Meyers Grosses Konversations-Lexikon*, 20:926. Leipzig: Meyer.

Zigeuner. 1935a. *Der Grosse Brockhaus*, 20:630. Leipzig: Brockhaus.

Zigeuner. 1935b. *Der Grosse Herder*, 12:1506. Freiburg: Herder.

Zigeuner. 1938. *Der Neue Brockhaus*, 4:804. Leipzig: Brockhaus.

Zigeuner. 1950a. *Der Kleine Brockhaus*, 2:686. Wiesbaden: Brockhaus.

Zigeuner. 1950b. *Der Neue Herder*, 2:5017–5018. Freiburg: Herder.

Zigeuner. 1956. *Der Grosse Herder*, 9:1441–1442. Freiburg: Herder.

Zigeuner. 1957. *Der Grosse Brockhaus*, 12:698, 699. Wiesbaden: Brockhaus.

Zigeuner. 1964. *Meyers Neues Lexikon*, 8: 891–892. Leipzig: Meyer.

Zigeuner. 1968. *Der Neue Brockhaus*, 5:604. Wiesbaden: Brockhaus.

Zigeuner. 1974. *Die Brockhaus Enzyklopaedie*, 20:684, 687. Wiesbaden: Brockhaus.

Zigeuner. 1977. *Meyers Neues Lexikon* (2nd ed.), 15:439. Leipzig: Meyer.

Zigeuner. 1979. *Meyers Enzyklopaedisches Lexikon*, 25:713, 714. Mannheim: Meyer.

Zigeuner: Die Nomaden unter uns. 1954. *Frankfurter Allgemeine Zeitung* (16 Jan.).

Zigeuner durften abreisen. 1959. *Bild am Sonntag* (21–22 Feb.), 3.

Zigeuner, ein arischer Stamm? 1936. *Das Schwarze Korps* (6 Aug.), 14.

Zigeuner erhalten ein Sippenarchiv. 1941. *Stuttgarter NS-Kurier* no. 74 (16 Mar.).

Zigeunerfreundlich? 1981. *Der Tagesspiegel* (16 Apr.).

Zigeuner in Panick. 1959. *Hamburger Abendblatt* (18 Feb.), 5

Zigeuner protestieren gegen ZDF-Fernsehfilm. 1981. *Süddentsche Zeitung* (28 Apr.).

Zigeuner-Romantik mit Mercedes, Champagner und sehr viel Trubel. 1949. *Kasseler Stadtausgabe* (2 Dec.).

Zigeuner und VVN. 1948. *VVN Nachrichten* no. 6 (2 Feb.).

Zigeuner und Wahlen. 1983. *Frankfurter Allgemeine Zeitung* (11 Jan.).

Zimmermann, Michael. 1989. *Verfolgt, vertrieben, vernichtet: Die nationalsozialistische Vernichtungspolitik gegen Sinti und Roma.* Essen: Klartext.

Zimmermann, Michael. 1996. *Rassenutopie und Genozid: Die nationalsozialistische "Lösung der Zigeunerfrage."* Hamburger Beiträge zur Sozial- und Zeitgeschichte. Hamburg: Christians.

Zimmermann, Michael. 1997. Ohne Zweifel ein Genozid—Unabhängig von den Zahlen. *Frankfurter Rundschau* (20 Feb. 1997).

Zimmermann, Michael. 2000. Zigeuner und Zigeunerpolitik in Deutschland. Eine Übersicht über neuere historische Studien. *WerkstattGeschichte* 25:35–58.

Zimmermann, Rainer. 1972. *Otto Pankok: Das Werk des Malers, Holzschneiders und Bildhauers.* Berlin: Rembrandt.

Zingari. 1950. *Enciclopedia Italiana di Scienze, Lettere ed Arti* (956ff.). Rome.

Zuckermann, Moshe. 1993. *Shoah in the Sealed Room: The "Holocaust" in Isreali Press during the Gulf War.* Tel-Aviv: Zuckermann. (In Hebrew.)

Zülch, Tilman (Ed.). 1979. *In Auschwitz vergast, bis heute vervolgt: Zur Situation der Roma (Zigeuner) in Deutschland und Europa.* Hamburg: Rowohlt.

Bibliography

Zülch, Tilman. 1980. "Französische Kriegsverbrechen im Algerienkrieg." *Pogrom* 11(77): 29–42.

Zülch, Tilman. 1981. Und auch heute noch verfolgt? *Zeitschrift für Kulturaustausch* 31(4): 397–410.

Zülch, Tilman. 1985. Das Vermächtnis der opfer von Gestern: Einsatz für die Opfer von heute. *Pogrom* 116/117: 19–25.

Zülch, Tilman, and Fritz Greussing. 1981. Vorwort der Gessellschaft für bedrohte Völker. In Donald Kenrik and Grattan Puxon (Eds.), *Sinti und Roma: Die Vernichtung eines Volkes im NS Staat*. Göttingen: Gesellschaft für bedrohte Völker, 9f.u.

Index

Index

Index

lic opinion, 147–151, 160–175; Origins, 3, 4; Compulsory sterilization, 36–38, 52, 119, 138–140, 157–158; Gypsy Lore Society, 17, 166

Hamburg, 57, 60, 63, 69, 70, 94, 102, 103, 104, 117, 121, 195
Hannover, 62, 115
Hauff, Karl, 101
Hapsburg Monarchy, 28, 74–75
Heck, Hocki, 212
Heidelberg, 208
Heile, Wilhelm, 71
Heinrich, John, 51
Herzog, Roman, 212
Hessdörfer, Karlo, 120, 122
Hesse, Hermann, 21, 22
Hesse, 57, 59, 60, 61, 64, 66, 67, 68, 77, 78, 82, 85, 88, 93, 96, 98, 113
Heuß, Herbert, 199
Heydrich, Reinhard, 38, 39, 40
Hiersemann, Karl-Heinz, 197, 198
Hildesheim, 147, 158
Himmler, Heinrich, 35, 38, 39, 40, 42, 44, 46, 47, 48, 49, 50, 52, 59, 62, 111, 133, 136, 152
Hindenburg, Paul von, 134ff
Hipler, Fritz, 22
Hitler, Adolf, 22, 24, 39, 40, 43, 44, 49, 55, 57, 101, 134, 138, 164, 170, 178
Hoegner, Dr. Wilhelm, 73, 74, 81, 85, 91, 196, 197
Holocaust, TV miniseries, 180–181, 185
Holzmann, Dr. Ernst, 77
Hohmann, Joachim S., 16, 188
Homosexuals, 94, 122, 183, 189, 219, 211, 213
Honecker, Erich, 203
Höß, Rudolf, 49, 51, 52
Hundhammer, Dr. Alois, 197–199
Hungary, 12, 13, 14, 49, 54, 79, 150

India, Indians, 3–4, 19, 42, 43, 54, 79, 150
Illingen (Saar.), 5
Israel, State of, 173, 181, 206, 207, 208

Jäger, Karl, 44
Jäckel, Eberhard, 213–214
Jaspers, Karl, 176
Jelpke, Ursula, 211

Jenische, xiv, 18, 158
Jews, Judaism, xvi, 4, 9, 16, 26, 28, 34, 36, 37, 38, 39, 40, 43, 44, 45, 51, 53, 55, 57, 59, 67, 83, 85, 87, 88, 91, 97, 98, 99, 109, 111–116, 117, 122, 126–127, 143, 148, 156, 157, 160–175, 189–192, 193, 194, 201, 203–214, 216, 219
Jochimsen, Lukrezia, 14–15, 147, 151, 158
Jochum, Paul, 79, 121
Junge Welt, 203, 205
Justin, Eva, 35, 36, 38, 121, 123, 129–142, 153, 173, 174
Jürgens, Hans, 141

Kääb, Arthur, 146
Karlsruhe, 105, 106, 107, 108
Karsten, Leo, 121
Karway, Rudolf, 199
Kassel, 59
Kawczynski, Rudolf (Rudko), 201
Kenrick, Donald, 54
Kielar, Wieslaw, 51
Kittel, Manfred, xii
Koblenz, xvii
Kocka, Jürgen, xiii
Kogon, Egon, 168
Kohl, Helmut, 179, 202, 205, 206–207, 209
Kollwitz Käthe, 209, 210
Krämer, Gustav, 78
Kricow, 102
Küster, Otto, 109, 116, 118, 119, 124

Lafontain, Luise, 102
Langbein, Hermann, 172
Latvia, 46, 47, 150
Laufen am Kocher, 60
Lehar, Franz, 22
Lewy, Gunter, 213f
Libau, 46
Lipset, Seymour, 163
Lithuania, 150
Lohse, Heinrich, 46
Lombroso, Cezare, 20
Lodz, 46
Lower Saxony (Niedersachsen), xvii, 60, 76, 86, 115, 117
Luenenburg, 60
Luschan, Felix von, 18, 37
Luther, Martin, 9

Margaret

- need to write about Heimler + Sikhi
- Barmann - discussion
- different experiences at Mourning.

Index